DATE DUE

DEMCO 38-296

Diversity and Complexity in Prehistoric Maritime Societies

A Gulf of Maine Perspective

INTERDISCIPLINARY CONTRIBUTIONS TO ARCHAEOLOGY

Series Editor: Michael Jochim, *University of California, Santa Barbara*
Founding Editor: Roy S. Dickens, Jr., *Late of University of North Carolina, Chapel Hill*

Current Volumes in This Series:

THE AMERICAN SOUTHWEST AND MESOAMERICA
Systems of Prehistoric Exchange
Edited by Jonathon E. Ericson and Timothy G. Baugh

THE ARCHAEOLOGY OF GENDER
Separating the Spheres in Urban America
Diana diZerega Wall

DIVERSITY AND COMPLEXITY IN PREHISTORIC MARITIME SOCIETIES
A Gulf of Maine Perspective
Bruce J. Bourque

EARLY HUNTER–GATHERERS OF THE CALIFORNIA COAST
Jon M. Erlandson

ETHNOHISTORY AND ARCHAEOLOGY
Approaches to Postcontact Change in the Americas
Edited by J. Daniel Rogers and Samuel M. Wilson

FROM KOSTENKI TO CLOVIS
Upper Paleolithic–Paleo-Indian Adaptations
Edited by Olga Soffer and N. D. Praslov

HOUSES AND HOUSEHOLDS
A Comparative Study
Richard E. Blanton

ORIGINS OF ANATOMICALLY MODERN HUMANS
Edited by Matthew H. Nitecki and Doris V. Nitecki

PREHISTORIC EXCHANGE SYSTEMS IN NORTH AMERICA
Edited by Timothy G. Baugh and Jonathon E. Ericson

REGIONAL APPROACHES TO MORTUARY ANALYSIS
Edited by Lane Anderson Beck

STYLE, SOCIETY, AND PERSON
Archaeological and Ethnological Perspectives
Edited by Christopher Carr and Jill E. Neitzel

Diversity and Complexity in Prehistoric Maritime Societies

A Gulf of Maine Perspective

BRUCE J. BOURQUE

Maine State Museum
Augusta, Maine
and Bates College
Lewiston, Maine

PLENUM PRESS • NEW YORK AND LONDON

loging-in-Publication Data

Bourque, Bruce J. (Bruce Joseph)
    Diversity and complexity in prehistoric maritime societies : a
Gulf of Maine perspective / Bruce J. Bourque ; with contributions by
Dosia M. Laeyendecker ... [et al.].
        p.   cm. -- (Interdisciplinary contributions to archaeology)
    Includes bibliographical references and index.
    ISBN 0-306-44874-2
    1. Turner Farm Site (Me.) 2. Indians of North America--Maine-
-North Haven Island--Antiquities. 3. Indians of North America-
-Maine--North Haven Island--Anthropometry. 4. Excavations
(Archaeology)--Maine--North Haven Island. 5. Maritime archaeology-
-Maine--North Haven Island. 6. North Haven Island (Me.)-
-Antiquities.   I. Title. II. Series.
E78.M2B678 1995
974.1'53--dc20   95-1085
                                                          CIP

ISBN 0-306-44874-2

© 1995 Plenum Press, New York
A Division of Plenum Publishing Corporation
233 Spring Street, New York, N. Y. 10013

10 9 8 7 6 5 4 3 2 1

Printed in the United States of America

Foreword

New England archaeology has not always been everyone's cup of tea; only late in the Golden Age of nineteenth-century archaeology, as archaeology's focus turned westward, did a few pioneers look northward as well, causing a brief flurry of investigation and excavation. Between 1892 and 1894, Charles C. Willoughby did some exemplary excavations at three small burial sites in Bucksport, Orland, and Ellsworth, Maine, and made some models of that activity for exhibition at the Chicago World's Fair. These activities were encouraged by F. W. Putnam, director of the Harvard Peabody Museum and head of anthropology at the "Columbian" Exposition. Even earlier, another director of the Peabody, Jeffries Wyman, spawned some real interest in the shellheaps of the Maine coast, but that did not last very long.

Twentieth-century New England archaeology, specifically in Maine, was—for its first fifty years—rather low key too, with short-lived but important activity by Arlo and Oric Bates (a Harvard student) prior to World War I. Later, another Massachusetts institution, the R. S. Peabody Foundation at Andover, took some minor but responsible steps toward further understanding of the area's prehistoric past.

Beginning in the 1970s, however, more long-term commitments to such Maine studies came from Harvard's Peabody Museum in the form of the work of graduate students under my own mentorship: Bruce J. Bourque and R. Michael Gramly. Some of Bourque's work is recorded in this volume, and Gramly has published his significant Vale site report elsewhere. That two more of my students—Steven L. Cox and Arthur E. Spiess—are professionally employed in Maine archaeology is a further source of personal pride. I must underline the fact, however, that the choice of their research venues was very much their own decisions; I did not collar them in Cambridge and point them Down East. Their contributions to Maine archaeology are a matter of record.

The quality of that published record is no better documented than in this lengthy monograph by Bruce Bourque. In these days of quick and sometimes dirty "pro forma" site reports turned out to meet federal requirements of Cultural Resource Management, this volume is "none of the above." It records the detailed and careful study of a rich 5,000-year-old coastal Maine site that has been carried out over a period of more than twenty years. No fewer than eight appendixes document the specialized analysis of many of the myriad data bits recovered from that one site. Too much on too little? Not at all, for it is only through monographic coverage that we can assemble the real building blocks for significant new ideas and syntheses.

This report and others like it (rare as they may be) are essential. If we are to address larger integrative questions (as Bourque does with care and, I feel, great success in Chapter 8), we must have more than flimsy stacks of data-rich and synthesis-poor "gray literature."

The title of this book includes what can be called a "catchword" of current scientific controversy: the hot topic of "Chaos and Complexity." Recently, I cannot seem to write a foreword without touching on this interesting area of intellectual discourse, but this time it is no stretch. It is indeed a well-established dogma in archaeology that large covering-terms are an essential tool of analysis. Whether they be chronological ("Early Woodland"), typological ("Clovis points"), or regional/environmental ("Boreal Archaic") in nature, these appellations cover large segments of time, artifacts, or geography. And yes, they are useful: They help "calm down" the immense diversity that one sees in these masses of data. They are "comforters," useful in allowing one to speak with others without the need to define all of the diversity and complexity that they cover so well. But there are consequences of such comforting regularity—the explanatory devices tend to attain or retain that same intellectual smoothness. Cultures thus spread evenly across the landscape, and, more importantly, the modes of this expansion are seen as more or less uniform throughout time and space.

Is this really what happens? Each of us has his or her own sense of reality in both his or her own lives and intellectual constructs. Some archaeologists today (called post-Processualists) would leave it at that—each to his or her own reality *and* vision of the past. (The post-Processualists are a vocal and verbally adroit group centered in England, and I for one will leave them there. They are of course welcome to their own special view of the past.) I think Bourque would agree, however, that while each of us sees the world individually, we must achieve some normal consensus to allow us to operate and communicate with others, and to move forward.

But general archaeological consensus on what one will call things and on what mechanisms of change seem reasonable does not indicate blanket agreement on what each archaeologist thinks happened in the past. Thus, I applaud Bourque's lengthy concluding chapter. It is bound to be controversial, but much of the data are in this volume, and Bourque's careful review of the intellectual history of previous scenarios of the past in the Northeast and beyond is well laid out for all to see. He has cited the reports, pointed out the specific artifact connections, and has drawn it all together. Of course, Bourque does argue for *diversity* and *complexity* in the past and about the nature of *how* some of the important changes took place, but he has earned that right. You may not agree, but give the book a good read; I trust you will enjoy it as much as I did.

STEPHEN WILLIAMS

Peabody Professor of American Archaeology, Emeritus
Harvard University

Preface

The Turner Farm site is located on North Haven Island, one of the Fox Island group in Penobscot Bay off the central Maine coast. Large-scale excavations there during the 1970s, followed by over a decade of analysis, have produced a body of data that, in its age, size, and comprehensiveness, is probably unparalleled among coastal sites in North America. It spans five millennia, from 5000 B.P. to the early historic period, and includes 6,500 catalogued artifacts of stone, bone, and fired clay, as well as 1,800 bone samples from which over 20 thousand vertebrate specimens have been identified.

The site has been known to archaeologists since the late nineteenth century, when amateurs collected artifacts from the beach in front of it and dug potholes in its eroding scarp. It was not until 1969, however, when I began a large-scale and long-term survey of the Fox Islands, that its great potential became apparent. As we excavated the site during the 1970s, archaeological interest in the Northeast increased dramatically, particularly in northern New England. This revival led to the publication of syntheses that explored relationships between the region's archaeological cultures, as well as their ties to those found elsewhere throughout eastern North America. Although these syntheses made some reference to the Turner Farm site, access to its data was limited to interim reports and personal communications based upon preliminary analyses. The two decades of research on this site that have now elapsed have changed, sometimes radically, the ways in which we view the prehistoric peoples of the Gulf of Maine and, indeed, those who lived throughout a much larger region. This volume presents the results of that research and explores its implications not only for eastern North America but for maritime societies in general.

Because seacoasts are among the most unstable ecological zones on earth, previous discussions of human adaptation to the sea often have been forced to construct composite cultural chronologies made up of numerous samples from disparate locations. Even so, such sequences often fail to reach very far back into the past because earlier sites have been differentially destroyed by coastal erosion. In this regard, the Turner Farm data set is doubly useful, for it provides a record of human coastal adaptation during the entire recent Holocene epoch at a single location. Granted that oceanographic conditions changed significantly in that location during the site's history, we believe that our reconstructions of

vii

those changes have allowed us to see through short-term microadaptational reactions to perceive more basic trends.

The volume is organized around a series of stratigraphic "packages" that are referred to as occupations and are numbered 1 to 4. The first occupation dates between 5000 and 4500 B.P. and pertains to the Small Stemmed Point tradition, which is found throughout much of southern New England and New York, but the existence of which in Maine was not even suspected when research began at the site. The second applies to the Moorehead phase, the culture which gave rise to Maine's well-known Red Paint cemeteries. The third applies to the Susquehanna tradition, representing the northernmost major habitation component of this unusual culture as well as the only cemetery with extensive bone preservation. Occupation 4 is conceptually different from earlier occupations in that the term refers to an uncertain number of components that apparently occurred in rapid succession after about 3000 B.P. that we could not reliably separate stratigraphically and that were therefore analyzed somewhat differently from earlier occupations.

ACKNOWLEDGMENTS

The Turner Farm project grew directly out of my dissertation research on the pre-history of the central Maine coast, which was funded by the National Science Foundation. Stephen Williams, then Peabody Professor of North American Archaeology and my advisor, assisted me in obtaining that grant, which, along with permission to use my parents' Maine summer home, made it possible during the summer of 1969 to explore archaeological collections and sites between Deer Isle and Frenchman's Bay. This is the region where Arlo and Oric Bates, Douglas S. Byers, Wendell S. Hadlock, Warren K. Moorehead, John H. Rowe, and Charles C. Willoughby, among others, had previously worked on sites spanning (we already knew in 1969) the past 5,000 years of prehistory. The viability of my dissertation topic rested on the fact that these data had led to the formulation of several models of regional prehistory that I hoped to test. Additional support came from the Polaroid Corporation, which provided a large stock of 4 × 5 film. This donation enabled me to build a large photo archive of Maine collections that are found throughout the Northeast, several of which include artifacts from the Turner Farm site.

As Penobscot Bay lies at the western margin of my initial geographic focus, I decided to visit the Fox Islands only in August, at the end of the 1969 season, just to make preliminary inquiries about potential archaeological resources. It soon became apparent that those resources would be so impressive as to require a rethinking of the whole scope of my thesis.

The Turner Farm project must be one of the most community-based, long-term archaeological projects ever undertaken in North America. The site itself was well known to all North Haven residents, many of whom had collected artifacts from the shoreline in front of the midden. Most welcomed the prospect of an archaeological team working on their island. Thus, as soon as I arrived, literally within hours, Eric Hopkins provided me with a boat, David and Roberta Cooper gave me a room in their newly opened Inn, local collector Stanley Smith offered me a tour of the Island's sites, and George Burr and Oscar Waterman granted me free access to their large and well-documented artifact collection, which included a large number of artifacts from the site.

With this auspicious beginning, I left the island to write my thesis and to begin a teaching career at Skidmore College. During the winter of 1970, Dean R. Snow offered me the opportunity to teach a field school for the State University of New York at Albany, and so during the summers of 1971 and 1972, with mixed crews of S.U.N.Y. and Skidmore students, I was able to return in force to begin research on the Fox Islands. Our efforts in 1972 were further augmented by generous donations from Mr. and Mrs. Garrison Norton, Mr. and Mrs. Thomas Watson, Jr., and Mr. and Mrs. John Crocker.

In 1971, after conducting test excavations at other North Haven middens, Turner Farm site co-owners William Rice and Dorothy Turner Ames granted us permission to begin excavations there. To them go special thanks for their unfailing support. Our crews became especially attached to Dorothy, who died in 1975, for she seemed intensely proud of our interest in what was literally the frontyard of her ancestral home. Our field crews were soon augmented by volunteers from the island. Through the years, these included Ellen Nichols, David Hopkins, Janet Bolen, Laura Van Agt, and others, along with Chuck Curtis, a local high school student with an interest in archaeology. With so substantial a crew, we were able early on to recover an excellent preliminary sample that provided our first indication of the site's real potential. That potential earned support from the National Geographic Society for the 1974 and 1975 seasons.

Throughout the entire project, the community of North Haven provided for our every need. The Coopers continued to house the crew and, after 1972, turned the responsibility of feeding them over to Georgiana Fleischman. Ellen Nichols provided space in her home for a field laboratory, J.O. Brown and Son and Y-Knot Enterprises took care of our boating needs, the family of C. Peter Strong entertained us, Waterman's store provisioned us, and Eliot Brown provided power equipment that saved us the backbreaking chore of backfilling our excavations each year.

Supervision of large crews such as those employed at the Turner Farm site required capable assistants. In the early years, Stephanie Hale Benoit, one of my students at Skidmore, provided that service. Over time, her efforts were augmented by Rene Descartes, Stewart Eldridge, Stewart McConnell, and David Morse. In 1972, when I arrived at the Maine State Museum, technician Robert Lewis began to assume what would become a critical role in the overall management of field operations and laboratory analysis for the project.

Although analytical work began in 1972, data recovery outstripped our efforts to keep up. I was grateful, therefore, for the interest in the project shown by David Morse, who wrote a master's thesis on the faunal remains, Richard Will, whose master's thesis dealt with the bone tools, and John Cross, who analyzed the ceramics for a college senior thesis. Over the years, the project has also benefited from collaboration with professionals in ancillary fields. I have been especially fortunate in obtaining assistance regarding paleoenvironmental reconstruction from Harold Borns, Ronald Davis, and especially Daniel Belknap, all of the University of Maine's Institute for Quaternary Studies. That effort was also aided by Dosia Laeyendecker of the Smithsonian Institution, who graciously provided wood identifications from our charcoal samples. Arthur Spiess, ably assisted by Robert Lewis, went far beyond his obligatory involvement in analyzing the huge faunal sample upon which so much of my interpretation of the site is based. Initial support for their efforts came from a 1980 National Science Foundation grant. Robert Stuckenrath, then of the Smithsonian Institution and the Quaternary Institute, generously provided radiocarbon dates. Robert Doyle, formerly director of the Maine Geological Survey, has provided long-term support in helping us define lithic use and procurement patterns.

Finally, my interpretation of this site and its significance to the prehistory of eastern North America has been shaped by many productive discussions with colleagues. Chief among them are Steven Cox, Steven Davis, Dena Dincauze, William Fitzhugh, Robert Funk, Moira McCaffrey, James Petersen, Brian Robinson, David Sanger, Christopher Turnbull, and Stephen Williams. To all these friends I extend my deepest gratitude.

Turner Farm Crew Members:

1971   Kathy Attfield, Polly Bickel, Anne Buhr, Rene Descartes, Margaret Gill, Stephanie Hale, Dan Levy, John Lieber, Sarah Reith, Lloyd Trinkoff, Laura Uhl

1972   Amy Cohen, Thomas Godfrey, Stephanie Hale, Janet Keeter, Robert Lewis, Michelle Morrison, David Morse, Mary Stanclift

1973   Janet Bolen, Charles Curtis, Jeffrey Groff, David Hopkins, Robert Lewis, Sandy Mayer, Michelle Morrison, David Morse, Ellen Nichols

1974   Stephen Brooke, Jeffrey Cody, Charles Curtis, Laura Grant, David Hopkins, Robert Lewis, Rick Lynch, Sandy Mayer, Stuart McConnell, Kevin McGuiggan, David Morse, Ellen Nichols

1975   Jane Carpenter, John Cross, Charles Curtis, Stuart Eldridge, Laura Grant, Stephanie Hale, David Hopkins, Robert Lewis, Steven Mason, Kevin McGuiggan, David Morse, Ellen Nichols

1977   Charles Curtis, David Hopkins, Robert Lewis, Ellen Nichols

1980   Charles Curtis, Robert Lewis

Contents

Chapter 1

Introduction

As analysis of the Turner Farm data has progressed, I have been surprised at the geographic extent over which we must range to understand what was happening at the site and, conversely, in the region for which the site provides new insights: from Labrador to Florida and from Nova Scotia to the Great Lakes. Analyses on scales as broad as this are possible mainly because of the unusually high quality of the data set. Most shell middens on the Gulf of Maine coast, as elsewhere, have excellent bone preservation—a critical aid to understanding, among other things, subsistence, technology, and mortuary behavior—and the primary reason why much of my research during the past quarter century has been devoted to these remarkable sites. Moreover, aside from the unique length of the Turner Farm sequence, most episodes of occupation there were multiseason, even year-round, reflecting a substantial proportion of each occupation's annual range of activities.

It is for all these reasons that the data set attained another unique quality: its large size. Even during our first week of excavation in 1971, we realized that the site would provide a truly unique opportunity to study issues long of interest in the Northeast. Thus we persisted over several seasons, ultimately exploring a volume of midden that is roughly comparable to the entire volume excavated at all other shell middens where we have worked.

The analysis of so large a corpus has been a long and sometimes trying process. Many of the trials arose from our decision to apply a broad range of analytical techniques, some of which were developed specifically for this project. Many were directed at one truly outstanding aspect of the collection: its faunal remains. Much effort went into quantifying and otherwise evaluating the relative importance of various species and into determining the seasons during which they were taken. Aside from commonly used seasonal indicators, such as antler shedding, presence of migratory species, and the like, we examined incremental growth patterns in a variety of hard tissue (e.g., teeth, mollusk shells, and fish otoliths and vertebrae). We also quantified the composition of the midden in order to estimate the relative dietary importance of its most abundant constituent element: mollusk shell.

Another major undertaking was radiocarbon dating the sequence. At this point we have dated 57 organic samples, giving us a fairly reliable chronological framework for the site's history (Appendix 2). From the outset, we decided to base that framework on charcoal dates, the standard material used in this region. Shell middens such as the Turner Farm site, however, produce such an abundance of organics that we found several opportunities to compare charcoal dates with dates from closely associated samples of other materials, sometimes with interesting results. This aspect of the analysis would have been costly, not only in time but also in money, had it not been for the very generous assistance of Robert Stuckenrath, then of the Smithsonian Institution, who ran most of our samples free of charge. We also asked Dosia Laeyendecker of the Smithsonian Institution to identify the tree species that had provided firewood, a source of data used to supplement published pollen analyses regarding forest composition. Her analysis confirms that prehistoric forests of North Haven Island were radically different from those found there today (Appendix 4).

As is the case for virtually all shell middens in the Gulf of Maine, an erosional scarp along the seaward limit clearly indicates that some portion of the site has been lost to erosion, and we suspected that other portions had been submerged because of coastal subsidence, a factor that has no doubt altered the physical environment throughout the site's catchment area. In order to take account of these changes, we sought the assistance of Daniel Belknap, of the University of Maine, in reconstructing land–sea relationships in the area. Our efforts in this regard began with explorations of areas where the site had been submerged beneath a salt marsh and encroached upon by beach deposits. Belknap's reconstruction, based on data from subbottom profiling and vibracoring, has been of great assistance in allowing us to evaluate the structure and content of the remaining portion of the midden (Appendix 5).

A variety of lithic types were used during the site's history, ranging from locally available rhyolites to cherts from far/distant sources. Because the ultimate point of use was the same for all types, we thought it especially important to examine patterns of lithic procurement and use during various time periods. Here we were fortunate in obtaining the assistance of Robert Doyle, former director of the Maine Geological Survey, who presents the results of his extensive analysis in Appendix 6.

The discovery of the Susquehanna tradition cemetery was a landmark event for eastern North American archaeology. There, for the first time, were preserved the uncremated human remains and bone technology of a people whose now boneless cemeteries have often been encountered in the Northeast, and whose technology so closely resembles that found among Archaic peoples throughout much of eastern North America (Appendix 3). George Armelagos, then of the University of Massachusetts, Amherst, agreed to take on the analysis of the human remains, and the work was eventually performed by two of his students, Lenore Barbian and Ann Magennis (Appendix 7).

The cemetery population also provided us with an opportunity to assess diet from a source completely independent of the Susquehanna tradition faunal sample: light-stable isotopes preserved in human bone (Figure 6.13). A comparison of the isotope values from this sample with others from central coastal Maine ranging in age from 4300 to 400 B.P. revealed one of the biggest surprises of the whole project: the site's Susquehanna tradition occupants, surrounded by the riches of the sea, apparently made little use of them, consuming less marine protein than any other coastal population known to us.

It is thus my hope that the data and analyses offered here will provide a framework through which the eastern Gulf of Maine can be better integrated into our understanding of not only the Northeast, but of all of eastern North America as well. Therefore, before proceeding to an account of our research, I will summarize the major issues to which it makes some contribution.

THE LATE ARCHAIC PERIOD IN THE NORTHEAST

Of the regional syntheses produced during the late 1960s and 1970s, the most influential for the Late Archaic period was by Tuck, who organized the data according to three traditions that he defined as "widespread cultural patterns," each conceived as "coterminous with what were, at the time of European contact, equally broad environmental zones" (Tuck 1978a:28). Tuck's first tradition, the Lake Forest, is a revision of Ritchie's (1938:106–107) Laurentian tradition, while the second, the Narrow Point, is an extrapolation from Ritchie's (1965, 1969a:216–219) Small Stemmed Point tradition. The third, the Maritime Archaic tradition, was first defined by Tuck (1971:350–357) and soon adopted by Fitzhugh (1972:129–130).

Tuck defined the Lake Forest tradition as a "whole cultural tradition" (in the sense of Goggin 1949, see below) that was confined mainly to the Great Lakes drainage basin where beech-maple-hemlock and maple-basswood forests were said to predominate, and where it persisted from 5000 to 3000 B.P. (Tuck 1978a:29). Fish were said to have been a more important component of the Lake Forest tradition diet than in more southerly traditions. Its technology included notched points similar to contemporaneous styles found throughout a broad area from the Koster site in Illinois to Tennessee and Arkansas. Its eastern expression took the form of Ritchie's Laurentian tradition, with its ground stone technology (including ground slate points), while farther to the west, around the Upper Great Lakes, an Old Copper "industry" developed instead (Tuck 1978a:31).

Tuck's Narrow Point tradition was said to extend over an ecologically homogeneous oak-hickory-chestnut and deer-turkey biome that stretched from the Atlantic coast through southern New York state into Michigan and as far west as Illinois (Tuck 1978a:34–36). Its basic economy was said to have developed by 5000 B.P. and perhaps to have persisted in southern New England until ceramics appeared in the sequence around 2700 B.P. According to Tuck, "The subsistence base was clearly the Virginia deer" and its Narrow point technology was typified by "narrow-bladed, thick stemmed, and sometimes broadly side-notched forms with a broken or unfinished base" (Tuck 1978a:35–36). Its adaptive pattern was considered to be probably uniform across its range despite differences between some assemblages owing to lack of communication between river drainages.

Tuck's Maritime Archaic tradition was mapped onto coastal areas between northern New England and Labrador where "the most important resources were in some way connected to the sea" (Tuck 1978a:32). Although "best known from the third and second millennia B.C.," evidence from the L'Anse Amour burial mound and from other sites nearby in the Strait of Belle Isle, southern Labrador, were taken as indications that the tradition had begun by 7000 B.P. (Tuck 1978a:33). Like its putative adaptive pattern, its material culture was said to be uniform over its range and to include a variety of chipped and ground stone forms, several types of specialized marine hunting equipment of bone, as well as a suite of magical or decorative objects. These artifacts were deposited with red ocher in burials, some of which were grouped into cemeteries.

Snow's (1980:187–233) discussion of the Late Archaic period adopted Tuck's tripartite scheme with its strong linkages between cultural traditions and putatively uniform ecological zones. Snow also affirmed that

> Tuck is on the right track when he suggests names for the first two traditions that reflect their adaptations, as much as geographic and physiographic correlates, and I propose that the same logic be extended to the third tradition. If this is done, a fairly obvious choice is "Mast Forest Archaic." (Snow 1980:188)

According to Tuck (1978a) and Snow (1980), all three traditions converge on the Maritime Peninsula, where both would assign what I (Bourque 1992a:34–39) have called the Moorehead phase to the Maritime Archaic tradition. Researchers working in the region, however, have generally not been enthusiastic about this scenario, but data from the Turner Farm site have not been widely available to address the issue. As pointed out below, those data suggest that the Moorehead phase, of which Occupation 2 at the Turner Farm site is one manifestation, derived from something akin to the Small Stemmed Point tradition rather than the Maritime Archaic tradition.

THE LAURENTIAN AND MARITIME ARCHAIC TRADITIONS AND THE MOOREHEAD PHASE

Ritchie originally defined the Laurentian as an "aspect," according to the Midwestern Taxonomic System (McKern 1939:308; Ritchie 1938:106–107). He (Ritchie 1955, 1958, 1980:79) later redefined it as a tradition in the sense of Willey and Phillips, that is, as "an archaeological unit possessing traits sufficiently characteristic to distinguish it from all other units similarly conceived, . . . spatially limited to the order of magnitude of a locality or region and chronologically limited to a relatively brief interval of time" (Willey and Phillips 1958:22). More recently, Ritchie (1958:626–628) described the Laurentian as

> an extensive cultural continuum, widely spread throughout northeastern North America, with its major area of development and diffusion within southeastern Ontario, southern Quebec, northern New England and northern New York. Its most diagnostic traits, occurring in considerable morphologic variety, comprise the gouge; adz; plummet; ground slate points and knives, including the semilunar form or ulu, which occurs also in chipped stone; simple forms of the banner stone; a variety of chipped-stone projectile points, mainly broad-bladed and side-notched forms; and the barbed bone point. (Ritchie 1980:79–83)

Although this redefinition refers to the Laurentian as a tradition, note that Ritchie commented explicitly upon its wide extent throughout the Northeast but remained vague about its temporal range.

The northeasternmost expression of the Laurentian tradition is the Vergennes phase, which Ritchie described as "centered along Otter Creek and Lake Champlain in western Vermont, but extending into Quebec and northern and eastern New York," and dating between about 4500 and 5500 B.P. (Ritchie 1980:84). Although rather elusive, with few clear components, the Vergennes phase was thought to be typified by large, side-notched Otter Creek points, ground slate points, and ulus (Ritchie 1961:40–41, 94–98; 1980:84–89).

Byers (1959:243–255) later defined the Boreal Archaic culture to include the Late Archaic Red Paint cemeteries of Maine along with nonmortuary sites in Maine and the

Maritime Provinces that had produced similar artifacts. He also extended the concept to cover similar assemblages north of the Gulf of St. Lawrence from Tadoussac, Quebec, to the Strait of Belle Isle area of Newfoundland and Labrador. Harp (1963) later used the term to describe materials recovered during his surveys at Port au Choix and other sites along the Strait of Belle Isle, and, presaging Tuck's Maritime Archaic tradition, also applied it to Late Archaic materials from the Nevin site in Maine. Harp later encountered similar materials in Late Archaic burials at Port au Choix (Harp and Hughes 1968).

Tuck's (1971) initial report on the extremely well preserved remains from other Late Archaic mortuary loci at Port au Choix included a new formulation, the Maritime Archaic tradition, which, like its intellectual predecessor, the Boreal Archaic, was said to include the peoples responsible for the Red Paint cemeteries from Labrador to central Maine. The Nevin site in Blue Hill, Maine, played a critical role in Tuck's extension of the tradition southward across the Gulf of St. Lawrence to Maine because several bone artifact styles from its red ocher-filled graves—virtually unique among Maine's Red Paint cemeteries—so closely resembled the new forms from similar graves at Port au Choix.

Tuck's use of Goggin's (1949:17) "whole cultural tradition" concept meant "not considering merely one or two aspects of technology or even an entire technology but instead combining the study of technology with what can be inferred about subsistence and settlement patterns, art, aesthetics, religion, and whatever other cultural data have been recovered by archaeologists" (Tuck 1978a:28). The clear intent of such a definition is to imply the broad-scale sharing of several "systems," including "technology, economy, social organization, aesthetics, religious beliefs, etc., as well as the all-important external factor of environment and the adjustments made to it which seem to be reflected in most of the above-named systems" (Tuck 1971:350). Tuck's use of the term *tradition* resembles Ritchie's in its vague specification of temporal span. Goggin stated only that a tradition might be thought of as "perhaps extending through some period of time and exhibiting normal cultural changes" (Goggin 1949:17).

When Willey and Phillips put forth their terminological system for cultural–historical integration, they cited Goggin (1949) as an example of the "blunting that is inseparable from increased generalization" of the tradition concept, which causes it "to lose its primary significance of long temporal continuity as a counterpoise to the broad spatial continuity represented by the horizon." They therefore proposed "a return to something like the original meaning of a tradition," which they understood to be "a (primary) temporal continuity represented by persistent configurations in single technologies or other systems of related forms" (Willey and Phillips 1958:37).

Unfortunately, both definitions of tradition have become embedded in the archaeological literature of the Northeast without distinction. As Snow (1980:190) has noted, it is just this kind of terminological ambiguity that may lie near the crux of some of the more protracted debates regarding the Late Archaic period in the Northeast. Snow's solution, however, was to shift the focus from the constituent technological elements used to define traditions (such as ground slate technology, narrow-stemmed projectile points, and the like) to ecologically defined "adaptations" (Snow 1980:190). Thus, Snow's reformulation not only underscored the comprehensiveness of Tuck's tradition concept along with its assertion that such traditions reflect zones of ecological uniformity, but it once again emphasized geographic factors at the expense of temporal continuity.

Snow's attempt to flesh out Tuck's scheme also ran afoul of his attempt to find room for previously published data, the initial interpretations of which have subsequently proven suspect. Thus he suggested a beginning date for the Moorehead complex—the putative manifestation of the Maritime Archaic in Maine—prior to 5000 B.P. on the basis of a single date from the Hathaway site, and an end date of about 3800 B.P. based on two dates from the Cow Point cemetery in New Brunswick (Snow 1980:206–208). While the latter date remains credible on the basis of recent data, the former conflicts with data from Turner Farm Occupation 1 and other sites discussed below. Snow also included within his Moorehead complex "notched points analogous to Otter Creek points and other points of the Lake Forest Archaic," ground slate semilunar knives (ulus), and certain gouge and adz forms that now appear to belong outside any conception of a Moorehead complex or phase (Snow 1980:206–213). Finally, Snow invoked pollen data as evidence that during the era of the Maritime Archaic in Maine "the woodland caribou (*Rangifer tarandus caribou*) lived in Maine . . . and was well adapted to the mature coniferous forest of the area" (Snow 1980:114–115, 199). Subsequent research has demonstrated neither the presence of caribou in Maine at this time nor particularly favorable conditions for them (Jacobson et al. 1987). In sum, Snow's conception of a Moorehead complex has proven to be too inclusive, too long, too terrestrially oriented, and, as we shall see below, to have been given an inappropriate ancestral affiliation.

The Ground Slate Point Problem

The origin of this technology has puzzled archaeologists since the nineteenth century (Abbott 1881:63–64). Holmes apparently was the first to point out similarities among "highly specialized slate spear or harpoon head(s), long, narrow, and bayonet-like . . . [which] form an unbroken chain of genetic, accultural, or fortuitous analogies entirely circling the globe where the land areas were most nearly continuous" (Holmes 1919: 24–25). During the 1940s, just prior to the advent of radiocarbon dating, both Gjessing (1944, 1948) and Spaulding (1946) regarded the slate point as one of several ground stone (and possibly bone) artifact forms whose origins lay in Eurasia, but which later underwent independent regional elaborations in the northwestern and northeastern regions of North America. Their formulations differed, however, in that "Gjessing favored an Arctic coastal diffusion, Spaulding a dissemination through the taiga or coniferous forest zone spanning the Old and New Worlds" (Ritchie 1969a:385). Bryan (1957) favored Gjessing's formulation and was apparently the first to associate ground stone technology with maritime hunting, which he postulated had its origin in an early culture that spread along the littoral margins of northern North America. Ritchie's review of the ground slate problem, however, emphasized the absence of detailed similarities between the Northwest Coast and the Northeast and concluded that these industries "arose independently of each other, beginning at approximately the same time, around 3000 B.C." (Ritchie 1969b:389).

De Laguna (1946) was among those who suggested that ground slate technology in the Northeast was derived from ancient Eskimo antecedents. Eventually, radiocarbon dating made it clear that Dorset Eskimo technology could not have given rise to ground slate tools in the Northeast, but in her defense de Laguna (1962) pointed out how poorly understood the relative ages of the region's prehistoric cultures had previously been, and she remained convinced that ground slate tool making in the two regions was somehow historically linked and that parallel or convergent developments probably occurred only "in some places" (de Laguna 1962:164). Ritchie (1962) used radiocarbon dates to argue for the clear temporal priority of the Indian over Dorset technology, and that the former had its origins about 5000 B.P. in the ground bone and hammered copper technologies of the Great Lakes. Similar to de Laguna, Meldgaard thought that early Dorset culture "smells of forest" and thus that it was strongly influenced by, or derived from, Indian cultures of Labrador and Newfoundland (Meldgaard 1960:593, 1962:95). Byers (1962:153), on the other hand, attributed resemblances between Dorset and Indian artifacts to chance, while Harp (1964:185) regarded any parallelisms between Indian and Dorset culture as the result of similar adaptations to forest exploitation and littoral hunting.

After it became apparent that ground slate technology had Indian and not Dorset origins, the idea that it was derived from a unified circumpolar culture became untenable. Fitzhugh elaborated upon Ritchie (1969a), noting that ground slate industries worldwide had developed independently, and suggested that they collectively be called the "Northern Maritime Technological complex" (Fitzhugh 1974:55). Fitzhugh also reaffirmed Bryan (1957), commenting that these technologies "flourished largely within the context of a maritime adaptation" and that "northern maritime cultures tend to develop ground slate tool complexes while interior adaptations do not" (Fitzhugh 1974:55, 1975b:376). At about the same time, Tuck (1971) also emphasized the connection of ground slate technology to maritime hunting in the Northeast and made this connection a key defining feature of the Maritime Archaic tradition.

Ground slate point technology in the Northeast still has not been reliably traced back before about 5500 B.P., although a few variable and generalized specimens have been recovered from various contexts dating to about 7000 B.P. (Fitzhugh 1978:488; McGhee and Tuck 1975:44–45, 114, 240–241; Petersen 1991:107–109, Figures 77–82; J. Wright 1972a:154–155). After about 5500 B.P. the technology ramified throughout much of the Northeast with specimens occurring as far west as Michigan (H. Thompson 1989), eastward down the St. Lawrence Valley, along its tributaries, and up and down the Atlantic coast from northern Labrador to the Kennebec River. It was during this post-5500 B.P. florescence that distinct styles developed. Although no ground slate points have been found at the Turner Farm site (and very few have been found in the handful of other early shell middens either), the presence there of bayonets made of swordfish rostra provides a new perspective on the possible origins of the ground slate point.

THE SUSQUEHANNA TRADITION IN MAINE

From its inception, the Susquehanna tradition has been regarded, at least implicitly, as related in some way to a series of "broadpoint" complexes found southward along the Atlantic slope to Georgia and even Florida (Bullen and Bryant 1965; Coe 1964:97; Ritchie 1980:151–152; Witthoft 1953). The southernmost expression of this broadpoint manifestation has been variously referred to as the Savannah River or Stallings Island phase, which may have begun before 4500 B.P. and persisted until about 4000 B.P. (Coe 1964:45; Oliver 1985a:132–136; Stoltman 1974; Willey 1966:256–257). More recently, Elliot et al. (1992) have defined the Mill Branch phase, dating between about 4200 and 3800 B.P., which, as we shall see, encompasses somewhat more comprehensively the attributes shared widely with Late Archaic broadpoint cultures to the northeast.

Although the Mill Branch phase may herald a new understanding of Late Archaic culture history in the Southeast, continuing vagaries of chronology there leave the origin of broadpoint technology and its associated traits in considerable doubt (Smith 1986:6–7). As pointed out in Chapter 6, its northern manifestations do not antedate 4000 B.P. This south-to-north temporal gradient is now generally taken to indicate that "many elements, if not the entire complex, have their ultimate origin in the Southeast" (Tuck 1978a:38). A similar spread westward across the Appalachians into the Ohio and lower Tennessee drainages, and beyond to the southern shores of Lake Huron, has also been suggested (Dragoo 1976:118; Oliver 1985a:133; Spence et al. 1990:99–102; Willey 1966:257). The temporal priority of broadpoints and associated technological elements in the Middle Archaic of the Midwest, however, suggests that a dispersal eastward from that region is more likely (see, e.g., Jeffries and Butler 1982:194–275, Jeffries 1987:37–66).

Opinions also vary regarding the significance of this expansion and the meaning of the similarities between its regional manifestations. Despite Witthoft's assertion that his "Susquehanna Soapstone culture . . . represents a very distinct and marked change in every detail of material culture and way of life from earlier times in the Susquehanna Valley," he did not regard it as intrusive because he thought its projectile point styles were derived from local prototypes (Witthoft 1953:14–15). Kent et al. followed suit, stating that "Transitional period cultures can be considered, by and large, as in situ developments which grew out of the Archaic of the northern Piedmont . . ." (Kent et al. 1976:92).

In fact, Witthoft (1949:10–11) and other archaeologists in the middle Atlantic states have construed the culture in evolutionary terms as "transitional" between the Archaic and Woodland stages (or periods) because the characteristic lithic technology is often found in association with steatite and ceramic vessels. Ritchie was among those who considered Susquehanna tradition sites in New York as part of a Transitional stage, noting that its artifacts were found on the same sites used by earlier and later groups, and concluding that there is "little to suggest on these and other sites any marked difference in the way of life of any of the various occupants" (Ritchie 1980:152). His use of the stage concept, as well as his denial that the Susquehanna tradition represented changes in local lifeways, I take to mean that he did not consider its appearance in New York primarily as the result of outside influences or immigration. Funk and Rippeteau (1977:21, 49) demonstrated significant behavioral novelties in the Frost Island phase of the Susquehanna tradition, yet they too regarded it as an in situ development (see also Kent et al. 1976:91–94; Tuck 1978a:37–38). Even in his most recent discussion of this issue, Funk (1993:225–226) adheres to the idea that the tradition was most probably a product of rapid but local cultural change. Funk acknowledges that "it is impossible to maintain that the Broadspear tradition originated in the Upper Susquehanna Valley or the rest of the Northeast," that "Broadspear-Susquehanna" complexes represent whole cultural systems in the study area, and that in Maine, at least, they follow hard upon the Moorehead phase with no evidence for in situ change; he nevertheless reasserts his belief that "those systems were products of diffusion and in situ development rather than migration" (Funk 1993:224–225). He identifies one possible thread of continuity from earlier times, "a complex mortuary ceremonialism with roots in prior Laurentian occupations" (Funk 1993:224–225). The evidence comes from two richly furnished cremation cemeteries found in close proximity in coastal Connecticut (Pfeiffer 1992:159–164). The earlier is the Bliss site, which dates to about 4700 B.P. and includes artifacts with clear Laurentian cognates. The second is the clearly Susquehanna-related

Griffin site. To me, close proximity by itself has little import, because in at least two Maine cases cemeteries included an early Moorehead phase component and a later, superimposed Adena-related one that can hardly be explained on the basis of cultural continuity (Bourque 1992a:130; Turnbull 1983). This evidence suggests that while prehistoric cultural traditions in a given region may occasionally have maintained an accurate knowledge of burial grounds over long periods of time, locational criteria for cemeteries—knolls of well-drained, coarse sediments, for example—are a more likely explanation for such juxtapositions.

Beyond the geographic proximity of the Bliss and Griffin sites, Funk lists similarities that are very widely encountered in Archaic contexts throughout the Northeast and beyond, such as dry bone cremation, the use of red ocher, the ritual killing of grave goods that are sometimes made of exotic materials, and the incorporation of plant and animal remains. For whatever reason, few such mortuary sites have been reported in southern New York and Connecticut, and I do not find these similarities between these virtually unique sites to be compelling evidence for cultural continuity. In sum, all these researchers, while recognizing the rapid and extensive reorganization of the archaeological record that the Susquehanna tradition heralds, have attempted to explain it in adaptive, diffusional, or evolutionary terms and have gone out of their way to disavow the possibility that immigration from the south might be a far more parsimonious explanation.

The Susquehanna tradition has been dealt with somewhat differently in New England. First, it has generally been regarded as fully Archaic rather than transitional even though steatite bowls have been found in Susquehanna sites there (Dincauze 1974:40; Snow 1980:247). Moreover, there has been less adherence to evolutionary models. Indeed, it was only in the 1970s that Dincauze first suggested that the appearance of the Susquehanna tradition involved the arrival of a new population, and that "the alternative explanation of trait diffusion does not suit the data" (Dincauze 1972:58). Even she was cautious, however, asserting that "no mass migration was involved, but rather an infiltration of small groups of people whose industrial traditions were markedly different from those of the resident population" (Dincauze 1974:27). Dincauze (1968:18, 80, 89–90) was also the first to note the presence of Susquehanna tradition artifacts in Maine, particularly at the Goddard and Eddington Bend sites.

Bourque identified additional Susquehanna tradition sites in Maine, including a cemetery at Eddington Bend on the Penobscot River, and commented that "Susquehanna tradition occupations may have replaced or overlapped those of the Moorehead phase at ca. 1800 B.C. or later but cannot be demonstrated to have interacted with it in any way" (Bourque 1992a:39–42). Sanger (1973:131–133) suggested that Susquehanna immigration had occurred along the coast as far east as the St. John River, and recently (Sanger 1991:56) reported points and drills, including some made of Maine-derived raw materials, across the Bay of Fundy in southern Nova Scotia.

Disconformities between Turner Farm Occupations 2 and 3 were found to be so striking that the most likely explanation seemed to be the replacement of earlier populations by immigrants from southern New England (Bourque 1975:43–44). More recently, Sanger and Bourque (1986) reconsidered the issue of Susquehanna tradition emergence in Maine and found themselves still in support of the immigration model. Finally, the distinct differences in human bone isotopic values between the Moorehead phase Nevin sample and the Susquehanna tradition Turner Farm sample provide additional support for the idea that the lifestyle of the latter is so different from the former as to suggest the intrusion of a new population from the south rather than derivation from earlier populations (Bourque and Krueger 1994).

Diffusion or Migration?

Willey may have been the first to suggest that the Savannah River-based Stallings Island population expanded out of its homeland into the lower Tennessee and Green rivers, and that the Indian Knoll site in particular represents "an actual movement of Eastern groups into this region" (Willey 1966:257). The notion that a similar population movement may have been responsible for a northward spread up the Atlantic coast was first suggested by Turnbaugh (1975). Turnbaugh's model links such a migration to a supposed warming trend (H. Wright 1971) and concomitant northward spread of the anadromous American shad (*Alosa sapidissima*). Subsequent paleoclimatic research, however, has failed to corroborate Turnbaugh's climatic-warming trend and, instead, indicates relatively rapid cooling during this period (Diaz et al. 1989; Webb et al. 1993:443–460; Zielinski et al. 1994:948). His hypothesis has been further discounted because of a widely held view that anadromous fishing has a much longer history in the Northeast than Turnbaugh's model would allow (Carlson 1988; Spiess 1992:171–185; Spiess et al. 1983).

Cook (1976) used archaeological data to critique Turnbaugh's model. His summary of several sites south of New England provides a convenient point of departure for reexamining the broadpoint migration debate. Cook incorrectly trivialized the numerous similarities found among the various expressions of the broadpoint phenomenon by asserting that it represents little more than the development of "a heavy-duty hafted knife . . . particularly useful to a maritime economy as practiced on various parts of the eastern seaboard during the second and third millennium B.C." (Cook 1976:353; see also Ahler 1971 and Dunn 1984).

Cook's diffusionist argument has been welcomed by archaeologists who are reluctant to consider population movement as a plausible explanation. Most recently, for example, Custer favored "a functional interpretation in which broadspears are viewed as a distinctive set of tools and knives unrelated to special groups (Custer 1989:151; see also Custer 1991:71). For New England, Cook had an especially strong influence on Snow's (1980) discussion of the Susquehanna tradition. Thus, in criticizing Turnbaugh's model Snow continued the preoccupation with lithic technology by asserting that "identifying components on the basis of diagnostic point types and going on to inferences having to do with phases and prehistoric populations may be a satisfying but nevertheless misleading archaeological exercise" (Snow 1980:254). As we shall see, however, data from Turner Farm Occupation 3 indicate that point types are hardly the extent of the evidence linking the Susquehanna tradition to the Late Archaic of the Southeast.

THE CERAMIC PERIOD

While there has been relatively lengthy discussion about possible population discontinuities during the Archaic period in Maine, there has been a general insistence that population continuity was maintained from the beginning of the Ceramic period until

European contact. Tuck (1975:145), for example, noted that despite evidence for "continual and sometimes rapid cultural change" beginning sometime prior to the Christian era, "no one seriously questions the essential population continuity to the present day" (Tuck 1975:145; see also Snow 1980:278). In part, this has been because linguistic data suggest that the eastern Algonquian languages spoken in this area when Europeans arrived were all closely related (e.g., Goddard 1978; Snow 1972:220, 1980:258–259, 304; Tuck 1975). It also reflects the fact that during the past 20 years considerably more effort has been devoted to the study of the Archaic period, with its complex technology and mortuary ritualism, than to the Ceramic period, which has been perceived to have a rather pedestrian archaeological signature compared to both the preceding Archaic and to contemporaneous ceramic-using cultures of the Midwest. But the root of this insistence is similar to that which caused archaeologists to regard the Susquehanna tradition as an in situ development despite its locally anomalous appearances—that is, a strong reliance on evolutionary models for culture change recently reinforced by a preoccupation with processual explanation.

In fact, however, ceramic data from Turner Farm Occupation 4, as well as from numerous other stratified shell middens, often fail to provide evidence for continuous, in situ development of ceramic styles such as might be expected of a long-resident population. The implications of these data for the population continuity model are considered below.

Linguistic Prehistory

The ongoing dialogue about the patterns of northeastern prehistory takes place against a backdrop of linguistic distribution that many archaeologists have felt compelled to address. Its main feature is the presence in what is now central New York and southern Ontario of an area historically occupied by Iroquoian-speaking peoples that separates two zones occupied by Algonquian speakers (Goddard 1978). Speculation about when and how this pattern became established has taken the form of attempts to attribute the development and spread of various archaeological patterns to one or another of these language groups (see Ellis et al. 1990:120–122 for a summary). Although the specificity of the various formulations has often far surpassed anything linguists have dared attempt, the variability among them has reflected diametric opposition more than a struggle toward consensus. Part of the disagreement seems to stem from the fact that, for linguists and archaeologists alike, linguistic prehistory has been at the top of few researchers' agendas and the resulting formulations have rarely gone beyond position simplistic archaeological–linguistic correlations. Of the recent entrants in the debate, Snow has the best claim to serious scholarship by virtue of having published a paper (Snow 1976) dealing solely with linguistic matters, as well as increasingly complex updates of his views (Snow 1980, 1992). His hypotheses are evaluated below.

Chapter 2

The Turner Farm Site

The Turner Farm site is located on North Haven Island in Penobscot Bay (Figures 2.1 and 2.2). North Haven is the second largest of the Fox Islands, which also include the larger island of Vinalhaven and 93 smaller islands. Like most of the 153 recorded prehistoric archaeological sites on the Fox Islands, the Turner Farm site is a shell midden situated on a relatively level terrace facing a gravel beach. It is one of the largest and deepest Fox Island sites, encompassing about 2,300 m² and reaching depths in excess of 1.5 m. Its deposits preserve what is probably the longest and most complex cultural sequence on the Gulf of Maine coast. The Fox Islands, which today are devoid of foxes, were so named in 1603 by English explorer Martin Pring (McLane 1982:95). Throughout most of the seventeenth and early eighteenth centuries they were part of the French colony of Acadia. Although numerous primary historic accounts refer to both Indian and French settlements on Penobscot Bay islands, apparently none were on the Fox Islands (see, e.g., Bourque 1989).

The first European settlers came mainly from Marshfield, Massachusetts, soon after the Treaty of Paris (1763) guaranteed English control of the region. Turner Farm was established about 1765 by the Thomas family and, through inheritance by a female descendant, recently became known as Turner farm. Because of its long tenure under local ownership, a detailed oral tradition of land use history was available. Active farming ceased in the late 1920s, but the property remained in the family until it was sold to summer residents in 1980. The original house still stands to the north of the site, and a boathouse, shown in Plate 2.1, stood on the beach immediately in front of the site until 1973. No other buildings have ever stood on the site. Although it is clear that the midden area has been extensively plowed, the residents have no recollection of this happening.

The first recorded excavations at the Turner Farm site were done surreptitiously by Arlo Bates and his son Oric in 1904. Because the site was only one of several shell middens explored by the Bateses during their summer cruises along the New England coast, Arlo's field notes provide only a few details:

> The deposit on the Turner Farm is very large, and extends for a considerable distance into the field. The family have an interesting collection of stone implements, and a remarkable amulet, a natural stone of animal shape pierced with holes for suspension [see Plate 7.8; actually a reworked steatite bowl sherd]. The farmhouse is not now inhabited, and I fear that our digging was not without a

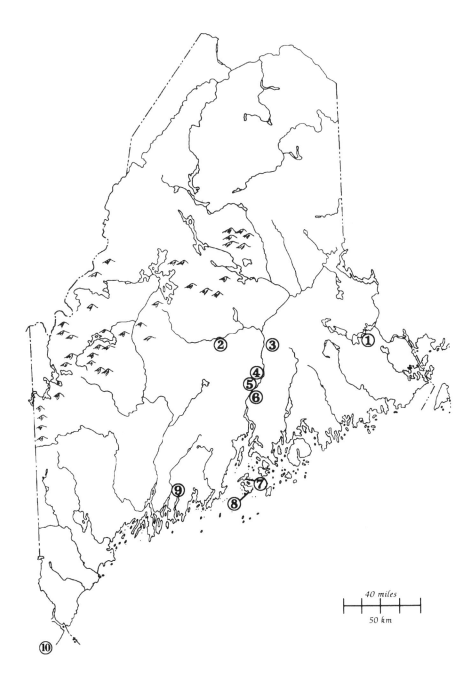

Figure 2.1. Map of Maine showing archaeological sites mentioned in the text: 1, 95.20; 2, Sharrow; 3, Hathaway; 4, Hirundo and Young; 5, Godfrey; 6, Eddington Bend; 7, Turner Farm; 8, Amburst Farm; 9, Davis-Tobie; 10, Seabrook.

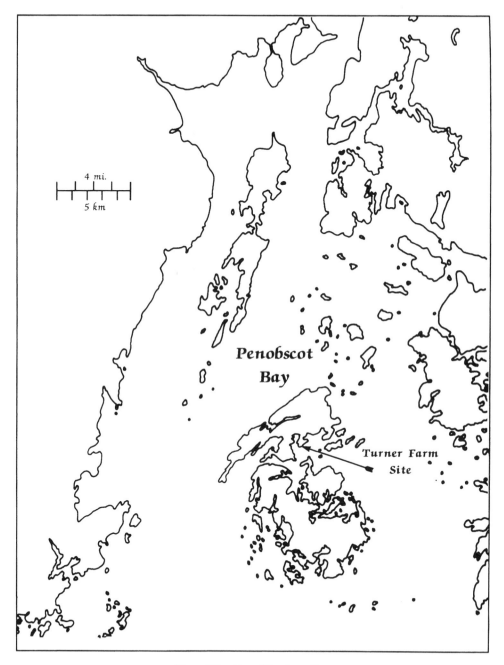

Figure 2.2. Map of Penobscot Bay.

Plate 2.1. View of the Turner Farm site taken in 1917.

flavor of lawlessness, as we had no leave. We dug in a bank on the shore, the top of the heap being eight or nine feet above tide-water. (Bates 1911:7–8)

Oric, who wrote a bachelor's thesis about this research while studying anthropology at Harvard University, reported one outcome of their clandestine operation: "Here the digging is not without its dangers, the head of the Turner family being a lonely savage who, in 1904, favored me with both barrels of his shotgun" (Bates and Winlock 1912:78). The Bateses nevertheless made at least one other excavation at the site in 1911, when they encountered a multiple human burial:

> In the bank of the heap at Turner's Farm turned up this summer [1911] a huddle of six skeletons. They were deep enough under the surface to have escaped the plough, say from twenty to twenty-four inches. They were in confusion, one on top of another, heads in different directions, positions unlike and irregular. The photographs show this poorly, but it is better indicated by the drawing [Figure 2.3] made by Bela Pratt [a painter, amateur archaeologist, and summer resident of North Haven] on the spot, which shows how the vertebrae of one skeleton (the one sent to Harvard marked A) was bent over a skull below it. The smaller and softer bones were badly decayed and crumbled, and of the six skulls only two were in fair condition. They had been broken by stones which had apparently been thrown in to fill the pit or by the weight of earth and passers above the surface. I examined the skulls rather carefully for any evidence that they had been crushed before

Figure 2.3. Field sketch by Bela Pratt of skeletons excavated by Arlo and Oric Bates in 1911.

burial, but I could find none. The breaks were (to me, at least) obviously made after interment. I do not know how much weight this find has, but it would seem a possible instance of interment in a pestilence. If the bodies were the result of a slaughter, especially a hand to hand conflict, it is hardly probable that the skulls would have remained whole. A burial would hardly have taken place in a kitchen midden on this scale of enemies [enmity?] unless the foe had been slaughtered on the spot, and moreover one of the skeletons was that of a woman. The inference which I made was that the plague was severe, and the Indians, departing in fear (they could hardly have remained with so wholesale a grave under so thin a covering of the porous nature made inevitable by the nature of the shell-heap,—no loam being in evidence—) had thrown the bodies into a hasty hole, tumbled in a number of stones from six to eight inches in diameter, and then covered the place with the shells they had displaced to make the grave. One of the skulls sent to Harvard was deformed, with cleft palate, etc. (Bates 1911:27–29)

Our excavations encountered a disturbance that is probably the result of their digging. Perhaps because of continued vigilance on the part of the Turners, we encountered no evidence of later excavation. During the late 1960s, when the owners were not often in residence on North Haven, local residents once again began to dig for artifacts there. In 1971, they agreed to cease digging and to leave their pits open for our inspection.

THE EXCAVATIONS

Our excavation began with a linear array of pits extending northward from the erosion scarp and passing near the collectors' pit, which had exposed deep, well-stratified deposits. We soon encountered in situ artifacts from the Late Archaic period, many of which closely resemble those from Maine's well-known Red Paint cemeteries (Moorehead 1922:20–151; Willoughby 1898, 1935/1973:6–80). Most evident were similarities to the bone and antler artifacts from Moorehead phase graves at the Nevin site in nearby Blue Hill Bay (Bourque 1992a:124–125; Byers 1979). The Nevin cemetery is unique among Red Paint cemeteries in that human skeletal material and bone grave furnishings were preserved by the alkalinity of the surrounding shell midden.

Coming as they did from a well-stratified midden rich in organic remains, these Archaic deposits were especially encouraging because so little data pertaining to the lives of Moorehead phase peoples had been recovered from either their cemeteries or the few habitation components attributable to them. Byers's excavations at the Nevin site had certainly encountered both, but he was unable to establish reliable stratigraphic control for any of the site's several components. Rowe (1940) had encountered Moorehead phase midden deposits at the Waterside site in Sorrento, but his explorations were hampered by extensive midden disturbance. Finally, although the Bateses (Bates 1911:12; Bates and Winlock 1911:87–88) and, later, Hadlock (1939:5–19) had encountered Moorehead phase materials at the Taft's Point site in Gouldsboro, apparently in stratified contexts (Bourque 1992a:23), no details were ever published.

Large-scale excavations in the midden ended in 1975. In 1977, excavations were undertaken in the salt marsh to the west of the midden (labeled "bog" on site plans in this volume) and in 1980 a small area west of the main excavation was opened as an exhibit for an American Quaternary Society field trip. In all, these excavations involved 4,275 ft^2 (398 m^2), about 17 percent of the midden's surface area, and 10,700 ft^3 (303 m^3), about 24 percent of the midden's total volume. Approximately 6,500 cataloged artifacts and 1,800 cataloged vertebrate bone samples were recovered.

The 1971 and 1972 seasons were undertaken as field schools sponsored by the State University of New York at Albany with additional support from private donors. Because the university provided British-system measuring equipment, this system remained in use throughout the project. Field work in 1974 and 1975 was supported by grants from the National Geographic Society. Throughout the project, citizens of North Haven contributed a great deal of support, assisting in the excavation, loaning equipment, arranging boat transportation, and granting us access to their homes for use as field laboratories. The analysis of faunal remains was supported by a grant from the National Science Foundation.

The site's complex stratigraphic sequence, which spans nearly five millennia from about 5000 B.P. to the early historic period, has been divided into sequential "occupations." Occupation 1 represents the scant remains of one or a few components dating between about 5000 and 4500 B.P. Occupation 2 apparently represents a single component dating somewhere between about 4500 and 4000 B.P. Occupation 3 includes either one extended or two closely spaced components dating between about 3800 and 3600 B.P.

Most strata postdating about 3000 B.P. included ceramic styles representing more than one time period, suggesting that the site at that time was more frequently occupied than in earlier times. The absence of clear stratigraphic discontinuities separating typologically definable components forced us to include all late deposits, except the uppermost plow zone, in a concatenation labeled Occupation 4. The following chapters are organized in accord with these four occupations, and present analyses of the artifacts, faunal remains, and human skeletal material from the site together with discussions of their significance to eastern North American archaeology. They are followed by a series of appendices that describe several ancillary research projects undertaken in connection with the overall project. Summary statements about that research, however, are integrated into the earlier chapters. Additional detailed reporting of faunal analysis can be found in Spiess and Lewis (1993).

Chapter 3

Methods and Techniques

HISTORY OF METHODOLOGY

While investigating prehistoric coastal exploitation on Martha's Vineyard, Massachusetts, between 1964 and 1967, William A. Ritchie (1980) encountered shell middens that resulted from long sequences of episodic occupation and that, therefore, had complex stratification. In excavating them, he developed methodology that involved opening groups of contiguous pits (sections) separated by balks to preserve evidence of stratigraphy for later recording. Because stratification of these sites was complex and finely structured, arbitrary levels were not used.

Generally, Ritchie recorded both point provenience and stratigraphic descriptions for all important artifacts. More ubiquitous items, such as flaking debris and bone refuse, were provenienced by section and stratigraphic level or by numbered feature. In addition to noting stratigraphic associations, depth-below-surface was recorded for all significant materials and features. Stratigraphic sections, by contrast, were drawn with reference to a local horizon above the surface, defined by line level, and ultimately keyed into a topographic map of the site.

Midden samples were collected systematically from a column in each balk. Features and other unusual deposits were sampled on a judgmental basis. An extended commentary was prepared for all radiocarbon samples detailing their context, associations, probable origins, and reliability for dating a specific depositional event. Horizontal plans were drawn for all features, and sometimes stratigraphic sections as well.

Since this was pioneering research for the Northeast, Ritchie employed small, carefully supervised crews, stressing the recovery of carefully documented samples. He also avoided the use of screens, relying instead upon meticulous excavation for comprehensiveness.

In 1968, when I served as Ritchie's crew chief in excavations of three shell midden sites on and near Deer Isle, Maine, I employed essentially identical excavation methods. Again, one of our main concerns was cultural history, but because these middens were composed mainly of *Mya* shell, their stratification proved to be less obvious than on Martha's Vineyard, where stratigraphic discontinuities were clearly defined by changes in mollusk species frequencies (see, e.g., Ritchie 1980:127–133). In the Deer Isle middens, stratigraphic discontinuities could often be observed during excavation, especially when they were defined by very thin shell-free deposits or "floors" separating thicker shell-rich deposits. In order to trace these discontinuities from section to section, however, we were forced to open linear arrays of pits and sometimes to remove the balks to expose long sections. Using this strategy, subtle changes in midden composition, such as shell fragment size, crushed blue mussel (*Mytilus edulis*) content, high fish bone or soil content, or even the orientations of clam valves, became stratigraphic indicators (see Bourque 1992a:234–235, 263).

EXCAVATIONS AT THE TURNER FARM SITE

Our excavation and sampling strategies at the Turner Farm site were similar to those described above (Figure 3.1, Plate 3.1). Excavation proceeded by opening 5-ft^2 sections, usually assigned to one excavator. Generally, excavators of each section worked independently. Where extensive, complex features were encountered, however, the simultaneous, coordinated excavation of several contiguous sections was sometimes attempted. Although partially successful, we found this approach difficult to expand very far because even the most obvious features merged with others or became difficult to trace for other reasons. Furthermore, the deeper the surface under scrutiny, the more time consuming the excavation of overlying midden became. This tension between stratigraphic control and horizontal exposure was never satisfactorily resolved.

Artifacts were cleaned, cataloged, and packed for shipment to the Maine State Museum soon after excavation. Objects needing preliminary stabilization were usually dealt with

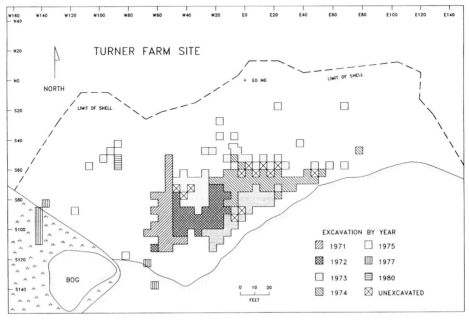

Figure 3.1.   Plan of excavations at the Turner Farm site.

Plate 3.1. View of 1972 excavations at the Turner Farm site taken from the roof of the boathouse shown in Plate 2.1.

during excavation with advice from the Museum's conservation staff. Complex conservation problems required field visits from the Museum's conservators, who also undertook long-term conservation and restoration of artifacts at the Museum after each field season.

Our long-term planning was constrained by uncertainties about renewed funding and owner permission on an annual basis. One result of these constraints was our decision not to attempt balanced sampling of the midden's surface area, a technique popular during the 1960s and 1970s as a means of reducing subjectivity in choosing where to excavate. Rather, we decided that the unique potential of the Archaic deposits should be our main focus. Thus, areas of the midden where Archaic deposits were not encountered were more lightly sampled than those containing Archaic deposits.

PROBLEMS OF RECOVERY

Because even experienced shell midden excavators vary in their ability to recover artifacts, bone refuse, and other materials of interest, researchers in the Northeast recently have turned to screening as a means of standardizing the rates of collection of important materials. In our experiments with the use of screens, however, we have encountered three problems that have caused us to avoid their use on a routine basis. First, although very small and commonly encountered items, such as fish bone and retouching flakes, are the most likely to be undercollected by trowelling, they are also the most likely to fall through a screen. One solution to this problem is to catch the first-stage screenings in a finer screen. While effective, this added step greatly slows the pace and increases the cost of excavation, and is thus likely to impede the sampling of horizontal variability on a larger scale. Our approach to the problem of undercollecting has been to rely on samples from balks in estimating the proportions of the more common midden constituents. Although such samples are less reliable than double screening for estimating the frequencies of less ubiquitous remains, this shortcoming is at least partially compensated for by other techniques described below.

Second, screening is physically destructive to fragile items, such as bone artifacts, fish bones, and pottery sherds. We have found that the careful manual collection of small bones in particular seems to enhance their identifiability, and thus to compensate adequately for presumed underrecovery.

Third, many excavators respond to the tedium of shell midden excavation by becoming lax in recovering faunal remains and artifacts of low interest, particularly when they know that they can ultimately rely on the screen. Our attempts to deal with the problem of tedium have focused on close supervision and providing extra assistance to those working on difficult recovery jobs. In sum, given budget limitations, the rapid rate of coastal site destruction, and assuming the availability of motivated field assistants such as those we employed at the Turner Farm, the problems presented by uniformly screening shell midden materials outweighed the advantages.

AMBIGUITY IN THE STRATIGRAPHIC RECORD

As at many stratified middens, artifacts and faunal remains were occasionally recovered from seemingly inappropriate contexts. A potential source of stratigraphic ambiguity in shell middens that has been the subject of considerable speculation in the Northeast is the postdepositional movement of artifacts. Hypothetical factors can be invoked to argue for both upward and downward disturbance of discrete objects. However, at the Turner Farm site, the primary direction of movement appears clearly to have been upward.

The evidence for upward movement comes from the distributions of artifact styles known to occur with specific periods (Table 3.1). Of particular importance are plummets, which date prior to about 4000 B.P., and ceramics, which date after about 2700 B.P. Despite their relatively small sample size ($N = 55$), plummets were frequently encountered above Occupation 2 strata. Ceramic sherds, by contrast, although far more abundant, were very rarely found below ceramic period contexts.

Plummet distribution provides a standard for evaluating the possible upward mixture of other probably early materials—particularly swordfish bone and pecking stones—whose cultural contexts at the Turner Farm site were less certain. The similarities between plummet and swordfish bone distribution strongly suggest that both originated exclusively in strata attributed to Occupation 2 (about 4400–4200 B.P.). This conclusion is supported by the total absence of swordfish remains from Ceramic period contexts elsewhere in the Penobscot Bay area. Pecking stone distribution, however, suggests that at least some were produced after Occupation 2 times.

The upward movement of artifacts seems to have been the result of discrete disturbance events, especially pit digging by the site's later occupants. This inference derives from the fact that movement rates in the midden were quite variable. Some spatially clustered artifacts—for example, Susquehanna bifaces (Plates 6.1–6.6)—fortuitously escaped upward movement to a large extent, while more uniformly scattered artifacts—for example, plummets (Plates 5.4–5.5)—did not. Furthermore, when the same materials were abundant in more than one stratum, their horizontal distributions showed a strong tendency toward congruence, suggesting that the stratigraphically inferior cluster was the immediate source for the superior one.

Another source of ambiguity is incorrect or ambiguous stratigraphic attribution (Table 3.2). This problem arose especially near discontinuities where shell-rich units may have

Table 3.1. Stratigraphic Distribution of Diagnostic Specimens

Level[a]	Pottery	Occ 3 points	Plummets	Swordfish	Pecking stones
FCS	77	4	0	1	14
NGF	5	0	0	0	2
MCS	95	0	0	0	5
1GF	112	1	0	8	17
CCS	93	3	3	9	10
2GF	57	3	1	8	5
B2GF	5	2	0	3	4
Occ 3	0	156	8	24	32
Occ 2	0	0	55	127	175
Occ 1	0	0	0	2	0
Total	444	169	67	182	264

[a]FCS, finely crushed shell; NGF, new gravel floor; MCS, moderately crushed shell and black soil; 1GF, first gravel floor; CCS, coarsely crushed shell and black soil; 2GF, second gravel floor; B2GF, below second gravel floor; Occ 3, Occupation 3; Occ 2, Occupation 2; Occ 1, Occupation 1.

Table 3.2. Summary of Provenience Data

Level	Bone lot samples	Diagnostic artifacts[a]
Plow zone	279	586
Occupation 4	753	1,317
Occupation 3	292	693
Occupation 2	368	301
Occupation 1	8	10
Disturbed	20	22
Mixed	99	36
Lack of data	10	23[b]
Total	1,829	2,988
Percent poor data	.5	.7
Percent poor stratigraphic provenience	5.4	1.2
Percent disturbed	1.1	.7
Total percent poor provenience	7.0	2.6

[a]Including pottery, scrapers, bone points, beaver tooth knives, bifaces, hammerstones, and plummets.
[b]Includes 9 from stone or bone bags.

been trodden into shell-free ones, or when such discontinuities were difficult to discern during excavation. The frequency of incorrect attribution is difficult to evaluate because few artifact or faunal classes can be exclusively attributed to specific temporal ranges using independent criteria. Generally, we suspect that the impact of misattribution on our analysis has been minimal. For example, no Susquehanna tradition bifaces were attributed to Occupation 2 strata even where they directly underlay these bifaces.

SITE STRUCTURE

As described in the following chapters, our excavations encountered well-preserved and clearly stratified midden deposits over large areas of the site (Figure 3.2, Plate 3.2). However, it soon became apparent that the midden had clearly sustained substantial damage resulting mainly from two factors. The first is relative sea-level rise, which has negatively impacted virtually all Fox Islands sites through bank-face erosion, beach transgression, and submersion (Figure 3.3). To the east, where the terrain rises several feet above sea level, photographs taken about 1919 show a stable, well-vegetated bank (Plate 2.1). Photos taken in the early 1960s, however, reveal breaches in vegetation and from that time to the mid-1980s erosion made significant inroads on the midden, keeping the bank largely unvegetated. Presently, the bank is once again largely stabilized by vegetation. The low-lying western portion of the site is being reworked or simply overridden by beach transgression, and our excavations through the beach, described below, indicate the presence of deeply buried midden. Appendix 5 discusses the impact of sea-level rise in detail.

The second source of disturbance is plowing, which probably occurred on a regular basis after the farm was established about 1765. The resulting plow zone is a homogeneous stratum of finely crushed shell and dark soil extending over the entire midden. It yielded artifacts from all the site's components, probably because even the earliest lie near the

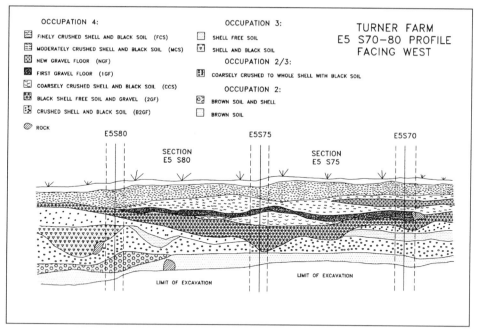

Figure 3.2. Stratigraphic section of the Turner Farm midden.

surface at the margins of the site and in shallow areas where ledge outcrops have been buried by midden deposition.

Although the site has been plowed and otherwise disturbed as recently as this century, a uniform shell-free sod (generally 8 cm thick) covered the entire midden. The presence of this sod suggests that restratification of such shell-rich deposits occurred rapidly after cultural deposition ceased.

Below the plow zone lay shell-rich strata interspersed with generally thinner shell-free deposits. The former are regarded as shell refuse. Some could be subdivided into smaller units representing discrete depositional episodes, but most were more massive, probably reflecting rapid accumulation. Most of the shell was extensively broken, presumably by postdepositional trampling. Only in the thickest strata did whole valves predominate (see, e.g., Appendix 1, column 3).

The shell-free deposits seem to have resulted from a variety of processes. Many were composed of fine, well-sorted gravel like that found on the modern beach but darkly stained by charcoal and organic residues. These deposits were referred to as beach gravel floors, and they range in extent from a few to several hundred square meters and seem to be living surfaces stained by fires and decayed organics. The smaller ones may have been house floors, while the more extensive ones may have been deposited to cover odoriferous waste or sharp shell fragments. Most features originate in or are otherwise associated with these floors. Some of the larger shell-free strata, like the sod mentioned above, are probably topsoils formed during periods of abandonment or reduced refuse disposal to which beach gravel was later added. Others, however, are composed of subsoil, probably redeposited

Plate 3.2. Photo of stratigraphic section shown in Figure 3.2.

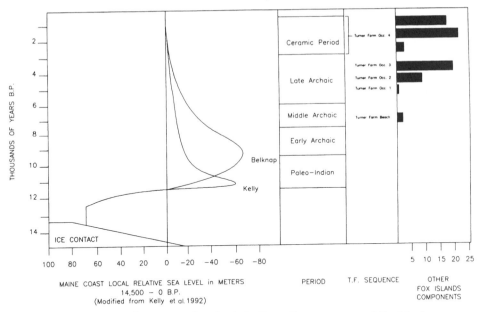

Figure 3.3. Comparison of Maine coastal sea level, the Turner Farm sequence, and Fox Islands component frequency.

from local high points to level the site (see, e.g., Figure 3.2, "Brown soil"). Projecting intermittently through a basal layer of stained subsoil matrix, probably the original surface, were outcrops of highly fractured acid volcanic bedrock.

Artifacts were comparably abundant in both shell-free and shell-rich deposits, and their horizontal distributions were fairly congruent as well. This congruity probably arose from the deposition of refuse near areas of food preparation and consumption. The greater abundance of bone refuse in shell-rich lenses indicates that the trampling of artifacts from shell-rich lenses into underlying floors was not a major taphonomic factor.

Discrete modern disturbances of the higher strata were encountered occasionally, mainly in the southern portion of the excavated area. Most contained historic artifacts, such as sherds of lead-glazed earthenware and nails. Some of the larger disturbances possibly reflect the operation of a hauling line for boats or a fish weir. Near the erosion scarp was an unusually large and deep disturbance, quite probably the pit from which Arlo and Oric Bates removed human remains.

SUBMERGED MIDDEN

In 1977, we explored the area where the midden, beach, and marsh converge. Our goal was to ascertain the extent to which the midden had been covered by beach transgression, and also to learn whether organic artifacts might be preserved in the peat of the marsh. A trench extending from the midden into the marsh (Figure 3.1) exposed a total of 125 ft² (about 12 m²) and reached a depth of 4 ft (about 1.2 m) below mean high tide (the level of the marsh surface). This work involved building a caisson of overlapping planks driven vertically into the peat, as well as the sporadic pumping of water. Blocks of peat were then removed, broken apart, and wet screened. The peat produced several recent carpentry scraps but no prehistoric artifacts except a few bifaces judged to be intrusions from the adjacent midden. Below the peat, however, we encountered a thin, dark deposit that yielded artifacts ranging in age from the Archaic to the Ceramic period. The artifacts were not beach tumbled and seemed to be in situ. Apparently, this deposit is a conflation of multiple strata whose shell dissolved in acid marsh water as they were submerged by rising sea level.

An additional two 5-ft² sections were excavated through beach deposits near the point where the beach comes into contact with the western end of the erosion scarp (Figure 3.4). Below 5 ft or more of beach gravel, both pits encountered a dark, cemented deposit that readily reacted with dilute HCl. Apparently this was midden from which the shell had dissolved after being submerged, but where precipitated shell carbonate has cemented the remaining midden elements into a kind of caliche. Like the artifacts from beneath the marsh, those recovered from the caliche showed no signs of beach tumbling but were not recovered in proper stratigraphic sequence. The deeper pit reached subsoil at 11.5 ft (about 3.5 m) below mean high tide.

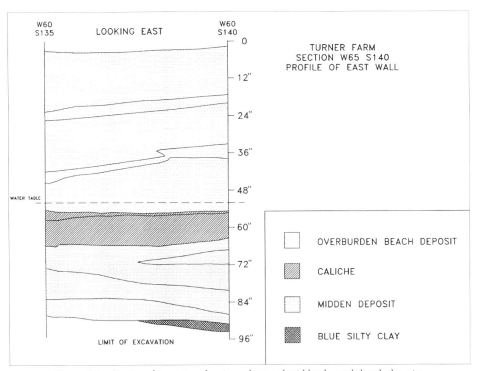

Figure 3.4. Stratigraphic section showing submerged midden beneath beach deposits.

CHRONOLOGY

Our chronology for the site is based largely on radiocarbon dates generously provided by Robert Stuckenrath, then of the Smithsonian Institution. Because Stuckenrath was interested in comparing radiocarbon dates on a variety of associated organic materials, we also submitted samples of antler, bone, shell, and swordfish rostrum.[1] These samples consistently yielded more recent dates than those on associated charcoal. This disparity strongly suggests that dissolved calcium carbonate from shells high in the midden has percolated downward, contaminating samples below them. Evidence of such percolation is ubiquitous in the white carbonate coating found on many lithic artifacts from the midden. We have therefore discounted noncharcoal dates in constructing an absolute chronology for the site. Unless otherwise specified, the dates given in the following chapters are on charcoal samples.

[1]Stuckenrath's laboratory reports did not specify whether the bone and rostrum dates were on apatite, collagen, or both.

Chapter 4

Occupation 1

INTRODUCTION

Occupation 1 represents a palimpsest of cultural remains found in contexts that were stratigraphically below midden deposits attributed to later occupations. While this stratigraphic ambiguity is cause for uneasiness regarding claims that the remains represent a single component, the internal consistency of artifacts from the submidden and of radiocarbon dates from Occupation 1 features, as well as corroborating evidence from other components of similar age, overcome the stratigraphic problem to a considerable extent.

The oldest artifact recovered from the Turner Farm site appears to be a Middle Archaic Stark point (Plate 4.1, no. 29.9.7934; see Dincauze 1976:29–37). It was found on the beach, where it probably was redeposited by erosion, and is not regarded as affiliated with Occupation 1.

The earliest in situ cultural remains came from three pits excavated into subsoil (Table 4.1, Figure 4.1). All contained shell and dark soil fill and a few faunal remains. Only one pit (Feature 15-1973) produced a chronologically diagnostic artifact, a small stemmed point.

Outside the features, on or just in subsoil, were found a series of flaked stone artifacts (Figure 4.1). Most common are small stemmed points (Plate 4.2, Table 4.2). An asymmetrically side-notched biface, an apparently water-rolled, expanding-stem point (Plate 4.3, lower left), and a few biface fragments were also recovered. Two small stemmed points recovered from stratigraphically higher contexts were probably displaced upward by later disturbance.

The small stemmed points ($N = 18$) are mostly made of quartz. Eleven have striking platform remnants at their bases and the remaining seven show no sign of purposeful basal thinning. This stem configuration suggests that they were set into socketed shafts. Their average length, width, and thickness do not differ significantly from small stemmed point assemblages from the Neville site (Manchester, New Hampshire; Dincauze 1976:52), the Seabrook Marsh site (New Hampshire), and the Nelson Island site (Newburyport, Massachusetts; Robinson 1985:13, 43), or the Davis-Tobie site on the Sheepscot River (Alna, Maine; Maine State Museum files).

Absent from Occupation 1 were small triangular bifaces and bifacial scrapers, which have often been found in association with small stemmed point components elsewhere

Plate 4.1. Stark point found on the beach in front of the Turner Farm site.

Table 4.1. Dates (B.P.) from Occupation 1

Date	Lab Number	Section	Sample Number	Feature Number	Material	Description
4410 ± 80	SI 1920	W25S105	2051		Swordfish	Subsoil
4970 ± 85	SI 2392	E40S65	67C	22-1974	Charcoal	Shell-filled pit
5210 ± 70	SI 2394	W35S105	13C	5-1972	Charcoal	Shell-filled pit covered by "subsoil"
5290 ± 95	SI 1925	E5S85	39C	15-1973	Charcoal	Black-soil-filled pit truncated by a later soil and shell-filled pit

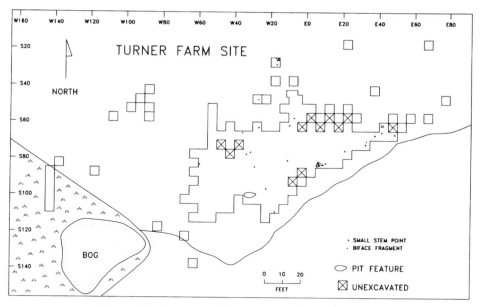

Figure 4.1. Distribution of Occupation 1 artifacts and features.

(e.g., Dincauze 1976:110–113; Robinson 1985:43). Also apparently absent from Occupation 1 are plummets, gouges, and other heavy stone artifacts, although it is probable that some such artifacts attributed to Occupation 2 actually originated in Occupation 1.

THE AGE OF OCCUPATION 1

One small stemmed point was found in a submidden feature (15-1973) dating to 5290 ± 95 B.P. (SI 1925), but subsequent analysis suggests that this feature represents at least two separate events. Its upper fill produced a large stemmed point attributed to Occupation 2 (Plate 5.1, lower left), an unusual expanding-stem biface (Plate 7.5, upper right), and charcoal samples that produced three additional dates that range from 4555 ± 95 B.P. (SI 1923) to 3710 ± 60 B.P. (SI 4242).

The small stemmed point from Feature 15-1973 is still regarded as probably associated with the earliest date. Moreover, charcoal samples from two other submidden contexts produced similar dates: 4970 ± 85 B.P. (SI 2392) and 5210 ± 70 B.P. (SI 2394; Table 4.1). As pointed out below (see also Table 8.1), these are early dates for this technology, but the parsimonious explanation of this data set is that small stemmed point technology and the submidden features all pertain to an occupation dating around 5000 B.P.

A swordfish rostrum fragment found below the midden yielded a date of 4410 ± 80 B.P. (SI 1920), but this date is suspect because the sample was likely contaminated by carbonates of more recent ages.

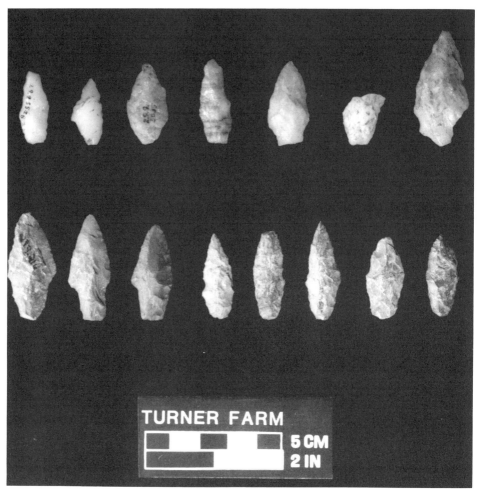

Plate 4.2.   Small stemmed points from Occupation 1.

THE IMPACT OF EROSION ON OCCUPATION 1

Seismic and sediment core data from Penobscot Bay indicate that Occupation 1 occurred near the end of several millennia of rapid rise in relative sea level (Appendix 5). While there remains some uncertainty regarding the level of Mean High Water (MHW) at the site during Occupation 1, it very probably stood more than 5 m below present levels. As Figure A5.7 indicates, it seems clear that the rise in MHW has eroded an extensive area that would have been available for habitation during Occupation 1 times.

It is significant in this regard that the three dated Occupation 1 features were found within 25 ft (8 m) of the erosional scarp, and that nearly half the small stemmed points were also found in the eastern portion of the midden just behind the erosional scarp between Features 15-1973 and 22-1974 (Figure 4.1). This area of the site has apparently been

Table 4.2. Stemmed Bifaces from Occupation 1[a]

Catalog number	Material[b]	Length	Width	Thickness
755	NYC	3.08	1.27	.48
849	Chesire quartzite	3.89	1.63	.74
1400	OHB	3.56	1.59	.65
1783	Quartz	3.01	1.59	.79
1854	NYC	3.05	1.42	.73
1991[c]	OHB	—	1.98	.84
3035	Quartz	3.04	1.55	.77
3694	Quartz	4.30	2.11	.97
3742	OHB	6.02	2.18	.89
4164	Quartz	3.07	1.22	.72
4223	NYC	3.28	1.20	.52
5019[c]	OHB	—	1.79	.62
5349	OHB	3.65	1.35	.51
5404	KTM	3.16	1.20	.48
5578[c]	Quartz	—	1.19	.50
5842[c]	Quartz	—	—	—
6008	Quartz	2.47	1.22	.55
6646	Quartz	2.31	1.31	.51
7643	Quartz	2.45	1.43	.58
n =		15	18	18
ave. =		3.36	15.10	.66
s.d. =		.91	.32	.15
min. =		2.31	1.19	.48
max. =		6.02	1.98	.97

[a]All measurements in centimeters.
[b]See Appendix 6.
[c]Incomplete specimen.

differentially protected from erosion by underlying bedrock. Consequently, what remains of Occupation 1 may be only a small remnant of its original extent. Since later occupations at the site produced both shell-filled features and shell-rich midden deposits, and since Occupation 1 features contained significant amounts of shell, attesting to shellfish exploitation, it seems reasonable to suggest that an Occupation 1 shell midden may have been completely eroded from the southern margin of the site.

FAUNAL REMAINS

Faunal remains from Occupation 1 are scant. All three features contained soft-shell clam (*Mya arenaria*). Feature 5-1972 also contained sea urchin (*Strongylocentrotus droebachiensis*). Vertebrate remains are limited to two deer (*Odocoileus virginianus*), one sea mink (*Mustela macrodon*), 21 postcranial fragments of swordfish (*Xiphias gladius*), one duck, and some cod (*Gadus callarias*; 55 vertebrae and 1 dentary fragment). The dated swordfish rostrum fragment referred to above is also regarded as belonging to Occupation 1. Some swordfish and cod remains attributed to Occupation 2 may actually have originated in Occupation 1.

Plate 4.3.   Bifaces found in "subsoil."

SIGNIFICANCE OF OCCUPATION 1

Early discussions of the Turner Farm site (Bourque 1975, 1976) avoided positing relationships between Occupation 1 and other components in the Northeast, despite obvious resemblances to Ritchie's (1965, 1980:218ff; see also Dincauze 1974:47–48) Small Stemmed Point tradition of southern New England and New York State. In large part, this avoidance was due to the fact that this was the first such assemblage to be reported from Maine. Its relationship to that tradition, therefore, was not initially apparent given the paucity of data then available from the region between its established range and Penobscot Bay.

It is now obvious that small stemmed point technology was prevalent at least as far eastward along the Gulf of Maine coast as Penobscot Bay. Most important, perhaps, is the Davis-Tobie site, where typical small stemmed points were found in association with a plummet, a gouge, an avoid atlatl weight, a grooved pebble "net weight," and a quartz biface scraper, all of which resemble specimens previously found in association with small stemmed points to the southwest (Dincauze 1976:62, 75; Robinson 1985:19, Figure 25; Staples and Athearn 1969:5–7). Also found in an isolated test section at the Davis-Tobie site was a quartz triangular point conforming to Ritchie's (1971a:127–128) Squibnocket triangle type. Two radiocarbon dates for this component are 4470 ± 150 B.P. (RL 748) and 4215 ± 340 B.P. (GX 14137). The only other dated small stemmed point component in Maine is the Rosie site in Topsham: 4385 ± 250 B.P. (GX 16266; Cox and Wilson 1991:27). Dates on human bone from the Small Stemmed Point tradition component at Seabrook Marsh are 4310 ± 255 B.P. (GX 4824G) and 4780 ± 185 B.P. (GX 4824A; Robinson 1985:40).

The easternmost known small stemmed point component on the Maine coast is at the Nevin site in Blue Hill Bay (Hamilton and Krader, personal communication, 1989). Small stemmed points have also been identified in Nova Scotia at the Bain site near Yarmouth, and at Rafter Lake in Halifax Co. (Sanger 1988a:89; Tuck 1984:19). Their occurrence there may be part of a once contiguous coastal distribution now broken by coastal submersion along the Bay of Fundy coast (Turnbull 1985:14). None have been reported in New Brunswick, even from the archaeologically rich Miramichi Valley, which suggests that Penobscot Bay may be near the northern limit of this technological complex.

The available evidence suggests that Occupation 1 is the oldest small stemmed point component yet identified in New England. The only one of comparable antiquity in southern New England is Bear Swamp in Berkeley, Massachusetts, which has a date of 4640 ± 80 B.P. (Y-2499; Staples and Athearn 1969:5). Taken as a group, these data call into question Ritchie's (1980:218ff) proposed Small Stemmed Point immigration from the lower Susquehanna drainage about 4200 B.P. Furthermore, the association of rod-shaped whetstones and atlatl weights with some components (e.g., Bear Swamp, Davis-Tobie, Rosie) supports Dincauze's (1974:47) assertion that the tradition developed in place from local antecedents around 5000 B.P.

The small Occupation 1 faunal sample warrants little extrapolation. However, given long-standing uncertainty about the onset of maritime exploitation in the Gulf of Maine, it is worth emphasizing that the exploitation of shellfish, cod, and swordfish is in evidence as early as about 5000 B.P. at the Turner Farm site and that the early importance of cod and swordfish is confirmed at the Seabrook Marsh site and apparently also at the earliest component at the Nevin site (Hamilton and Krader, personal communication 1989; Robinson 1985:52–61). Such data suggest a much stronger maritime adaptation for the people who used small stemmed point technology than was previously recognized.

Chapter 5

Occupation 2

INTRODUCTION

Discovery of the midden deposits and underlying altered subsoil that are now attributed to Occupation 2 was indeed a happy event, for it fulfilled the promise of intact Archaic coastal components suggested by private artifact collections from the Fox Islands that I had studied earlier (Bourque 1992a). Writing over two decades after that discovery, when archaeologists in the Northeast casually discuss Archaic occupations extending back to 8000 B.P., I can recall both the fascination that Late Archaic cultures of the Northeast have held for American archaeologists since the inception of the discipline and the pitiful weakness of the data pertaining to the lives of these people that was available until quite recently.

In 1971, new ideas about who the "Red Paint people" were, about their relatedness to other eastern cultures with elaborate mortuary ceremonialism, about their social and economic behavior, and about their relationship to later cultures of the Northeast became a renewed focus of interest as active research in the region revived following a long period of quiescence. As I hope to demonstrate below, examination of the remains of Occupation 2, combined with recent research on older collections from other Maine Late Archaic sites, has contributed much to our understanding of the Red Paint people.

STRATIGRAPHY

Occupation 2 deposits were encountered in 131 of 163 excavated sections. They include discontinuous lenses of dark-stained, relatively shell-free subsoil matrix overlain by shell-rich refuse. In the excavated area, Occupation 2 shell refuse covered about 90 percent of this surface. Forty features were attributed to these strata (Table 5.1, Figure 5.4). The first published statement on our excavations at the site (Bourque 1975:36) suggested that three human burials encountered there just a few months earlier were associated with Occupation 2. Subsequent excavation, however, revealed that they were actually part of a large cemetery associated with Occupation 3.

Table 5.1. Features from Occupation 2

Feature number	Section	Description	Dates
2-1972	W50S85	Hearth	
3-1972	W50S90	Cooking pit	
9-1972	W30S90	Hearth	
12-1972	W40S90	Hearth	2705 ± 60 B.P. (SI 1926A)
			3115 ± 60 B.P. (SI 1926B)
13-1972	W30S95	Small soil- and shell-filled pit	
15-1972	W25S95	Pit in subsoil	3745 ± 75 B.P. (SI 2406)
16-1972	W20S95	Pit in subsoil	
20-1972	W20S90	Pit in floor	
27-1972	W15S90	Hearth	
28-1972	W20S100	Dog burial	
5-1973	W10S90	Hearth	
6-1973	W10S90	Hearth below Feature 5-1973	
10-1973	E0S90	Dog burial	
14-1973	E5S75	Hearth	
16-1973	E5S75	Black soil-filled pit in subsoil	
17-1973	W0S80	Hearth on subsoil	
20-1973	E10S80	Hearth on subsoil	
22-1973	E10S80	Cache in subsoil	3480 ± 90 B.P. (B 6031)
24-1973	E10S80	Dog burial	4390 ± 55 B.P. (SI 1921)
14-1974	E0S75	Pit in subsoil	2970 ± 65 B.P. (SI 2402)
15-1974	E20S80	Pit in subsoil	
20-1974	E50S65	Hearth	
23-1974	W10S75	Pit in NW corner of section	
24A-1974	W5S75	Shallow pit, foreshaft and plummet	4135 ± 85 B.P. (SI 2395)
25-1974	E20S70	Pit in SW corner of section	
26-1974	E0S70	Dog burial	
28-1974	W5S70	Pit	
31-1974	W10S80	Shell-filled pit	
43-1974	E25S75	Dog burial	
5-1975	W30S80	Shell- and soil-filled pit in subsoil	
8-1975	W10S50	Red ocher patch	
2-1972	W50S85	Hearth	
17-1975	W35S90	Pit in subsoil	
20-1975	W35S80	Large shell-filled pit	
21-1975	W35S85	Shell-filled pit in subsoil	
25-1975	W30S50	Hearth	
27-1975	W40S70	Pit	
29-1975	W40S70	Shell-filled pit in subsoil	
31-1975	W25S50	Small brown soil-filled pit	
32-1975	W45S65	Whole shell-filled pit in subsoil	
36-1975	W30S75	Dog burial	

In this and in more recent components, artifacts were comparably abundant in both shell-free and shell-rich deposits, and their horizontal distributions were fairly congruent as well. This congruity probably arose from the deposition of refuse near activity areas.

Stratigraphic data suggest that Occupation 2 was a single, fairly brief episode spanning only a few years. No complex stratigraphy developed, all deposition occurred on the subsoil surface, and no subsequent covering of shell refuse with beach gravel occurred, as it did in later occupations. Moreover, the discreteness of artifact clusters described below suggests a single, unbroken sequence of occupation and deposition.

THE AGE OF OCCUPATION 2

Dates attributed to Occupation 2 deposits range from 4555 ± 95 B.P. (SI 1923) to 2705 ± 60 B.P. (SI 1926a; Table 5.2). Most of the younger dates are on antler, bone, and shell, which, as pointed out above, consistently produced dates younger than expected. The oldest date is from upper fill of the same feature (15-1973) that produced the small stemmed point and associated date discussed in Chapter 4. Thus, the age of Occupation 2 is probably best reflected by a single charcoal date: 4390 ± 55 B.P. (SI 1921; see Table 8.1).

THE IMPACT OF EROSION ON OCCUPATION 2

Analysis of data from seismic profiles and sediment cores throughout Penobscot Bay indicates that Mean High Water stood approximately 4 m below modern levels during Occupation 2 times (Appendix 5). This suggests that significant areas of the Occupation 2 midden have been submerged or destroyed by erosion. As shown in Figure A5.7, the loss has probably been most extensive in the low-lying, southwestern portion of the site. Occupation 2 deposits probably extend beneath the modern barrier beach and marsh to the south and west of the midden, although our limited excavations there encountered no evidence.

Table 5.2. Dates (B.P.) from Occupation 2

Date	Section	Sample number	Feature number	Material	Description	Lab number
2705 ± 60	W40S90		12-1972	Antler	Hearth	SI 1926a
2970 ± 65	E0S75	62C	14-1974	Swordfish	Pit in subsoil	SI 2402
3115 ± 65	W40S90		12-1972	Antler	Hearth	S1 1926b
3445 ± 70	E40S65-70	72C		Swordfish	Subsoil surface	SI 2401
3480 ± 90	E10S80	57C	22-1973	Charcoal	Cache	B 6031
3665 ± 55	W25S105	42C		*Mercenaria*	Basal midden	SI 2403
3710 ± 60	E5S85	63C	15-1973	*Mya*	Pit (top)	S1 4242
3745 ± 75	W25S95	37C	15-1972	*Mya*	Pit with needle	SI 2406
3785 ± 75	E5S85	41C	15-1973	*Mya*	Above Fea. 51-1973	SI 2408
3920 ± 25	E15S80			Ivory	Walrus tusk	OS 1832 AMS
4005 ± 55	E5S85	44C	15-1973	Charcoal	Pit (upper)	SI 4241
4050 ± 220	W60S90	196C		Charcoal	Midden base	GX 2464
4135 ± 85	E0S70-75	69C	24a-1974	*Mya*	Foreshaft, plummet	SI 2395
4390 ± 55	E10S80	53C	24-1973	Charcoal	Dog burial	SI 1921
4555 ± 95	E5S85	54C	15-1973	Charcoal	Pit	SI 1923
Too small	E0S75	61C	24a-1974	Charcoal	Foreshaft, plummet	SI 2391

ARTIFACTS FROM OCCUPATION 2

Lithic Artifacts

Flaked Stone

Bifacial blades are the most numerous flaked stone artifact class from Occupation 2. Bifaces with contracting to parallel stems predominated (N = 19, Table 5.3, Plate 5.1). Fifteen had unthinned bases, retaining what appears to be a remnant of a striking platform. Most are narrow and thick (mean width/length ratio = 0.35; mean thickness/width ratio = 0.37). Nine had clearly asymmetric blades. Only two showed signs of dulling along stem margins. Most are made of green to gray porphyritic Kineo-Traveler rhyolite, which is widely available in the Penobscot Bay region in the form of glacially transported cobbles and boulders (see Appendix 6). Other locally available lithic types were also used.

Long, thick, narrow-stemmed bifaces very similar to those of Occupation 2 have been recovered from central and eastern Maine, including from several habitation and mortuary components between the Kennebec and St. John valleys (e.g., Hadlock 1939:10–11, Plate 6c, 1–3; Sanger 1973:207–208; Nevin Collection, R.S. Peabody Foundation; Wilder Col-

Table 5.3. Stemmed Bifaces from Occupation 2[a]

Catalog number	Length	Width	Thickness	Basal stem width
335	11.2	2.8	1.6	1.1
579	7.9	2.3	0.9	1.0
1394	—	3.3	0.9	1.4
1271	8.3	2.5	1.8	0.8
1396	8.8	2.2	0.9	1.3
1401	9.9	2.3	0.9	0.7
1525	7.0	2.3	1.2	0.7
1528	7.6	3.7	1.2	0.9
1557[b]	—	—	—	0.6
1748[b]	—	1.9	0.6	1.3
1825	6.7	2.2	1.0	1.4
1952	12.3	3.6	1.2	1.4
2101	3.9	2.3	0.6	1.1
2147	6.3	2.5	0.8	0.8
3016[b]	—	2.5	1.2	1.2
3533	4.5	3.7	0.9	1.2
4122	8.3	2.3	0.8	1.4
5010	8.3	2.2	0.9	0.8
5097	6.6	3.1	1.1	—
n =	15	18	18	18
mean =	7.8	2.7	1.0	1.1
s.d. =	2.2	.6	.3	.3
min. =	4.5	1.9	.6	.6
max. =	12.3	3.7	1.8	1.4

[a]All measurements in centimeters.
[b]Incomplete specimen.

Plate 5.1. Bifaces from Occupation 2.

lection, Maine Historical Society). They clearly are derived from earlier stemmed point styles of the Small Stemmed Point tradition. They also resemble point styles to the south and west (Funk 1993:223). Funk has recently pointed out, for example, that contemporaneous points from central and southern New York, including the narrow-stemmed Lamoka point, consistently retain striking platform remnants on their bases (Funk 1993:193, 224). Another likely southern analog is the narrow-stemmed form of the Lackawaxen phase of the Delaware Valley (Kinsey 1972b:335–337). Other flaked stone forms associated with Occupation 2 include a small, variable series of bifaces and unifaces (Plate 5.2). Like the Moorehead phase points, Funk has recently argued that all these southern point styles are derived from the Small Stemmed Point-related Sylvan Lake phase of the middle Hudson Valley (Funk 1993:223).

Pecked, Ground, and Polished Stone Tools

Pecking Stones.   These are by far the most numerous stone tool class from Occupation 2 (N = 125, Plate 5.3). Nearly all are roughly fist-sized pieces of rhyolite that have been shaped by repeated impacts against other rocks, creating surfaces composed of accumulated shatter cones. Ultimately, those that did not break became remarkably spheroidal. A few rounded pebbles of more granular rock had similar wear. Sixty-two rhyolite specimens retain areas of weathered cortex, while 38 retain flake scars suggesting that they may have originated as cores.

Weights ranged from 27.1 to 1,151.4 g and averaged 258 g. The smallest seem too light for effective reduction of pecked stone forms and may have been used in combination with iron pyrites to make fire. They are sometimes, but not always, associated with other artifacts or lithic debitage, suggesting that they were used for both pecking and flaking.

Plummets.   Plummets were second in abundance only to pecking stones in the lithic artifact sample (N = 55). Generally, appropriately shaped pebbles were minimally modified by pecking, and some only by grinding a groove for suspension.

The sample is divisible into two weight classes. Small plummets weigh between 20 and 420 g (N = 36, Plate 5.4). The larger ones weigh between 610 and 1,260 g (N = 13, Plate 5.5). Similar size dichotomies have been noted at other Late Archaic sites with large samples, such as the Goddard site in Brooklin, Maine (Bourque and Cox 1981:9) and the Nelson's Island site in Newburyport, Massachusetts (Robinson 1985:16). Large plummets were probably used to weight fishing lines furnished with bone hooks. The much more numerous small ones, however, seem too light for line weights. Fitzhugh (1985:92) has made the same observation for small plummets from the Labrador coast. Robinson (1985:59) has suggested that they served as sounding weights, but they are far too numerous on Moorehead phase sites to have served this function exclusively. In view of the scarcity of bird bone from Occupation 2, it is unlikely that they were tied together for use as bolas for bird hunting. Small plummets from Occupation 2 contexts at the Turner Farm site and from some Moorehead phase cemetery assemblages intergrade morphologically with stylized zoomorphic forms, suggesting a magico-religious function (Plates 5.6a and 5.6b).

Unlike pecking stones, plummets were widely scattered throughout the main excavation and generally were not found in clusters. No difference in their distribution by weight class was observed.

Plate 5.2. Bifaces from Occupation 2.

Plate 5.3. Pecking stones from Occupation 2.

Plate 5.4. Small plummets from Occupation 2.

Adzes and Gouges.   Adzes and gouges from Occupation 2 resemble those encountered in Moorehead phase cemeteries in both form and raw materials (N = 40, Table 5.4, Plates 5.7, 5.8). They generally fall near the middle of the Moorehead phase size range and closely resemble those from the Cow Point cemetery on Grand Lake, New Brunswick (Sanger 1973:200). Most adzes and gouges seem to be discards, broken either during manufacture or use. Gouge bits (N = 6) lack the marked concavity seen in many specimens from cemetery assemblages (see, e.g., Moorehead 1922, Figures 19, 20, and 41; Snow 1969, Plates 17, 18, 25, and 26). Adz bit cross sections are plano-convex (N = 3) or symmetrically convex (N = 1). Most preserved polls (4 of 5) are battered or spalled as if they have been driven by a mallet.

Whetstones.   The few whetstones from Occupation 2 were so designated on the basis of unnaturally smooth, or polished, flattened surfaces (Plate 5.9). They bear little resem-

Plate 5.5. Large plummets from Occupation 2.

blance to carefully shaped, perforated specimens from Moorehead phase cemeteries (see, e.g., Moorehead 1922, Figures 35, 55; Sanger 1973:202, Plate 14; Willoughby 1935/1973:77).

Artifacts of Bone and Other Hard Tissue

Bone artifacts, particularly the elaborate and highly specialized forms, were relatively more common in Occupation 2 deposits than in any other component at the site. Many close analogues have been found at Late Archaic coastal components elsewhere in the Northeast, especially at the Nevin (Bourque 1992a:124–125; Byers 1979), Waterside (Rowe 1940), and Taft's Point (Hadlock 1939) sites in Maine. More general resemblances are found at Port au Choix in Newfoundland (Tuck 1976).

Plate 5.6. a) Zoomorphic plummet from Turner Farm Occupation 2 (same artifact as Plate 5.4, upper left). b) Small plummets and zoomorphic forms from various Moorehead phase sites.

Replicative experiments conducted by Will (1981), as well as analysis of bone debris, indicate that most artifacts were made from blanks of cervid bone diaphyses broken along incised grooves. Will (1981:56) shaped such blanks by scarping with a rhyolite flake drawn at an acute angle. The resulting surfaces exhibited a series of subparallel striated facets very similar to those found on most Occupation 2 bone artifacts (Plate 5.10). Perforations were made by either gouging or drilling.

Bayonets

Most bone artifacts from Occupation 2 are long and pointed and probably were used to arm piercing weapons ($N = 49$). The most carefully worked are referred to as bayonets ($N = 5$, Table 5.5, Plates 5.11, 5.12), so named because of their resemblance to the distinctive

b

Plate 5.6. (*Continued*)

narrow, hexagonal ground stone bayonets of Moorehead phase cemeteries (see, e.g., Figure 8.2). The Turner Farm specimens are made from swordfish rostra. Most have hexagonal cross sections, though the number of facets varies from five to eight. These facets are not simply tooling marks but rather are design features comparable to those of ground stone bayonets.

Two bayonet bases in the sample have stems—nearly as broad as the blade in one specimen complete enough to preserve this feature. None have fully preserved lengths. Two have zigzags incised on their blades (Figure 5.12).

The only previously reported swordfish rostrum bayonets are from Grave 5 at the Nevin site and from basal strata at the Waterside shell midden (Byers 1979:48; Figure 8.5).

Table 5.4. Adzes and Gouges from Occupation 2

Catalog number	Condition	Catalog number	Condition
3/350	Complete	2114	Poll
160	Poll	3023	Complete
233	Poll	3192	Midsection
260/5122	Poll	3693	Bit
550	Midsection	4006	Poll
708	Poll	4059	Poll
717	Midsection	4217	Midsection
1200	Complete	4199/5393	Midsection
1211	Bit	4221	Midsection
1282	Poll	5096/5792	Bit
1403	Bit	5121	Midsection
1479	Poll	5180	Midsection
1526	Midsection	5343	Midsection
1553	Midsection	5359	Poll
1606	Poll	5432/6234	Midsection
1636	Midsection	5776	Poll
1671	Midsection	5889	Midsection
1703	Bit	5932/6315	Bit
1950	Complete	6284	Midsection
1951	Complete	6291	Poll

The Nevin specimen apparently no longer exists. The Waterside specimen, however, is clearly hexagonal in cross section and of similar proportions to those from the Turner Farm.

Elongate Forms with Triangular Cross Sections

These artifacts are made of swordfish rostrum or cervid (probably moose, *Alces alces*) bone ($N = 6$, Table 5.6, Plate 5.13). They have triangular cross sections and pointed tips. None is complete and the form of their proximal ends is unknown. One specimen bears a simple zigzag motif along its widest side and another has a row of rectanguloid lugs along one edge (Plate 5.14). Again, a possible analogue to this class may be found in ground stone bayonets from the region (see, e.g., Figure 8.4).

Bone Blades

Twelve elongate artifacts regarded as bone blades were recovered from Occupation 2 (Table 5.7, Plate 5.15). They are made of both deer and moose bone. No bone blades have survived intact but the best preserved specimens (Plate 5.15, the three on the left) are probably close to their original length. Their cross sections are tabular but most retain a natural longitudinal ridge on their dorsal side. Blade widths range from less than 1.2 cm to over 3.0. Thicknesses range from .6 cm to 1.7 cm. Some of this variability may be the result of resharpening. In dorsal view, some are bilaterally symmetric and some seem to be asymmetric because of wear. Preserved tips are slightly upturned, suggesting a transition from diaphysis to epiphysis. Three bear finely incised decoration.

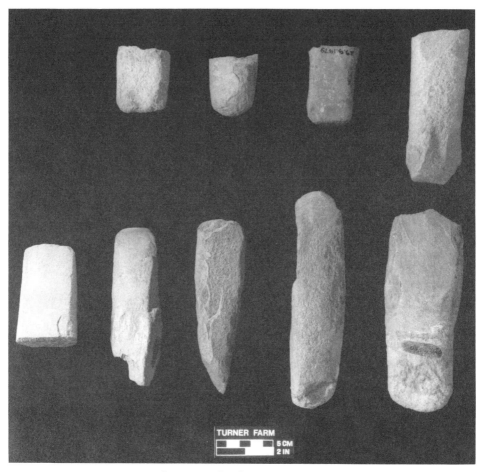

Plate 5.7.   Adzes from Occupation 2.

In form and decoration, these blades are virtually identical to 34 "daggers" recovered from the Nevin site (Byers 1979, Figures 22–28; Bourque 1992a:195; see Table 5.8, Plate 5.16, Figure 5.1). Also apparent are general resemblances to bone daggers from Port au Choix and the Lamoka phase of New York, which, however, are undecorated (Ritchie 1980:53, 61; Tuck 1976:32–33, Plate 23).

Three intact basal portions have attributes suggesting that sinew or vegetable fiber may have been applied to form a handle. This inference is supported by the presence on the Nevin specimens of grooves apparently worn by such lashing (Bourque 1992a:195). If so, these tools may have been hand-held daggers or knives, as Byers (1979:32) suggested. However, they may also have been used as lance tips in the manner described for the Gaspé region during the late seventeenth century by Nicholas Denys (1677/1908:428).

Finally, one stemmed blade of mammal bone (Plate 5.17) was recovered from Occupation 2. Badly broken, it is illustrated in Figure 5.2 with suggested reconstruction. One side has a raised medial ridge, while the other is convex except for a shallow flute at its base.

Plate 5.8.   Gouges from Occupation 2.

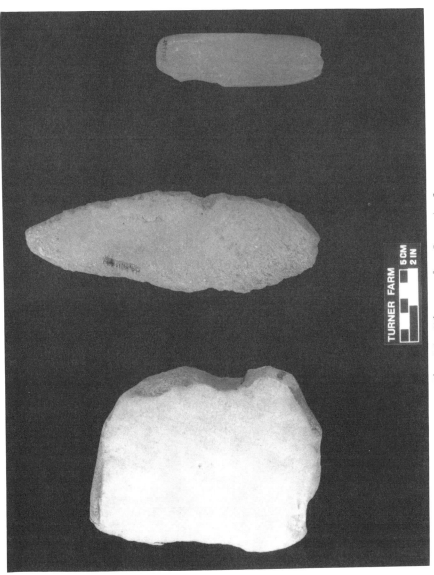

Plate 5.9. Whetstones from Occupation 2.

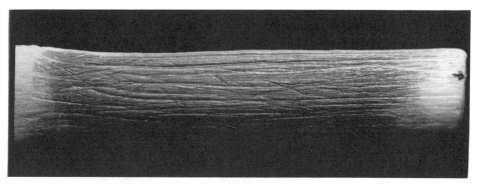

Plate 5.10.   Faceted surface of bone experimentally modified by scraping with a rhyolite flake.

Barbed Weapons

The second most numerous class of bone tools from Occupation 2 ($N = 25$, Table 5.9) is unilaterally barbed weapons. The most common form is made of mammal bone ($N = 7$) or swordfish rostrum ($N = 1$) and has between two and four closely set barbs near the tip (Plate 5.18). The largest of these bears a single band of incised decoration diagonally across its midsection, similar to that found on bone daggers. These distinctive weapons have been encountered at other Moorehead phase shell midden components, including the Waterside site (Rowe 1940, Plate 7a) and the Stanley site on Monhegan Island.

Five larger barbed spears made of swordfish rostrum resemble the smaller ones in having relatively short distally barbed sections (Plate 5.19). Where preserved, the bases are either tapered or cut and snapped. None are perforated and only one has a slight notch at the base that may have helped prevent it from pulling loose from a shaft.

The remaining barbed bone weapons from Occupation 2 vary in form but have relatively long barbed segments with low-angle barbs (Plate 5.20). Their raw materials include antler ($N = 1$), swordfish rostrum ($N = 2$), swordfish fin ray ($N = 2$), and cervid bone ($N = 4$). Two have gouged basal perforations for line attachment. One of these has a single, well-defined barb near its base, resembling harpoon tips recovered from both the Nevin and the Port au Choix sites.

Table 5.5. Bayonets from Occupation 2[a]

Catalog number	Length	Width	Thickness	Number of facets	Decoration
252/258	17.7*	2.1*	1.1*	6	Present
456	9.1*	2.2*	1.1	6	Present
2045	22.4*	2.3	1.2	6	Absent
6128	12.2*	2.3	1.5	5	Absent
6562	17.6*	2.1	1.2	8	Absent

[a]All measurements in centimeters.
*Incomplete measurement from broken specimen.

Plate 5.11.   Swordfish rostrum bayonets from Occupation 2.

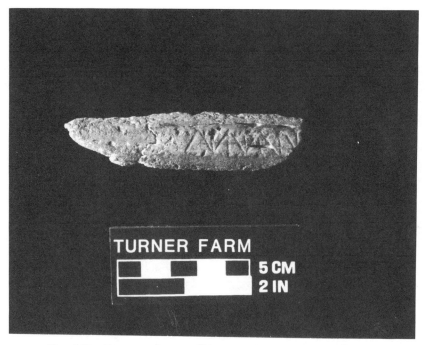

Plate 5.12. Zigzag motif on swordfish rostrum bayonet from Occupation 2.

An open-socketed toggling harpoon of swordfish rostrum was recovered from a basal Occupation 3 deposit but is regarded as probably from Occupation 2 (Plate 5.21). The proximal end is missing and the flat side has a series of shallow undulating depressions just above the socket that may have resulted from wear. Two open-socketed harpoons from Moorehead phase graves at the Nevin site are more narrow and rounded in cross section than this specimen.

Table 5.6. Elongated Triangular Forms from Occupation 2

Catalog number	Length	Width	Thickness	Decoration	Species
466	8.0*	2.1*	1.4*	Present	Moose
1116	8.2*	2.0*	1.3*	Absent	Swordfish
1738	12.7*	2.5*	1.2*	Absent	Swordfish
1799	12.2*	1.4*	1.3*	Absent	Moose
1945	22.0*	1.9	1.6	Absent	Moose
7949	11.6*	1.9	1.1	Absent	Moose

*a*All measurements in centimeters.
*Incomplete measurement from broken specimen.

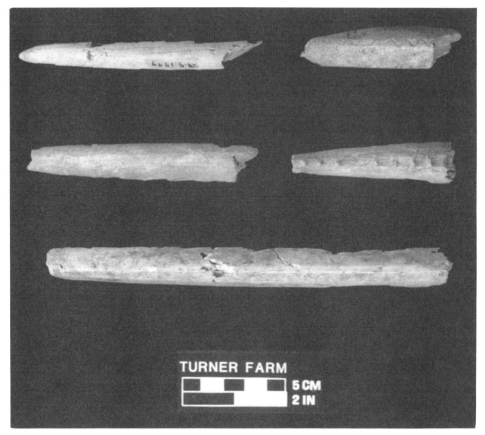

Plate 5.13. Elongate forms with triangular cross sections made of bone and swordfish rostrum from Occupation 2.

Modified Beaver Incisors

Beaver incisor tools from Occupation 2 constitute the largest bone tool class of the assemblage ($N = 44$; Plate 5.22, Figure 5.9; Table 7.4). Most had distal ends ground obliquely to the sides and buccal surface to create a sharp cutting edge. The angles between these cutting edges and the sides of the teeth, from apex to tip, range from 10° to 90°. Four incisors were split or ground linguo-buccally to produce an enamel edge along the full length of the artifact (Plate 5.22, lower right). Five fragmentary worked incisors of indeterminate form were also recovered. Ground beaver incisors have been found in Moorehead phase contexts at the Waterside (Rowe 1940, Plate 7) and Nevin sites (Byers 1979:25, Table 2). Several were also recovered at Port au Choix, including one in an antler haft (Tuck 1976:48, Figure 21). However, most previous discussions of such tools pertain to samples

Plate 5.14. Details of three specimens shown in Plate 5.13.

Table 5.7. Bone Blades from Occupation 2[a]

Catalog number	Length	Width	Thickness	Decoration	Species
96	17.8*	2.4	1.0	Absent	Moose
228	18.1*	1.6*	0.8*	Present	Deer
291	23.1	2.3	0.9	Absent	Deer
1016	14.7*	3.0*	1.3	Absent	Moose
1946	10.7*	2.5*	1.3	Absent	Moose
2017	19.7*	2.5	1.7	Absent	Moose
2280/2331	9.5*	1.2*	0.6	Present	Deer
2334	6.6*	1.6*	0.8*	Absent	Deer
6010	12.5*	2.5*	1.0*	Absent	Moose
6096	15.3*	2.4*	1.1*	Present	Moose
6626	20.8*	2.3	0.7	Absent	Deer
7187	10.4*	1.4*	0.7*	Present	Deer

[a]All measurements in centimeters.
*Incomplete measurement from broken specimen.

from various Ceramic period sites, where incisor tools exhibit considerable diversity. Further discussion of their morphology and use will therefore be deferred to Chapter 7.

Socketed Antler and Bone

Four modified shed antler beams were recovered from Occupation 2 strata (Plate 5.23). They were cut distally and the soft core was gouged out to form a deep socket (Table 5.10). Two had smoothed exterior surfaces. Another had its brow tine and burr removed. No wear patterns were observed on these specimens, but their form suggests that they served as hafts for stemmed bifaces. Similar specimens come from the Nevin and Waterside sites (Byers 1979:57, 64; Rowe 1940:10, Plate 7). Byers's suggestion that they were hafts for beaver incisors seems unlikely in view of the large diameter of their sockets. Rowe (1940:10) suggested that they were used as handles for large bone points or short reworked slate points.

Three socketed moose phalanges were also recovered from Occupation 2 strata (Plate 5.24). None was extensively modified externally. They resemble socketed caribou phalanges from Port au Choix, which Tuck (1976:234) called "bangles."

Foreshafts

Three long cylindrical objects of swordfish rostrum are probably harpoon foreshafts (Plate 5.25). All have one forked end; two have prongs that terminate in a slightly expanded lip, probably to retain lashing. Only one specimen is complete enough to establish its original length at approximately 20.5 cm. Very similar foreshafts occur in two other Moorehead phase assemblages in Maine. At least two were found by Hadlock at Taft's Point (Bourque 1992a:23, 192) and a well-preserved decorated specimen was found at the Nevin site (Byers 1979, Figure 22). Much longer foreshafts of marine mammal bone were found at Port au Choix. The ends of the Port au Choix specimens terminate in a variety of forked, spatulate, and pointed forms, as well as in sockets (Tuck 1976:33–34, 217, 221). It is

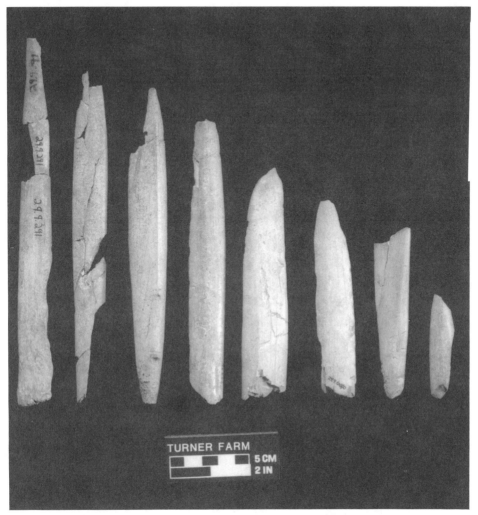

Plate 5.15. Bone blades from Occupation 2.

Table 5.8. Bone Blades from Occupation 2[a]

	(n = 12)		(n = 12)		(n = 12)
Length	n = 2	Width	n = 4	Thickness	n = 7
	ave. = 21.4		ave. = 2.4		ave. = 1.1
	s.d. = 1.7		s.d. = 0.1		s.d. = 0.4
	min. = 19.7		min. = 2.3		min. = 0.6
	max. = 23.1		max. = 2.5		max. = 1.7

[a]All measurements in centimeters.

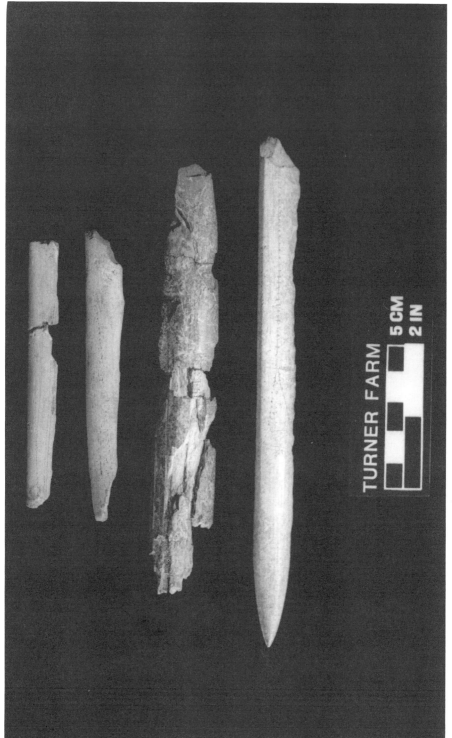

Plate 5.16. Decoration on bone daggers from Occupation 2.

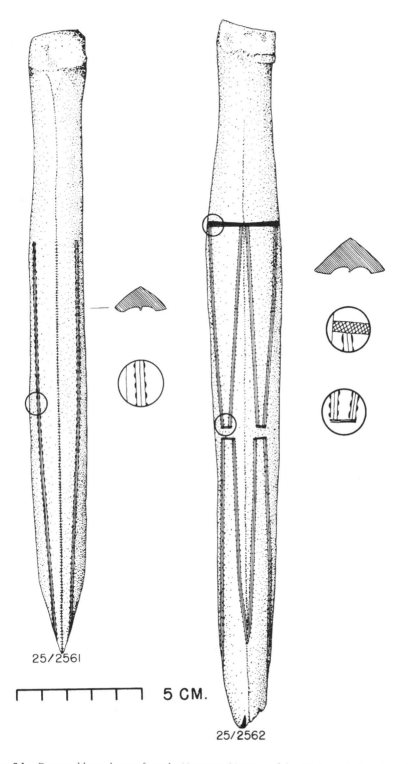

25/2561

5 CM.

25/2562

Figure 5.1. Decorated bone daggers from the Nevin site (Courtesy of the R.S. Peabody Foundation).

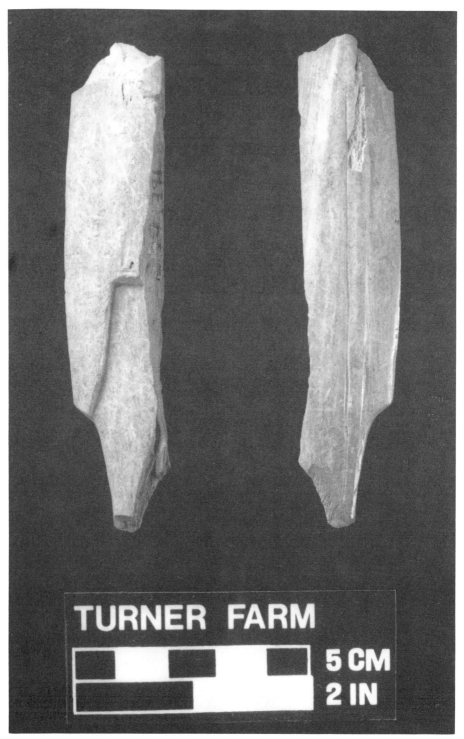

Plate 5.17. Stemmed blade of mammal bone from Occupation 2.

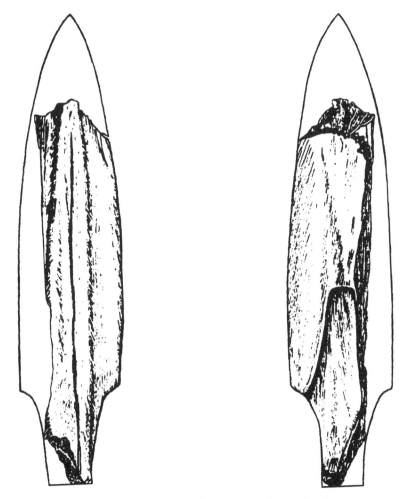

Figure 5.2. Stemmed blade illustrated in Plate 5.17 showing suggested original profile (Drawing: Don Bassett).

unclear whether the notched ends of any of these foreshafts are proximal or distal, or with what artifact forms they were used. Byers (1979:70) suggested that the Nevin specimens were notched to receive the single-barbed bone harpoons that were found in association. Tuck (1976:38) also suggested that the Port au Choix shafts were intended to receive bone harpoons. However, the forked ends on historic Inuit foreshafts attach to wooden shafts and the harpoons are set into sockets on the distal end. One specimen from the Turner Farm site has the remnant of such a socket.

Fishhooks

The practice of hook-and-line fishing during Occupation 2 times is attested to by three barbed fishhooks (Plate 5.26). One is made of a single piece of mammal bone; the other two

Table 5.9. Barbed Spears and Harpoons from Occupation 2[a]

Catalog number	Length	Width	Thickness	Material	Number of barbs
37	4.6[c]	—	.6	Swordfish[d]	>1
331	4.6[c]	—	.6	Swordfish[e]	>3
367	7.4	1.1	.6	Cervid	3
368	5.8[c]	—	.6	Cervid	>2
515	4.0	1.0	.6	Cervid	4
688	4.2[c]	—	.6	Cervid	>1
689	6.6[c]	—	.8	Swordfish[d]	>1
699[b]	6.5[a]	1.1	.6	Cervid	4
724	4.1	.7	.4	Cervid	4
737	5.8	.9	.7	Cervid	3
1646	3.4[a]	.6	.4	Cervid	>2
1713/1907	6.9[c]	—	.5	Swordfish[e]	>1
1815	7.6[c]	.6	.5	Swordfish[d]	4
1833	4.6[c]	—	.7	Swordfish[d]	>2
1937[b]	10.5[c]	1.8	1.0	Moose	1
1939	20.0[c]	1.9	.8	Swordfish[d]	6
2270	4.8[c]	—	.5	Cervid	>1
3409	7.6[c]	—	.7	Swordfish[d]	>2
4090	6.3[c]	—	.8	Antler	>1
5039/6118	9.1[c]	—	.6	Swordfish[d]	>4
5854	6.8[c]	—	.7	Cervid	>2
5857	4.6	1.3	.7	Cervid	2
5925	4.9	.8	.4	Cervid	4
6559	2.7	.5	.3	Mammal	2
6639	2.5	—	—	Cervid	>1

[a]All measurements in centimeters.
[b]Specimen has basal perforation for line attachment.
[c]Incomplete measurement from broken specimen.
[d]Rostrum.
[e]Fin ray.

are modified turtle scapulae designed to receive separate bone barbs. The shank of the mammal bone hook has clearly defined flanges for line attachment, while the preserved end of one turtle scapula specimen is grooved. Hooks resembling the former specimen were recovered at the Early Owasco period Maxon Derby site in Onondaga County, New York (Ritchie and Funk 1973:208, Plate 102). No analogues for the compound specimens have come to our attention.

Bird Ulna Tubes

Two modified Canada goose (*Branta canadensis*) ulnae were found along with several other artifacts in Feature 22-1973 (Plate 5.27, Figure 5.3). When discovered, they lay parallel and in contact with each other, suggesting that they were attached when buried. They appear to be a matched pair from one individual. The papillae have been removed by scraping. Their distal epiphyses have also been removed and the proximal ends modified by grinding or scraping. Elongate holes have been gouged or scraped near the proximal ends.

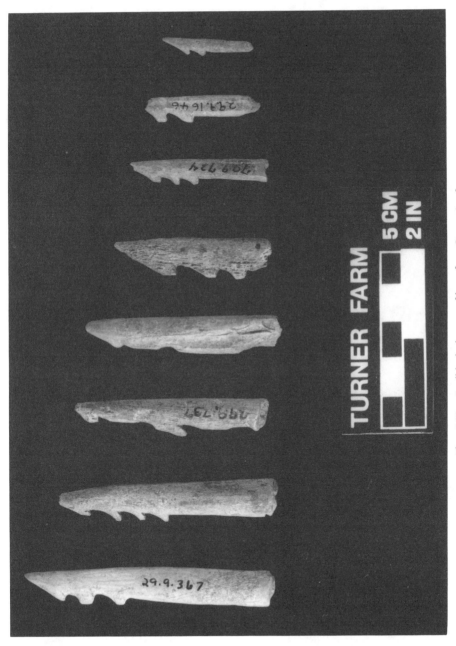

Plate 5.18. Small barbed spears of bone from Occupation 2.

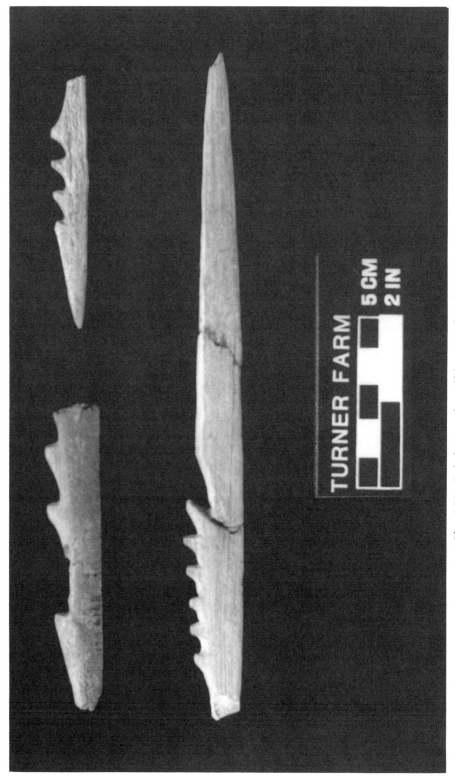

Plate 5.19. Barbed spears of swordfish rostrum from Occupation 2.

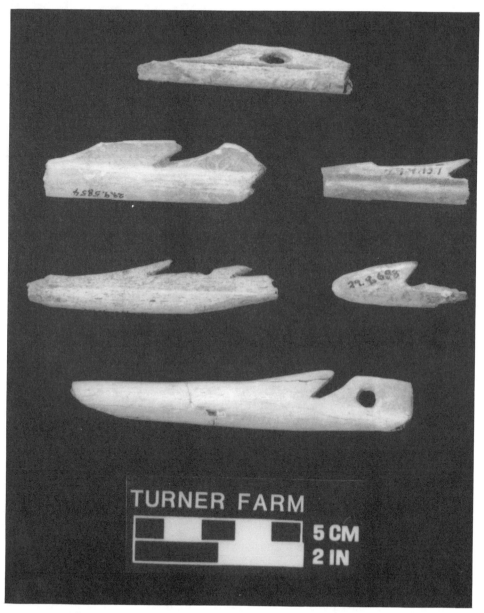

Plate 5.20. Barbed weapons from Occupation 2 made of various bony tissues.

Plate 5.21.   Open-socketed harpoon of swordfish rostrum attributed to Occupation 2.

Plate 5.22. Modified beaver incisors from Occupation 2.

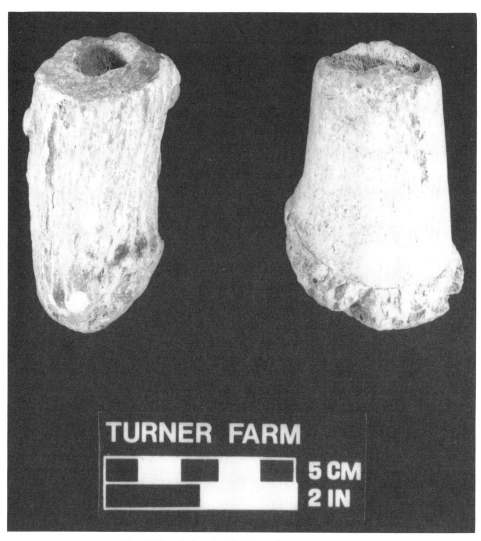

Plate 5.23.   Socketed antler beams from Occupation 2.

Table 5.10. Socketed Antler Beams from Occupation 2[a]

Catalog number	Length	Socket diameter	Socket depth	Removals
434	7.5	1.7	2.7	Brow tine and burr
6384	6.6	1.4	3.4	Burr and surface
7150	4.8	.9	2.0	Burr and surface
7151	5.2	1.4	2.6	None

[a]All measurements in centimeters.

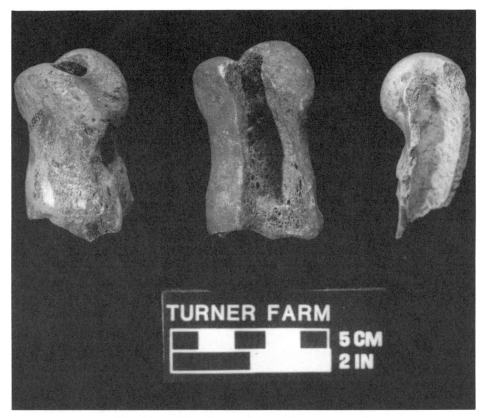

Plate 5.24.   Socketed moose phalanges from Occupation 2.

The distal ends also have multiple perforations. Finally, both bear similar incised motifs just distal to the elongate holes.

A single larger specimen with different incised decoration was recovered from Grave 9 at the Nevin site (Byers 1979:68). Several specimens from Port au Choix, particularly Tuck's nos. 6 and 7, are also similar (Tuck 1976:238). It is interesting to note that his nos. 1 and 2 were found with their perforations "perfectly aligned . . ., leaving little doubt that the two tubes were once tied together" (Tuck 1976:73). Tuck suggests that the Port au Choix bone tubes with multiple perforations are flutes or whistles. The Turner Farm specimens do not produce a musical note when played as a flute, although they might if the small perforations on their distal ends were plugged.

Bone Needle

A single bone needle (Plate 5.28) was recovered from Feature 15-1972. We suspect that this small shell-filled pit excavated into subsoil dates to Occupation 2, although it may

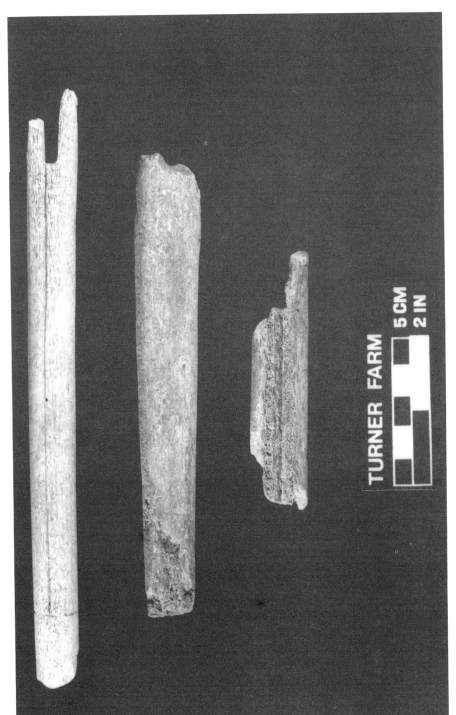

Plate 5.25. Foreshafts of swordfish rostrum from Occupation 2.

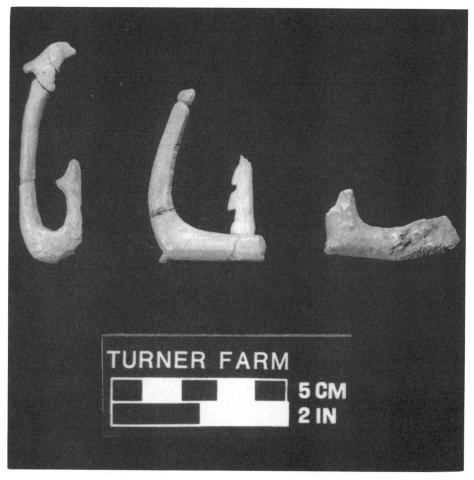

Plate 5.26. Barbed bone fishhooks from Occupation 2.

pertain to Occupation 3. The eye of the needle was made by gouging. The surface bears a polish probably derived from use.

At least four similar but larger needles were recovered from the Nevin site midden and burials (Bourque 1992a:24–25, 193, Figure 17; Byers 1979:25), and thirteen were recovered at Port au Choix (Tuck 1976:41–43, Plate 32). As Tuck points out, the thread used with these needles may have been either beaten animal sinew or spun vegetable fiber.

Bird Effigy

A single stylized bird's head carved from mammal bone was included in the same cache (Feature 22-1973) as the modified goose ulnae (Plate 5.29). The eyes and beak are clearly defined by incised lines. The proportions, orientation of the head, and hooked beak resemble a cormorant (*Phalacrocorax*) or perhaps a merganser (*Mergus*). The tail end is

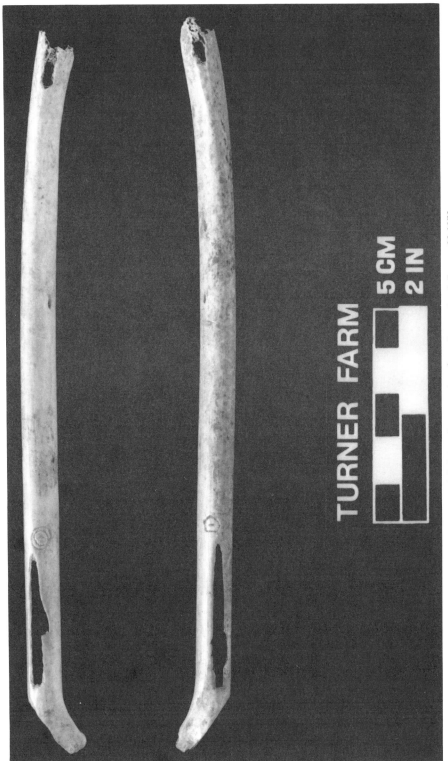

Plate 5.27. Modified Canada goose ulnae from Occupation 2 Feature 22-1973.

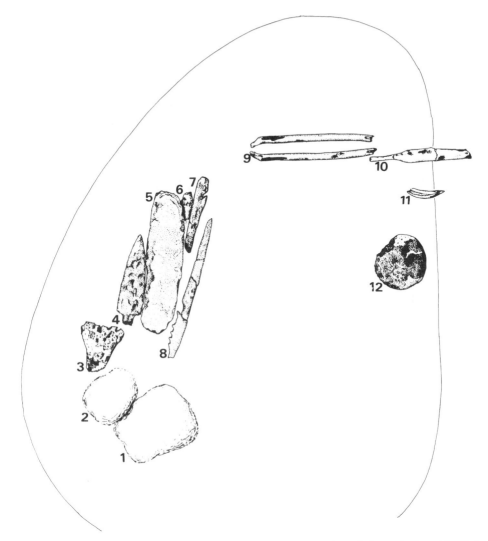

Figure 5.3. Cache of artifacts from Occupation 2 Feature 22-1973. Key: **1**—rock; **2**—rock; **3**—unidentified vesicular substance; **4**—stemmed point; **5**—adz; **6**—bone dagger; **7**—bone harpoon; **8**—swordfish rostrum spear; **9**—modified Canada Goose ulnae; **10**—bird effigy; **11**—beaver incisor tool; **12**—pecking stone (drawing: Patricia Arey).

broken, but clear impressions of lashing suggest that it may have been part of a larger composite artifact—perhaps a complete bird effigy. Its presence in the cache, which was near an ocher-furnished dog's grave (Feature 24-1973), suggests that it may have had magico-religious significance.

Similar renditions of birds' heads were among the numerous effigies from Port au Choix (Tuck 1976:57–58, Figures 23–26). Although none appear to have been part of a larger artifact, the similarities between these and other bone artifacts from the Turner Farm, Nevin, and Port au Choix sites support the notion of a shared artistic and symbolic tradition.

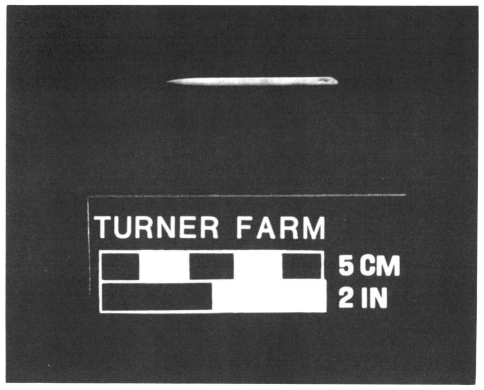

Plate 5.28.   Eyed bone needle attributed to Occupation 2.

HORIZONTAL PATTERNING

The distributions of features, artifacts, and bone refuse define two zones, one near the shore and the other farther inland. Each zone, in turn, includes an eastern and a western cluster (Figures 5.4–5.10). This patterning defines four "activity areas" (Figure 5.6). The shoreward zone includes a roughly linear array of three burned rock features surrounded by dense scatters of artifacts, flaking debris, and bone refuse. Several small fragments of tightly curled birch (*Betula papyrifera*) bark were recovered near these burned rock features. Five dog burials also came from the shoreward zone.

Inland from the shoreward zone was a series of small pits, a moderately dense scatter of refuse, and several small artifact clusters, frequently dominated by pecking stones. Some of these clusters were associated with dense scatters of debitage and seem quite task specific.

In the shoreward zone, dense scatters of artifacts and debitage were found near burned rock features and a bone refuse concentration in Area 1. Two clusters of debitage occurred behind the features, but artifacts were less abundant. As in the interior, the few artifact clusters that did occur often were dominated by pecking stones and, to a lesser extent, by plummets. The association of pecking stones with debitage is less marked here than in the interior zone.

Plate 5.29. Bird effigy carved from mammal bone from Occupation 2 Feature 22-1973.

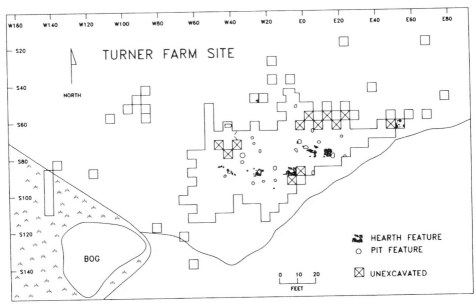

Figure 5.4. Distribution of Occupation 2 features.

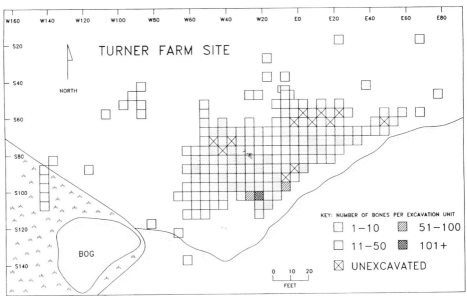

Figure 5.5. Occupation 2 bone refuse density.

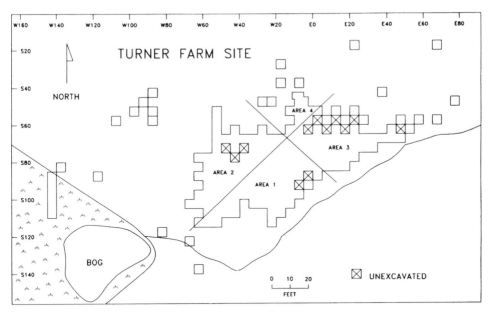

Figure 5.6. Occupation 2 activity areas.

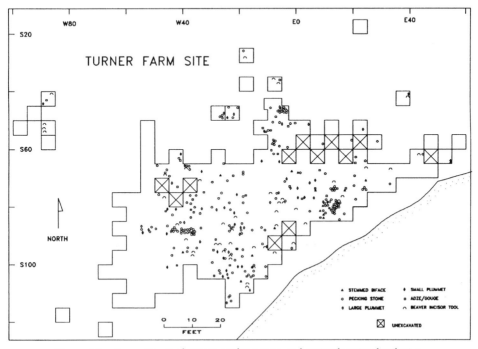

Figure 5.7. Occupation 2 adz/gouge, pecking stone, and projectile point distribution.

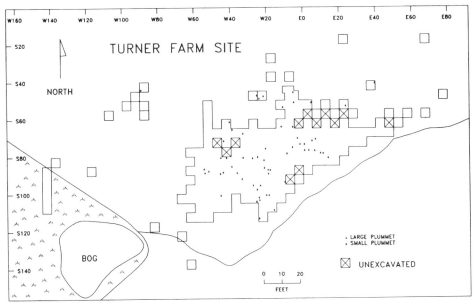

Figure 5.8. Occupation 2 plummet distribution.

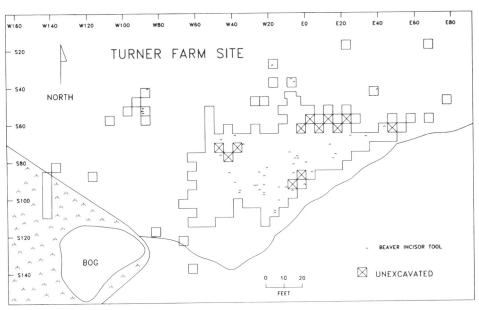

Figure 5.9. Occupation 2 beaver incisor tool distribution.

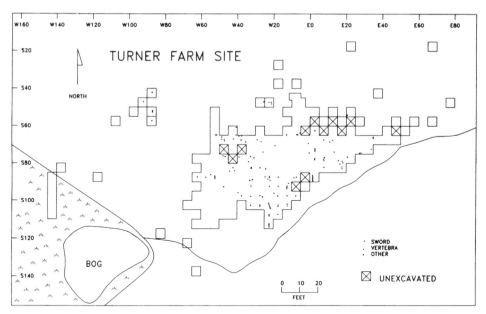

Figure 5.10. Occupation 2 swordfish bone distribution.

The distribution of cultural remains in Occupation 2 exhibits a general east–west symmetry, and it may also be that inland Areas 2 and 4 were specifically linked to their contiguous shoreward ones. However, important differences were encountered between all areas. Area 1, for example, was unique in producing a large amount of bone refuse and an artifact cluster with no well-defined hearth in association. Moreover, artifacts and bone were generally most abundant in the low, southwestern sections of the excavation (Area 1), adjacent to the modern beach. Area 4 differs from Area 2 mainly in the scarcity there of bone and features.

Some of these inter-area differences are probably the result of postdepositional distur-bance. For example, a bone and artifact cluster like that in Area 1 may have been eroded to the south of Area 3, which now abuts the erosion scarp. Inland, Area 4 lacks bone refuse, particularly seal bone, which was abundant in Area 2. It is probable that Area 4 was badly disturbed by a series of graves originating in Occupation 3 strata. This inference is supported by the anomalously high seal bone count in overlying strata.

Artifact Distribution

Large clusters of pecking stones occurred in Areas 2, 3, and 4, while in Area 1 pecking stones were numerous around hearth areas and in the shoreward refuse scatter (Figure 5.7). This pattern suggests that while pecking stone clusters in Areas 2, 3, and 4 reflect task-specific scatters, pecking stones in Area 1 had been dispersed along with general refuse.

Despite their gross similarity, shoreward Areas 1 and 3 have distinctively different artifact suites. Area 1 has absolutely and relatively (respectively) more beaver incisor tools and plummets than any other, while Area 3 produced three times as many flaked stemmed bifaces and more than twice as much worked stone and debitage as Area 1. However, this apparent distinctiveness is somewhat diminished when all areas are considered. For example, all stemmed bifaces were found in Areas 1 and 2. Furthermore, some of the other differences among these areas can be attributed to postdepositional erosion. For example, both beaver incisor knives and plummets are more numerous in the shoreward portion of Area 1 and would have been lost if erosion had proceeded to the extent it has in Area 3. Nevertheless, the discreteness of horizontal artifact distribution at various scales observed in Occupation 2 is sufficiently striking to indicate the spatial differentiation of specific activities.

DOG BURIALS

The most prominent features in Occupation 2 were found in the shoreward zone. Of special importance are six dog burials (see Table 5.1). The dogs ranged from newborn to medium-sized adult. Two, the newborn and the largest adult, were accompanied by red ocher. The larger of these (Feature 24-1973) was placed near the cache (Feature 22-1973) described above, suggesting that the pit is related to the burial. All this evidence of special treatment strongly suggests the importance of dogs to Occupation 2 populations. No other evidence of this practice has been reported from other Moorehead phase sites, however, although the general absence of bone preservation in most Red Paint cemeteries may have obscured the presence of dog burials there.

FAUNAL ANALYSES

This section is based on detailed faunal analyses presented in Spiess and Lewis (1993). It differs significantly from previously published comments (Bourque 1975, 1976) that relied on preliminary impressions prior to detailed stratigraphic analysis. The most important changes pertain mainly to Occupation 2, and occurred during the past decade as we became aware of the site's complexity. Perhaps most importantly, high estimates of seal abundance in Occupation 2 were incorrect, while estimates of cod and shellfish were too low.

Faunal Remains

Cervids

Well-preserved cervid remains appear to dominate the faunal sample heavily during excavation. As pointed out below, however, various marine protein sources were more important in the diet. The data indicate that from Occupation 2 onward, deer of all ages were hunted mainly during the colder months. It is interesting to note that the deer sample from Occupation 2 represents, on average, larger and older individuals (especially males), than any later occupation. Seasonality data on the Occupation 2 deer hunt suggest that most carcasses were brought to the site between the months of October and March. The hunt may have ceased altogether during the summer. Whether it resumed much before the rut in October is unclear. The fact that climatic conditions were probably milder on the Maine coast in the fourth millennium B.P. than at present would not have altered the timing of the rut, which is under endocrine control and triggered by day length, not by temperature (Verme and Ullreg 1984:110). Thus, deer were taken primarily after their fall buildup of fat reserves—in their prime, from a nutritional standpoint. At present, deer tend to leave small, exposed islands for larger ones or the mainland between September and January (Schemnitz 1975). Therefore, large islands, such as North Haven and Vinalhaven, may actually have seen an increase in deer population during the hunting season. A milder than modern climate may also have allowed more deer than at present to migrate to the islands.

Moose account for only eight bones, all possibly from one individual. However, our estimate of relative numbers of individuals represented, based on phalange and dewclaw frequencies, indicates that moose contributed 2 percent of the cervid individuals and 12 percent of cervid live weight.

The apparent importance of deer in the diet of Occupation 2 inhabitants, and indeed of all later occupants, seems inconsistent with the site's easy access to marine resources. The inconsistency is underscored by light-stable isotopic ratios in human bone from several Maine coastal populations, which confirm the importance of marine protein in the diets of these populations (Bourque and Krueger 1994). The inconsistency is explained by the differential extent to which terrestrial and marine vertebrates were utilized and their remains deposited at the site. Fish were mainly valuable for their flesh, oil, and (in the case of swordfish) rostra; other parts may well have been discarded near where the fish were captured. On the other hand, terrestrial game, and deer in particular, had many useful parts that would have assured their transportation to the site as complete carcasses. Furthermore, mammal bone is relatively much more likely than fish bone to survive in identifiable condition and to be recovered during excavation.

Bear

The Black bear (*Ursus americanus*) is represented by only four bones (0.5 percent of the deer bone count). None provided information on season of death.

Mustelids

Occupation 2 deposits produced 86 bones probably of the extinct sea mink (*Mustela macrodon*), only two of the surviving mink *Mustela vison*, and three of indeterminate species—equivalent to 9 percent of the deer bone count. A single, sectioned sea mink canine suggests death in late winter or early spring.

The beaver sample includes 18 postcranial items (12 unworked), in addition to 45 worked incisors. This amounts to 7 percent of the deer bone count. No specimens provided data on season of death. Furthermore, given the scarcity of beaver habitat on the Fox Islands, these incisors are probably curated items obtained on the mainland.

Marine Mammals

Marine mammals are poorly represented in the Occupation 2 sample. Only 27 phocid bones were recovered, equivalent to 2.6 percent of the deer bone count. This is a lower ratio than for any later component. Species include gray seal (*Halichoerus grypus*), harbor seal (*Phoca vitulina*), and harp seal (*Phoca groenlandica*). Because gray seals are much the largest, their bones are relatively easy to identify. To counter this potential bias, seal species identification was based on auditory bullae, the densest and most diagnostic bone for all species. A minimum of four gray seals, six harbor seals, one harp seal and one other *Phoca* (species indeterminate) is represented.

The gray seals probably were taken between January and March, when they hauled out for molting and whelping (Cameron 1970). A single, sectioned tooth supports this interpretation. Harbor seals were probably also taken during their molting and whelping season, which falls between June and July in this region (Boulva and McLaren 1979).

One marine mammal element of interest is a small walrus tusk, probably female or juvenile. It was recovered from apparently undisturbed midden just below the suspected Bateses' disturbance mentioned in Chapter 2 and has been radiocarbon dated at 3920 ± 25 B.P. Its age and the fact that it was found stratigraphically below a bone dagger suggest that it probably pertains to Occupation 2. The otherwise warm-water nature of the Occupation's marine faunal assemblage suggests that it originated in the Gulf of St. Lawrence or farther north.

Fish

The relative importance of fish and terrestrial mammals is methodologically difficult to ascertain. As discussed above, fish were much more likely to have been processed off site. Moreover, their bones are small, frail, and difficult to quantify. All these factors suggest that our faunal analysis significantly underrepresents fish, especially small species.

Cod: Cod (*Gadus* spp.) are the most abundant species in the Occupation 2 sample, with 169 bones (114 vertebrae), or 15.9 percent of the large mammal bone count. The distribution of cod bone in Occupation 3 strata is spatially congruent with that of Occupation 2, suggesting their further underrepresentation in Occupation 2.

Swordfish: Swordfish (*Xiphias gladius*) hunting was clearly a major activity during Occupation 2 (Figure 5.10). However, the attribution of some swordfish bone is unclear. Some attributed to Occupation 2 probably derived from Occupation 1, and, as stated above, those recovered from higher strata probably pertain to Occupation 2. Furthermore, evaluating the relative dietary importance of swordfish compared to cod or deer is complicated by the high frequency of rostrum fragments, a raw material of considerable importance.

Swordfish remains have consistently been found at sites of the Small Stemmed Point tradition and Moorehead phase, including Taft's Point (Hadlock 1939), Waterside (Rowe 1940), Nevin (Byers 1979), Stanley (Sanger 1975:62), and Seabrook Marsh (Robinson 1985:103–105). Since swordfish inhabit warm waters, including the Gulf Stream, and are not now common in the Gulf of Maine, their prevalence in Late Archaic sites indicates warmer water temperatures in the past (Bigelow and Schroeder 1953:351–357). Probably they were summer visitors in the Gulf (Spiess et al. 1983:101–103). Currently, swordfish are taken by either harpoon or by hook. Archaeological evidence suggests that harpooning was the technique used during Occupation 2.

Sturgeon: Establishing either sturgeon (probably *Acipenser sturio*) abundance or dietary importance relative to other species is complicated by the fact that only the large dermal scutes are well calcified enough to survive in a shell midden. However, the potential contribution per individual is significant, since most adult females (larger than males) weigh up to 250 lb (Bigelow and Schroeder 1953:81). Only 12 fragmentary scutes were recovered from Occupation 2 deposits. Possibly only a single individual is represented.

Sturgeon were common in the Gulf of Maine in historic times. Large individuals might have been encountered near the Turner Farm site any time during the year except between May and July when sturgeon enter rivers to spawn. Historically, sturgeon were lured at night by torchlight and speared in the belly as they rolled near the surface (Spiess and Lewis 1993:291). Barbed harpoons from Occupation 2 seem appropriate for such a strategy.

Flounder: Of the 91 identifiable flounder bones recovered (8.6 percent of the large mammal bone total), only 53 could be identified to species. Fifty were from winter flounder (*Pseudopleuronectes americanus*), and three were from yellowtail or smooth flounder (*Limanda ferruginea* or *Loipsetta putnami*). The growth status of six vertebrae suggest that flounder were taken during more than one season, but we have not determined which ones. Winter and smooth flounders inhabit a wide range of water depths, including shoals, where they can be speared easily (Bigelow and Schroeder 1953:276–285). Yellowtails generally prefer deeper water and may have been taken by hook and line (Bigelow and Schroeder 1953:271–275).

Other Fish Species: Other species represented in the sample include tomcod (*Microgadus tomcod*, 14 bones), sculpin (*Myoxocephalus scorpius* and *M. octodecimspinosus*, 14 bones), herring (*Clupea* spp., five bones), Atlantic salmon (*Salmo salar*, two bones from large individuals), pollack (*Pollachius virens*, three bones), haddock (*Melanogrammus aeglefinus*, one bone), striped bass (*Roccus saxatilis*, one bone), spiny dogfish (probably *Squalus acanthias*, one back spine), and alewife (*Alosa pseudoharengus*, one bone). As a group they probably represent incidental catches and, for the larger species, opportunistic capture.

Birds

Our attempts to identify avian remains is hampered by the scarcity of diagnostic traits that might distinguish species in the same size range and also by the varying body proportions among birds of similar gross size. For example, leg bone epiphyses of raptors in our sample might be identified to species, while diaphyses and axial elements are indistinguishable from several "larger than duck" species.

Unlike fish, birds are likely to be brought whole to the home base. If so, they were of very minor dietary importance during Occupation 2. The total bird bone count is 164 (15.5 percent of the large mammal bone count), lower than for any later component.

Despite the small size of the bird sample, it is diverse. Most important are ducks (bone count, 47) and duck-sized birds (bone count, 37). Other birds range in size from swan to small alcid. Duck species include eider (*Somata mollissima*, one bone), scaup (*Aythya marila* and *Aythya affinis*, three bones), bufflehead (*Bucephala albeola*, one bone), common merganser (*Mergus merganser*, 11 bones), small ducks (including Anatinae and Aythyinae, four bones), and a single bone from a black duck-sized bird. Great Auk (*Pinguinus impennis*) was represented by 11 bones.

Low bone counts and a diverse range of species suggest that birds were of minor dietary importance. Birds were nevertheless symbolically important during this period as evidenced by the bird effigy discussed above, and by similar carved birds' heads found at roughly contemporaneous sites ranging from Maine to Port au Choix (Tuck 1976).

Crustaceans

The chitinous shells of crustaceans do not survive in Maine shell middens. Neverthe-less, there is good reason to suspect that these species, primarily the lobster (*Homarus americanus*), were significant food sources.

Mollusks

Throughout the stratigraphic sequence, the vastly predominant mollusk species was *Mya arenaria*. However, Occupation 2 strata produced the highest relative frequencies of blue mussel (*Mytilus edulis*), the only quahog (*Mercenaria*), and the only significant amounts of sea urchin (*Strongylocentrotus droebachiensis*). Like swordfish, the presence of quahog, which is now extinct east of the Kennebec River, indicates warmer than modern water temperatures. The relative scarcity of blue mussel and the absence of sea scallop (*Placopec-ten magellanicus*) are surprising, for both are still commercially fished in the area.

The clam shell from Occupation 2 represents approximately 9,760 kg of clam meat. Unfortunately, no comparable statistic is available for fish, bird, or mammal species. Assessing mollusk dietary significance is further complicated by the probability that clam flesh was extensively used as bait for hook-and-line fishing, as suggested by the bone hooks recovered from Occupation 2 deposits. Furthermore, Claassen (1986:34) has noted that the nutritional value of some mollusks fluctuates seasonally.

A comparison of deer bone weight with total excavated shell weight from the site's different components indicates the relatively great importance of *Mya* in Occupation 2.[1] This finding is particularly significant in light of the prevalent notions that a shift toward shellfishing occurred much later in prehistoric New England.[2]

A total of 22 clam valves from Occupation 2 were analyzed for season of death. Six were taken between late October and early February and 13 were taken between late February and early April. These data strongly suggest that shellfish were collected primarily during the late winter, probably as a food source of last resort. This pattern accords well with Samuel de Champlain's account of shellfish exploitation in the Gulf of Maine about A.D. 1600.[3]

Horizontal Distribution of Faunal Remains

The relative frequencies of taxa represented in the faunal assemblage differ signifi-cantly in horizontal distribution. Bird and cod were generally abundant in the shoreward zone and scarce in the interior, while small clusters of single species (for example two clusters of cod and two of duck bone) were encountered in the shoreward zone, but not

---

[1]The only higher ratio occurs in the plow zone, where it has been increased by taphonomic factors.

[2]See, e.g., Sanger (1975:71), who suggested that such a shift occurred on the Maine coast about 3500 B.P., and Snow (1972:215, 1978:65), who suggested a shift about 2000 B.P. See also Braun 1974 for a discussion of southern New England data.

[3]"During the winter, in the deepest snows, they hunt elks (?) and other animals, on which they live most of the time. And unless the snow is deep, they scarcely get any reward for their pains, since they cannot capture anything except by a very great effort. . . . When they do not hunt, they live on a shell-fish called the cockle" (Biggar 1922–1926:55).

in the interior. Seal bone was relatively much more common in Area 2 (6 percent of the total bone count) than in Areas 1 or 3 (2 percent each).

Swordfish remains exhibited markedly differential distribution. The ratios of rostrum to other bone are 15:28 in Area 1, 16:19 in Area 2, and 26:14 in Area 3. Four of the five vertebrae came from Area 2.

Spiess and Lewis (1993) cite several lines of evidence supporting the idea that Area 2 was where dogs were kept and fed seal meat not favored for human consumption. First, the presence of dogs at the site during Occupation 2, and their importance to its human occupants, is attested by carefully prepared dog burials. Second, ethnographic analogy suggests that seal meat was not a prominent part of the human diet during Occupation 2, and what bone there is is clustered in Area 2, away from the densest scatter of other food species remains. Third, many seal bones at the site have ragged epiphyseal ends, suggestive of dog chewing. Finally, Area 2 lacks bird and fish bones that might have caused dogs to choke.

Faunal Summary

Faunal remains suggest that cervids constituted the primary source of protein in the Occupation 2 diet (Figure 5.11). Isotopic data from the Nevin skeletal population, however, indicate a protein diet dependent upon carnivorous fish or sea mammals (Figure 6.13). The relative abundance of swordfish and cod remains suggests that these species, rather than terrestrial or marine mammals, were the primary protein source. In addition, the prevalence of heavy woodworking tools in most Moorehead phase sites supports the inference that marine hunting, particularly swordfishing, was undertaken from stout, seaworthy vessels, probably dugouts.

The major source of terrestrial protein, and probably fat, was deer, particularly between October and March. Moose were rarely taken. Harbor, gray, and occasionally harp seals were taken in small numbers during the same seasonal range. The extent to which they were used as human food remains unclear. Bear and beaver were also taken in small numbers, probably during the cold months. The scarcity of beaver postcranial elements probably reflects limited availability on the Fox Islands. Mustelids, particularly *Mustela macrodon*, were taken in small numbers, possibly during late winter and early spring.

Shellfish, particularly *Mya arenaria*, played a significant role in the diet toward the end of winter. During the spring, birds and their eggs also contributed. Fish, particularly flounder, may have been caught during spring as well, but the main fishing season was summer, when substantial amounts of swordfish and cod were probably brought to the site from offshore fishing stations such as the Candage site on Vinalhaven (Bourque 1992b) and the Stanley site. These activities probably continued into autumn, giving way to a reliance on mammals in November.[4]

[4]This reconstruction is based on the modern distribution of cod, with large individuals being found in deep water and smaller individuals inshore. Recently, Robert Steneck (personal communication, 1990) has proposed an alternative model suggesting that prehistorically cod were a dominant carnivore inshore as well, and that they have recently been fished to extinction there.

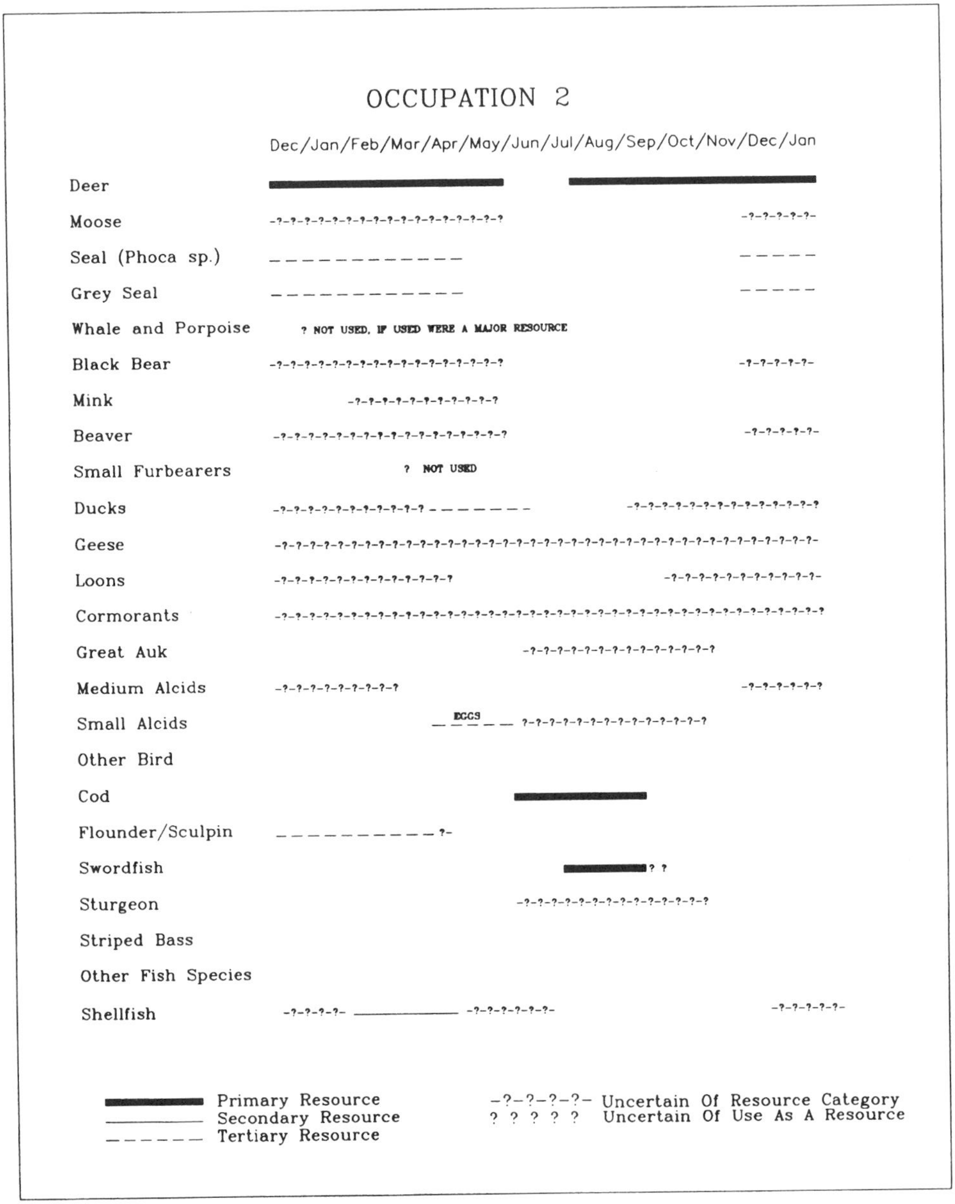

Figure 5.11. Faunal seasonality from Occupation 2 (Spiess and Lewis 1993).

SUMMARY

The deposition of numerous artifacts and abundant refuse around hearth clusters in Areas 1 and 3, as well as the scarcity of task-specific scatters near them, suggests that domestic activity focused there. Houses probably also clustered there. The interior zone reflects a different, more limited range of activities. Area 2 yielded a relatively high artifact count, and faunal remains were comparably abundant, although they differed in important ways from those in the shoreward zone. Finally, Areas 2 and 4 both have prominent task-specific scatters. All available data—including stratigraphic and horizontal patterning, faunal diversity, and artifact joins—suggest contemporaneity among all areas.

Faunal data suggest that Occupation 2 represents a more or less year-round (or at least extended multiseasonal) habitation. Brief periods of total abandonment cannot be ruled out, but the site probably served at least as the central base for a community for at least one year. Perhaps the most likely season for abandonment was the spring, when anadromous fish runs may have attracted many to riverine camps. However, equally plausible is the notion that some people, perhaps elders and small children with their mothers, remained at the site year round.

SIGNIFICANCE OF OCCUPATION 2

The cultural attribution of Maine's Red Paint cemeteries has concerned archaeologists for a century. At issue has been the association of nonmortuary components with the cemeteries. Hadlock (1939) made little of the fact that his excavations at the Taft's Point site produced artifacts similar to those from the cemeteries. Rowe (1940) encountered bayonets of slate and swordfish rostrum, beaver incisor knives, gouges, and plummets in early levels of the Waterside site and recognized the similarity of the stone tools to the cemeteries. Rowe even defined the "Moorehead complex" as a "designation for the peculiar range of tool types occurring in the 'Red Paint' graves," and at the Waterside midden, the Nevin site, and Taft's point as well (Rowe 1940:7–8, 15–16, Plate XIV). Then, beginning in the mid-1950s, amateur excavators at the Goddard site recovered several cemetery-like artifacts from nonmortuary contexts, but their activities drew little professional attention (Bourque and Cox 1981:7–11; Mellgren 1974; Mellgren and Runge 1958).

When the pace of archaeological research in Maine increased during the late 1960s, attention once again focused on defining a cultural context for the cemeteries. Bourque (1992a:16–36) summarized the extant data for the period prior to 1970, noting similarities between the cemeteries and habitation sites such as Taft's Point, Waterside, Nevin, and Goddard, attributing all to the Moorehead phase. The Turner Farm was omitted from the list because the collection then available presented no clear indication for so old a component.

Great interest was focused on Maine's Red Paint cemeteries in 1971 by Tuck's postulation of a Maritime Archaic tradition, in which he included them. That same year, our excavations at the Turner Farm site first encountered a component, later attributed to Occupation 2, that ultimately produced an assemblage closely resembling grave furnishings found in the cemeteries—particularly those at the Nevin site, the only one with substantial bone preservation.

The comparability of the Occupation 2 and Nevin artifact assemblages is crucial because Byers (1979:70–71) was reluctant to regard the latter as Archaic in age, despite Rowe's earlier observations and Tuck's (1971) publication of the Port au Choix cemetery which demonstrated close typological relationships in grave furnishings between the two sites. Byers (1979:25) used very stringent criteria for admitting Nevin artifacts to the category of grave furnishings, but nevertheless included gouges, ground slate points, plummets, and swordfish rostrum foreshafts on the list. He had earlier included the gouges, slate points, and plummets in his discussion of the "Boreal Archaic levels" at the Ellsworth Falls sites, yet he did not refer to them in discussing the age of the Nevin burials (Byers 1959, 1979:70–71). He also noted that swordfish remains have been found exclusively in sites having Archaic components, and that "no evidence of swordfishing has been found in later sites" (Byers 1959:250). Once again, however, he made no reference to swordfish in discussing the age of the Nevin burials. The extensive similarities between the Occupation 2 assemblage and grave furnishings from the Nevin burials, I believe, places most, if not all, the Nevin burials clearly within the Moorehead phase.

Having established a linkage between Occupation 2 and the Red Paint cemeteries, we can address the long-standing question of whether the people interred in cemeteries also exploited marine resources. The first to suggest that Maine shell middens postdate the earliest coastal occupations may have been Loomis and Young, who thought that basal shell-free strata at sites they investigated indicated that "the original object, of coming to the sea shore, was not clams but rather fishing; and possibly hunting, but especially fishing" (Loomis and Young 1912:20). Moorehead also felt "safe in suggesting that the Red Paint People did not live at the shell heaps or at least they did not accumulate shell heaps" (Moorehead 1922:149). Willoughby, however, noted that artifacts similar to those found in Red Paint cemeteries had occasionally been recovered from at least five Maine shell middens, and concluded that what we now refer to as Archaic peoples were "responsible for at least the beginnings of some of these middens" (Willoughby 1935/1973:48, 202).

Hadlock downplayed the association of mollusk shell with the plummets and slate bayonets he encountered at the Taft's Point midden and, moreover, wished to make it clear that he did "not regard the artifacts found in the prepottery horizons as having been made and used by those people known as the Red Paint people of Maine" (Hadlock 1939:5–7, 29). He did, however, acknowledge the presence of "over twenty-five sections of swordfish sword" in the site's basal levels (Hadlock 1939:14). Next to deal with this issue was Rowe (1940), who made it clear that artifacts of his Moorehead complex were associated with swordfish and shell at the Waterside site.

Bourque (1992a:23–26) reviewed evidence from several sites for the exploitation of shellfish and large fish species, including swordfish, during Moorehead phase times. Snow, however, characterized these people as "terrestrial hunters and fishermen that applied their skills in a maritime setting when on the coast, but overlooked the potential productivity of unfamiliar shellfish populations" (Snow 1972:211). Snow reiterated his view that shellfishing began only about 2000 B.P. on the Maine coast, stating that "its adoption would have entailed a significant re-adjustment of the pre-existing [nonmaritime] pattern" (Snow 1974:137). In a similar vein, Sanger (1975:61–62) cited the late (after about 4000 B.P.) onset of substantial biological productivity in the Gulf of Maine as a prerequisite for extensive maritime exploitation, particularly of shellfish.

Occupation 2 deposits at the Turner Farm clearly demonstrate the substantial exploitation of shellfish by about 4500 B.P. Moreover, the faunal data indicate that shell refuse alone is a poor indicator of maritime exploitation. Indeed, faunal data from the Turner Farm and other coastal Moorehead phase components, as well as isotopic data from the Nevin burials, make clear the dominant role marine vertebrates played in the economy of the Moorehead phase.

These data, however, do not support the notion that the Moorehead phase had an economy like that of Tuck's Maritime Archaic tradition. Indeed, it reflects an adaptation to climatological conditions that are even more temperate than those prevalent in the Gulf of Maine today and quite unlike those of Newfoundland/Labrador in the past or at present.

Chapter **6**

Occupation 3

INTRODUCTION

Although some long-standing uncertainties about the Late Archaic in the Northeast had been somewhat clarified by Occupation 2, our rapidly evolving appreciation of the data provided by Occupation 3 promised to raise new uncertainties about what has been alternately referred to as the Terminal Archaic, or the Transitional period. When we began excavations at the Turner Farm site in 1971, the Susquehanna tradition was a recently proposed concept that tied together significant, if somewhat locally anomalous, data sets and presented interesting points of similarity with other contemporaneous data sets over wide areas of eastern North America. Like the Moorehead phase, most of the relevant data came from cemeteries and little of it revealed much about the people responsible for them.

Our early recognition of Susquehanna tradition midden deposits was initially helpful merely because they sealed the critical Occupation 2 deposits below them. After we encountered the cemetery with its wealth of data on mortuary behavior and bone technology, however, Occupation 3 began to take on the importance reflected in the relative attention it has been accorded in this volume.

STRATIGRAPHY

Deposits attributed to Occupation 3 were somewhat less extensive than those of Occupation 2, being encountered in 110 of 163 excavated sections. Its lower, shell-free lenses generally overlay Occupation 2 shell lenses, and resemble other extensive shell-free "floors" in the midden. The large shell-rich lenses that overlay the lower shell-free lenses probably arose during Occupation 3, by the accumulation of refuse on the occupied surface. The numerous features (Table 6.1, Figure 6.1) originated mainly in the shell-free lenses.

Table 6.1. Features from Occupation 3

Feature number	Section	Description	Dates
2-1971	W55S80	Pit in subsoil	
4-1971	W35S105	Shell-filled pit	
7-1972	W35S95	Shell-filled pit	3630 ± 85 B.P. (SI 1919)
18-1972	W30S100	Hearth	
19-1972	W25S100/W20S100	Hearth	3650 ± 75 B.P. (SI 1922)
21-1972	W20S80	Pit	
25-1972	W15S90	Hearth/shallow pit	
26-1972	W20S75	Pit in subsoil	
1-1973	W10S90	Hearth/house floor	
2-1973	W15S100	Hearth/house floor	
3-1973	W15S105	Hearth/house floor	3515 ± 80 B.P. (SI 1924)
4-1973	W20S105	Hearth (part of Feature 19-1972)	
7-1973	W5S85	Pit (shell-filled) in subsoil	
13-1973	E5S75	Pit down to subsoil	
21-1973	E20S75	Hearth	
23-1973	E20S75	Pit	
4-1974	E25S75	Hearth	
7-1974	E25S75	Pit	
8-1974	E25S75	Pit	
9-1974	E25S75	Pit	
12-1974	E20S80	Hearth on subsoil	3280 ± 50 B.P. (SI 4243)
17-1974	E15S75	Two preforms and axe	
18-1974	E15S75	Hearth	
19-1974	E15S75	Pit (soil and shell) in subsoil	
24-1974	W5-10S70	Hearth and floor	3710 ± 80 B.P. (SI 2390)
27-1974	E15S70	Pit in subsoil	
28-1974	E0S65-70	Pit in subsoil	3450 ± 75 B.P. (SI 2396)
29-1974	W15S85	Hearth	
30-1974	W25S70	Primary inhumation	3105 ± 75 B.P. (SI 2399)
			3270 ± 75 B.P. (SI 2397)
32-1974	W15S65	Pit (shell-filled) into subsoil	
33-1974	W15S65	Pit (shell and dark soil)	
34-1974	W25S70/W20S70	Primary inhumation	
35-1974	W20S70	Pit (contains two human bones)	
36-1974	W15S75	Hearth and pit subsoil	
37-1974	W10S75	Pit in west wall	
38-1974	W10S75	Cremation	
39-1974	W15S75	Secondary inhumation	2660 ± 100 B.P. (GX 14968-G)
			3205 ± 75 B.P. (SI 2400)
			3610 ± 90 B.P. (SI 2404)
40-1974	W10S75	Small pit in subsoil	
41-1974	W10S55	Cremation	3855 ± 75 B.P. (SI 2405)
42-1974	W10S55	Cremation	4020 ± 80 B.P. (SI 2393)
3-1975	W10S60	Cremation (part of Feature 41-1974)	

(Continued)

Table 6.1. (*Continued*)

Feature number	Section	Description	Dates
6-1975	W30S70	Primary inhumation	3700 ± 220 B.P. (GX 14806)
			3870 ± 115 B.P. (GX 14807)
9-1975	W10S50	Cremation/Primary burial	3470 ± 59 B.P. (GX 19997-AMS)
			3490 ± 235 B.P. (GX 15745-A)
			3662 ± 60 B.P. (GX 15745-G-AMS)
			3770 ± 260 B.P. (GX 15745-G)
11-1975	W10S50	Cremation (part of Feature 19-1975)	
12-1975	W10S50	Cremation	
13-1975	W35S90	Hearth and pit	
14-1975	W10S50	Cremation (part of Feature 41-1974)	
15-1975	W15S55	Pit (brown soil and shell)	
16-1975	W15S55	Pit (brown soil and shell)	
18-1975	W30S65	Primary inhumation	3280 ± 180 B.P. (GX 15744-A)
			3480 ± 75 B.P. (SI 4248)
			3700 ± 85 B.P. (S1 4247)
			3825 ± 65 B.P. (SI 4249)
			3825 ± 75 B.P. (GX 15744-G-AMS)
			3945 ± 230 B.P. (GX 15744-G)
19-1975	W5S55	Cremation	
22-1975	W5-10S50	Cremation (part of Feature 42-1974)	
24-1975	W10S40	Cremation	
26-1975	W30S50	Pit in subsoil	
28-1975	W20S40	Cremation	
30-1975	W15S55	Secondary inhumation (cremated bone in fill)	
33-1975	W5S50	Primary inhumation	
34-1975	W11.5S46.25	Cremation	
35-1975	E10S55	Cremation	

THE AGE OF OCCUPATION 3

Dates from reliable Occupation 3 contexts (Table 6.2) span more than a millennium, from 4020 ± 80 B.P. (SI 2393) to 3105 ± 75 B.P. (SI 2399). The more recent dates are on shell, which, once again, is considered an unreliable dating medium in the Turner Farm context. The earliest date is on carbonized wood from a cremation. Its context seems very well defined and its extreme age may reflect the use of old wood in a cremation event. The wide range of dates from the burial labeled Feature 18-1975, spanning 665 years (using 1 *SD*), supports the notion that wood of widely varying ages was available. The conifer-dominated woods of the area today would not provide trees of such varying ages. However, the hardwood-dominated forests suggested by charcoal analysis (Appendix 4) probably would have. Dates regarded as most reliable range from 3870 ± 115 B.P. (GX 14807) to 3480 ± 75 B.P. (SI 4248; Table 8.1). Evidence presented below, however, suggests that Occupation 3 actually consisted of at least two episodes.

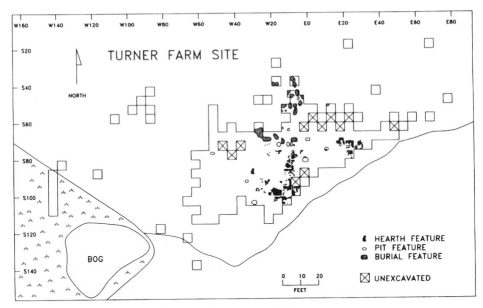

Figure 6.1.   Occupation 3 features.

THE IMPACT OF EROSION ON OCCUPATION 3

The rate of relative sea-level rise in Penobscot Bay had slowed considerably by Occupation 3 times and the extent of loss to erosion of Occupation 3 and later components must be much less extensive than for earlier components (see Appendix 5). Excavations through the modern beach and the salt marsh nevertheless encountered Occupation 3 and later components more or less in situ.

ARTIFACTS

Nearly equal proportions of the Occupation 3 lithic artifact sample came from the midden and burials. Specimens found in the midden [N^m] numbered 330, while specimens found in the burials [N^b] numbered 373 (Table 6.3). Those from the midden were generally heavily worn or broken. Only a few simple bone artifacts were recovered from the midden. Artifacts from the burials were generally little worn, but had often been burned, heat shattered, or ritually broken. Bone artifacts from the burials were relatively much more abundant and complex.

Flaked Stone

Flaked bifaces dominated the artifact sample, particularly in the midden (Tables 6.3, 6.4). Most bifaces are large, thin, and in styles typical of the early Susquehanna tradition throughout the Northeast (see, e.g., Dincauze 1968:19; Ritchie 1980:158). The series also

Table 6.2. Dates (B.P.) from Occupation 3

Date	Section	Sample number	Material	Feature number	Feature	Lab number
2660 ± 100	W15S70-75	4362	Human bone	39-1974	Secondary inhumation	GX 14968-G
3105 ± 75	W25S70	64C	Human bone	30-1974	Primary inhumation	SI 2399
3205 ± 75	W15S70-75	66C	Human bone	39-1974	Secondary inhumation	SI 2400
3270 ± 75	W25S70	63C	*Mya*	30-1974	Primary inhumation	S1 2397
3280 ± 180	W30S65		Human bone	18-1975	Primary inhumation	GX 15744-A
3450 ± 75	E0S65-70	60C	*Mya*	28-1974	Pit in subsoil	SI 2396
3470 ± 60	W105S0	127C	Charcoal	9-1975	Cremation	GX 19997-AMS
3480 ± 75	W30S65	153C	Charcoal	18-1975	Primary inhumation	SI 4248
3490 ± 235	W10S50		Human bone	9-1975	Primary inhumation	GX 15745-A
3515 ± 80	W15S105	194C	Soil sample	3-1973	House floor	SI 1924
3610 ± 90	W15S70-75	65C	Charcoal	39-1974	Secondary inhumation	SI 2404
3630 ± 85	W35S90-95	14C	Charcoal	7-1972	Pit	SI 1919
3650 ± 75	W20S100	31C	Charcoal	19-1972	Hearth	SI 1922
3662 ± 59	W10S50		Human bone	9-1975	Primary inhumation	GX 15745-G-AMS
3700 ± 220	W30S70	148C	Charcoal	6-1975	Primary inhumation	GX 14806
3700 ± 85	W30S65	152C	Charcoal	18-1975	Primary inhumation	SI 4247
3710 ± 80	W5-10S70	68C	Charcoal	24-1974	House floor	SI 2390
3770 ± 260	W10S50		Human bone	9-1975	Primary inhumation	GX 15745-G
3825 ± 65	W30S65	154C	Charcoal	18-1975	Primary inhumation	SI 4249
3825 ± 76	W10S50		Human bone	18-1975	Primary inhumation	GX 15745-G-AMS
3855 ± 75	W10S55	70C	Charcoal	41-1974	Cremation	SI 2405
3870 ± 115	W30S70	6657	Human bone	6-1975	Primary inhumation	GX 14807-G
3945 ± 230	W30S65		Human bone	18-1975	Primary inhumation	GX 15744-G
4020 ± 80	W10S55	71C	Charcoal	42-1974	Cremation	SI 2393

resembles contemporaneous Late Archaic lithic technologies farther afield—to the south as far as Florida and to the west perhaps as far as Kansas (McElrath 1993:149–150; Milanich 1994:85–104; Reid 1984).

Because those from the burials probably are less reduced by wear and resharpening than those from the midden, and because other published Susquehanna samples from New England are generally also from burials (see especially Dincauze 1968), descriptions of stone tools are based primarily on the burial sample.

Like the Susquehanna tradition-related biface technologies to the south (see, e.g., Cresson 1990; Dincauze 1968:15–29; Funk 1993:197), the biface sample from the midden and burials is basically divisible into classes representing a production sequence.

Preforms

The preforms have straight, convex, or concave bases (N^m = 29, N^b = 38; Plate 6.1). Longer and wider than most finished tools, few preforms show evidence of use, such as fine retouch or edge dulling. They apparently are thinned quarry blanks intended for later

Table 6.3. Lithic Tool Types
from Occupation 3

Artifact type	Total	Midden	Burials
Preforms[a]	67	29	38
Mansion Inn blades	80	39	41
Miscellaneous	11	11	0
Tapered-stem blades	68	23	45
Contracting-stem points	71	66	5
Straight-stem points	34	32	2
Expanding-stem points	193	73	120
Notched points	13	2	11
Boats blades	28	9	19
Drills	90	38	52
Gravers	4	0	4
Gouges	9	1	8
Adzes	13	1	12
Grooved axes	3	1	2
Pendants	3	0	3
Whetstones	5	0	5
Beveled cobbles	7	1	6
Scrapers	4	4	4

[a]Not counting Mansion Inn blades.

modification. Many retain thick striking platform remnants at their widest point, above the base (see, e.g., Plate 6.2). This indicates that they were made from large, broad flakes. In this regard, they differ markedly from the relatively thick, narrow bifaces of Occupations 1 and 2, which, as described above, were laterally retouched blades that retained striking platform remnants at the base of the stem.

Our experiments with flaking rhyolite, the material used for most of the Occupation 3 bifaces, suggest that the kind of broad flakes needed for Occupation 3 bifaces can most easily be obtained from massive blocks. Many bifaces were of Kineo-Traveler Rhyolite, the source of which lies 185 km to the north. Widely distributed southward by glacial transport, it occurs in boulders that, on the coast at least, rarely attain the large size needed to generate such flakes. This distribution suggests that this raw material, at least, was obtained by traveling up the boulder train at least far enough to encounter large boulders. The other extensively used raw material was Vinalhaven banded-spherulitic rhyolite, the source of which is located less than 5 km west of the Turner Farm site.

Many preforms conform to Dincauze's (1968:16–23) Mansion Inn type. They are comparable in length to her Watertown variety of that type, but are wider and thicker as well. They exceed her smaller Dudley variety in all dimensions.

Boats Blades

Boats blades are the longest bifaces and have bases that are pointed or nearly so ($N^m = 9$, $N^b = 19$; Plate 6.3). They bear close resemblance to Dincauze's (1968:26–27, Plate

Table 6.4. Summary of Statistics for All Bifacial Tools from Occupation 3[a]

Artifact type		Midden				Burials			
		Length	Width	Thick	Base W[b]	Length	Width	Thick	Base W[b]
Preforms[c]	N =	11	22	25	19	18	27	30	2
	Ave =	8.68	4.52	1.41	3.72	10.04	5.42	1.32	2.40
	SD =	1.94	1.04	.42	1.29	1.68	.92	.33	.56
	Min =	5.70	2.70	.80	1.60	6.70	2.90	.70	2.00
	Max =	12.70	6.60	2.30	6.60	13.70	7.10	2.10	2.80
Mansion Inn	N =	12	33	36	0	22	35	37	33
blades	Ave =	7.56	4.65	1.21	0.0	9.26	6.10	1.34	2.89
	SD =	2.81	1.06	.34	0.0	1.57	1.07	.33	.62
	Min =	4.60	2.80	.60	0.0	6.40	3.50	.60	1.60
	Max =	15.60	7.00	2.10	0.0	12.40	8.20	2.10	4.50
Tapered-stem	N =	0	18	22	19	20	37	41	28
	Ave =	0.0	3.83	.81	2.08	9.17	4.40	.73	2.29
	SD =	0.0	.65	.11	.61	1.20	.73	.14	.45
	Min =	0.0	2.60	.60	1.10	6.90	2.80	.40	1.70
	Max =	0.0	5.10	1.00	3.60	11.60	5.80	1.10	3.60
Contracting-	N =	18	57	61	65	2	2	4	2
stem	Ave =	6.28	3.94	.96	1.56	6.75	4.30	.92	1.80
	SD =	1.02	.73	.16	.25	1.48	4.24	.24	.28
	Min =	4.40	2.20	.70	1.00	5.70	4.00	.60	1.60
	Max =	8.10	6.00	1.50	2.10	7.80	4.60	1.10	2.00
Straight-stem	N =	18	26	31	31	1	0	2	0
	Ave =	6.89	3.40	.84	1.70	11.70	0.0	1.05	0.0
	SD =	1.62	.61	.14	.28	0.00	0.0	.07	0.0
	Min =	3.10	2.20	.60	1.20	11.70	0.0	1.00	0.0
	Max =	10.40	4.80	1.30	2.30	11.70	0.0	1.10	0.0
Expanding-	N =	17	60	67	66	70	90	111	93
stem	Ave =	6.04	3.32	.75	2.04	7.71	3.96	.76	2.25
	SD =	1.04	.56	.14	.32	2.22	.90	1.20	4.03
	Min =	4.70	1.90	.50	1.50	3.50	2.30	.50	1.50
	Max =	8.40	4.70	1.10	3.00	13.80	6.70	1.10	3.40
Notched	N =	0	0	0	0	0.0	5	7	7
	Ave =	0.0	0.0	0.0	0.0	0.0	3.22	.70	2.21
	SD =	0.0	0.0	0.0	0.0	0.0	.31	.10	.43
	Min =	0.0	0.0	0.0	0.0	0.0	2.70	.60	1.50
	Max =	0.0	0.0	0.0	0.0	0.0	3.50	.90	2.80
Boats blades	N =	0	6	5	6	8	12	15	1
	Ave =	0.0	4.70	1.06	4.28	13.1	5.40	1.21	5.20
	SD =	0.0	.66	.26	.71	3.16	.59	.19	0.00
	Min =	0.0	4.10	.70	3.50	10.40	4.60	.90	5.20
	Max =	0.0	5.60	1.30	5.50	18.00	6.40	1.50	5.20
Drills	N =	2	9	6	9	16	26	31	24
	Ave =	8.30	2.24	.98	2.24	8.64	2.10	.66	2.10
	SD =	2.40	.65	.23	.65	2.83	.37	.17	.38
	Min =	8.60	1.40	.70	1.40	4.60	1.20	.50	1.20
	Max =	10.00	3.50	1.40	3.50	13.80	2.80	1.20	2.80

[a]All measurements in centimeters.
[b]Base W = base width.
[c]Not counting Mansion Inn blades.

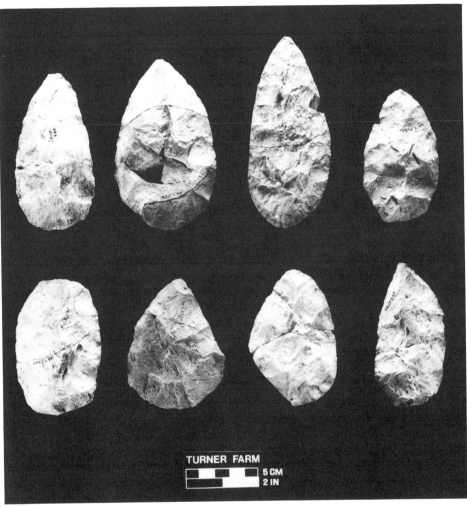

Plate 6.1. Preforms from Feature 24-1975.

XV, nos. 1–4) definition of the type, but are thicker. One biface fragment from the midden appears to be the base of a Boats blade with side notches, similar to those reported by Dincauze and observed in the Griffin site assemblage from Old Lyme, Connecticut (Pfeiffer 1990:96). Evidence for their use is inconclusive. No edge grinding was observed on either the midden or the burial samples, but they seem unlikely to be precursors of any other finished forms. Though the sample is small, Boats blades from the midden cluster horizontally with expanding-stem points, which were apparently a later stemmed point form in the Occupation 3 sequence.

Plate 6.2. Mansion Inn blades from Occupation 3.

Plate 6.3. Boats blades from Occupation 3.

Tapered-Stem Blades

This class has stems with concave margins of uniform radius (N^m = 23, N^b = 45; Plate 6.4). A few stem margins are parallel at the base, but none diverge to form an expanding stem. Average tapered-stem blade length is not significantly different from other bifaces, but they are slightly narrower and considerably thinner, being among the thinnest tools in the flaked tool assemblage (Table 6.4). They have been encountered in other collections from contemporaneous Maine sites, including a cemetery at the nearby Eddington Bend site (W. Smith 1926:58–73). Similar specimens were illustrated by Dincauze (1968; Plate III, nos. 1, 2, Plate VII, no. 5, Plate VIII, nos. 2, 3, Plate XVI, nos. 2–6), who included them with

Plate 6.4. Tapered-stem blades from Occupation 3.

Watertown blades. Tapered-stem blades cluster in the northern, particularly the northeastern, portion of the excavation, and therefore seem primarily associated with expanding-stem points.

The function of these blades is unclear. Generally they appear unworn, although 20 show signs of stem-edge dulling, suggesting hafting or preparation for it. The majority would perhaps have received final stem modification before hafting.

Stemmed Points

All stemmed points are finished bifaces. Those from the midden show clear signs of wear in their patterns of retouch, breakage, and stem polish. They are smaller than preforms and equal to or smaller than tapered-stem blades in length, blade width, and stem width. They can be differentiated from the former by the compound curvature of their stem margin below the blade, and further subdivided into three varieties: those with stems that slightly contract (narrowest at the base, $N^m = 66$, $N^b = 5$), have parallel edges ($N^m = 32$, $N^b = 2$), or expand (narrowest point above the base, $N^m = 73$, $N^b = 120$). Basal configurations range from slightly convex to slightly concave.

Contracting- and straight-stemmed points (Plate 6.5) are similar to Ritchie's (1971b:47, Plate 27) Snook Kill type and to Dincauze's (1972:41–42, Plate XVI) Atlantic blades. Farther afield, similarities are found in the Genesee points of Funk's (1976:261–263) Batten Kill phase, Lehigh points of central Pennsylvania, Koens-Crispin points of the Delaware Valley, and broad-bladed points of the Satchell phase of southwestern Ontario, all of which date to about 3800 B.P. (Funk 1993:196; Kenyon 1980; Regensberg 1971; Ritchie 1971b:24–25; Witthoft 1953:16–22, Plate 10). All these styles resemble Coe's (1964:45) Savannah River Stemmed type, which dates to about 4000 B.P. (see below). Those with expanding stems closely resemble Ritchie's (1971b:53–54, Plate 31) Susquehanna Broad and Dincauze's (1968:23–26) Wayland notched and Dudley notched types, especially the former (Plate 6.6). The Turner Farm expanding-stem sample has smaller blades than Wayland notched points, but their stem dimensions are the same. They exceed Dudley notched points in all dimensions.

In the Northeast, as in the Savannah River series of the Southeast, the continuum of stem form from contracting to expanding has appeared to be a progressive phenomenon (see, e.g., Funk 1993:197; Kraft 1970:72; Oliver 1985b:136; Ritchie 1980:140–141; Robinson and Bolian 1987:28–29, 32, 38–39; Truncer 1990:11; Turnbaugh 1977:139–153). The Turner Farm data support this model. Decreasing blade thickness decreases with time at the Turner Farm site; points with contracting stems (including specimens from the midden) are significantly thicker than those with expanding stems. We have not been able to determine whether this pattern is true in other areas of the Northeast. Both contracting- and straight-stem points are also thicker than tapered-stem blades, further indication that the latter may be contemporaneous with the late, expanding-stem forms. Despite considerable discussion, the issue of whether these points functioned as weapon tips or knives remains unresolved (see, e.g., Custer 1991; Oliver 1985a:203–205).

Notched Points

These stemmed bifaces can only be described as corner- or side-notched ($N^m = 2$, $N^b = 11$; Plate 6.7). They are smaller than stemmed points and more variable in form,

Plate 6.5.   Bifaces from Feature 18-1975, Occupation 3.

but all have a markedly narrow angle between the blade base and stem margin, constituting a notch. Two fire-damaged fragments probably were heat fractured in a cremation, although they were found outside burial features. They may be made of exotic chert and, if so, are the only exotics recognized in the Occupation 3 sample. It is interesting to note that a similar fire-broken notched fragment came from the Eddington Bend Susquehanna tradition cremations, which produced four other corner-notched fragments of apparently exotic chert.

There appear to be few contemporaneous analogues for these artifacts in the Northeast. The closest are from the Small Point phase of the Terminal Archaic sequence proposed by Spence and Fox for southern Ontario (Spence and Fox 1986:6–11, Figures 1.5, 1.6). There, some sites have produced drill bits that closely resemble those of the Susquehanna

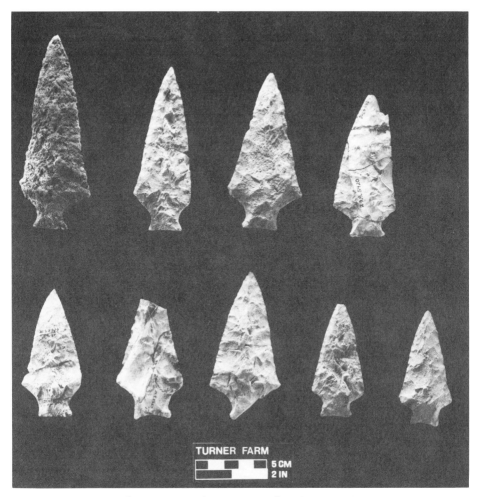

Plate 6.6.   Expanding-stem points from Occupation 3.

tradition (e.g., at the Hind cemetery, burials 18a and 20), although Spence and Fox present the Small Point phase as spatially juxtaposed and culturally distinct from it.

Scrapers

Recovered from the midden were four bifacial blades with extensive rounding and polishing along an excurvate edge at one end (Plate 6.8). These tools, more commonly made on stemmed points, occur widely in Susquehanna tradition and related contexts. Although they are generally referred to as scrapers, one Turner Farm specimen examined under low-power magnification had wear that appeared to indicate abrasion against wood, suggesting that the tool had been used as a wedge (John Shea, personal communication

Plate 6.7. Notched points from Occupation 3.

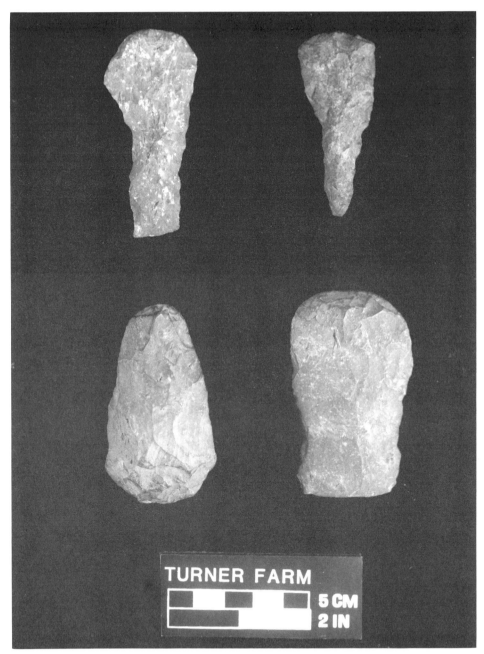

Plate 6.8. "Scrapers" from Occupation 3.

1989; see, e.g., Dincauze 1968:17–18; Ellis et al. 1990:103; Kinsey 1972a:208; Kraft 1972:13, 1990:73, Figure 5; Turnbaugh 1977:141–142). Whether these tools are comparable to visually similar artifacts from the Southeast remains to be seen (see, e.g., Claflin 1931:Plate 14; Waring 1977:Figure 67; Webb 1974:261–263, Figure 35c).

Drills

These extremely narrow bifaces flare at the base, usually to a straight basal margin resembling those of expanding-stem points, although some bases are ovoid (N^m = 38, N^b = 52; Plate 6.9). Specimens recovered from the midden are relatively short, apparently reduced in length by wear and resharpening. Those from mortuary features are much longer and appear unused. Close analogues have been found in several Maine Susquehanna contexts as well as in contemporaneous contexts in southern New England and much farther to the south (see, e.g., Dincauze 1968:28–29; Funk 1976:262; Webb 1974:256,

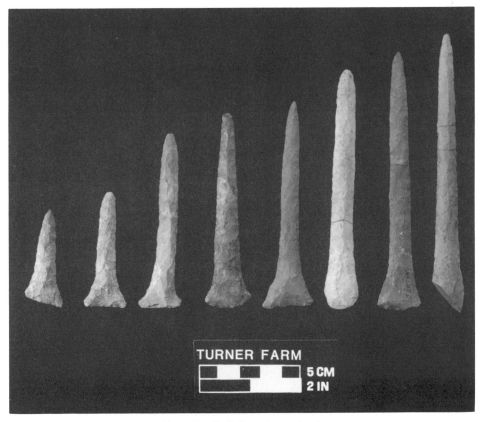

Plate 6.9. Drills from Occupation 3.

Figure 33a). While it is possible that some Occupation 3 drills were made on reworked points, as has been claimed for drills of the Frost Island phase in New York and the Southeast (Funk 1993:197; B. Smith 1986:10), many from the mortuary features are too long to have been produced by reworking points, typical preforms, or tapered-stem blades as defined above. Southern Susquehanna tradition and related technologies, where drills are shorter, often possess broad lateral extensions at the blade base and thus are often regarded as having been reworked from stemmed points (see, e.g., Bullen and Green 1970:25; Claflin 1931:37–38, Plate 65; Cresson 1990:126; Dincauze 1968:28–29; Funk 1993:197; Kraft 1972:13; Webb 1974:256–257, Figure 33b). These southern "cruciform" drills are usually attributed to contexts dated after about 3600 B.P., while at least some drills from Occupation 3 apparently are earlier (see, e.g., Kraft 1990:68–69; Pfeiffer 1990:101). Thus, the absence of the cruciform drills at the Turner Farm site and elsewhere in Maine may reflect temporal differences primarily.

The manner in which drills were used at the Turner Farm site remains uncertain, largely because use wear is not apparent on the few specimens examined. Dincauze (1968:28–29) reported drill-like wear on only one specimen in her limited sample and "push-pull" wear on another. Webb (1974:257–258) observed that the nonwinged drills from Indian Knoll that closely resemble those from Occupation 3 "would have served admirably to produce the deep conical holes in antler projectile points," an artifact class in evidence in Occupation 3.

Gravers

Made on small, thin flakes by minimal, fine, unifacial retouch, these tools went unrecognized during excavation and all specimens were later recovered from tool fragment lots from burial contexts ($N^m = 0$, $N^b = 4$; Plate 6.10). That they constitute a formal tool type is indicated by the discovery of a similar graver in a Susquehanna tradition component on Mashipacong Island in northernmost New Jersey (Kraft 1990:68, Figure 6) and at Indian Knoll (Webb 1974:259, Figure 33d), as well as at the Eddington Bend site. Funk's (1993:197) "retouched flake tools" may also refer to such gravers.

Ground Stone Tools

Ground stone tools are much less frequent in Occupation 3 strata than in Occupation 2, particularly relative to flaked stone tools. The small sample nevertheless demonstrates interesting variability. Most are adzes and gouges designed for heavy woodworking. They are generally made from a metasiltstone that was not used during Occupation 2 (Plates 6.11, 6.12; see Appendix 6). Smaller adzes were shaped by flaking and sharpened by grinding. One specimen has a broad, shallow pecked hafting groove across its dorsal surface. The larger ones were shaped by pecking and then ground over much of their surface. Their dorsoventral asymmetry is much less marked than in the Occupation 2 sample, and indeed some may have been hafted as axes. Most polls show evidence of battering. The bits of several specimens from burials have been purposely shattered. Adz lengths range from 11 to 24.5 cm ($N^m = 1$, $N^b = 12$). Gouges are finished in a similar manner, but unlike the adzes, have considerable dorsoventral asymmetry ($N^m = 1$, $N^b = 8$). Their grooves extend less than

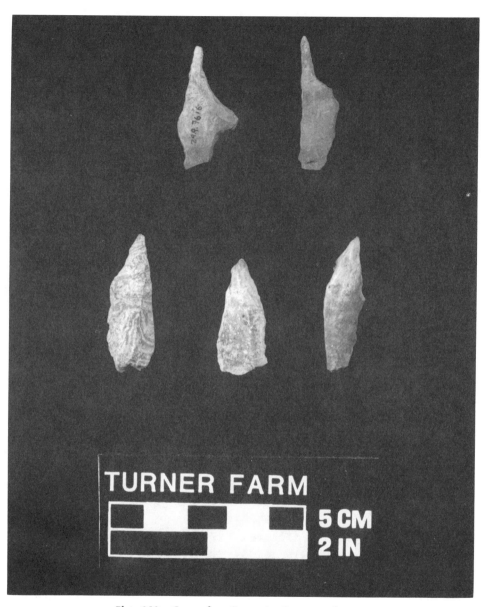

Plate 6.10. Gravers from Occupation 3 mortuary features.

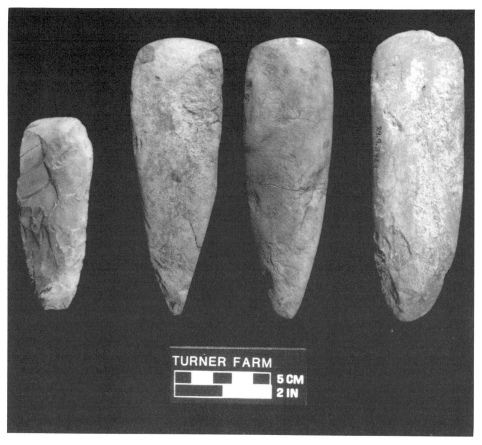

Plate 6.11.   Adzes from Occupation 3.

half the length of the tool and generally are better defined than those on gouges from Occupation 2.

Grooved Axes

Three axes were recovered by excavation, and a fourth large one (partial length = 29 cm) from the Ames family collection is tentatively assigned to Occupation 3 on the basis of its morphology (N^m = 1, N^b = 2; Plate 6.13). All were pecked and ground, the three largest ones having some degree of lipping around the groove. Two specimens from burials had purposely shattered bits. Similar grooved axes are commonly encountered in unstratified interior Maine sites where Susquehanna bifaces occur. General analogues have been found throughout the range of contemporaneous Susquehanna tradition-like biface technology (see, e.g., Claflin 31:29–30, Plate 48; Dincauze 1968:31–33, Plates IX, XI; Sassaman and Lewis 1990:52–54; Webb 1974:272, Figure 38b), though relatively rarely with the groove lipping comparable to that seen on the two specimens from the Turner Farm burials and on other Maine examples.

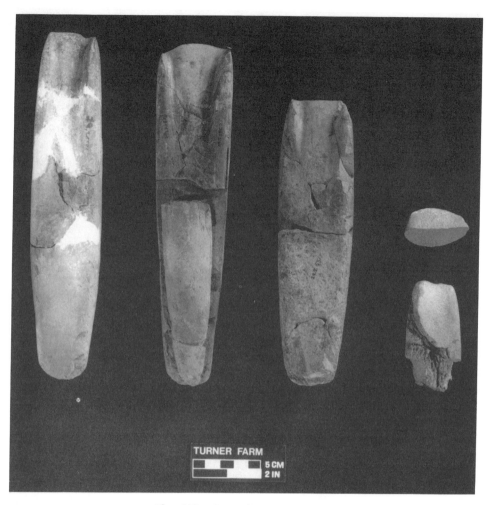

Plate 6.12. Gouges from Occupation 3.

Grooved axes have a long history in eastern North America, in the Northeast beginning by Middle Archaic times (Dincauze 1976:42, 72–73; Maymon and Bolian 1992:120, 126). They apparently went out of use in the Gulf of Maine drainage by the beginning of the Late Archaic and have not been reported from any Small Stemmed Point tradition or Moorehead phase context. Thus, their reappearance in Occupation 3 and related Maine contexts heralds a distinct reintroduction.

Pendants

Three unique ground slate pendants were recovered from Feature 12-1975, a multiple cremation burial. The crescentic one has a notch, probably representing a mouth, and a suspension hole at the apex. It is thin and quite flat in cross section and may represent a

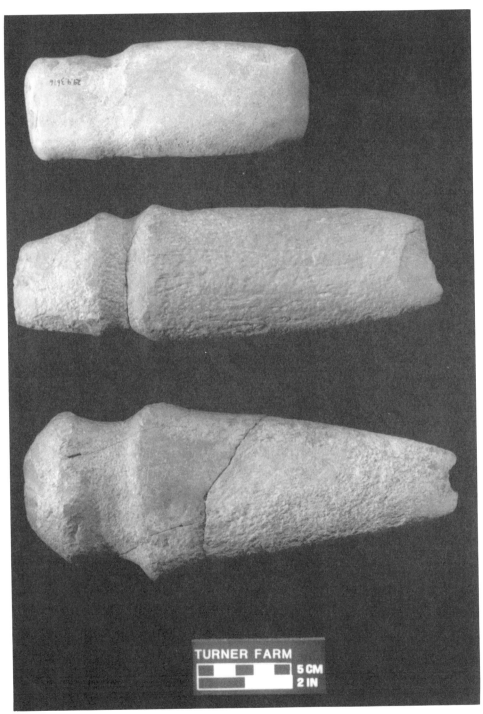

Plate 6.13.   Grooved axes from Occupation 3.

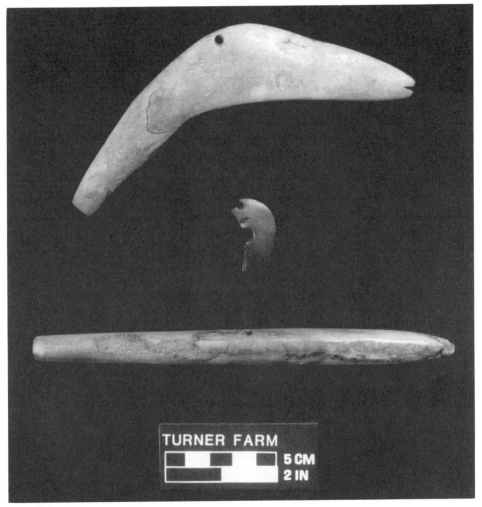

Plate 6.14.   Ground slate pendants from Occupation 3 mortuary Feature 12-1975.

bird's head or the profile of a marine mammal. The long and asymmetrically tapered one can best be described as a bar amulet. It has a **D**-shaped cross section and is pierced in the center. The discoidal specimen was originally perforated with two probable suspension holes. All three are apparently without analogues from any northeastern Archaic context.

Whetstones

These soft, abrasive, siltstone pebbles and small cobbles exhibit a variety of grinding wear ($N^m = 0$, $N^b = 5$; Plate 6.15). One has a series of scratches and grooves on its tabular surface. Two rod-shaped specimens from Feature 24-1975 exhibit longitudinal smoothing, as if from honing the gouges also found in that feature. The remaining two have well-

Plate 6.15.   Whetstones from Occupation 3.

defined grooves suitable for smoothing a small-diameter wooden shaft. All these tools resemble the grooved hones encountered by Dincauze (1968:38–39) and listed for select sites farther south by Cook (1976:346).

Beveled and Grooved Cobbles

This variable class comprises smooth subtabular water-worn cobbles of elliptical outline with abraded margins usually at or near one end ($N^m = 1$, $N^b = 6$; Plate 6.16). All are of fine-grained rock. The wear varies from a flat facet to a well-defined groove, with intermediate examples exhibiting a series of subparallel, shallow striations over the area of the facet. All grooves and striations slant from upper left to lower right, viewed with the edge held vertically. When held in the right hand in an anatomically comfortable position, such grooves would be formed by moving the artifact to and from the user. The faceted examples closely resemble Dincauze's (1968:37–38) beveled hammers that she regarded as biface flaking tools similar to quartz specimens reported from Orient phase sites by Ritchie (1959:60, 70). Other cobbles have grooves that appear to be the equivalent of what Dincauze referred to as "steps" across the faceted surface. Cross (1990:227–228) has recently suggested that prolonged use of faceted cobble hammers produces first the striations and finally the step pattern. Cross notes that these cobble hammers are found solely in Susquehanna tradition contexts, including the Griffin site (Pfeiffer 1980:132). This association accords well with Dincauze's observation that finishing flakes were apparently driven off her Susquehanna tradition bifaces by blows from "a broad, flattened hammer face" (Dincauze 1968:16). Although Cross (1990:228) has produced wear similar to faceted abraiders on antler billets used for flaking, Dincauze commented that "porphyritic felsites [rhyolites] are refractory materials, and probably required a heavier hammer" (Dincauze 1968:16). The absence of heavy antler billets from Occupation 3 supports this conclusion.

Bone Artifacts

Bone and antler were apparently much less important as raw materials during Occupation 3 than during Occupation 2. Moreover, Occupation 3 bone artifacts differ from those of Occupation 2, even when their basic functions are similar (e.g., the harpoons shown in Plate 6.17). That swordfish rostrum was not used at all is strong evidence that the unworked swordfish bone found in Occupation 3 midden deposits was derived from Occupation 2 deposits.

Techniques of bone and antler tool manufacture also differed from those of Occupation 2 and from those of later times as well; virtually all Occupation 3 specimens had ground or polished surfaces rather than the scraped ones found on those from Occupations 2 and 4 (Will 1981). As in the Occupation 2 sample, incised decoration ranges from crude to very delicate. Both samples exhibit exclusively geometric motifs, but their specific forms are distinctly different.

Barbed Weapons

All barbed weapons came from mortuary features. They include a large antler harpoon, a barbed bone spear and five socketed antler tines, which appear to be toggling harpoons

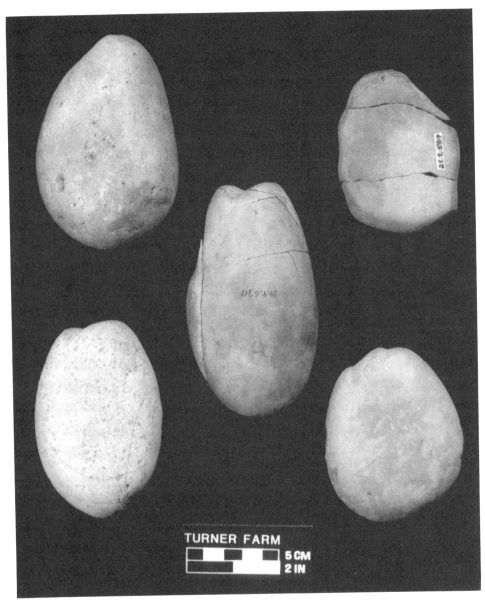

Plate 6.16. Beveled and grooved cobbles from Occupation 3.

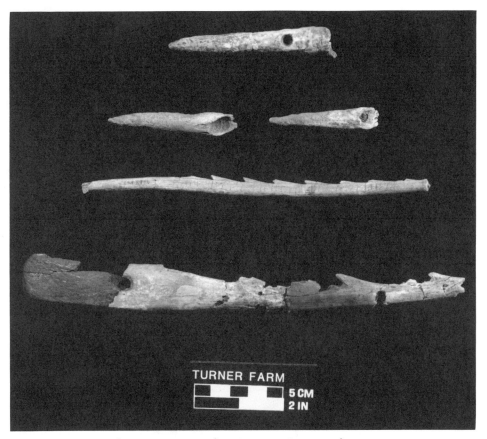

Plate 6.17. Harpoons from Occupation 3 mortuary features.

(Figure 6.2, Plate 6.17). No similar harpoons are known from earlier contexts in eastern North America, although similar specimens have been found in undated, but presumably later, contexts in southern New England (see, e.g., Willoughby 1935/1973:217, Figure 121b; James Bradley, personal communication 1993). Analogues for the socketed antler tines are absent from earlier or contemporaneous northeastern assemblages but similar specimens have been reported from approximately contemporaneous contexts at the Indian Knoll site in Kentucky, and at the Bilbo and Stallings Island sites on the Savannah River (Claflin 1931:26; Waring 1977:165–166; Webb 1974:239).

Beaver Incisor Tools

A substantial sample of beaver incisor tools was recovered from Occupation 3 (N^m = 22, N^b = 0; Figure 6.3, Table 7.4). This sample resembles that from Occupation 2 in the relative frequencies of its various styles and is regarded as completely derived from it by upward mixture and possibly by excavator error (N^m = 25, N^b = 0; Figure 6.3, Table 7.4). This conclusion is based on two factors. First, despite the very high proportion of Occupa-

Figure 6.2. Antler harpoon from Occupation 3 mortuary Feature 9-1975 (Drawing: Don Bassett).

tion 3 bone tools that came from burial features, no beaver incisor tools were included. Second, the areas where most Occupation 3 specimens were recovered are congruent with Occupation 2 concentrations or were areas where Occupation 3 burials had disturbed underlying Occupation 2 strata.

Gaming Pieces

Ten hemispherical objects (three of antler, three beaver femur heads, and four deer femoral heads) were found in Feature 18-1975, a burial (Plate 6.18). All femoral heads were from immature animals as shown by unfused epiphyseal surfaces; some had their unfused undersides smoothed by grinding. They resemble the button-shaped "waltes" used as dice by recent Indians in this region (see, e.g., Speck 1940:173).

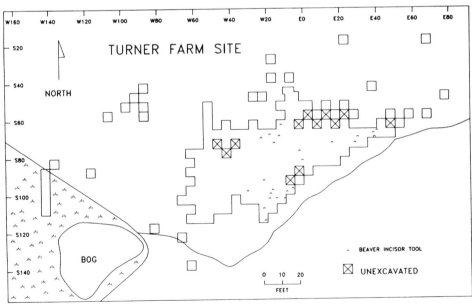

Figure 6.3. Beaver incisor tool distribution from Occupation 3.

Bone Dice?

These interesting artifacts are made from cervid long-bone diaphyses. They range from 5.9 to 8.1 cm in length and 1.8 to 2.3 cm in width ($N^m = 7$, $N^b = 0$; Plate 6.19). Dense striations along the edges of all but one specimen suggest that they were shaped by grinding. The marrow cavity side of all specimens bears well-defined parallel incisions. Traces of red ocher remain in the grooves of one specimen. Although the function of these artifacts is unknown, five were found together with an isolated deer astragalus, suggesting that they are gaming pieces similar to those used throughout aboriginal North America during the historic period (see, e.g., Culin 1975:44–225).

Decorated Bone Objects

Four decorated calcined bone objects were recovered from secondary cremation deposits (Figure 6.4, Plate 6.20). The head of a comb from Feature 38-1974 bears very delicate incised decoration with differing, rigidly geometric motifs on opposite sides. This is the earliest comb known from New England and, aside from one from Frontenac Island, the earliest from the Northeast (Ritchie 1980:116, Plate 39, no. 11). It is remarkable in two respects. First, it differs from later northeastern bone combs in originally having (probably) eight tines instead of the usual three to six, and a top that appears to have contracted upward instead of expanding (see, e.g., Bourque 1992a:301; Mason 1981:274). Second, neither of its decorative motifs remotely resemble those found on other decorated combs in the Northeast. Relatively precise analogues for both motifs, however, are to be found on roughly contemporaneous specimens from the Indian Knoll cemetery in Tennessee (see, e.g., Webb 1974:318). The possible significance of these similarities is discussed below.

Feature 41-1974 produced a calcined fragmentary cylindrical object that closely resembles the button-headed bone pins from the same late Savannah River Archaic sites that produced the socketed antler projectile points noted above (Claflin 1931:23–24, Plate 37g, k, m, Plate 38b, c; Waring 1977:169, Figure 62a). Its surface bears trianguloid fields set off by short oblique dashes and filled with very fine (about 20 per cm) cross-hatching. This specimen is also unique in the Occupation 3 sample because its surface bears well-defined scraping facets like those on Occupation 2 bone tools. Two other objects from Feature 38-1974 are a flat bone pin with broad, oblique, parallel bands crossed obliquely by very fine, closely spaced parallel lines incised (about 3 per cm) on one side and a flat bone fragment decorated with cross-hatching. Finally, a probable fragmentary deer auxiliary phalange tip bearing fine, zigzag incisions came from Feature 12-1975.

Undecorated Bone Pins

Other examples of long, pointed bone artifacts include three made from bone splinters found in mortuary Feature 19-1975 (Plate 6.21). Once again, these artifacts are without regional analogues of similar age, but do have analogues from southeastern sites such as Indian Knoll and Stallings Island (Claflin 1931:Plate 27j; Webb 1974:208, 214, Figures 24, 26). Several other cylindrical midsections and tip fragments may also be parts of bone pins.

Plate 6.18.   Bone "gaming pieces" from Occupation 3 mortuary Feature 18-1975.

Plate 6.19. Bone "dice" from Occupation 3.

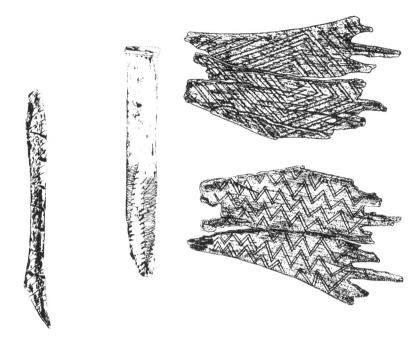

Figure 6.4. Decorated bone objects from Occupation 3 mortuary features (see Plate 6.20). From left to right: diagonally incised flat bone pin, Feature 38-1974 (drawing: Patricia Arey); button-headed bone pin, Feature 41-1974 (drawing: Patricia Arey); comb, Feature 24-1975 (drawing: Don Bassett).

Bone Gouges

Numerous calcined fragments of an indeterminate number of bone gouges were found in cremation burials (Plate 6.22). One additional unburned specimen came from a primary burial (Feature 9-1975). All had been smoothed by grinding over most of their surface. The relatively great breadth of their bits suggests that they were made from moose long bone. All the burned specimens from the cremations had very sharp bits that may have been used for hide scraping. The specimen from Feature 9-1975, however, was very dull, as if from extensive wear. At least one bone gouge was recovered from cremations at the Eddington Bend cemetery and a generally similar tool was recovered at Frontenac Island in western New York (Ritchie 1945:106–107).

Rattle Parts

From a cremation deposit (Feature 12-1975) came modified scutes from the carapace of a box turtle (*Terrapene carolina*) and a painted turtle (*Chrysemys picta*), along with 18 small spheroidal quartz pebbles (Plate 6.23). Modified scutes of box and painted turtle were also found in burial Features 41b-1974, 42-1974, and 9-1975, again associated with

Plate 6.20. Decorated bone objects from Occupation 3 mortuary features.

Plate 6.21. Undecorated bone pins from Occupation 3 mortuary features.

Plate 6.22. Bone gouges from Occupation 3 mortuary features.

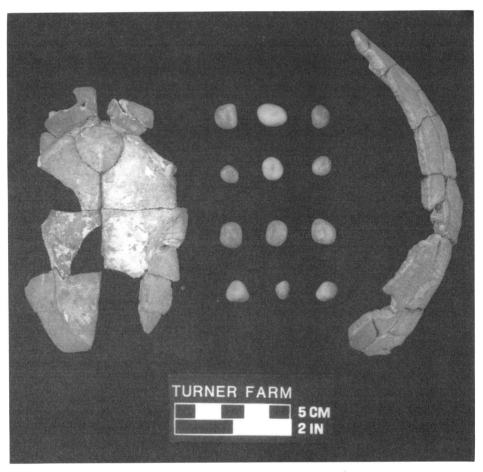

Plate 6.23.   Rattle parts from Occupation 3 mortuary features.

rounded quartz pebbles. Probably all represent rattles. Such rattles are unknown on the Maritime Peninsula or farther northeast prior to Occupation 3, but are widespread in earlier and contemporaneous Archaic assemblages to the south and southwest, including the Savannah River and the Tennessee Basin (see, e.g., Ritchie 1980:118, Plate 41, nos. 1, 3, 4; Webb 1974:224, 233, Figure 29).

Other Bone Artifacts

A residual sample of worked bone and antler fragments from burial contexts has been so extensively damaged that the original forms and functions of many items cannot be determined. Identifiable ones include simple awls, two of which have eyes at the proximal end, and several antler tine fragments with surfaces ground smooth that appear to be fragments of stone flaking tools.

Copper Beads

Feature 12-1975, a well-furnished cremation deposit, yielded 12 cylindrical, rolled copper beads (Plate 6.24). This discovery is of special interest for two reasons. First, copper is one of very few exotic raw materials recovered from Occupation 3 deposits. Second, it represents the largest sample of copper artifacts from any Susquehanna tradition context, the others being limited to a small adz from the Mansion Inn cremation cemetery in Sudbury, Massachusetts, and two tiny fragments from a pit feature at the Cobbosseecontee Dam South site in Manchester, Maine (Bourque 1992c:18; Dincauze 1968:35).

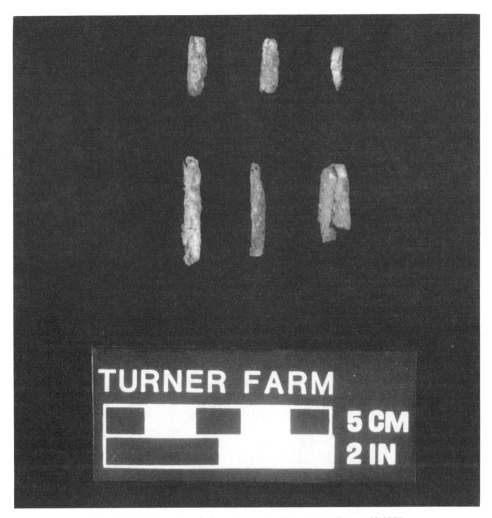

Plate 6.24.   Copper beads from Occupation 3 mortuary Feature 12-1975.

HORIZONTAL PATTERNING

Occupation 3 produced numerous large hearth clusters, small pits, and other striking features, most of which originated in shell-free deposits that were overlain by Occupation 3 shell midden. In the south-central area of the excavation we encountered a cluster of contracting-stem points (Figure 6.5). This cluster was approximately coterminous with an area of shell-free surface, probably stained subsoil, and overlying shell midden. Central to this cluster was a large feature complex including an extensive cobble pavement (Feature 19-1972), an extensive array of hearths, and the house floor encompassing Features 1-1973, 2-1973, 3-1973, 4-1973, 25-1972, 29-1974, and 24-1974. The intensity of activity in this focal area apparently led to the reworking of some features, making their exact limits and relationships difficult to define. This area also has discrete bone refuse clusters in its southern and western portions, and also to its north.

To the north of this contracting-stem point and feature cluster we encountered a large concentration of expanding-stem points (Figure 6.6). It too was associated with a shell-free surface with overlying shell midden. This area included a large depression in subsoil, perhaps a concave house floor complex (Feature 21-1973), associated with a nearby pit (Feature 26-1972), a hearth area (Features 17-1974, 18-1974, 21-1973, 4-1974, and possibly 12-1974), and a cluster of pits (Features 19-1974, 7-1974, 8-1974, and 9-1974). A second hearth cluster (Feature 21-1974) may also be associated, although two clusters of early contracting-stem points were found adjacent to it, suggesting that it predates the other features.

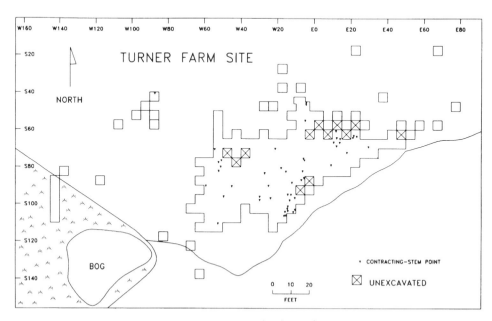

Figure 6.5. Contracting-stem point distribution from Occupation 3.

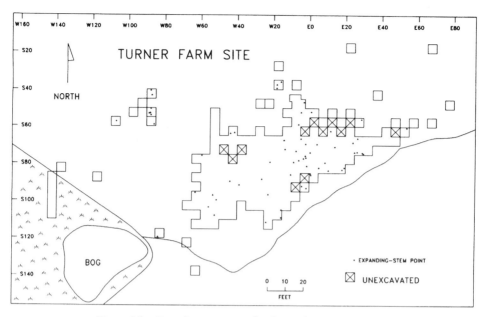

Figure 6.6.   Expanding-stem point distribution from Occupation 3.

Other Artifact Clusters

Contracting-stem points clustered in the eastern portion of the excavation, just inland from a series of pit and hearth features, but our excavations there were too limited to allow precise characterization of their distribution (Figure 6.5). Expanding-stem points were numerous in sections near the northwest limit of excavation. They are separated from the main cluster by interposed contemporaneous burials, but their significance is otherwise difficult to evaluate given the limited extent of our excavations. Straight-stemmed points cooccurred with both contracting- and expanding-stem clusters, suggesting that they are chronologically intermediate (Figure 6.7). Preforms, tapered-stem blades, and drills also were recovered from both areas (Figures 6.8–6.10). The latter two classes, however, were more abundant in the expanding-stem cluster, and Boats blades were almost exclusively associated with them (Figure 6.11).

In sum, these artifact clusters cannot be separated on the basis of available radiocarbon dates, nor do their stylistic differences warrant considering them as completely discrete. Nevertheless, stylistic differences suggest that the southern cluster was the focus of an earlier episode of occupation than the northern one.

FAUNAL ANALYSES

The faunal sample from Occupation 3 differed in two respects from that of Occupation 2. First, in addition to the bone refuse resulting from routine consumption of game, we

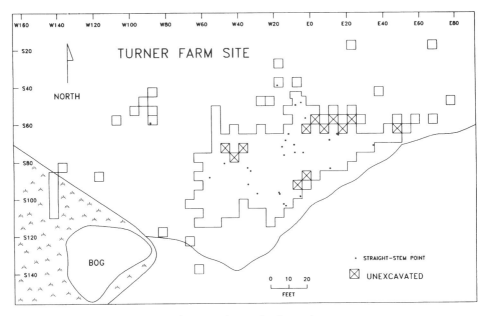

Figure 6.7. Straight-stemmed point distribution from Occupation 3.

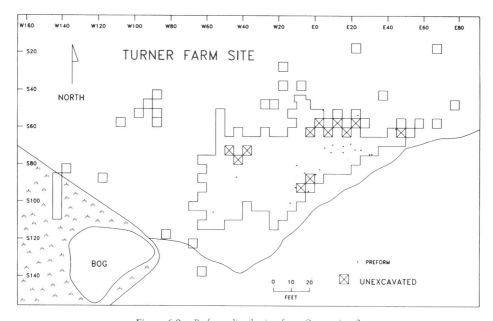

Figure 6.8. Preform distribution from Occupation 3.

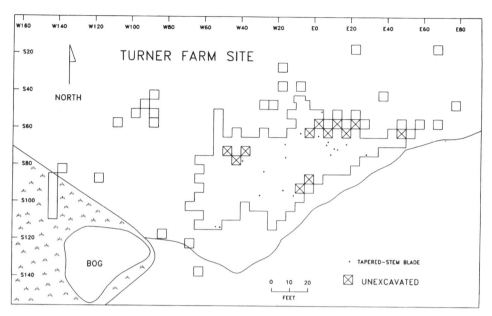

Figure 6.9. Tapered-stem blade distribution from Occupation 3.

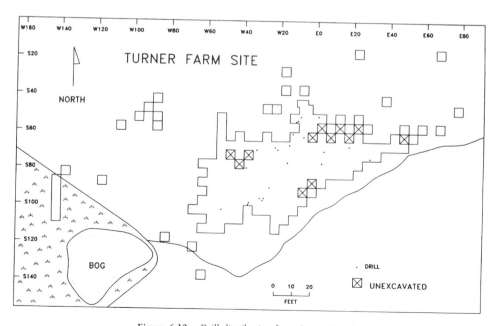

Figure 6.10. Drill distribution from Occupation 3.

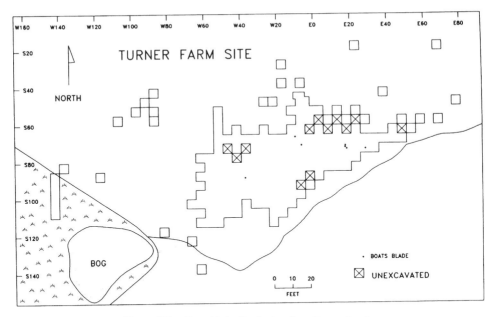

Figure 6.11.   Boats blade distribution from Occupation 3.

recovered samples of dietarily significant fauna which had played a role in mortuary ceremonialism. Secondly, while it was readily apparent in the Occupation 2 sample that mammal bone was in great demand as a raw material for the manufacture of tools and weapons, we found very little such evidence for Occupation 3, aside from the few, albeit sometimes impressive, bone artifacts from mortuary features.

Faunal Remains

In the field, the apparent dominance of cervid bone was even more impressive in Occupation 3 deposits than in Occupation 2. Moreover, unlike the latter, the absence of any strong indicators of marine vertebrate dietary importance in Occupation 3 reinforced human bone isotope data (Figure 6.13; Bourque and Krueger 1994) in setting this population off as the least maritime-oriented in the site's history.

Cervids

As in Occupation 2, deer were the predominant prey species represented in the faunal sample (Figure 6.12). Total bone count is 1,061, very close to that of Occupation 2, but representing a decline from two-thirds of the terrestrial mammal kill to approximately one-half, based on weight estimates. As in Occupation 2, metapodial proximal ends are relatively more abundant than diaphyses and distal ends, perhaps because of butchering patterns that separated and discarded lower limbs by severing the metapodials.

Deer were taken year round, although tooth and parietal bone data suggest that the

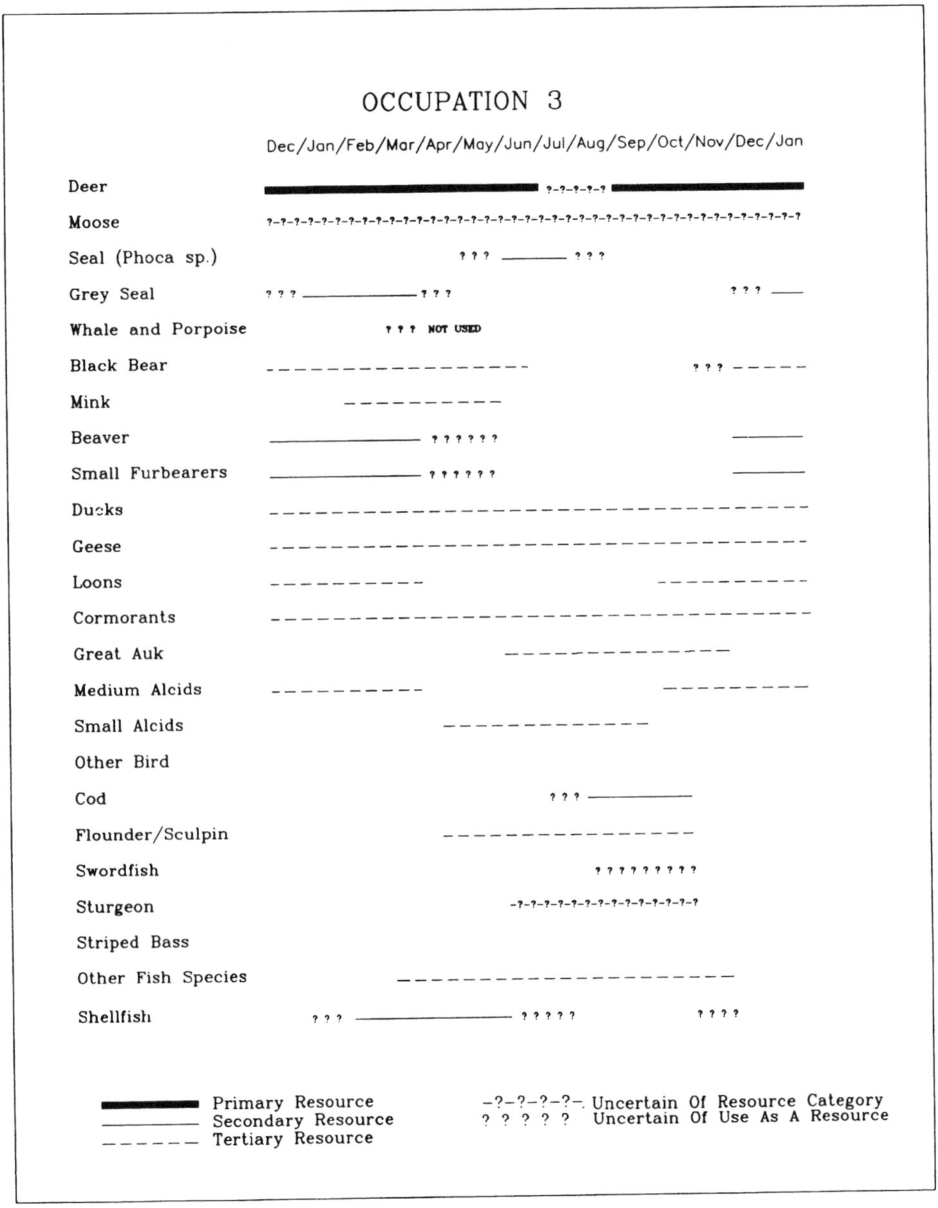

Figure 6.12. Faunal seasonality from Occupation 3 (Spiess and Lewis 1993).

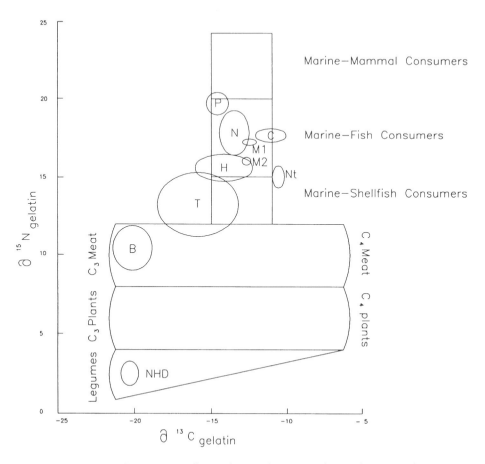

Figure 6.13. Ranges of $\partial^{15}N_{gelatin}$ versus $\partial^{13}C_{gelatin}$ for coastal Maine populations, the Port au Choix cemetery, Newfoundland (Tuck 1976), and the Boucher cemetery, Highgate, Vermont (Krigbaum 1989), modified from Bourque and Krueger 1991. B = Boucher humans; C = Crocker site humans, c. 1000–1200 B.P., North Haven Island; H = Sixteenth-century Penobscot Bay humans; M = Protohistoric humans from Moshier Island, Casco Bay; N = Nevin cemetery humans, Blue Hill; Nt = Late Prehistoric humans from Nantucket Island, Massachusetts (Medaglia, Little, and Schoeninger 1990); NHD = North Haven deer, 4000–1000 B.P.; P = Port au Choix humans; T = Turner Farm cemetery humans.

The ellipses represent the first standard deviations. Archaeological data indicate that the Boucher (B) protein diet was probably devoid of marine protein, while the Port au Choix (P) diet was probably rich in marine protein. $\partial^{15}N_{gelatin}$ values for the Nevin (N) population reflect a marine contribution nearly as high as that of the Port au Choix population, but lowered somewhat by the unusually low $\partial^{15}N_{gelatin}$ values of legume-fed Maine coastal deer (NHD). The $\partial^{13}C_{gelatin}$ values of the Port au Choix population reflect high-latitude phytoplancton depletion, while those of the Crocker site (C) and Nantucket (Nt) individuals apparently reflect the importance of flounders in the diet, as flounders feed among the detritus from meadows of Spartina (C_4 metabolism). The elevated $\partial^{13}C_{gelatin}$ values are not seen in the Moshier Island (M) data probably because flounder were not important in their diet. $\partial^{15}N_{gelatin}$ and $\partial^{13}C_{gelatin}$ values for the Turner Farm (T) population appear to fall essentially on a mixing line between marine fish consumers and terrestrial C_3 meat eaters, skewed slightly to the right by their consumption of legume-fed deer. Those of the sixteenth-century Penobscot Bay humans (H) may reflect a decline in marine exploitation as the result of increased emphasis upon terrestrial (fur) hunting after the arrival of European traders in the region.

majority were killed between May and January. This pattern contrasts with the absence of summer-killed deer in Occupation 2. Another change from Occupation 2 is the marked relative increase in skeletally immature deer (33 to 53 percent) relative to deer aged between 3 and 8+ years based on M3 wear (25 to 11 percent). Moose bone frequency relative to deer rose from 0.7 percent in Occupation 2 to 1.2 percent in Occupation 3, an increase from 2 to 4.5 moose killed per 100 deer. Calculations of the relative dietary contribution suggest that moose provided fully 25 percent of cervid meat (up from 12 percent in Occupation 2). These data support the notion that changes observed in the Occupation 3 deer sample reflect increased hunting pressure on large mammals, although an increase in moose abundance cannot be ruled out. The year-round capture of deer, the increase in skeletally immature deer, and the relative increase in moose also support the human bone isotope data, which indicate increased hunting pressure on terrestrial mammals during Occupation 3.

Rodents

Beaver bone, excluding worked incisors, amounts to 9.3 percent of the deer and seal bone count (N = 104), an increase of 260 percent over Occupation 2. Yet the large, fleshy hind limbs are underrepresented in the sample compared to Occupation 2. Possibly, this change reflects an increase in the importance of beaver fur over meat. A single, sectioned molar from Occupation 3 indicated death between December and March. Other rodent bones include one muskrat and three porcupine (one postcranial bone).

Mustelids

Mink bone (N = 154, mostly M. macrodon) amounts to 13.6 percent of the deer and seal bone count, representing a large relative increase from 4.9 percent in the Occupation 2 sample. One sectioned canine indicated a probably late winter kill, in agreement with most of the mustelid seasonal indicators throughout the Turner Farm sequence. Six otter bones were recovered from Occupation 3.

Bear

Bear remains include 13 bones, or 1.2 percent of the deer bone count, only a slight increase over the bear–deer ratio for Occupation 2. No indicators of season of death were recovered.

Other Terrestrial Mammals

A single red fox (Vulpes vulpes) tooth and 18 dog bones (12 postcranial) make up the rest of the terrestrial mammal bone sample.

Sea Mammals

Only a relatively small number (N = 74) of phocid remains were recovered from Occupation 3 deposits, but bone count and phocid count relative to deer increased from

Occupation 2 (7.0 versus 2.6 percent). Based on auditory bullae, the jump was much greater, from 25 to 45 percent. However, in the area where Occupation 3 cremations cluster, seal bone appears to have been mixed upward from Occupation 2 deposits as a result of grave digging. The ratio of gray to harbor seals remains about equal (15 to 16), and the few available seasonal indicators suggest that both gray (3 teeth) and harbor (2 teeth) seals were taken during their respective molting seasons.

Fish

Cod is the most abundant species ($N = 104$; 9 percent relative to the large mammal bone count). Statistics derived from upward mixture of Occupation 2 artifacts suggest that approximately 18 percent of these bones were derived from Occupation 2 contexts. If so, the relative frequency of cod to large mammal bone from Occupation 3 reflects a decrease of over 50 percent from Occupation 2. Three cod vertebrae suggest capture in September and October, later than was apparently the case during Occupation 2.

Next in abundance was flounder bone ($N = 106$; 9.1 percent relative to the large mammal bone count). As in Occupation 2, winter flounder are largely predominant. These statistics are comparable to those of Occupation 2. However, vertebrate annulus analysis suggests that flounder catches occurred at diametrically opposite seasons from Occupation 2, though, as stated above, we have not determined what those seasons were.

Swordfish bone from Occupation 3 included five rostrum fragments, five vertebrae, and 60 other postcranial fragments. All are regarded as derived from earlier occupations. The horizontal distribution of swordfish bone is quite congruent with that of Occupation 2 (compare Figures 5.10 and 6.14), and their relative frequency is comparable to upwardly displaced plummets (Figure 6.15). Moreover, no swordfish bone was recovered from burial contexts.

Only nine fragments of sturgeon scute were recovered from Occupation 3 strata, and it is probable that some of these were derived from lower strata. Sculpin, striped bass, tomcod, cunner, and eel complete the list of fish species identified for Occupation 3. The cunner bones probably came to the site in the guts of larger fish.

Birds

The bird bone total for Occupation 3 is 345, which amounts to 29.7 percent of the large mammal bone count. This is an increase of 15.5 percent over Occupation 2. In general, the range of birds taken does not differ markedly from Occupation 2, but auk decline from 15 percent in Occupation 2 to 7 percent in Occupation 3. The bones of small alcids sometimes contain medullary bone deposits indicating death just prior to egg laying. The duck relative bone count increases from 48 to 57 percent in Occupation 3. Although eider decline from 27 percent to 7 percent of the duck bone count, the scaups, black ducks, and small Aythyinae remain comparable in relative frequency.

Shellfish

Soft-shelled clams are even more predominant in Occupation 3 than in Occupation 2, largely because of the total absence of quahog. The total weight of fresh clam shell deposited

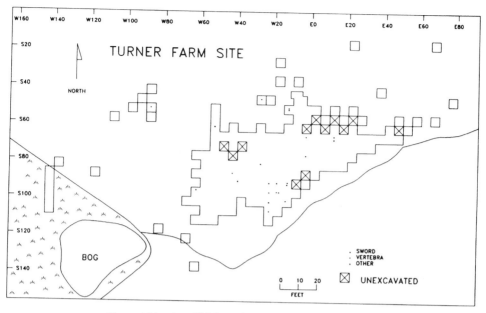

Figure 6.14. Swordfish bone distribution from Occupation 3.

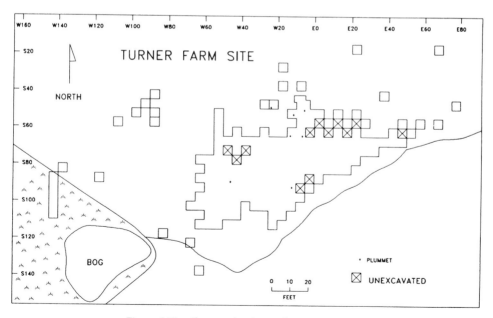

Figure 6.15. Plummet distribution from Occupation 3.

in the excavated portion of Occupation 3 was 12,740 kg (compared to 15,020 kg in Occupation 2). This leads to an estimate of 8,280 kg of clam meat for Occupation 3, down from 9,760 kg in Occupation 2.

Mollusk collection, as in Occupation 2, appears to have been between February and April. The absence of quahog from Occupation 3 and later components at the site probably reflects a drop in water temperature. Isotopic analyses of clam shell that may shed light on this issue are currently underway.

Other Fauna

Four turtle carapace fragments, probably from snapping turtle (*Chelydra serpentina*), were recovered from the Occupation 3 midden.

Horizontal Distribution of Faunal Remains

Contracting-Stem Point Cluster

Feature 19-1972, a large cobble-pavement hearth produced an extensive faunal sample dominated by deer (N = 113, minimum number of individuals [MNI] = 8). However, in this area of the site bone derived from Occupation 2 was mixed into Occupation 3 strata by cultural turbation. This disturbance is indicated by the presence of 21 swordfish bones there, directly over the major Occupation 2 cluster of this species. Therefore, a proportionate reduction of the deer bone count drops the number to 102.

An interesting aspect of the Feature 19-1972 deer sample is the absence of any broken metapodial diaphysis fragments, despite the presence of 6 proximal and 10 distal ends. Such fragments were identified nearby and widely elsewhere in Area 1, as well as in Occupation 2 strata. Their absence from Feature 19-1972 may indicate merely the consumption of these fragments as raw material for tool making or their dispersal elsewhere on the site as a normal part of metapodial processing. However, it may also imply the ritualized consumption of deer marrowbone, with the shaft fragments selectively deposited elsewhere.

Other species represented in Area 1 include seal (N = 4), mink (N = 2), beaver (four postcranials), dog or wolf (*Canis lupus*; N = 6), black guillemot (N = 1), an unidentified bird (N = 1), and cod (2 vertebrae). Seasonal indicators from Area 1 remains suggest that they were deposited during two periods: August to September and December to February. A single *Phoca* canine represents probable death in June or July.

To the east of Feature 19-1972 is a large, slightly concave shell-free lens, heavily strewn with hearth rocks (Features 1-1973, 2-1973, 3-1973, and 25-1972). Here, deer dominate the faunal sample. Feature 3-1973 produced 23 swordfish rostrum fragments, indicating the presence of intrusive Occupation 2 faunal remains.

At the north end of this complex lay Feature 24-1974, which yielded a substantial faunal sample. It included no swordfish, and therefore is less likely to reflect contamination from Occupation 2. It, too, is dominated by deer (N = 37; MNI = 5), but small numbers of mink, beaver, harbor and gray seal, bear, great auk, possibly loon, scaup, *Anas*, and cod bones were also found. The scaup and cod bones indicate fall and winter use of this feature.

Bone refuse density and species representation surrounding the features of Area 1 are comparable to samples from within them, except for a very dense scatter of bone shoreward of the large feature complex described above and another more limited bone scatter in W45S110. Both scatters contain relatively few deer bones. A light scatter of refuse was encountered in the southwestern portion of the excavation—again, relatively low in deer and also in fish content.

Expanding-Stem Point Cluster

Features in this area yielded very little bone refuse. Hearth Feature 12-1974 contained 10 deer bones (MNI = 2), pit Feature 19-1974 produced one deer bone, and pit Feature 7-1974 produced two cod skull fragments. Refuse was more dense surrounding the features, however. South of Feature 21-1972, a possible house pit, was a moderately dense cluster notable for its relatively low cod content. To its east, surrounding the hearth cluster, was a denser scatter of bone refuse, again notable for its low fish bone count. Farther east, near the limit of excavation, bone density rose again, and again fish bones were scarce.

It is noteworthy that fish bone counts were uniformly low in areas of Occupation 3 where underlying Occupation 2 strata were also low in fish bone. This congruence suggests that, taken as a whole, the Occupation 3 sample overrepresents not only swordfish but all fish species.

Summary of Dietary Data

Faunal data indicate that the marine component in Occupation 3 was much smaller than in Occupation 2. The decline is most apparent in fish and shellfish. A slight relative increase in seal bone in the Occupation 3 sample pales in significance compared to the increases seen in later components, where fish once again also rise in importance.

Another impressive faunal indicator is the sharp decline in bone weaponry from Occupation 2 times, when foreshafts, spears, harpoons, fishhooks, and perhaps bayonets all suggested extensive maritime exploitation. All these data are further supported by human bone isotopic data indicating that although faunal remains underrepresent the contribution of marine protein to the Occupation 3 diet, they nevertheless do support the notion that Susquehanna tradition populations consumed markedly less marine protein than both earlier and later coastal dwellers (Figure 6.13). Moreover, the Turner Farm Susquehanna tradition population was apparently much more variable in marine protein intake than other populations investigated. Factors influencing this diversity may have included differing geographic origins of the cemetery population or differing food preferences. No significant relationship between age or sex and marine dietary intake was noted.

BURIALS

In 1915, W. B. Smith excavated at least eight cremation burials interspersed with Moorehead phase "Red Paint Graves" at Eddington Bend, just above the head of tide on the Penobscot River (Moorehead 1992:134–143). He noted that the cremation pits were well defined and, therefore, had been dug "much later" than the ocher-filled graves. He also presented a schematic diagram showing a cremation pit intersecting an ocher-filled one, implying, though not stating explicitly, that this relationship also indicated their relative ages.

The association of such burials with what is now labeled the Susquehanna tradition in New England was first clearly established by Dincauze (1968). Susquehanna burial components have now been identified at two additional Penobscot area sites (Bourque 1992a:40; Borstel 1982) and elsewhere across the northeast, including Quebec (Dumais 1978:69–71).

The Occupation 3 cemetery at the Turner Farm site was encountered unexpectedly in 1974, and was explored only to the extent necessary to define its approximate limits (Figure 6.16). Nevertheless, a substantial sample was recovered. The sample is unique in three important respects. First, it is in intimate association with extensive contemporaneous occupation remains. Second, bone preservation in the noncremation burial features, and even in some cremation deposits, is relatively good. Third, all excavations of both burials and associated midden deposits were conducted under controlled conditions. These characteristics provide an unparalleled opportunity to elucidate a broad range of Susquehanna tradition mortuary behavior and to relate it to a broader cultural context. The diverse

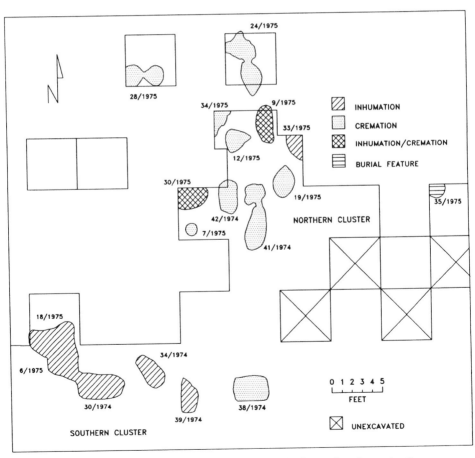

Figure 6.16. Detail of Figure 6.1 showing burial distribution from Occupation 3.

mortuary features and their contents are described in the following paragraphs. Appendix 3 presents the data in tabular form.

The mortuary features are divisible into two basic types: those containing secondary cremation deposits typical of previously encountered Susquehanna tradition cemeteries, and those containing unburned human inhumations, which are reported here for the first time in a Susquehanna context. All secondary cremation deposits include the remains of multiple individuals, often in direct association with abundant, varied grave furniture. The inhumations include two multiple secondary and seven primary inhumations.

The excavated area of the cemetery is divisible into two spatially distinct clusters: a southern one composed mainly of inhumations, and a northern one where secondary cremation deposits predominate. The only contracting-stem points from the burials came from Feature 18-1975 in the southern cluster, while only straight-stemmed and expanding-stem points were found in the secondary cremation deposits. This dichotomy suggests that the cemetery spread northward through its period of use, and that simple inhumations were initially the predominant burial form but were replaced or supplemented by secondary cremation deposits in time. This pattern supports the inference based on differential stemmed point distribution in Areas 1 and 2 that Occupation 3 may actually represent a relatively long period of use, a palimpsest of two or more components. A human-bone gelatin radiocarbon date of 3825 ± 76 (GX-15744-G-AMS) from Feature 18-1975 in the southern cluster and another of 3662 ± 59 (GX-15745-G-AMS) from Feature 9-1975 in the northern cluster suggest that Occupation 3 spanned more than two centuries. The comments on human remains presented below are summarized from Barbian and Magennis (1994).

The Southern Cluster

A contiguous cluster of inhumations was encountered in the southern portion of the cemetery. The inhumations include an adult male (Feature 18-1975); a female (aged > 50 years), a child, and an infant (Feature 6-1975); and a single subadult (Feature 30-1974). An additional single probable female (Feature 34-1974) was interred just to the east of Feature 6-1975. All lay in shallow graves excavated through a thin Occupation 2 midden deposit into subsoil. This burial group is unique among Archaic burials in northeastern North America in that the adults in Features 18-1975 and 6-1975 have occipitally flattened skulls, and the subadult in Feature 30-1974, while lacking conclusive evidence for skull deformation, has cranial proportions suspiciously like the other two, and unlike the rest of the cemetery population (Plates 6.25–6.27). Interestingly, the only other such occurrence reported in eastern North America was at Indian Knoll, a site that bears numerous other resemblances to the Susquehanna tradition (Snow 1948:Figure 31).

About 2 ft (0.6 m) east of Feature 34-1974 was a multiple secondary burial (Feature 39-1974). Two feet farther east was found a richly furnished, multiple, secondary cremation deposit (Feature 38-1974).

Features 18-1975, 6-1975, and 30-1974

The close proximity of these five primary inhumations and the occipital deformation of at least two suggest that they are perhaps a family group. The male in Feature 18-1975 lay

Plate 6.25.   Occipitally deformed skull from Occupation 3 mortuary Feature 18-1975.

Plate 6.26.   Occipitally deformed skull from Occupation 3 mortuary Feature 6-1975.

Plate 6.27.   Occipitally deformed (?) skull from Occupation 3 mortuary Feature 30-1974.

fully flexed on his right side, head east, facing north (Plate 6.28; see color insert opposite page 160).

Covering and in direct contact with the thoracic and abdominal area, was a black carbonized lens that was covered in turn by another thin lens of redeposited shell and brown soil, both of which included occasional flecks of red ocher. The black lens was composed primarily of carbonized organic matter, including wood charcoal. Three dates on this charcoal average to 3668 B.P. Within the lens were 12 complete or fire-broken flaked bifaces, seven Boats blades, and five contracting-stem points, as well as 27 charred antler fragments, carbonized plum (*Prunus*) pits, and the waltes-like bone objects described above (Plate 6.18). Ocher traces in the lens probably derived from the original grave fill. Bone gelatin from skeleton dated at 3825 ± 76 B.P. (GX 15744-G-AMS) and 3945 ± 230 B.P. (GX 15744-G).

The female in Feature 6-1975 lay unevenly flexed on her left side, head north, facing east, away from both the male and the remains of two children. The mandible was missing. The skeleton of one child lay on its back with legs partially flexed to the right. Though articulated, it was badly fragmented and partially disintegrated. It appeared to have been disturbed after decomposition. The incomplete remains of an infant (aged 0–0.5 years) were identified among the child's bones in the laboratory, but were not recognized as a separate individual in the field. Red ocher was found throughout the feature, but was particularly abundant in the chest area of the child. Bone gelatin from the adult skeleton dated at 3700 ± 220 B.P. (GX 14806) and 3870 ± 115 B.P. (GX 14807).

As in Feature 18-1975, the three individuals were covered by redeposited midden that contained scattered charcoal fragments, possibly derived from the same black lens that covered part of it and nearby Feature 18-1975. A single complete drill made on a contracting-stem point was found in the grave fill, along with a single mammal bone. Another drill bit was associated directly with the skeletons.

A shallow trench originating in a thin, shell-rich lens overlying the graves, but itself overlain by ceramic period (Occupation 4) midden, intruded into the grave fill. The trench was filled with black organic matrix mixed with crushed shell. Charcoal from the fill dated at 3700 ± 220 B.P. (GX 14806). The missing adult mandible and disarranged bones may be attributable to this disturbance.

The contiguity of these three features suggests their near simultaneity. However, it is unclear how much time elapsed between the inhumations and the deposition of the black lens that overlay Feature 18-1975 and part of Feature 6-1975. The lens lay directly upon part of the Feature 18-1975 individual, but it both lay upon and was covered by redeposited midden probably derived from Occupation 2 deposits. It may thus have been deposited at the same time as the inhumations, as the graves were being filled, or at some later time, after one or both had been partially reopened.

The available data are inadequate to resolve this issue unambiguously. However, the missing mandible and disarticulation of infant bones in Feature 6-1975 seem best explained as the result of reopening the grave, perhaps for the emplacement of the black lens some time after the inhumation.

There is evidence to suggest that the lens represents a fire within the grave, or the stillhot remains of one kindled elsewhere. Arguing in favor of burning in situ are the carbonized ovoid objects, all but one of which were close together in a linear array suggesting careful placement before being burned. However, although they were found in direct association with the black lens, none of the human bone in Feature 18-1975 showed signs of burning. The available data, then, suggest that Feature 6-1975 may have been reopened at the time of a fire, or that the still smoldering remains of one was placed in direct contact with the individual in Feature 18-1975 at the time of his burial, the human bone probably remaining unburned because burial occurred in the flesh.

Finally, it should be noted that Features 18-1975 and 6-1975 provide evidence for the temporal priority of the southern cluster—or at least of the primary inhumations there—for they alone produced the presumably early contracting-stem and straight-stemmed points similar to those that characterize the southern midden area of Occupation 3.

Feature 30-1974 contained the articulated remains of a single subadult, partially flexed on the left side, head to the east, facing south, away from Features 18-1975 and 6-1975. No grave furnishings were encountered. The femurs were missing. A shallow excavation from just above the grave fill intruded into the burial, primarily in the area of the missing femurs. Redeposited midden filled the intrusive excavation.

Dates from this feature include one on shell in the intrusive pit (3270 ± 75 B.P., SI 2397), and another on human bone (3105 ± 75 B.P., SI 2399). These dates, like others on calcareous tissue from the site's older levels, are suspect of contamination by calcium percolation from overlying shell deposits. The fact that this individual's skull was possibly occipitally flattened like those in neighboring Features 6-1975 and 18-1975 suggests contemporaneity with them, and the charcoal and bone gelatin dates from those features are regarded as the more reliable.

Feature 34-1974

The probable adult female in Feature 34-1974 was a primary inhumation resting on the right side, head to the northwest, facing southwest. Red ocher was scattered around the skeleton, but no other grave furnishings were recovered. Grave fill included a mixture of subsoil, beach gravel, and finely crushed clam shell. A small mound of grave fill, probably visible from the surface during Occupation 3, surmounted the skull. A later midden-filled pit intruded into this burial, apparently removing most of both femurs and other leg bones.

Feature 38-1974

Because it is the sole cremation deposit encountered in the southern cluster, Feature 38-1974 may postdate the other burials there. It occupied a discrete, basin-shaped depression, and included the remains of at least four adults (including a male and a female), one subadult, and numerous animal bones and artifacts, all of which were embedded in a black, charcoal-rich matrix. Fragments of beech (*Fagus*) charcoal and a beechnut were found in the grave fill. No radiocarbon dates were obtained from this feature.

Like other cremation features described below, this one was carefully scrutinized for signs of purposeful artifact placement, but none was apparent. Moreover, subsoil surrounding the pit showed no reddening or other indication that a fire had burned there.

The human remains are unique in that complete individuals appear to have been cremated. Burning was incomplete, however, and red ocher staining was quite apparent on the unburned bones.

Artifacts from this feature, as from most other secondary cremation deposits, were often extensively fire damaged, and fragments often were missing. For these reasons, artifact counts represent minimum numbers that may underestimate the original frequencies by as much as 100 percent, even for some of the flaked stone tool samples.

Flaked stone grave goods from Feature 38-1974 were abundant, including a preform, a Mansion Inn blade, a Boats blade, 10 tapered-stem blades, two untyped blades, at least five expanding-stem points, a corner-notched point, two drills, and two gravers. The only ground stone tool was an adz. Bone tools included a large, eyed needle or bodkin (Plate 6.29), an awl, and fragments of worked antler. Animal bones, apparently representing food offerings, are predominantly those of a duck-sized bird, with smaller amounts of seal and deer bone and a red fox maxilla. All but one fragment of seal acetabulum are calcined, indicating that all these animal parts were purposeful inclusions.

Feature 39-1974

This feature represents a treatment of the dead very different from the simple, primary inhumations described above. It included four skulls, three of which were associated with postcranial bones. All were buried in a large (approximately 1.5 × 3 m), shallow depression

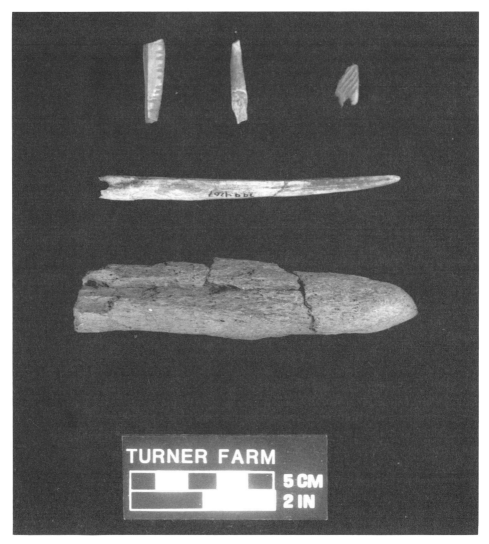

Plate 6.29.   Bone tools from Occupation 3 Feature 38-1974.

excavated into subsoil. The remains were organized into clusters resembling secondary "bundle" burials of individuals. Subsequent analysis of these clusters, however, demonstrated that these bundles include the bones of at least five individuals.

Grave furnishings were meager, including only some red ocher around the isolated skull and two biface fragments, one from a Boats blade. The latter actually may have been a chance inclusion since, although found within the grave, it was some distance from the bones.

The pit was filled by lenses of dark brown to black soil mixed with many fragments of fire-cracked rock. Some of the covering lenses contained finely crushed shell, while others contained finely divided charcoal. Three dates, two on human bone and one on charcoal from grave fill, range from about 3600 to 2500 B.P. The older charcoal date (3610 ± 90 B.P., SI 2404) is regarded as the most reliable. No reddened soil or charred bone was noted, so it is likely that burning occurred outside the grave. While the bones in Feature 39-1974 clearly do not represent primary inhumations, they do include an articulated spinal column.

Three bone samples from Feature 39-1974 reflect the lowest relative consumption of marine protein in the Turner Farm cemetery population series (Bourque and Krueger 1992). One sample was selected from each of the three bundles in the feature on the supposition that parts of the same individual would not be included in more than one bundle. This selection was made before we had determined that the clusters did not represent single individuals. However, the differing isotope values from each sample appear to support the likelihood that the three did, in fact, come from different individuals.

The Northern Cluster

Cremation Burials

Feature 24-1975. Grave furnishings from this secondary cremation deposit comprise the largest and richest from the extant cemetery sample, both in artifacts and animal bone. Surprisingly, however, its human bone content was the lowest of all cremation burials, including the remains of only one adult and one subadult (MNI) and weighing merely 4.3 kg. These bones were smoked but not calcined. All were placed in a basin-shaped pit excavated into subsoil and were found in a black carbon-rich matrix including fire-broken and damaged artifacts (Plate 6.30). The pit was covered with brown subsoil, probably backfill from the original pit excavation.

Flaked stone artifacts included 10 preforms, 22 Mansion Inn blades, three Boats blades, five tapered-stem blades, 21 expanding-stem points, at least three drills, three gravers, and a possible wedge. Ground stone tools included five adzes, five gouges, three whetstones, a notched and three beveled cobbles, an anvil stone, and a fragment of a stone rod. Ground edged stone implements included five adzes and five gouges. Bone artifacts included at least one barbed spear, a toggling harpoon, five bone gouges, an eyed awl, two bone beads, and several worked bone and antler tine fragments. A total of 863 animal bone fragments (9.8 kg) represent a moose, a deer lower foreleg (marrow bone), a probably complete beaver, dog, porcupine, and a medium-sized bird.

Feature 24a-1975. This feature comprised a basin-shaped pit similar to that of Feature 24-1975, which intersected its northern limit. Initially we considered it a part of Feature 24 and so designated it 24a. However, subsequent analysis has failed to demonstrate any further evidence of association.

The fill of Feature 24a-1975 included black soil mixed with cremated human bone. The deposit was covered with probable redeposited subsoil and midden, including shell fragments. Its contents are very sparse in comparison to Feature 24, but included at least two tapered-stem blades, a Boats blade, and six other fragmentary bifaces. No nonhuman bone was found.

Plate 6.30. Secondary cremation deposit Feature 24-1975.

Feature 28a-1975 and 28b-1975. Feature 28a-1975 was a small, secondary cremation deposit including skeletal remains ranging from unburned to calcined, and a small artifact sample, all in a black matrix. Artifacts include an expanding-stem point, two drills, three other biface fragments, fragments of a bone gouge (Plate 6.22), and 18 antler fragments.

Feature 28b-1975 lay just to the west of 28a and closely resembled it in size and structure. Its western side remains unexcavated. The excavated portion produced a small artifact sample including four expanding-stem points, a drill tip, and three additional biface fragments and one fragment of worked bone.

The human remains from Features 28a and 28b (accidentally combined in the field) represent one adult and two subadults. Features 28a and 28b produced only four fragments of animal bone, all from large mammals of indeterminate species.

From the area where 28a and 28b overlapped came one tapered-stem blade, a drill base, and a biface tip. No fragments could be joined with materials listed above.

Feature 12-1975. This feature was a basin-shaped pit excavated through an Occupation 2 feature (Feature 8-1975) and midden into subsoil to a maximum depth of approximately 12 in. (30 cm). In its base was a secondary cremation deposit that included human remains and at least one carbonized beechnut.

This basal deposit was covered by altered subsoil tinted by red ocher, and included several green rhyolite flakes. The fill was probably derived from grave back dirt including ocher and flaking debris from Feature 8-1975.

Over this fill lay another secondary cremation deposit, this one with numerous skull fragments but few postcranial elements. Flaked stone artifacts included three preforms, two Mansion Inn blades, two Boats blades, a tapered-stem blade, at least seven expanding-stem points, two corner-notched points, and at least three drills. Ground stone tools were limited to one gouge and one probable adz fragment. Other inclusions were modified box and painted turtle scutes and 18 pebbles that may represent shell rattles (Plate 6.23), three ground slate pendants, two ungual phalanges from raptorial birds, 12 small cylindrical copper beads (Plate 6.24), and 15 fragments of deer antler that may represent flaking tools or awls. This deposit was covered by a reddish, probably ocher-stained, soil—again apparently derived from grave back dirt. Above this was a third deposit of burned remains including calcined bone, but no artifacts. The final fill of this grave was a dark shell-free soil of unknown origin capped by a thin lens of shell midden.

The scant remains of two adults (one a male) and three subadults were recovered. Particularly underrepresented are skull parts, although one cranial fragment conjoined with another from Feature 19-1975. This feature was unique in yielding a large and diverse faunal sample, most of it calcined. Species represented include moose, deer, gray seal, beaver, dog, American eel, Canada goose and other birds, and turtle.

Feature 19-1975. This basin-shaped pit was excavated through a thin Occupation 2 midden into subsoil. A secondary cremation deposit was then placed in it and covered with basal midden material, probably grave back dirt. Bones from four adults and five subadults were included in the deposit. Individuals are not evenly represented by skeletal element; cranial bones are overrepresented. Most bones were dry when burned and were completely calcined.

Most grave furnishings were badly fire-damaged. Flaked artifacts included at least six preforms, six Mansion Inn blades, five tapered-stem blades, 39 expanding-stem points, six corner-notched points, and at least four drills. Other stone tools included a grooved axe, a beveled cobble, a grooved abrading stone, and four limonite nodules—possibly the remains of iron pyrite fire strikers. Bone tools included four gouges, a barbed spear, an eyed awl, a tubular bead, a porcupine incisor, and several worked bone and antler fragments. Faunal remains included bone from at least one moose, one deer, one sea mink, and fragments of turtle shell, as well as several unidentifiable mammal fragments.

Features 41a-1974 and 41b-1974.   These contiguous features were not recognized as discrete in the field. As a result, some of their human and nonhuman bone contents cannot now be separated. Feature 41a is a secondary cremation deposit in an ovoid pit dug into subsoil. It reached a maximum thickness of about 8 in. (20 cm). Adjoining its southern end was Feature 41b, a long, ovoid pit or trench also containing cremation remains, this time spread into a thin deposit reaching a maximum thickness of about 3 inches (8 cm).

The artifactual contents of Feature 41a-1974 included three preforms, four tapered-stem blades, thirteen expanding-stem points, and at least four drills. One biface fragment was part of a Mansion Inn blade from a cremation deposit in Feature 9-1975 located just to the north. Charcoal (including maple [*Acer* sp.]) from its fill dated to 3855 ± 75 B.P. (SI 2405). Stone artifacts from Feature 41b-1974 included one preform, one tapered-stem blade, two expanding-stem points, a drill, a biface fragment, and a gouge. Bone artifacts were limited to a scute from an unburned left-costal scute from a painted turtle, and the calcined tip of a probable awl.

Human bone recovered from this complex included at least four adults (at least one male) and six subadults. As in Feature 28a-1975, bone fragments ranged from unburned to calcined.

The combined faunal sample from these features included fragments from deer, sea mink, bird, and fish (probably flounder). Deer bone dominates the assemblage, including at least two individuals represented by lower leg bones. Both features were covered by redeposited rocky midden, probably of Occupation 2 origin.

Feature 42-1974.   This secondary cremation deposit was encountered in three separate sections, in two consecutive field seasons, by two different excavators, and extended into an unexcavated portion of the site. It appears to have been an ovoid pit excavated into subsoil to a maximum thickness of 6 in. (15 cm) and filled with a secondary cremation deposit. This deposit was then covered by subsoil matrix. Charcoal from the pit fill produced a date of 4020 ± 80 B.P. (SI 2393).

Human remains included at least seven individuals, including two adults and five subadults. Most bones appear to have been dry when burned. Grave furnishings were abundant: eight preforms, four tapered-stem blades, 13 expanding-stem and two straight-stemmed points, five drills, three gouges, one adz, a beveled cobble, and the fragmentary carapace of box turtle, probably from a rattle. The bones of at least seven deer, five dogs, one phocid, one large and one small bird, as well as 71 unidentifiable mammal bones, were also recovered. Two beechnuts and charcoal fragments of ash (*Fraxinus* sp.) were also identified.

Feature 7-1975.   This small, discrete, secondary cremation deposit included the remains of at least five individuals ranging from less than 6 months to greater than 18 years of age, all very poorly represented. Both dry and fairly fresh bones were included and most were calcined. Some, particularly those of the subadults, were ocher stained. Only one tapered-stem blade and three expanding-stem blades were included. Faunal remains include the calcined left maxilla of a cat (*Felis* sp., probably bobcat), a few bones of deer, and one Canada goose humerus. Four beechnuts were also recovered.

Feature 34-1975. This secondary cremation deposit was encountered in the northwest limit of a section partially opened to complete the excavation of Feature 12-1975. From its black matrix came the remains of one adult and one subadult. The bones ranged from smoked to calcined. Their state of desiccation when burned is unclear. Two expanding-stem points, a utilized flake, and two fragments of bird bone were also recovered from this fill.

Feature 35-1975. This partially excavated feature appears to lie at the eastern limit of the cemetery. It extends into unexcavated midden to the northwest of section E10S55. No human remains were recovered, but its artifact content suggests that it is a burial feature. Grave furniture included five preforms, four Mansion Inn blades, and two beechnuts.

Complex Burials

Feature 9-1975. This feature included the flexed, primary inhumation of a woman (aged > 55 years) covered by a complex sequence of lenses, including secondary cremation deposits that included the remains of one, or possibly two, adults and five subadults (Plate 6.31; see color insert opposite page 160). Most bone fragments are calcined but some are only smoked. The grave was deeper than most, penetrating 18 in. (46 cm) into the subsoil through a thin Occupation 2 midden.

The primary inhumation lay in the bottom of this grave, tightly flexed on the right side, arms folded against the chest, hands below the chin. The head lay to the north, facing west. Red ocher covered some of the postcranial skeleton and spread to the surrounding grave floor and fill, which consisted mainly of redeposited subsoil. Dates regarded as most reliable for this inhumation are from human bone gel: 3770 ± 260 B.P. (GX 15745-G) and 3662 ± 59 B.P. (GX 15745-G-AMS).[1] Over the skull lay a very thin ash-like layer, and above this, resting just above the left ear and cranium, in redeposited subsoil, was a dense cluster of artifacts. They included an adz, a gouge, and a grooved axe, all broken with parts missing or out of

[1]Cross (1990:120, 122) regards the unburned interments from the Turner Farm cemetery as predating Occupation 3. This view has recently been reiterated by Barbian and Magennis (1994:2–4, 18). Cross's opinion is based upon his participation as a crew member in the excavation of Feature 9-1975, and is reflected in his original field notes. It was no doubt influenced as well by the surprise we all felt when first confronted with Susquehanna tradition inhumations, which had never before been discovered. In fact, after the 1974 season I (Bourque 1975:36) stated that "while no artifacts were found with the [then known] inhumations, they will be regarded as associated with Occupation 2, *pending radiocarbon dates* (emphasis added)." Neither Barbian nor Magennis ever visited the site or studied its collection, and their views derive from their association with Cross as graduate students at the University of Massachusetts.

From a stratigraphic perspective, the problem with this interpretation is the intimate association—indeed the direct contact—in Features 6-1975, 18-1975, and 9-1975 of the burned deposits and the human remains they cover. From the perspective of horizontal distribution, the precise congruence of these burned deposits and sets of human remains is difficult to explain if they derive from separate components. Further difficulties arise from the Susquehanna tradition artifacts found in direct association with them. Finally, radiocarbon dates now demonstrate the full comtemporaneity of the unburned human remains with the rest of Occupation 3.

place, suggesting preburial breakage; an expanding-stem point; two long bone pins (Plate 6.21); four socketed antler tines (possibly toggling harpoons, Plate 6.17); a large, unilaterally barbed antler harpoon (Figure 6.2); and a bone gouge (Plate 6.22). Covering the arms and chest was a deposit of finely divided gray material, possibly graphite or phyllite. Fragments of the maxilla of a young but very large canid, probably a timber wolf, rested on the forearms. In the abdominal area were fragments of painted turtle plastron and six rounded quartz cobbles, probably from a rattle (Plate 6.23). Possible food remains associated with the burial include deer, dog, Canada goose, other birds, and cod.

A black, charcoal-rich lens covered most of the skeleton. In it were several fire-broken lithic artifacts: six preforms, one Mansion Inn blade, two Boats blades, six tapered-stem blades, five expanding-stem points, one adz, one gouge, one beveled cobble, and six quartz pebbles. The Mansion Inn blade conjoined with a biface fragment from Feature 41-1974a, a secondary cremation deposit located less than 5 ft south of Feature 9-1975. Several antler and worked-bone fragments and two beechnuts were also included. A discrete ocher-rich lens which produced a date of 3470 ± 60 (GX 19997-AMS) covered this black layer, followed by another black, organic-rich lens. Redeposited subsoil filled the rest of the grave cavity.

A small, basin-shaped pit was later excavated through this depositional sequence down to the level of the upper red ocher deposit. Into this pit were placed cremated human remains that included both dry and fresh bones. These cremated remains appeared to be divided into two lenses. A single, perforated bone object, probably an awl, was found in the upper deposit. This secondary cremation deposit was then filled with more redeposited subsoil that included two flaked stone drill bits. As with Features 18-1975 and 6-1975, the amount of time separating the inhumation and the subsequent deposits is difficult to determine. However, since there is no evidence that an intervening grave fill had been removed to allow the placement of the later deposits, the entire deposit probably represents a closely contiguous series of events.

Features 30-1975 and 33-1975. These two features included both unburned primary inhumations and cremated bone. Partial excavation limits our understandings of them. Neither feature yielded artifacts, and their attribution to Occupation 3 is based on stratigraphy, their proximity to the other burials, and the presence of cremated bone.

Feature 30-1975 was a basin-shaped pit extending at least 13 in. (33 cm) into subsoil. Only the southeastern portion of the feature was excavated. The recovered remains represent one substantially disarticulated female aged > 55 years. The presence of a second individual is indicated by the recovery of an additional patella and part of a femoral condyle.

The unburned bones were covered by stained subsoil matrix including cremated human bone. Red ocher was spread around the abdominal and pelvic area. Scant skull and other bone fragments of one adult and a probable subadult, all completely calcined, lay in the abdominal area. Also found were fin rays from tomcod (*Microgadus tomcod*), probably the remains of a recent meal but possibly included as a food offering. Additional faunal remains were quite abundant in the fill, comparable in volume to the human bone. The only species identified is dog.

Feature 33-1975 was also a basin-shaped pit excavated through a thin midden deposit into subsoil to a depth of at least 20 in. Only the extreme southwestern limit of this feature was exposed, and human remains recovered include only a single human toe bone.

Comparison of Burial and Midden Artifacts

Susquehanna tradition lithic technology is noteworthy because of the extreme length and width attained by very thin bifaces made from rather intractable raw materials. One goal of our analysis was to evaluate whether blades from Occupation 3 mortuary contexts exhibit these characteristics to a greater extent than those from the midden—in other words, to determine whether grave furnishings were of especially high quality. The Turner Farm site provides the first opportunity for such a comparison in a Susquehanna context because of the close association there of the large midden and mortuary lithic tool samples.

Recent analysis of late Ceramic period lithic artifacts from the Goddard site conducted by Steven Cox (personal communication, 1989) demonstrated that "whole" blades and projectile points from midden contexts were consistently smaller than broken ones—that is, those with bases present but tips missing. This pattern strongly suggests that broken specimens were discarded before being reduced by resharpening, while unbroken specimens probably were discarded after being "worn out." Cox's observation prompted us to make a similar comparison for the midden-derived sample from Occupation 3 (Table 6.5). For this sample, significant differences between broken and complete specimens were found for contracting-stem points (blade widths [complete narrower than broken] and preform thickness [complete thicker than broken]). The first instance may be the result of more wear and subsequent resharpening of the complete specimens, as predicted by Cox's model. In the case of blades, the trend is in the opposite direction from that predicted by Cox and probably reflects accidental breakage during thinning.

Despite the absence of marked differences between complete and broken specimens from the midden, further comparisons between midden (Table 6.5) and burial (Table 6.6) samples, except for length, used data from broken midden specimens only. Dimensions of all tools from the burials, both broken and complete, were included because breakage in this sample was assumed to be unrelated to normal wear.

This comparison reveals that the lengths and widths of burial specimens generally are greater than those from the midden, and moreover, that tapered-stem blades from burials were thinner than those from the midden. Maximum and minimum stem widths of expanding-stem points were also significantly greater for the burial sample. Thus, greater care in manufacturing, or quality, does indeed seem to be evident in the burial assemblage. A possible exception is the lot from Feature 18-1975, presumably the earliest grave in the sample. A caveat about this conclusion is that even the broken tools from the midden may have sustained significant width reduction during use.

Finished Tools as Grave Furniture. The question of whether bifaces from the burial sample were hafted, as if ready for use, is complicated by two problems. The first is that any orderly placement of grave offerings that might reflect parallel orientation (bundles) of similar hafted artifacts has been randomized by secondary deposition. Noncremation burial features yielded too few tools to assess whether they were placed in any particular order. The second problem is that edge wear on bifacial point stems, which is found in both midden and burial samples, might be either due to preparation for hafting or the result of haft wear. We have not pursued this issue exhaustively. Frequency tabulations, however, indicate that in both midden and burial samples such stem-edge wear occurs on no blades and few tapered-stem blades, but on most points. These similarities thus suggest either that

Table 6.5. Summary of Statistics for Complete versus Broken Bifaces
from Occupation 3 Midden[a]

Artifact type		Complete				Broken		
		Length	Width	Thick	Base W[b]	Width	Thick	Base W[b]
Preforms[c]	N =	11	11	11	8	11	14	11
	Ave =	8.68	4.66	1.60	3.84	4.37	1.28	3.64
	SD =	1.94	1.01	.42	1.10	1.09	.36	1.45
	Min =	5.70	2.90	1.10	2.20	2.70	.80	1.60
	Max =	12.70	6.00	2.30	5.30	6.60	1.90	6.60
Mansion Inn blades	N =	12	11	12	0	22	24	0
	Ave =	7.56	4.84	1.35	0.0	4.55	1.4	0.0
	SD =	2.81	.99	.41	0.0	1.10	.28	0.0
	Min =	4.60	3.50	.80	0.0	2.80	.60	.0
	Max =	15.60	7.00	2.10	0.0	6.20	1.60	0.0
Tapered-stem	N =	0	0	0	0	18	22	19
blades	Ave =	0.0	0.0	0.0	0.0	3.83	.81	2.08
	SD =	0.0	0.0	0.0	0.0	.65	.12	.61
	Min =	0.0	0.0	0.0	0.0	2.60	.60	1.10
	Max =	0.0	0.0	0.0	0.0	5.10	1.00	3.60
Contracting-stem	N =	18	18	18	17	39	43	48
points	Ave =	6.28	3.59	.98	1.49	4.11	.95	1.58
	SD =	1.02	.58	.19	.27	.74	.15	.24
	Min =	4.40	2.20	.70	1.00	2.50	.70	1.00
	Max =	8.10	4.40	1.50	2.10	6.00	1.40	2.00
Straight-stemmed	N =	18	16	18	18	10	13	13
points	Ave =	6.89	3.46	.87	1.68	3.31	.82	1.72
	SD =	1.62	.74	.16	.27	.34	.11	.30
	Min =	3.10	2.20	.60	1.20	2.80	.60	1.30
	Max =	10.40	4.80	1.30	2.10	3.80	1.0	2.30
Expanding-stem	N =	17	15	17	16	45	50	50
points	Ave =	6.04	3.11	.78	1.99	3.39	.74	2.05
	SD =	1.04	.65	.14	.31	.52	.13	.32
	Min =	4.70	2.10	.60	1.50	1.90	.50	1.60
	Max =	8.40	4.50	1.00	2.60	4.70	1.10	3.00
Notched points	N =	0	0	0	0	0	0	0
	Ave =	0.0	0.0	0.0	0.0	0.0	0.0	0.0
	SD =	0.0	0.0	0.0	0.0	0.0	0.0	0.0
	Min =	0.0	0.0	0.0	0.0	0.0	0.0	0.0
	Max =	0.0	0.0	0.0	0.0	0.0	0.0	0.0
Boats blades	N =	0	0	0	0	6	5	6
	Ave =	0.0	0.0	0.0	0.0	4.70	1.06	4.28
	SD =	0.0	0.0	0.0	0.0	.66	.26	.71
	Min =	0.0	0.0	0.0	0.0	4.10	.70	3.50
	Max =	0.0	0.0	0.0	0.0	5.60	1.30	5.50
Drills	N =	2	2	2	2	7	4	7
	Ave =	8.30	2.30	.80	2.30	2.23	1.08	2.22
	SD =	2.40	.71	.20	.71	.69	.22	.69
	Min =	8.60	1.80	.70	1.80	1.40	.90	1.40
	Max =	10.00	2.80	.90	2.80	3.50	1.40	3.50

[a]All measurements in centimeters.
[b]Base W = base width.
[c]Not counting Mansion Inn blades.

Plate 6.28. Primary burial in Occupation 3 Feature 18-1975.

Plate 6.31. Primary burial in Occupation 3 Feature 9-1975. Note the expanding-stemmed point and the socketed antler tine in direct contact with the cranium.

Table 6.6. Summary of Statistics for Complete versus Broken Bifaces
from Occupation 3 Burials[a]

Artifact type		Complete				Broken		
		Length	Width	Thick	Base W[b]	Width	Thick	Base W[b]
Preforms[c]	N =	18	16	17	1	11	13	3
	Ave	10.04	5.37	1.36	4.30	5.48	1.25	4.60
	SD =	1.68	1.09	.30	0.0	.63	.37	.36
	Min =	6.70	2.90	.70	4.30	4.20	.70	4.20
	Max =	13.70	7.10	1.80	4.30	6.40	2.10	4.90
Mansion Inn blades	N =	22	19	22	20	16	15	13
	Ave =	9.26	6.04	1.39	3.01	6.17	1.26	2.70
	SD =	1.57	1.21	.28	.62	.91	.39	.61
	Min =	6.40	3.50	1.00	2.20	4.40	.60	1.60
	Max =	12.40	8.10	2.10	4.50	8.20	1.90	4.10
Tapered-stem blades	N =	20	19	20	10	18	21	18
	Ave =	9.17	4.51	.73	2.38	4.28	.72	2.23
	SD =	1.20	.74	.13	.58	.72	.14	.37
	Min =	6.90	2.80	.50	1.70	3.10	.40	1.70
	Max =	11.60	5.80	1.00	3.60	5.80	1.10	2.90
Contracting-stem points	N =	2	1	2	1	1	2	0
	Ave =	6.75	4.00	.75	1.60	4.60	1.10	0.0
	SD =	1.48	0.00	.21	0.00	0.00	0.00	0.0
	Min =	5.70	4.00	.60	1.60	4.60	1.10	0.0
	Max =	7.80	4.00	.90	1.60	4.60	1.10	0.0
Straight-stemmed points	N =	1	0	1	0	0	1	0
	Ave =	11.70	0.0	1.10	0.0	0.0	1.00	0.0
	SD =	0.00	0.0	0.00	0.0	0.0	0.00	0.0
	Min =	11.70	0.0	1.10	0.0	0.0	1.00	0.0
	Max =	11.70	0.0	1.10	0.0	0.0	1.00	0.0
Expanding-stem points	N =	70	60	70	57	30	43	36
	Ave =	7.71	3.95	.76	2.21	3.98	.77	2.29
	SD =	2.22	.94	.12	.41	.85	.12	.39
	Min =	3.50	2.40	.50	1.60	2.30	.60	1.50
	Max =	13.80	6.70	1.10	3.40	6.10	1.00	3.10
Notched points	N =	0	0	0	0	5	7	7
	Ave =	0.0	0.0	0.0	0.0	3.22	.70	2.21
	SD =	0.0	0.0	0.0	0.0	.31	.10	.43
	Min =	0.0	0.0	0.0	0.0	2.70	.60	1.50
	Max =	0.0	0.0	0.0	0.0	3.50	.90	2.80
Boats blades	N =	8	8	8	0	4	7	1
	Ave =	13.10	5.40	1.21	0.0	5.40	1.20	5.20
	SD =	3.16	.60	.17	0.0	.66	.22	0.00
	Min =	10.40	4.60	1.00	0.0	4.70	.90	5.20
	Max =	18.00	6.40	1.40	0.0	6.30	1.50	5.20
Drills	N =	16	15	16	15	11	15	11
	Ave =	8.64	2.09	.66	2.09	2.12	.66	2.12
	SD =	2.83	.42	.18	.42	.30	.18	.30
	Min =	4.60	1.20	.50	1.20	1.80	.50	1.80
	Max =	13.80	2.70	1.20	2.70	2.80	1.00	2.80

[a]All measurements in centimeters.
[b]Base W = base width.
[c]Not counting Mansion Inn blades.

points from mortuary features were hafted, or that they had been completely prepared to receive a haft.

Burial Summary

It has been clear since Dincauze's (1968) work on the Susquehanna tradition that this group constructed cemeteries in the sense of Goldstein (1980:8). Unusually favorable preservation conditions at the Turner Farm site, however, have revealed a much greater complexity of burial ritual than previously has been encountered. Moreover, because of the probable northward shift of burial activity over time, the Turner Farm cemetery may overcome the dilemma recognized by O'Shea:

> A short use-life minimizes the potential for diachronic change, but may provide an insufficient sample for meaningful analysis, whereas the large cemetery, ideal for social analysis, often has the greatest potential for diachronic distortion. (O'Shea 1984:14)

Thus, at least some of this complexity seems best explained as the result of changes in mortuary ritual practices over time. Early burials tend to be sparsely furnished primary inhumations such as those in the southern cluster. Later burials were lavishly furnished, multiple, secondary cremation deposits and were predominant in the northern cluster.

The temporal priority of inhumation over cremation is also evident in central New York, where broad, straight-stemmed Genesee points were occasionally found with extended primary burials in the Frontenac Island cemetery, while at the Piffard site at least 50 slightly younger Perkiomen points were found in a secondary cremation deposit (Ritchie 1980:104–125, 153–154). The trend toward increasingly rich burial furniture is also apparent in other New England Susquehanna tradition cemeteries. Two caches of fire-broken, contracting-stem points and preforms were discovered at the Amburst Farm site on Vinalhaven and at the Nevin site (Bourque 1992a:43, 191; Byers 1979:70), and also at the Young site in Alton, Maine (Borstel 1982:58–65). Their simplicity contrasts with the multiple, richly furnished features of both the Turner Farm site and Eddington Bend cemeteries (W. Smith 1926:60–73). A similar contrast is to be found between Dincauze's (1968:82) early Call group, especially the Hoffman site in Andover, Massachusetts (Bullen and Hoffmann 1947:189), and the sites of the Mansion Inn phase.

Manipulation of the Dead

Dincauze's analysis of Susquehanna tradition cemeteries in eastern Massachusetts relied heavily on data recovered by amateurs who had recorded few details about grave structure and nonartifactual contents. She did note the possibility of "postponed inhumation" and "periodic artifact-burning and burial ceremonies," but her analysis left unresolved the sequence of events that occurred between death and burial in a secondary cremation deposit with grave furnishings (Dincauze 1968:75).

While some of the diversity exhibited by the mortuary features may be explained by temporal factors, most of it reflects manipulation of the dead, suggesting their ongoing importance in a ritual context. The amount of time that elapsed between ritual events is unclear, but the available data suggest that it may have been appreciable, perhaps spanning a generation or more. First, the secondary inhumations obviously reflect a period of curation following death. Second, both fresh and dry bone was found in all secondary cremations. Moreover, incomplete individuals were represented in all but Feature 38-1974, suggesting that elements of the recently deceased were combined with elements of the previously deceased, stored or exhumed for inclusion in the ritual. Third, some primary inhumations were reopened, and bones were removed, perhaps for inclusion in secondary cremation deposits. Finally, all other inhumations, possibly excepting Feature 33-1975, had cremation deposits incorporated into the grave fill. None of these intrusive crematory deposits approached the size and richness of offerings found in the secondary cremation burials, but they clearly were purposeful deposits, not merely accidental juxtapositions of later burials.

Extensive manipulation of human remains has been noted in several post-Archaic contexts throughout the Northeast and elsewhere in eastern North America, but it has been less frequently noted among Archaic cultures of the Northeast (Thomas 1974; Ubelaker 1974). Dincauze (1968:65) alluded to the possibility that the dead may have been stored out of the ground at some New York Susquehanna tradition sites. At the Nevin site, Byers (1979:24–71) encountered clear evidence for the burial of disarticulated remains; at the Seabrook Marsh site there is clear evidence for manipulation including the reopening of graves and the commingling of individuals (Robinson 1985:35–40). Thus, the practice may in fact have been widespread in the region among many culturally disparate groups.

As recently pointed out, several researchers during the 1970s and 1980s argued that "structure and organization of the mortuary domain [reflects] the structure and organization of a society" (Charles and Buikstra 1983:123). Moreover, many of these studies "attempted to measure or characterize the degree of structuring or organization of cemeteries—with the stated or implied assumption that the more complex the society in question is, the more structured or organized the cemetery will be" (Charles and Buikstra 1983:123). The measures of structure and organization, however, have proved problematic, particularly against any absolute scale. In this regard it might be useful to consider the relative degree of manipulation of the dead as one relatively absolute scale. At the very least, diachronic changes in such behavior over time in a given region should prove useful as a relative scale for measuring, if not complexity, at least the strength of "ritual affirmation of corporate structure" (Charles and Buikstra 1983:124). This possibility will be reconsidered in Chapter 8.

The precise nature of Susquehanna mortuary ceremonialism will never be known in its full detail. However, the preservation of bone in the Turner Farm burials has provided some interesting specimens that may be relevant in this regard. The presence of bone from edible animals may have been intended for consumption in the afterworld, but it may also have been intended for immediate consumption as a part of a mortuary feast. Another aspect of ritual behavior—gaming—is suggested by the placement of what appear to be bone dice in Feature 18-1975. We know from the discovery of other probable gaming pieces in the Occupation 3 midden that such games were probably played by these people, and the existence of gaming as part of mortuary ritual was a common practice during historic times throughout much of North America and elsewhere (Ventur 1980). It is interesting in this regard to note that dice have frequently been found in prehistoric graves in the Southeast (Ventur 1980:86).

Seasonality

Dincauze (1968:66, 1975:30–31) has suggested that the high frequency of charred nuts in southern New England Susquehanna tradition cemeteries may reflect autumnal rituals. Subsequently, hickory nuts, hazel nuts, and acorns were recovered from Susquehanna tradition cremation burials at the Griffin site in Connecticut (Pfeiffer 1980:131). Beechnuts and plum pits recovered from several secondary cremations at the Turner Farm site provide further support for the notion that autumn was the preferred season for rituals involving burial, but the scarcity of seasonal data leave open the possibility that mortuary rituals occurred at other times as well.

Burial Furnishings

There is a marked dichotomy between the bone artifact samples recovered from the midden and those from the cemetery. Even before encountering the burials, we were puzzled by the virtually complete absence of bone tools from Occupation 3 midden deposits. This absence was later underscored when we began to encounter elaborate bone and antler artifacts along with lithic artifacts as burial furniture. It is further underscored by the strong likelihood that bone tools are much more likely to have been destroyed by cremation, skewing the true ratio heavily in favor of the diminutive midden sample.

Adding to the puzzlement is the fact that, although they lack local prototypes, bone grave furnishings exhibit great variety, sophistication of design, and careful finishing. They also include sophisticated weapons apparently designed to capture marine vertebrates, an activity only weakly attested by the faunal and human bone isotopic data. Our initial impression was that these might have been accidental inclusions derived from Occupation 2. This now seems quite unlikely because both their forms and modes of manufacture—by grinding and polishing—are distinctly different from those of Occupation 2, from the Moorehead phase component at the Nevin site (Byers 1979), or from any later component in the Fox Islands area. The virtual absence of bone at most other known Susquehanna mortuary components—for example from Dincauze's (1968:39–40) cemetery sample or the Griffin site (Pfeiffer 1992:211–212)—leaves us with little basis for further regional comparisons. As noted above, however, instructive comparisons can be made to the bone technology of the Late Archaic period in the Southeast. The possible significance of these long-distance similarities will be considered in Chapter 8.

Grave goods more clearly suggestive of symbolic significance are the maxillae of predatory mammals—including wolf (Feature 9-1975), red fox (Features 19-1975 and 38-1974), and cat (Feature 7-1975); and turtle-shell rattle fragments (Features 41a-1974 and 42-1974), often accompanied by small quartz pebbles (Features 12-1975, 9-1975). Similar faunal remains from the eastern Massachusetts cemeteries and from the Griffin site include maxillary fragments and teeth from dogs (Dincauze 1986:Plate XIX; Pfeiffer 1992:211). Other faunal remains from the Turner Farm burials seem, for the most part, to represent food offerings. Comparable remains from the Griffin site include only a single deer bone (Pfeiffer 1992:211). Dincauze (1968:Plate XIX) illustrates several bone and antler fragments that probably also represent food offerings.

Dincauze argued that the artifacts from her cemeteries "were clearly not a special class of burial goods, but rather were derived from the entire range of material goods available to the depositors" and that most were "used, worn out, broken or unfinished." She concluded that "they were, in a magical sense, dead" (Dincauze 1968:65, 75). At the Griffin site, by contrast, "Many of the tools were unused and retained sharp edges. However, several features revealed sets of artifacts that had been rejuvenated or resharpened" (Pfeiffer 1992:212). As pointed out above, lithic grave furnishings from the Turner Farm burials, while not always pristine, can hardly be described as worn out. Instead, although most are utilitarian forms also encountered in the midden, they were often little worn and may have been specially manufactured as burial furniture. Furthermore, although several—most obviously the grooved axes from Features 9-1975 and 19-1975—appear to have been ritually broken, even unbroken bifaces may also have been "killed" by the breakage of some other part, such as a handle or shaft, which was not preserved.

In sum, grave furnishings of stone, bone, and antler, while generally of utilitarian design, were made special (compared to specimens discarded in the midden) by virtue of unusual quality, or by careful curation that caused them rarely, if ever, to be discarded in the midden. Some, such as the carnivore maxillae, the turtle-shell rattles, and perhaps the harpoon of antler, may have been completely symbolic in the Susquehanna context. Taken as a whole, the ideotechnic flavor of the Occupation 3 cemetery furnishings is impressive.

SIGNIFICANCE OF OCCUPATION 3

Definition of the Susquehanna Tradition

Technologically, Occupation 3 differs profoundly from Occupation 2. The predominance of flaked stone over bone forms stands in sharp contrast to Occupation 2, as do the production techniques and morphology of both flaked stone and bone artifacts. Faunal remains reflect differences of comparable magnitude in subsistence activities. Finally, though the discovery of interments and red ocher in the cemetery initially appears to diminish the previously attested dichotomy between Moorehead phase inhumation and Susquehanna tradition cremation, there remain profound differences between these two mortuary patterns.

John Whitthoft (1953) first defined a Susquehanna Soapstone culture in the Susquehanna River valley area, pointing out similarities shared by a whole group of bifaces, including those of the Susquehanna Soapstone culture. These included the Lehigh Broad point of Pennsylvania, the Perkiomen point of the Schuylkill Valley area, the Snook Kill point of eastern New York, Savannah River points of the Southeast, and "corner-removed" points of New England. To the stone pots and points, Byers (1959:239) added grooved axes and spear-thrower weights. Ritchie (1969a:152–153) noted the association of Perkiomen points with Vinette I pottery, scrapers and drills made from points, and chipped and ground adzes. Around 1960, amateurs working in Massachusetts began to invoke Witthoft's and Ritchie's notions about Susquehanna Soapstone culture to explain mortuary features there (see Brennon 1960; Robbins 1959:82–90; Dincauze 1968:5–6). Finally, Ritchie pointed out the recovery of Perkiomen points from 13 cremation and inhumation graves at the Piffard site in Livingston County, New York (Ritchie 1980:153–154).

By 1969, both Ritchie (1969a:222) and Dincauze (1968:89) were referring to a Susquehanna tradition in New York and southern New England. Concurrently, others (e.g., Bourque 1992a:39–43, 122; Finch 1971) were demonstrating its presence in northern New England. Numerous additional Susquehanna-related components have since come to light over a larger area of the Northeast extending to the Niagara Peninsula of Ontario (Kenyon 1980; Spence and Fox 1986:5–7), and northward to Pointe-du-Buisson, Quebec (Clermont and Chapdelaine 1982:33–39), and Ruisseau-des-Caps, Kamouraska County, Quebec (Dumais 1978:69–71). The assemblages from all these sites share often striking similarities and, as noted previously, they also resemble contemporaneous or earlier Archaic complexes over a much larger region. Discussion of these relationships is deferred to a later chapter.

Occupation 3 clearly conforms to the main themes of Dincauze's and Ritchie's conception of the Susquehanna tradition, and particularly to Dincauze's Watertown phase. Its huge artifact sample, stratigraphic integrity, and bone preservation, however, permit the addition of numerous new artifact forms and aspects of mortuary behavior to the known Susquehanna repertoire. Chief among these artifact forms are the corner-notched bifaces, ground stone pendants, copper beads, and the full range of bone and antler artifacts from the burials. The range of mortuary behavior has also been expanded to include a variety of inhumation forms, including primary and secondary burial as well as combinations of burial and cremation. A final important addition is that of occipital flattening among what may have been a single, early Susquehanna tradition family.

The Age of the Susquehanna Tradition

While there is a growing consensus about what constitutes the Susquehanna tradition in the Northeast, uncertainty remains about when it began. Witthoft initially suggested a beginning date of about 3500 B.P. for his Susquehanna Soapstone culture, and Ritchie (1980:136) concurred, citing a comparable Snook Kill phase date from eastern New York. Ritchie (1980:156–178) also postulated the derivative Frost Island and Orient phases, describing the latter as illustrating "the stone-pot-using Transitional stage of cultural development on Long Island, linking the preceramic Late Archaic with the Early Woodland ceramic stage, which was becoming established in the area toward the end of Orient times." Dincauze's (1968) analysis of cremation cemeteries from eastern Massachusetts revealed a comparable progression, beginning with the Watertown phase and ending with the Coburn phase.

Dincauze (1972:58) later defined an ancestral Atlantic phase, which she considered as "a northeastern member of a linked series of related cultural entities which extended, in a probably unbroken chain, northward from northern Florida into New England in the early centuries of the fourth millennium B.P." Her (Dincauze 1972:57, 1975:29) Atlantic and Watertown phases were given beginning dates of c. 4100 B.P. and c. 3600 B.P., respectively. Dates from the Turner Farm site suggest somewhat later beginning dates for these two phases.

As noted above, the diversity of stemmed point styles and burial styles, as well as the density of cultural remains and features, suggests that Occupation 3 spans a significant period of time, probably longer than Occupation 2 and perhaps representing discrete episodes of occupation. These data are thus in accord with the notion that an Atlantic phase-like population arrived in Penobscot Bay sometime between 3800 and 3700 B.P. at about the same time that the Moorehead phase ended (Bourque and Cox 1981:11; Sanger 1973:132). From the Mud Lake Stream site in southwestern New Brunswick have come two earlier dates on a Susquehanna component: 4000 ± 180 B.P. and 4010 ± 180 B.P. (Deal 1986:72–78). These are associated with early-looking contracting-stem points and with features that possibly reflect mortuary ceremonialism. This evidence may indicate the presence in the Gulf of Maine region of Susquehanna tradition occupation slightly preceding Occupation 3, although, as noted by Deal, it is not definitive in this regard. Moreover, the standard deviations overlap those of the earliest reliable Turner Farm dates.

Lithic technology indicates that this population developed in conjunction with its southern Susquehanna tradition contemporaries from an Atlantic-like to a Watertown-like phase. It even seems to have contributed grave furnishings in the form of flaked stone tools made of Vinalhaven banded-spherulitic rhyolite and Kineo-Traveler rhyolite to burials in southern New England (Bourque 1994; Dincauze 1968:94, 1974:41–42). The numerous radiocarbon dates available from Occupation 3 deposits can thus clarify the somewhat uncertain chronology of the early phases of the Susquehanna tradition in New England and New York.

Turner Farm dates suggest that Dincauze's beginning date for her Atlantic phase is too early by at least 200 years. Dincauze also thought that the Watertown phase succeeded it only after about 3600 B.P., while the Turner Farm dates suggest that the transition had occurred probably prior to 3700 B.P. If accurate, these revisions indicate a much greater degree of dynamism during the early phases of the tradition than is suggested by the traditional chronology, which extends it over nearly half a millennium.

Numerous sites on the Fox Islands and elsewhere in Maine have yielded lithic assemblages resembling that from Occupation 3, but nowhere has there been found significant evidence of the later phases of the Susquehanna tradition as it is manifest to the south, particularly in the form of the Orient phase and analogous expressions (Dincauze 1968:71–88; Pfeiffer 1992:73–89; Ritchie 1980:164–178). Indeed, no model for population size, structure, or lifestyle has been suggested, nor have reliable assemblages been identified for the period between about 3600 and 2700 B.P.. Thus, the data available suggest either that the Susquehanna tradition penetration into Maine persisted for no more than about two centuries, and was followed by a period of marked depopulation, or, less probably, that its archaeological signature was so extensively diminished and transformed by factors unknown that its continuity with later populations has been unrecognized.

Chapter *7*

Occupation 4
The Ceramic Period

TERMINOLOGY

As I recall, the term "Ceramic period," was coined by David Sanger and me in Ottawa when we first met at the 1968 meeting of the Canadian Archaeological Association. Our research interests had recently converged in Maine and I recall that we were anxious to establish a few ground rules which might allow us to shed terminological baggage derived from other regions. I think we were both equally anxious that one particular term, Woodland, not be extended northeastward yet again in reference to ceramic-making peoples of later prehistory in Maine and the Maritimes (see Sanger 1987:85–86 for a similar retrospective).

The Woodland concept is an artifact of the Midwestern Taxonomic System, one of two typological patterns characterized by the production of ceramic pottery (McKern 1939: 309–310; Willey and Sabloff 1980:112–113). However, it soon took on a whole series of associated cultural "traits," of which horticulture and complex mortuary ceremonialism (often equated with mound building) were paramount (Anonymous 1943). William H. Sears (1948) urged that the Woodland concept be limited to the presence of ceramic technology, but the three original traits have continued to be included in most general definitions of Woodland, modified and variably emphasized by regional specialists (see, e.g., Funk 1983:334; Griffin 1983:254; Willey 1966:268–269). An even more radical modification has been proposed by Custer (1989:141–184) for the Delmarva Peninsula, which extends the term back to 5000 B.P. to include most of what has been previously regarded as the Late Archaic period.

In the Maine-Maritimes region, some recently proposed typological schemes for the Ceramic period (e.g., Black 1988, 1992:9–10; Petersen 1985) also continue to use the term Woodland without addressing the discrepancies between the concept and archaeological reality, specifically the scarcity of complex mortuary ceremonialism and the total absence of horticulture throughout much of the region to which it is being applied. Sanger (1987:85–86) has recently reaffirmed his preference for "Ceramic period" over "Woodland" as a label for the period of ceramic production in Passamaquoddy Bay and elsewhere in the Gulf of

Maine. Fortunately, others working in the Maritimes (e.g., David 1978, 1988; Deal 1986) seem to be following suit. In fact, if adopting the term ceramic period was a good idea a quarter century ago, it is now an even better one, for not only have recent modifications continued to blunt the term Woodland as an instrument of nomenclature but, as we shall see below, the appearance of ceramics signals the reemergence of a rich archaeological record following a post-Archaic lapse during which that record is curiously silent.

CERAMIC PERIOD STRATIGRAPHY

The strata assigned to Occupation 4 exhibit more complexity than those of earlier components, apparently because of more frequent episodes of occupation (Tables 7.1, 7.2). This complexity has been reduced to the following units:

1. *Below the Second Gravel Floor* (B2GF, maximum thickness: 11 in [28 cm]): The sequence begins with a group of intermittent shell midden lenses overlying and occasionally mixing with Archaic period deposits or, sometimes, subsoil. Such lenses were encountered in 41 of 163 (25 percent) sections of the main excavation. They were defined as

Table 7.1. Features from Occupation 4

Feature number	Level	Section	Description	Date
12-1973	MCS	W10S100	Hearth	
2-1974	MCS	E0S75	Hearth	
1-1971	1GF	W55S85	Circular lens of ash	
10-1972	1GF	W25S95	Pit	
14-1972	1GF	W25S90	Hearth	
17-1972	1GF	W45S100	Pit or burrow	
22-1972	1GF	W25S85	Pit	
23-1972	1GF	W25S75	Hearth	
24-1972	IGF	W20S75	Hearth	
9-1973	1GF	E0S90	Pit	
3-1974	1GF	E10S75	Hearth	
5-1974	1GF	E30S75	Hearth	
11-1974	1GF	E10S75	Pit	
2-1975	1GF	E5S60	Hearth	
23-1975	1GF	W35S70	Hearth	
11-1972	CCS	W25S95 and W25S95	Hearth	
10-1974	CCS	E10S75 and E15S75	Pit	
4-1975	CCS	W30S70	Pit	
10-1975	CCS	E15S60	Hearth	
1-1972	2GF	W50S95	Hearth	
8-1973	2GF	E5S85	House floor	
11-1973	2GF	E5S75	Hearth	
19-1973	2GF	E20S75	Blocked-end tube	1955 ± 50 B.P. (SI 4240)
1-1974	2GF	E40S70	Hearth	
6-1974	2GF	E40S70	Pit	
16-1974	2GF	E45S70	Hearth	
21-1974	B2GF	E40S65	Pit in subsoil	3185 ± 65 B.P. (SI 4244)

Table 7.2. Dates (B.P.) from Occupation 4

Date	Level	Section	Sample number	Feature number	Material	Association	Lab number
115 ± 65	1GF	W35S90	147C		Charcoal		SI 4246
175 ± 70	MCS	W55S90	7C		Charcoal		SI 4239
875 ± 70	1GF	W60S85	4C		Charcoal		SI 4238
1200 ± 100	CCS	W55S110	197C		Charcoal		GX 2465
1955 ± 50	2GF	E20S75	37C	19-1973	Charcoal	Blocked-end tube	SI 4240
2105 ± 75	2GF	E15S75	120C		Charcoal		SI 4245
2275 ± 130	B2GF	W55S105	195C		Charcoal		GX 2463
2530 ± 65	B2GF	W55S105	44C		Sea urchin	Points and pottery	SI 2407
2575 ± 75	B2GF	W55S105	43C		Mya	Points and pottery	SI 2398
3185 ± 65	B2GF	E40S65	81C	21-1974	Charcoal		SI 4244
3280 ± 50	B2GF	E20S80	78C	12-1974	Charcoal		SI 4243

post-Archaic primarily by artifact content, which differs markedly, even at the level of debitage, from Occupation 3. The B2GF label stands for "below second gravel floor," indicating that the lenses underlay a more extensive unit labeled "second gravel floor." Four dates from B2GF lenses range from 2275 ± 130 B.P. (GX 2463) to 3280 ± 50 B.P. (SI 4243).

2. *Second Gravel Floor* (2GF, maximum thickness: 14 in [36 cm]): This relatively shell-free stratum was encountered in 83 of 163 (51 percent) main excavation sections. It is composed of dark soil and beach gravel, suggesting that it represents an old topsoil resulting from an extended hiatus in occupation, later augmented by culturally derived organics and beach gravel. Most features clustered near the eastern end of our main excavation, although considerable bone and pottery deposition occurred elsewhere (Figure 7.1). Two dates from this unit are 1955 ± 50 B.P. (SI 4240) and 2105 ± 75 B.P. (SI 4245).

3. *Coarsely Crushed Shell* (CCS, maximum thickness: 19 in [48 cm]): Overlying 2GF was an extensive, often thick series of shell-rich lenses that probably accumulated during its occupation. They were encountered in 134 of 163 (82 percent) main excavation sections, more than any other stratigraphic unit aside from the special case of the plow zone. A few features, mainly hearths, seemed to originate on localized depositional discontinuities within the CCS, suggesting some occupation of short-lived surfaces during its accumulation (Figure 7.2). Faunal remains are differentially distributed by species. Deer bone becomes increasingly concentrated over the eastern part of the site where underlying features of 2GF were concentrated. Moose, mink, bird, and fish bone, by contrast, clustered in the south-west, an area where CCS lenses were less abundant. This scale of differential faunal distribution is comparable to that encountered in later Occupation 4 strata. All differ from earlier occupations in that they seem to reflect larger-scale patterning, perhaps seasonally rather than functionally organized. A single date of 1200 ± 100 B.P. (SI 2465) was obtained from CCS.

4. *First Gravel Floor* (1GF, maximum thickness: 13 in [33 cm]): This shell-free stratum closely resembles 2GF in composition. However, it was more extensive, being encountered in 126 of 163 sections of the main excavation (77 percent versus 51 percent for 2GF). Numerous features originated in it, clustering in two areas, just east and west of the center of

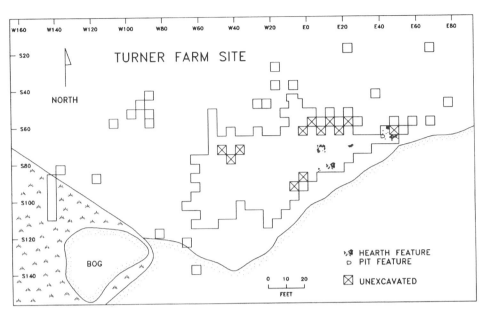

Figure 7.1.   Occupation 4, Second Gravel Floor features.

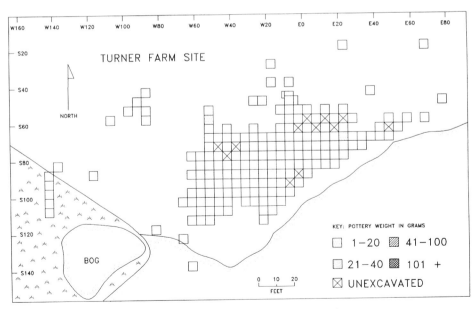

Figure 7.2.   Occupation 4, Coarsely Crushed Shell features.

our main excavation (Figure 7.3). Probably only the 875 ± 70 B.P. (SI 4238) date has significance, with the other date representing intrusive material or misinterpreted stratigraphy.

5. *Moderately Crushed Shell* (MCS, maximum thickness: 15 in [38 cm]): These shell-rich lenses overlie the 1GF. They resemble those of CCS in species composition, but their shell is somewhat more extensively crushed (655 kg shell/m^3 of midden for MCS versus 522 kg/m^3 for CCS). MCS shell is not as extensive as CCS, being encountered in only 63 of 163 sections (39 percent versus 82 percent). The MCS lenses are the latest, uppermost undisturbed midden deposits. However, the single radiocarbon date of 175 ± 70 B.P. (SI 4239) must reflect an undetected recent intrusion. Only two features were attributed to MCS (Figure 7.4).

6. *New Gravel Floor* (NGF, maximum thickness: 6 in [15 cm]): This relatively shell-free stratum was not recognized as a major stratigraphic unit in the field. Only later, during distributional analysis of the ceramic sample, was it reconstructed from profiles and floor plans. It has now been identified in 7 of 163 sections (4 percent). It represents a depositional discontinuity and occupied surface similar to 1GF and 2GF, but of briefer duration, and may have been comparable to them in horizontal extent before much of it was incorporated into the plow zone. Excavations in sections W90S45, W95S50, and W100S55 encountered a shell-free floor that has a stratigraphic position comparable to the NGF, but its isolation from the main excavation makes the contemporaneity of these two strata uncertain.

7. *Finely Crushed Shell* (FCS; maximum thickness: 15 in [38 cm]): Over most of the excavation, this uppermost stratum was highly uniform in thickness and composition, which includes finely crushed shell and dark soil. Historic period artifacts were frequently encountered in it, as were a mixture of materials representing all earlier components. The absence of discrete features or other fine structure, such as those encountered in deeper

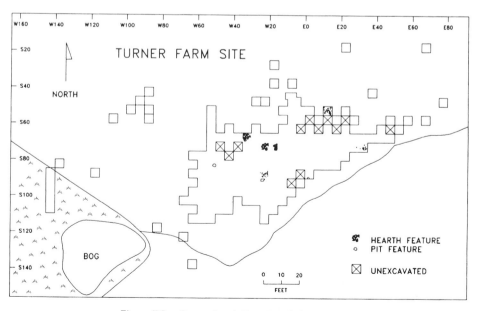

Figure 7.3. Occupation 4, First Gravel Floor features.

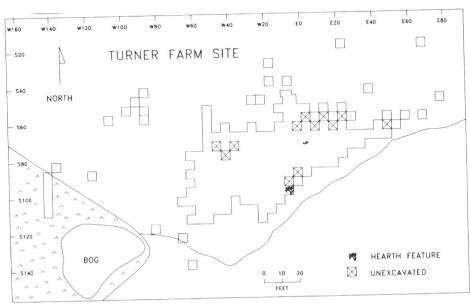

Figure 7.4. Occupation 4, Moderately Crushed Shell features.

strata, conforms to what one would expect if the midden surface had been homogenized by plowing. No one we asked could remember the site being plowed, but it is one of the few large arable areas near the farmhouse, and must have been plowed land at some time.

8. *Sod*: The midden is capped by shell-free sod averaging 6 cm in thickness and composed of black midden soil. During excavation, it was removed, shaken to loosen large clods and clinging plow zone, then set aside for later replacement. Such a sod over a presumably recent plow zone must be the result of ant and earthworm transportation of fine-grained deposits within the midden upward from shell-bearing strata below. This modern sod is the basis for our model of the development of shell-free strata encountered deeper in the midden.

ARTIFACTS

Lithics

Lobate-Stemmed Points

Lobate-stemmed bifaces have thick blades with lenticular cross sections, excurvate edges, and (usually) expanding stems with round bases ($N = 50$; Plate 7.1, Table 7.3). All are made of local materials—that is, local fine-grained volcanics and metavolcanics, as opposed to exotic cherts. They were found in B2GF, but are most common between 2GF and 1GF. Only two specimens were found in higher undisturbed contexts. This stratigraphic distribution suggests that they were in use during the period when ceramic pottery technology was introduced and persisted until sometime after 2000 B.P.

Plate 7.1.   Lobate-stemmed points from Occupation 4.

Table 7.3. Summary Statistics for Occupation 4 Bifaces[a]

Artifact type		Length	Width	Thickness
Triangles	N =	7	15	12
	Ave =	3.54	3.31	.66
	SD =	.97	.63	.15
	Min =	2.40	2.20	.50
	Max =	4.80	4.30	.90
Side-notched	N =	24	36	34
	Ave =	4.12	1.99	.71
	SD =	.84	.33	.13
	Min =	2.50	1.30	.50
	Max =	5.80	3.10	1.10
Corner-notched	N =	7	17	19
	Ave =	4.91	2.18	.71
	SD =	1.13	.27	.15
	Min =	3.10	1.75	.40
	Max =	6.40	2.60	1.10
Narrow-stemmed	N =	30	66	64
	Ave =	5.50	1.90	.72
	SD =	1.21	.34	.15
	Min =	3.60	1.20	.50
	Max =	8.40	2.90	1.10
Lobate-stemmed	N =	33	45	48
	Ave =	5.65	2.68	1.05
	SD =	.79	.41	.24
	Min =	3.40	2.00	.60
	Max =	7.10	4.10	1.70

[a]All measurements in centimeters.

Similar points have been encountered at numerous sites, usually in ambiguous stratigraphic contexts, at least as far east as Passamaquoddy Bay, New Brunswick, and possibly in the Miramachee drainage in New Brunswick as well (Allen 1981:339; Davis 1978:55, Plate 5; Sanger 1971b:Plate IIIa, b).

Narrow-Stemmed Points

Narrow-stemmed points are similar in length to the lobate-stemmed sample but are significantly thinner and narrower (N = 67; Plate 7.2, Table 7.3). Their cross sections are lenticular and most have gracefully excurvate blade margins. Their stems are parallel-sided to slightly contracting, rather long, and basally thinned; this last attribute distinguishes them from superficially similar points from Occupation 2 and other Moorehead phase components. Their distribution parallels that of lobate-stemmed points. It seems likely that the latter functioned as knives while the more gracile narrow-stemmed points armed lances or atlatl darts.

Like lobate-based points, narrow-stemmed points are also commonly found in probably Terminal Archaic and early Ceramic period Maine coastal contexts—including Site 29.159, a single-component shell midden on Butter Island in upper Penobscot Bay, which

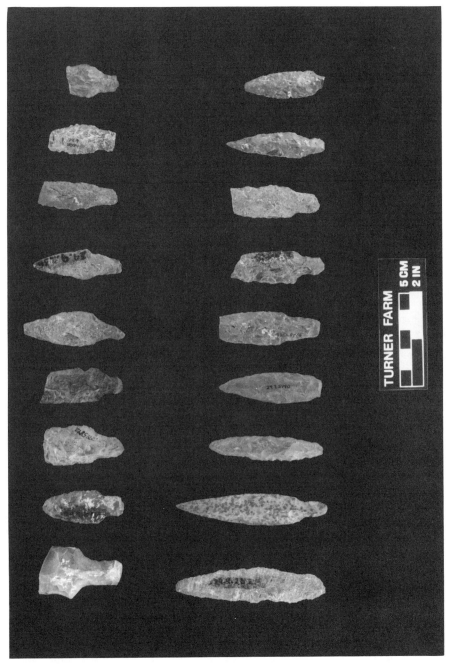

Plate 7.2. Narrow-stemmed points from Occupation 4.

produced three radiocarbon dates on charcoal: 1850 ± 150 B.P. (Beta 5916), 1950 ± 100 B.P. (Beta 5917), and 2010 ± 150 B.P. (Beta 5918). Their superficial resemblance to the narrow-stemmed points of the Moorehead phase was noted by Kingsbury and Hadlock (1951), and Tuck (1975:142) suggested that they were derived from that form. This now seems unlikely for two reasons. First, the two forms are separated by a span of at least 1,500 years, a period that includes the Susquehanna tradition incursion into Maine, southwestern New Brunswick, and southern Nova Scotia. Second, narrow-stemmed points of the Ceramic period are relatively thin, have lenticular cross sections and thinned stem bases, whereas most Moorehead phase stemmed points are thick, with lozenge-shaped cross sections and stem bases that retain striking platform remnants.

Notched Points

This class of points (Plate 7.3, Table 7.3) includes points with side (N = 36) and corner notches (N = 19). Found in small numbers in B2GF, notched points were more abundant in 1GF and higher. Some resemble the huge, highly uniform sample from the Goddard site in nearby Blue Hill Bay (Bourque and Cox 1981:13–16), but in drastically smaller numbers relative to cord-wrapped-stick-impressed pottery. The same relative scarcity has been noted at numerous other Ceramic period sites in Penobscot Bay, suggesting that some important reorganization of the population's economic activity occurred during late prehistory along this area of the coast.

Triangular Points

The small sample of triangular points clearly belongs late in the Ceramic period sequence (N = 19; Plate 7.4). It corresponds approximately with Ritchie's (1971:31–34, Plates 15 and 16) size ranges for the Madison and Levanna types. The occurrence of numerous similar points at many other Maine components indicates that they are a highly standardized point style probably used to tip arrows. The small Turner Farm sample leaves unresolved whether triangular points replaced notched bifaces or were used contemporaneously.

Eared-Stem Points

Eared-stem points have a slight expansion at the base (N = 8; Plate 7.5). Bourque (1976:37, Figure 1g, h, i) originally implied that the form was confined to Occupation 2, but they are now regarded as a minority form in various stratigraphic contexts (including Occupation 4), where they appear to be variants of the narrow-stemmed point style.

Other Bifaces

The large sample (N = 270) in the category of "other bifaces" is too variable to describe easily. Although many appear to be preforms, this residual sample appears to include numerous expedient tools, suggesting fewer formal constraints on biface tool manufacture than in earlier assemblages.

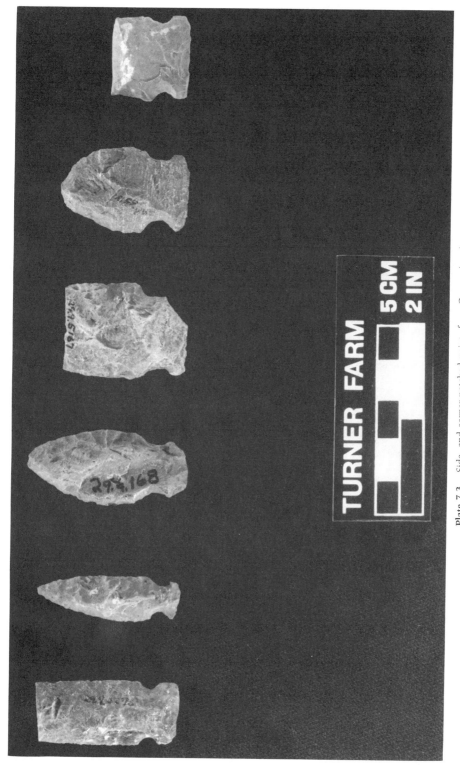

Plate 7.3. Side- and corner-notched points from Occupation 4.

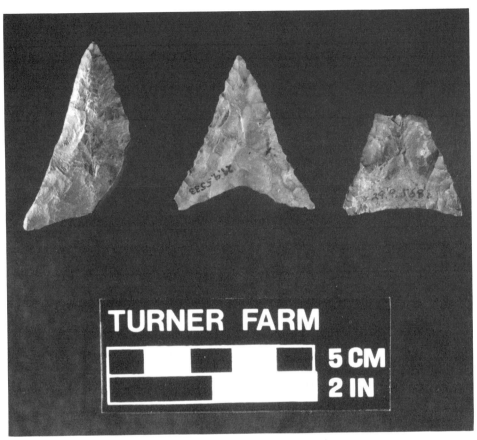

Plate 7.4.   Triangular points from Occupation 4.

Scrapers

Scrapers are ubiquitous in Ceramic period sites throughout the Maine-Maritimes region and occur in comparable frequencies in Occupation 4 deposits (N = 177; Plates 7.6, 7.7). Components of this period throughout southern Maine are notable for the large numbers of scrapers made of high-quality, exotic lithics originating from sources as far away as Ramah Bay, Labrador (Cox, 1995). Evidence from the Goddard site, however, indicates that the exotic-to-local ratio of scrapers and other tools rises dramatically for sites dating after about 1000 B.P. (Bourque 1994). The Turner Farm sample includes 40 exotic chert scrapers (22 percent of the scraper sample, including Munsungan, New York, and Nova Scotia cherts), which is comparable to the ratios from other multicomponent Ceramic period samples in the region (Appendix 6).

Scraper frequencies relative to midden shell weight are fairly constant from B2GF to the plow zone. This contrasts with bone points and incisor tools (discussed below), which increase markedly in frequency relative to shell weight through Occupation 4 strata. Their

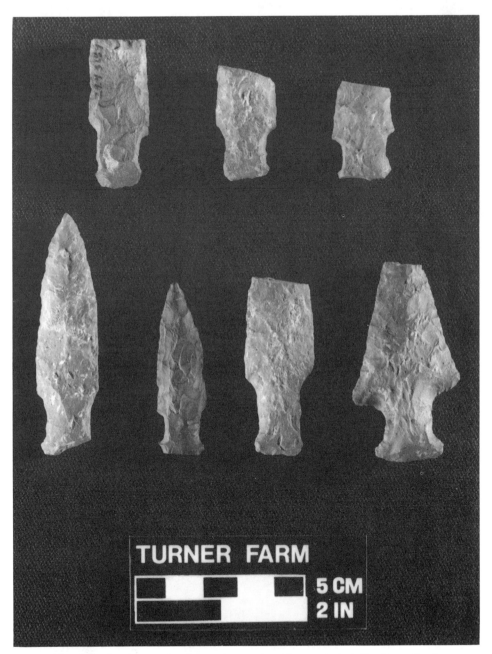

Plate 7.5. Eared-stem points from various stratigraphic contexts, including Occupation 4.

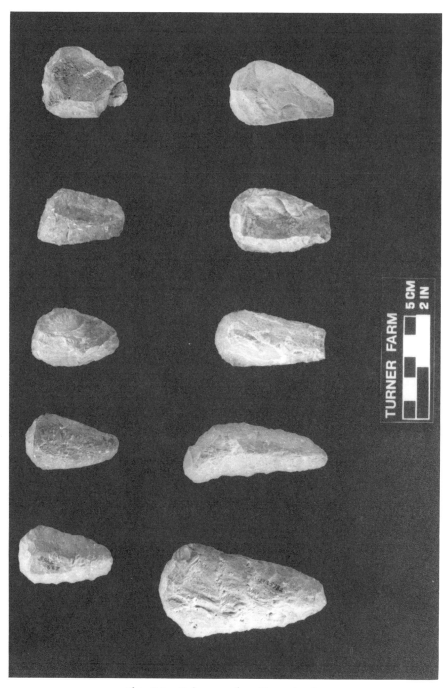

Plate 7.6. End scrapers from Occupation 4.

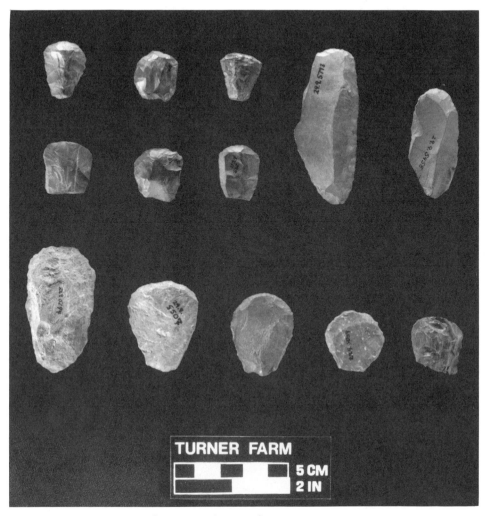

Plate 7.7. End scrapers from Occupation 4.

sizes are quite variable, and based upon limited data from other sites in the region, we expected to find a trend of decreasing scraper size through time (Sanger 1971a; 1987:121). No such trend is apparent, however.

The functions of scrapers remain unknown. Scraper edges rarely show rounding or polish, such as might be expected from use on hide or other soft materials. Rather, they became dulled by the accumulation of minute step fractures such as would occur from scraping a hard surface such as bone or perhaps dense wood. Bone artifacts from Ceramic period strata, which universally have scrape-marked surfaces, may well have been shaped by these tools.

Other Lithic Artifacts

Three additional artifacts deserve mention because all pertain to a little-understood cult phenomenon in the Northeast usually referred to as the Middlesex phase (Bourque 1994:29–34; Ritchie 1980:201–205). The first is the steatite gorget from the Turner family collection (Plate 7.8). The fact that it is apparently made of a bowl sherd suggests an Occupation 3 provenience. Its form, however, generally resembles the two-holed pendants commonly reported from Adena/Middlesex mortuary contexts (see, e.g., T. L. Ford 1976; Plates 27–31), not from Susquehanna tradition contexts. It is therefore provisionally regarded as pertaining to Occupation 4. The second artifact is a stemmed point also from the Turner family collection (Plate 7.8). It is made of a lustrous exotic chert and closely resembles points from other eastern Adena-related contexts (see, e.g., T.L. Ford 1976, Plates 16 and 17). The third artifact is a tubular pipe of Ohio pipestone (Figure 7.5). It was found on a house floor (Feature 19-1973), which produced a date of 1955 ± 50 B.P. (SI 4240). In the Northeast, such pipes also are most commonly found in Adena/Middlesex mortuary features, most of which predate the birth of Christ. It is interesting to note that these mortuary features tend to occur in clusters separated by substantial distances, and that one such cluster appears to focus on the Penobscot Bay area (Bourque 1994:30). The social mechanism that caused the dispersal of Adena-derived artifacts and their uneven distribution throughout the Northeast remains unclear. No major focus of Adena-related activity is apparent at the Turner Farm site, but its occupants during the few centuries before Christ were somehow involved in long-distance communication with the Adena heartland.

Bone Artifacts

Artifacts of bone, antler, and tooth are more numerous in Occupation 4 deposits than in earlier ones. Their typological variety, however, is more restricted.

Bone Points

Simple, bipointed bone points (N = 607) were shaped by scraping splinters of cervid bone (Plate 7.9). Most have a blunt end, often with wear-polish and step fractures, and a sharper beveled end that shows no such polish or damage.

Bone points in this sample average 7.2 mm in width (range = 5.4 to 9.0 mm) and 5.1 mm in thickness (range = 3.0 to 6.6 mm). Mean length is 58 mm (range = 86 mm to 41 mm). Variability in width and thickness is low. Length variability, however, is high and probably reflects length reduction by resharpening.

Bone point frequencies increase dramatically between B2GF and MCS. The largest sample came from the plow zone, but a comparison of bone point frequency relative to shell weight actually indicates a sharp decline in relative frequency above MCS, the high specimen count being due to the high frequency of identifiable fragments broken by plowing.

This style of bone point is ubiquitous in Ceramic period components along the coasts of Maine and the Maritime Provinces, but seems to be most common in central coastal Maine (see, e.g., Bourque 1992a:103–104, 297–298; Davis 1978:25, 60; Sanger 1987:53; Smith and Wintemberg 1929:24–25). The most comprehensive analysis of this tool class

Plate 7.8. Steatite gorget and stemmed point of exotic chert from the Turner family collection.

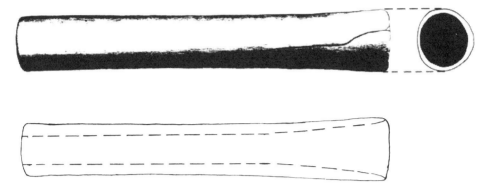

Figure 7.5. Tubular pipe from Occupation 4 Feature 19-1973.

remains that of Tyzzer (1936:266–271), who studied 339 Maine specimens whose dimensions are very close to those of the Turner Farm sample.

The function of these ubiquitous artifacts remains problematic. They do not closely resemble the probable arrow points from a late-sixteenth-century burial in Winthrop, Massachusetts (Willoughby 1924/1978:5). They do generally resemble ethnographic Naskapi gullet hooks (e.g., Speck 1935:120), artifacts from coastal British Columbia that are routinely identified as hook barbs, and generally similar forms from New York that are identified as fish gorges (e.g., Ritchie 1980:110, 233). Closer analogues were recovered from the Late Archaic Crawford Knoll site in southwest Ontario (Ellis et al. 1990;112). Maine bone points, however, are generally much more asymmetric than the similar artifacts from other areas. Moreover, the fish species closely associated with them at the Turner Farm and elsewhere in the area are flounder, whose mouths are far too small to be taken by hooks with barbs even as long as the shortest specimens. Finally, other Ceramic period coastal sites have produced extremely long bone points which could not have functioned in this way (Bourque 1992a:297).

The consistent pattern of damage to the blunt ends of bone points, along with the occasional observation of grooves apparently worn by lashing on their tapered ends, suggests that they were lashed to a shaft for use as thrusting weapons. Tyzzer (1936:266–271) replicated wear patterns he observed on archaeological specimens by using bone points as arrow tips. Similar wear patterns, however, may have been caused by their use as the central tips of leisters. Positive correlations between flounder bone and bone point frequencies at some Deer Isle sites support such an inference (Bourque 1992a:296). At the Turner Farm site, both flounder and bone points once again exhibit a comparable relative increase between B2GF and MCS. In the plow zone, flounder decreases in relative frequency even more sharply then bone points, due in part, no doubt, to differential breakage of the more delicate flounder bone.

Beaver Incisor Tools

This artifact class, which was common in Occupation 2 strata but absent during Occupation 3, made a strong comeback in Occupation 4 (N = 112; Plate 7.10, Table 7.4). The relative

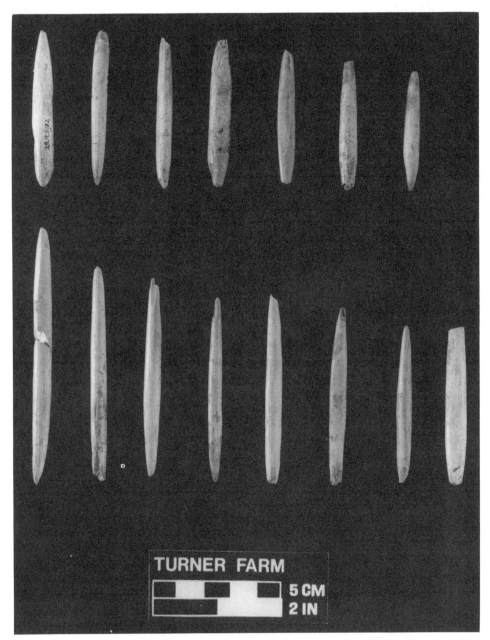

Plate 7.9.   Bone points from Occupation 4.

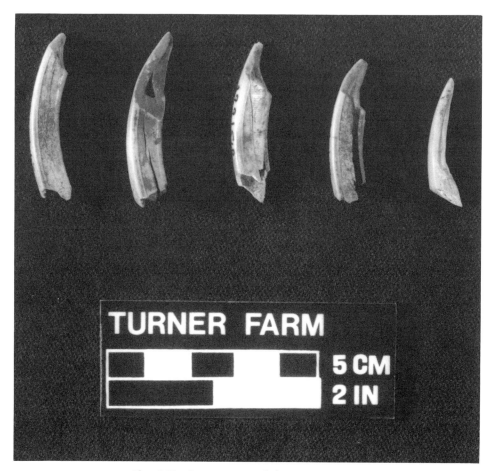

Plate 7.10.   Beaver incisor tools from Occupation 4.

frequency of incisor tools to kilogram of shell declines slightly above B2GF, in CCS and MCS. In the plow zone they exhibit a drastic decline, comparable to that of flounder bone.

Occupation 4 incisor tool forms sometimes resemble those from Occupation 2, but their variability increases significantly, which makes then difficult to characterize. Two separate angles describe the attitude of the modified surface to the natural features of the tooth; one refers to the angle at which this surface intersects the buccal enamel surface, and another describes the cross-section angle of the enamel and the worked surface. The shape of the modified surface may also be planar, concave, or complex. Finally, certain forms show a preference for mandibular incisors only.

Convex or planar modified surfaces are common in Archaic levels, while concave surfaces dominate the Ceramic period sample. Davis (1978:26) studied 49 Ceramic period incisor tools from the Minister's Island site in Passamaquoddy Bay, New Brunswick. All incisors in that sample were mandibular, and modified on their left sides. In the Turner Farm sample, by contrast, 14 of the 68 (21 percent) measurable specimens were maxillary,

Table 7.4. Modified Beaver Incisors

Kind	Occupation 2	Occupation 3	Occupation 4	Kind	Occupation 2	Occupation 3	Occupation 4
AD	3	0	5	AK	7	7	35
AE	14	2	5	BA	0	0	6
AF	2	2	1	BB	0	0	4
AG	1	0	0	BC	0	0	4
AH	2	0	4	CL	4	3	12
AI	4	1	13	MBTF	4	7	19
AJ	3	1	4				

Total Occupation 1   44
Total Occupation 2   22
Total Occupation 3   112

AD—Specimens in this type are polished at an angle betwe 10° and 27°, inclusive, at their distal end. AE—This type is similar to AD except that the polished angle varies from 28° to 45°, inclusively. AF—This type is also simlar to the above two, except that the polished angle varies from 46° to 60°, incluvisely. AG—Specimens in this type probably belong to one of the three listed above. They possess a polished angle at their distal ends, but are broken so that the angle could not be measured. Note: The majority (80 percent) of specimens belonging to these types are manufactured from lower incisors; lower right predominate. AH—This type is characterized by specimens which possess a gouge at one end. The gouge is highly polished. All of the specimens are manufactured from lower left incisors. AJ—Artifacts in this type are polished on their occlusal face only along their labial edge. They are all manufactured from upper incisors (upper left predominate) in this sample. AK—Specimens in this type are also worked on only one end. The modified surface is polished to a tapering point. The items are manufactured from both upper and lower incisors. BA—The lingual surface of specimens in this type are scraped flat. The ends are squared and polished. These incisors are short (2.10–2.90 cm long). BB—This type is similar to type BA except that specimens are medium length (2.91–3.70 cm long). BC—This is similar to the above two types except that specimens are long (3.71–4.50 cm long). Note: Specimens included in techno-shape types BA, BB, and BC are all manufactured from lower incisors. CL—Incisors in this type are split mesio-distally and ground along one or both edges. Two specimens appear to have modification at one end. They are both lower incisors. Al of the other examples are uppers (three are indeterminate as to left or right; the rest are upper left incisors; Will 1981:100–105, Plate 14).

and 8 of 96 (8 percent) were modified on their right sides. The presence of both left- and right-side modification may reflect the handedness of the user, and Davis's sample may, by chance, have been derived exclusively from right-handed people.

Use wear on these tools takes the form of striations perpendicular to the enamel working edge, extending back along the trailing (lingual) surface. No such wear was observed on the buccal enamel surface. This suggests that the buccal edge was forced against the work (probably wood) with the trailing surface held at the lowest possible angle. Presumably, this manner of use would compress the hard enamel cutting edge against the dentin, while heavy use in the opposite direction would cause the enamel to delaminate.

Taking all these variables into consideration, it is still possible to construe beaver incisor tools as analogous to ethnographically attested "crooked knives" (which are drawn toward the user), as suggested by Robins and Black (1988:139). However, they are perhaps more likely to have been used in a whittling motion, with the enamel forced away from the worker.

Another form ($N = 14$) virtually absent from Occupation 2 is cut or ground perpendicularly to the long axis at both ends. Davis (1978:26) illustrates one plausible method of hafting such tools transversely in an antler beam for use as routers to cut grooves, presumably in wood. Willoughby (1936;223) illustrated two such antler tines with associated beaver incisor tools from coastal Maine sites, and such routers have also been recovered from many other prehistoric contexts in the Northeast (see, e.g., Black 1992: Plates 5–10; Loring 1985:126–127; Ritchie 1980:232–233).

Occupation 4 strata yielded 15 of the 21 incisors that are split mesiodistally and ground along one or both edges. Similar examples described by Tyzzer (1943:357) may not actually be culturally modified, because desiccation of archaeological specimens often causes similar breakage. The Turner Farm specimens, however, show clear signs of grinding on the split surface.

Barbed Bone Spears and Harpoons

All barbed bone artifacts are probably made of cervid bone. All appear to be designed for the capture of small to medium-sized animals (N = 7; Plate 7.11). An ethnographic analogue is provided by an account by the English explorer James Rosier, who wrote that Indians from the Pemaquid area had arrows armed with "the long shanke of a Deere, made very sharpe with two fangs like a harping iron (harpoon)" (Quinn and Quinn 1983:303).

Barbed bone spears are relatively common in Ceramic period middens east of the Fox Islands around Deer Isle and Frenchman's Bay (Bourque 1992a:231, 275, 299). Therefore, the scarcity of such forms in contemporaneous components at the Turner Farm is surprising.

Perforated Teeth

These obviously ornamental artifacts include canines from one bear and five smaller mammals, and a moose incisor (Plate 7.12). Their rarity in the midden probably reflects careful curation.

Bone Hooks

Two nearly identical hooks were recovered from CCS and 1GF (Plate 7.13), and a third was found by an amateur. The three are so similar as to suggest a well-developed style not attested, so far, at other Ceramic period sites in the Northeast. They are much smaller than the Occupation 2 hooks and are similar in size to modern flounder hooks.

Other Bone Artifacts

Many mammal and bird diaphysis segments show casual modification as awls (Plate 7.14). A variety of other artifacts from Occupation 4 strata include:

- Two short bone diaphysis beadlike segments.
- Large-diameter modified fish (halibut?) vertebrae (beads?) (Plate 7.15).
- A barbed ivory shaft, probably a spear or leister tip (Plate 7.16; Willoughby 1935/1973:215i), in the Turner family collection. This artifact can be linked with Occupation 4 on the basis of a similar fragmentary specimen of bone recovered from 1GF. Examples of this highly standardized form are known from several sites on the central Maine coast. A complete specimen in the Burr/Waterman collection was recovered by scallop draggers in the early twentieth century. Another was brought up on an anchor in nearby Vinalhaven Harbor (Willoughby 1935/1973:215g). Additional fragments have been found in other Ceramic period coastal components (see, e.g., Bourque 1992a:299, Figure 117, 2nd from left).

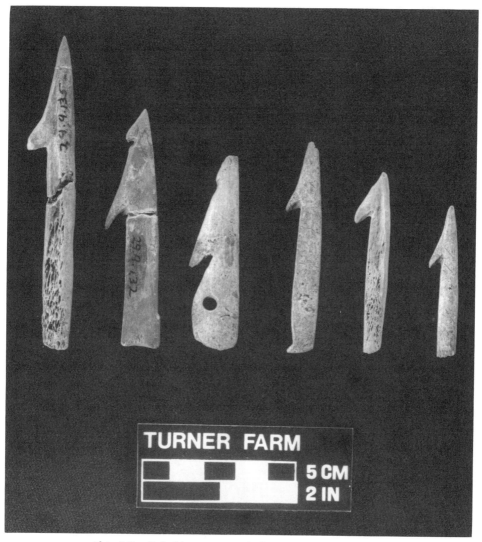

Plate 7.11. Barbed bone spears and a harpoon from Occupation 4.

CERAMIC STYLES AND DISTRIBUTION

Archaeologists throughout Maine and the Maritimes are currently working toward termi-nological consensus regarding ceramic styles and their temporal ranges. Although that consensus has not yet been achieved, I think that most would agree that the vast majority of the region's ceramics can be accommodated within a few broad stylistic groups. This discussion is organized according to my perception of those basic groups, and the data are presented according to a series of formalized hierarchical ware/type definitions defined in Bourque (1992a:90–102). Not mentioned are numerous additional motifs that occur in

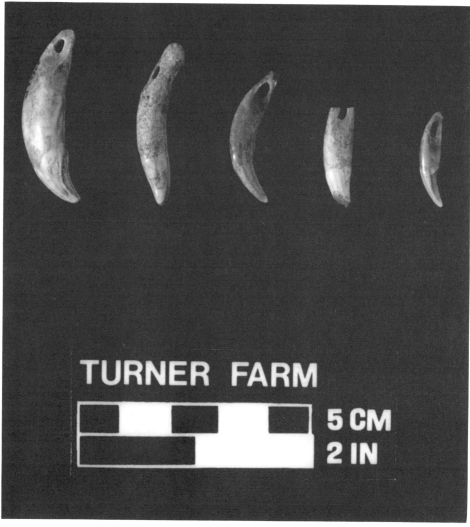

Plate 7.12.   Perforated teeth from Occupation 4.

combination with the predominant patterns, such as short incisions, punctuations, lip notches, and fingernail impressions. While encountered fairly commonly, their variety defies easy summary.

Vinette I

Adopting ceramic type names from an area as far removed from Maine as New York risks masking subregional differences. However, pottery conforming closely to Ritchie's (1980:194) Vinette I type is found so ubiquitously throughout the Northeast that its invocation here seems warranted.

Plate 7.13.   Bone hooks from Occupation 4.

Such pottery from Occupation 4 is friable, densely tempered with coarse grit, and generally shows evidence of coiled (or filleted) construction along breaks. It is cord maleated on both surfaces, often nearly vertically on the exterior and horizontally on the interior (Plate 7.17). No rim sherds were recovered.

Vinette I is clearly the earliest ceramic style in the Turner Farm sequence. It is common in 2GF, is most abundant in overlying CCS, and is present in small amounts, probably due to disturbance and compressed stratigraphy, in higher strata (Figures 7.6–7.10). Its horizontal distribution is in both strata clusters in three areas of the main excavation: the southwest, north central, and northeast (Figures 7.6, 7.7). This congruence suggests that it was used by the first occupants of the 2GF surface, was incorporated by them into shell refuse deposited on that surface, and had gone out of use by the time 1GF developed. Radiocarbon dates available for Occupation 4 are of little help in defining the temporal

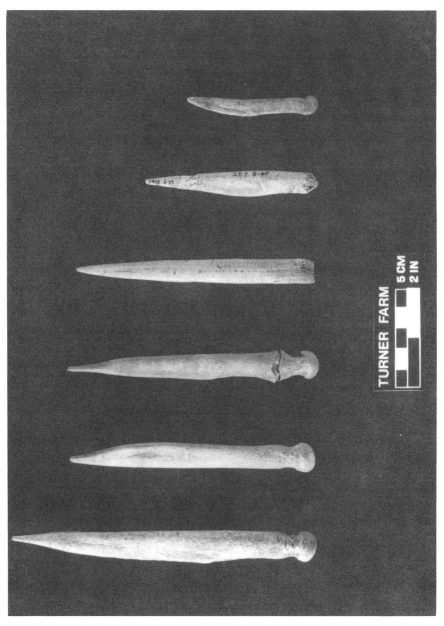

Plate 7.14. Bone awls from Occupation 4.

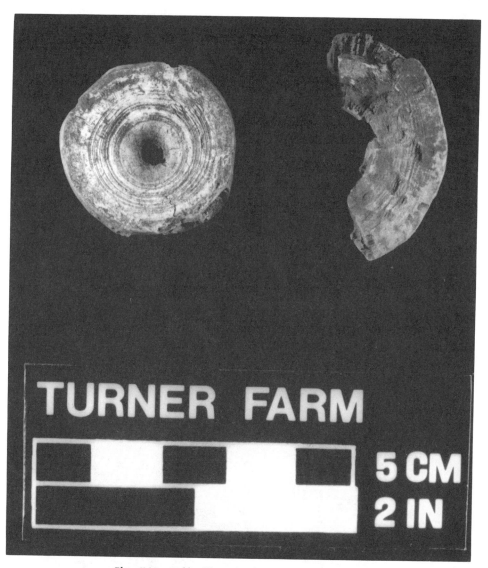

Plate 7.15.   Halibut(?) vertebra beads from Occupation 4.

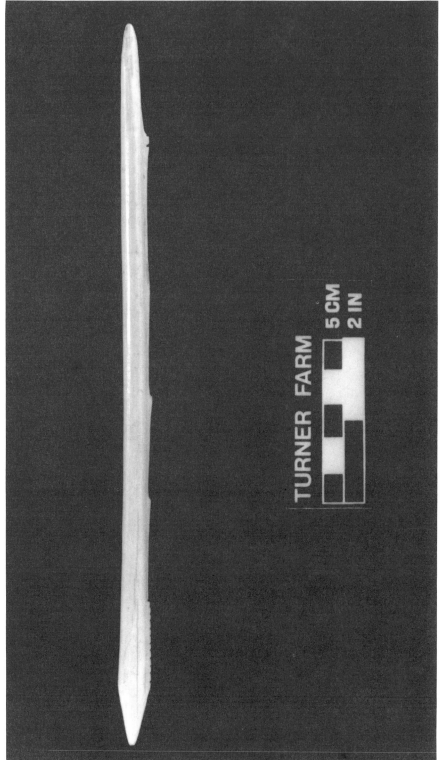

Plate 7.16. Barbed ivory leister tip from the Turner family collection.

Plate 7.17. Vinette I pottery from Occupation 4.

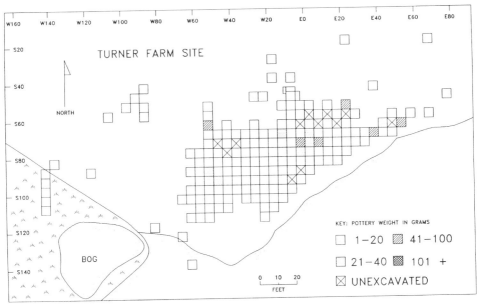

Figure 7.6.   Vinette I pottery from the Second Gravel Floor.

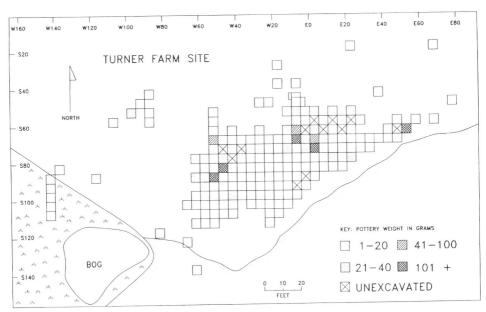

Figure 7.7.   Vinette I pottery from the Coarsely Crushed Shell.

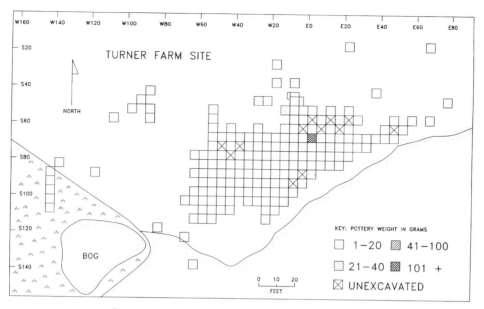

Figure 7.8. Vinnette I pottery from the First Gravel Floor.

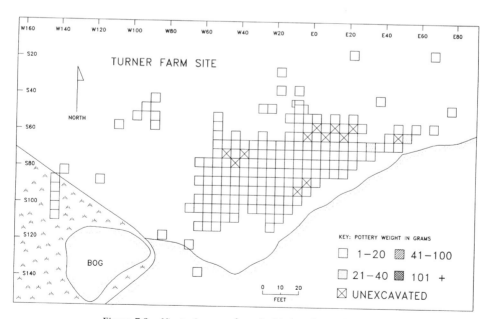

Figure 7.9. Vinette I pottery from the Moderately Crushed Shell.

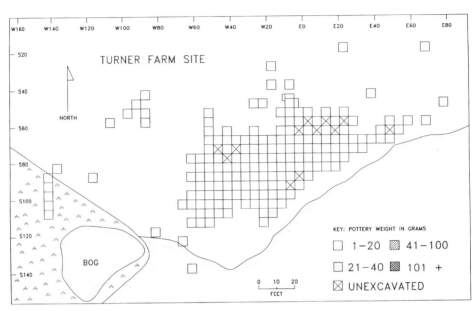

Figure 7.10. Vinette I pottery from the Plow Zone.

range there of Vinette I. In New Hampshire, it may date prior to 3000 B.P. (Howe 1988:82). Dates from other Maine sites, however, suggest a temporal range from about 2700 B.P. to perhaps as late as 2300 B.P. (Belcher 1989:179–181; Cox and Wilson 1991:32–33).

Pseudo-Scallop-Shell-Stamped

Originally, I (Bourque 1992a:93–94) included pottery with pseudo-scallop-shell-stamped decoration in my definition of Wiesenthal Ware, which included other decorative motifs as well. The criteria listed there apply well to the Turner Farm pseudo-scallop-shell-stamped sample: thin (about 9–12 mm), generally well-knit ware with variably coarse grit temper; straight rim profiles with simple rounded to pointed lips, sometimes flared in or out; rim interiors undecorated (Plate 7.18). Absent from the Turner Farm sample are punctate or incised decoration.

Data from other sites (Peterson and Sanger 1991:131–137) indicate that pottery fitting this general description succeeded Vinette I in northern New England. However, data from the Maritimes suggest that there it may have been contemporaneous with or even earlier than Vinette I (Allen 1981). The Turner Farm data support a sequential interpretation (Figures 7.11–7.15). Like Vinette I, pseudo-scallop-shell-stamped ceramics were found on 2GF, with traces below 2GF in B2GF, while some sherds appear to have been displaced upward as far as the plow zone (Figures 7.11–7.15).

An anomalous concentration was encountered in MCS in section W0S85. Evidence of a recent disturbance immediately to the east of this cluster suggests that the pottery may actually have been brought up in back dirt during the Bateses' excavation of the burials, described in Chapter 2.

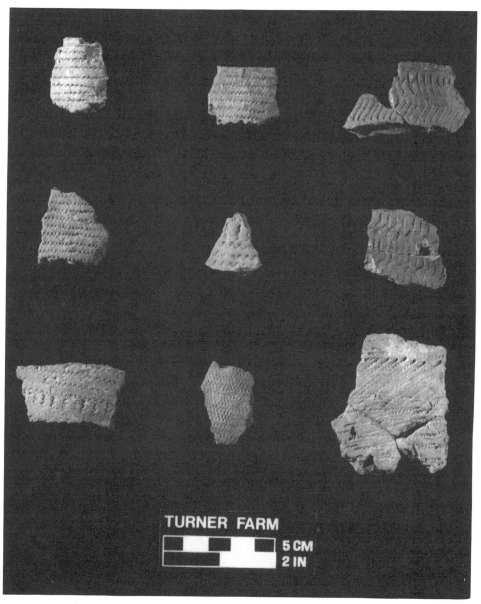

Plate 7.18.   Pseudo-scallop-shell-stamped pottery from Occupation 4.

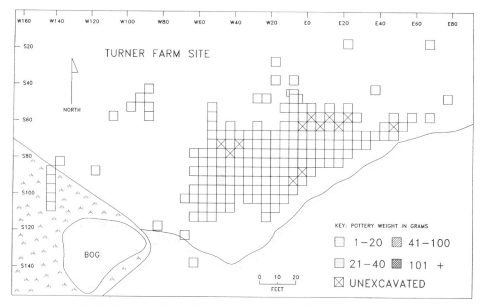

Figure 7.11. Pseudo-scallop-shell-stamped pottery from below the Second Gravel Floor.

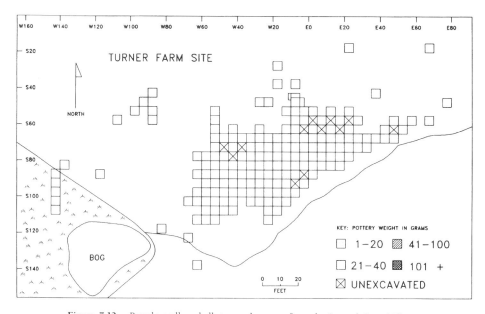

Figure 7.12. Pseudo-scallop-shell-stamped pottery from the Second Gravel Floor.

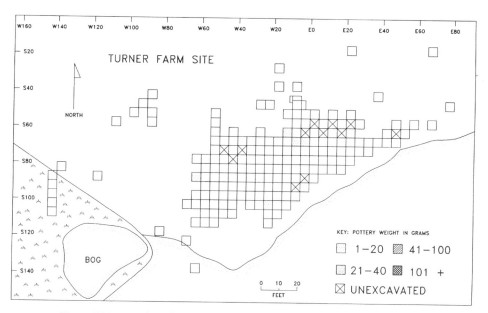

Figure 7.13. Pseudo-scallop-shell-stamped pottery from the Coarsely Crushed Shell.

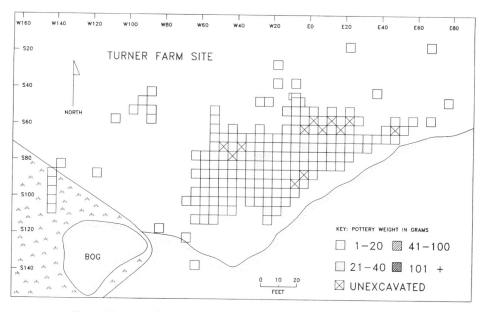

Figure 7.14. Pseudo-scallop-shell-stamped pottery from the First Gravel Floor.

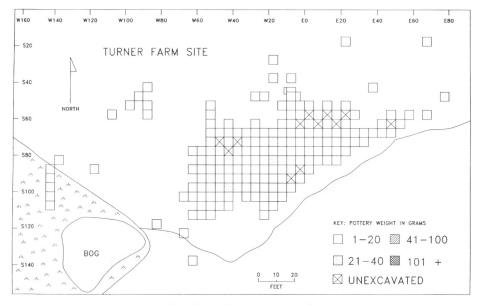

Figure 7.15. Pseudo-scallop-shell-stamped pottery from the Plow Zone.

Dentate-Rocker-Stamped

Most sherds bearing dentate-rocker-stamped decoration conform to a subset of the attributes I (Bourque 1992a:94–97) used to define Eaton Ware. It is thicker than pseudo-scallop-shell-stamped pottery (10–20 mm), generally more coarsely tempered and less well knit (Plates 7.19, 7.20). Occasionally, coil breaks were observed, although breakage usually occurred by lamellar failure and spalling, suggesting extensive paddle-and-anvil thinning. Absent, or rare, in the Turner Farm sample are interior rim decoration, extreme lip eversion, collaring, castellation, and unrockered (linear) stamping.

Dentate-rocker-stamped pottery was found in large quantities in 2GF and CCS above it. It is also very abundant in 1GF. None was encountered in the NGF, but moderate amounts were found in MCS and the plow zone. Its horizontal distribution in 2GF and CCS resembles that of Vinette I. Since data from other components indicate that the two styles are not contemporaneous, this congruence suggests that separate occupations occurred in the same areas of 2GF, resulting in overlapping areas of trash deposition. In 1GF, its distribution is quite different from that in 2GF and CCS, clustering near the center of the main excavation. Its distribution in MCS and the plow zone reflects that of 1GF, suggesting upward mixture. In sum, dentate-rocker-stamped pottery was used by later occupants of 2GF. It clearly remained in use when 1GF was occupied, and was again incorporated into refuse left on that surface.

A small sample of thin dentate-stamped pottery, resembling pseudo-scallop-shell-stamped pottery in its paste characteristics and vessel forms, was sorted separately from thicker specimens in anticipation that they might be earlier, as was apparently the case on

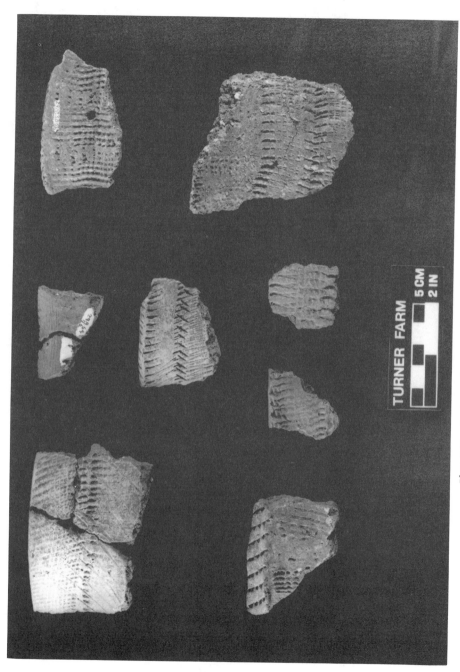

Plate 7.19.   Dentate-rocker-stamped pottery from Occupation 4.

Plate 7.20. Dentate-rocker-stamped pottery from Occupation 4.

Deer Isle (Bourque 1992a:93–97; Plate 7.21). This hypothesis could not be confirmed on the basis of the Turner Farm sample.

Cord-Wrapped-Stick-Impressed

Cord-wrapped-stick-impressed pottery, as here defined, constitutes a major subset of Grindle Ware (Bourque 1992a:97–98). Cord-wrapped-stick-impressed pottery appears always to be coil or fillet constructed and rarely exhibits the kind of lamellar disintegration seen in dentate-rocker-stamped sherds (Plate 7.22). Generally, cord-wrapped-stick-impressed sherds have darker surfaces than dentate-rocker-stamped pottery, suggesting either a higher organic content in the clay or reduced contact with oxygen in firing.

Surface treatment is characterized by impressions of cordage strands, probably wrapped around a stick or paddle edge. Rim interiors are never so decorated. While some

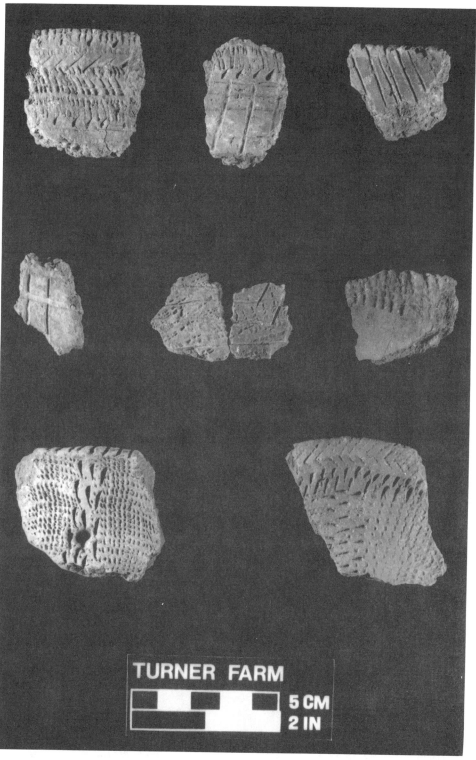

Plate 7.21. Thin dentate-stamped pottery from Occupation 4.

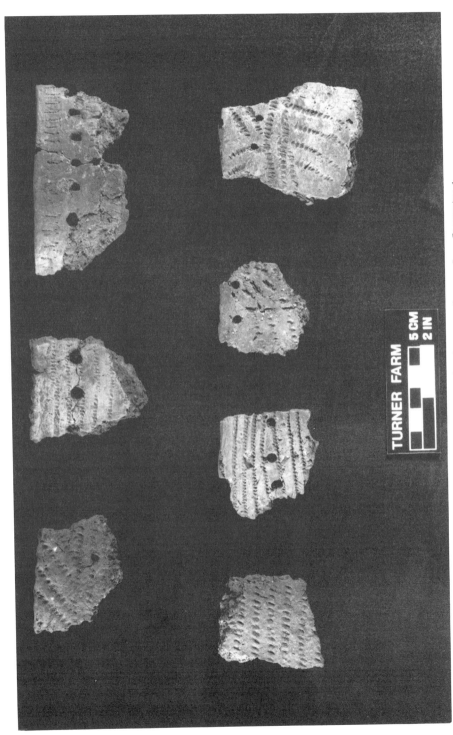

Plate 7.22.   Rim sherds of cord-wrapped-stick-impressed pottery from Occupation 4.

such impressions superficially resemble dentate stamping, close examination usually reveals the rounding of the cordage ply impressions, which contrasts with the rectilinear margins of dentate-rocker-stamped impressions. Most rim forms are simple, though occasional collaring is evident (e.g., Plate 7.23).

Relatively small numbers of cord-wrapped-stick-impressed sherds were encountered in 1GF. The NGF, despite its limited extent, produced more sherds. However, the great majority came from MCS and the plow zone. Though neither dentate-rocker-stamped nor cord-wrapped-stick-impressed sherds were tightly clustered on 1GF, their distributions seem dissimilar. Their distributions in MCS are similar, but both also resemble those of other styles as well, probably because of repeated occupation of the same areas.

The temporal relationship between cord-wrapped-stick-impressed and dentate-rocker-stamped pottery in 1GF is ambiguous. Possibly the styles were in part contemporaneous. Indeed, a few sherds from other sites in the area bear both dentate stamping and cord impressions. Generally, however, vessel construction characteristics, even those found in close proximity, are different. In sum, the available data from the Turner Farm site, and other sites in the Penobscot Bay area, strongly suggest separate time spans for these two styles, and that two episodes of occupation and dumping occurred in the same area of 1GF. If this interpretation is correct, both 1GF and MCS were accumulating and being modified over a long time span. The few radiocarbon dates currently available are inadequate to resolve this issue.

A small sample of vessels with structural characteristics and stratigraphic distributions similar to that of cord-wrapped-stick-impressed pottery are decorated with a variety of simple stamps and punctations (Plate 7.24). The impressions are often made by a cord-wrapped stick.

Cord-Maleated

This style was not recognized in Bourque 1992a. However, in recent years it has been encountered at late prehistoric, and possibly early postcontact, Maine sites (Petersen and Sanger 1991:151–156). At the Turner Farm site, it is characterized by relatively sparsely shell-tempered sherds that are generally much thinner (6–11 mm) than those with cord-wrapped-stick-impressed decoration (Plate 7.25). Cord impressions occur only on vessel exteriors and rim forms are simple. The small sample recovered from the Turner Farm comes primarily from the NGF and the plow zone above it.

Collared-Incised

Like cord-maleated pottery, this style was not recognized in Bourque 1992a. Subsequently, however, it has been noted at numerous Maine sites (Petersen and Sanger 1991: 156–160). It closely resembles pottery from late prehistoric to early postcontact contexts from a wide range of the Northwest Atlantic coastal settings—from Massachusetts Bay to Red Bay, Labrador (see, e.g., Clermont et al. 1983:66–116; Pendergast and Trigger 1972; Petersen 1990; Tuck 1985:246–247; Willoughby 1924/1978:7–8). Its very thin walls may be cord maleated, resembling thin cord-maleated pottery. Otherwise, it is distinctly different from all earlier pottery of the region in that it has a collared rim, visible in profile on both the interior and exterior, and bodies that are globular, lacking the straight sides and

Plate 7.23. Cord-wrapped-stick-impressed vessel from Occupation 4.

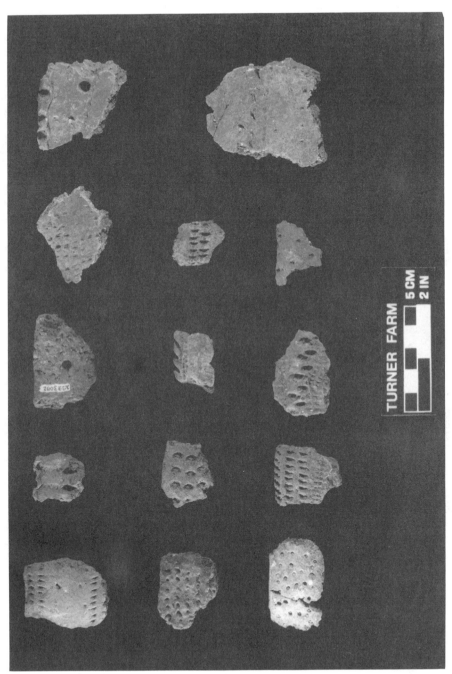

Plate 7.24.　Stamped and punctated pottery from Occupation 4.

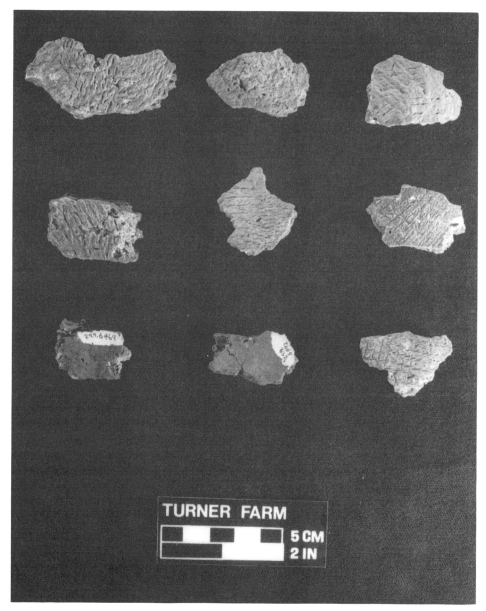

Plate 7.25. Thin, shell-tempered, cord-maleated sherds from Occupation 4.

pronounced conoidal base common in earlier forms. The collars of the two Turner Farm vessels bear typical triangular fields defined by incised lines. The body of the larger vessel (Plate 7.26) is cord maleated, while that of the smaller vessel is smooth.

The two collared-incised vessels from the Turner Farm were found within 5 ft of each other high in the stratigraphic sequence, but from sections peripheral to the main excavation that could not be accurately included to our stratigraphic analysis.

Plate 7.26.   In situ fragments of a collared-incised vessel from Occupation 4.

The great majority, and most elaborate examples, of collared-incised pottery have been recovered at sites on the north shore of the St. Lawrence, an area occupied by Iroquoian speakers between A.D. 1300 and A.D. 1600 (Pendergast and Trigger 1972:285–286). It has therefore often been casually identified as "St. Lawrence Iroquoian" pottery and Petersen (1990:35–36) has gone so far as to suggest that vessels of this type found in northern New England as far south as the Maine coast are "actual Iroquois ceramics." Support for obverse associations of the more traditional cylindrical-conoidal base form with Algonquian speakers might be derived from the fact that such vessels are observed in late sixteenth-century Algonquian-speaking contexts (see, e.g., Hulton 1984:74, Plate 44). However, the contemporaneity of the two forms in New England remains to be demonstrated, and it is possible that collared-incised pottery completely postdates the cylindrical-conoidal base style there. Moreover, St. Lawrence Iroquoian-like ceramics have been recovered from numerous southern New England contexts where Iroquoian occupation, or even trade, seem implausible (see, e.g., Willoughby 1973:195). Thus, while the presence of some Iroquoian imports to Maine cannot be ruled out at present, it appears more likely that collared-incised pottery represents a late ceramic horizon style manufactured throughout much of New England as well as in the St. Lawrence Valley.

Plain

Sherds bearing no surficial decoration were encountered in all ceramic-bearing strata. In general, they seem to be in proportion to the amount of pottery found in each level, except in the plow zone, where they seem overrepresented. It is tempting to see in this distribution the result of limited decoration of later pottery styles, but overall vessel design and decorative layout in this region is still very little understood.

FAUNAL REMAINS

The stratigraphic distribution of pottery styles described above clearly indicates that shell-free floors were occupied more than once and that the refuse from these multiple occupations is mingled in the overlying shell lenses. Therefore, the faunal samples from these units do not represent discrete sets of faunal remains resulting from single components. Although this handicaps our efforts to characterize specific changes in faunal exploitation through time, significant diachronic trends remain apparent (Figures 7.16–7.18). The sections that follow characterize the faunal remains by major group and describe trends in the faunal sample.

Cervids

Deer remained fairly common throughout Occupation 4. No significant changes in the processing of this species were noted, with the exception of a slight rise in the recovery rate of metapodial diaphysis fragments over Archaic levels. During Occupations 2 and 3, the lower leg was often separated by breaking the metapodial. The Occupation 4 sample, on the other hand, suggests that these meatless bones were conserved for later extraction of their marrow. Although not a strongly marked trend, it is in accord with numerous other subtle

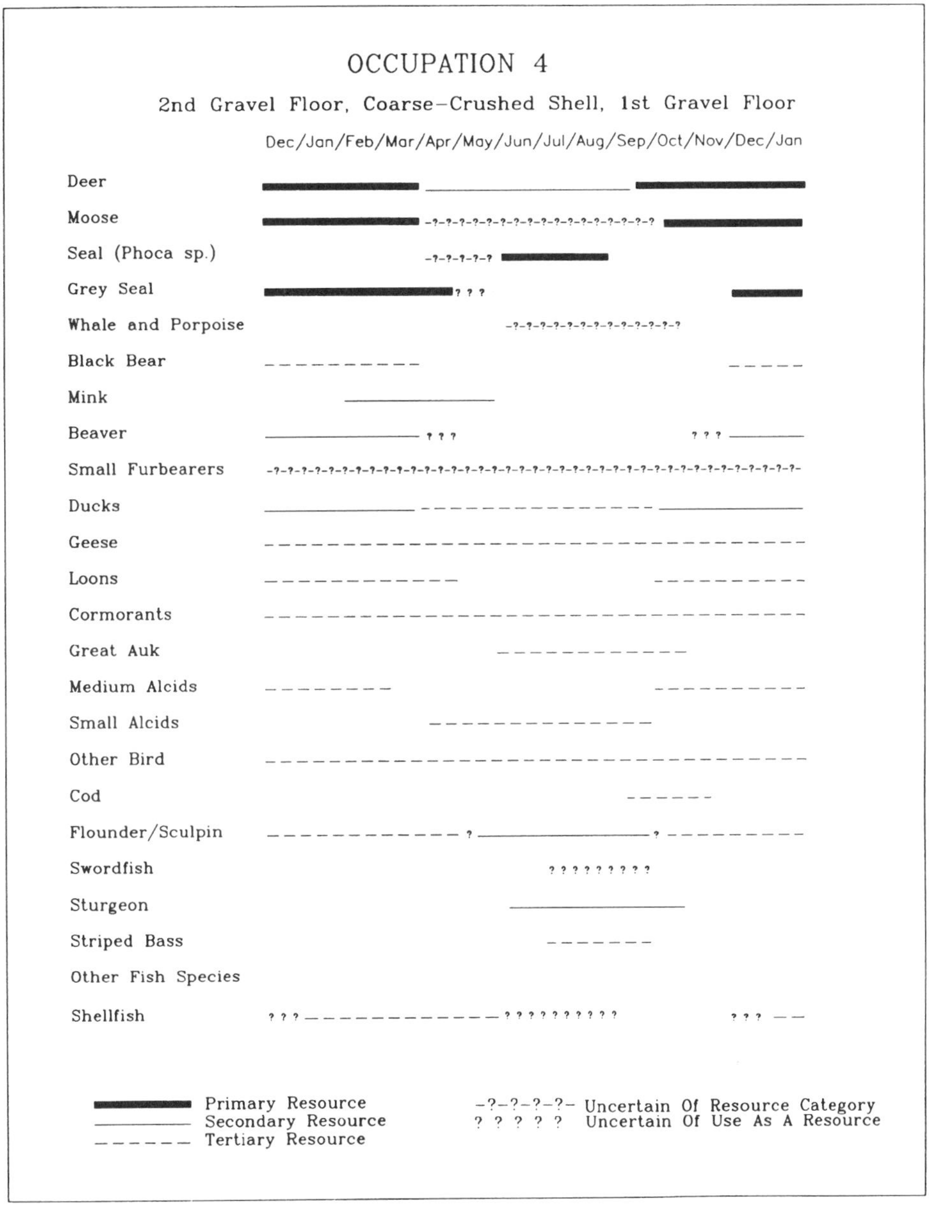

Figure 7.16. Faunal seasonality from Occupation 4: Second Gravel Floor, Coarsely Crushed Shell, First Gravel Floor (Spiess and Lewis 1993).

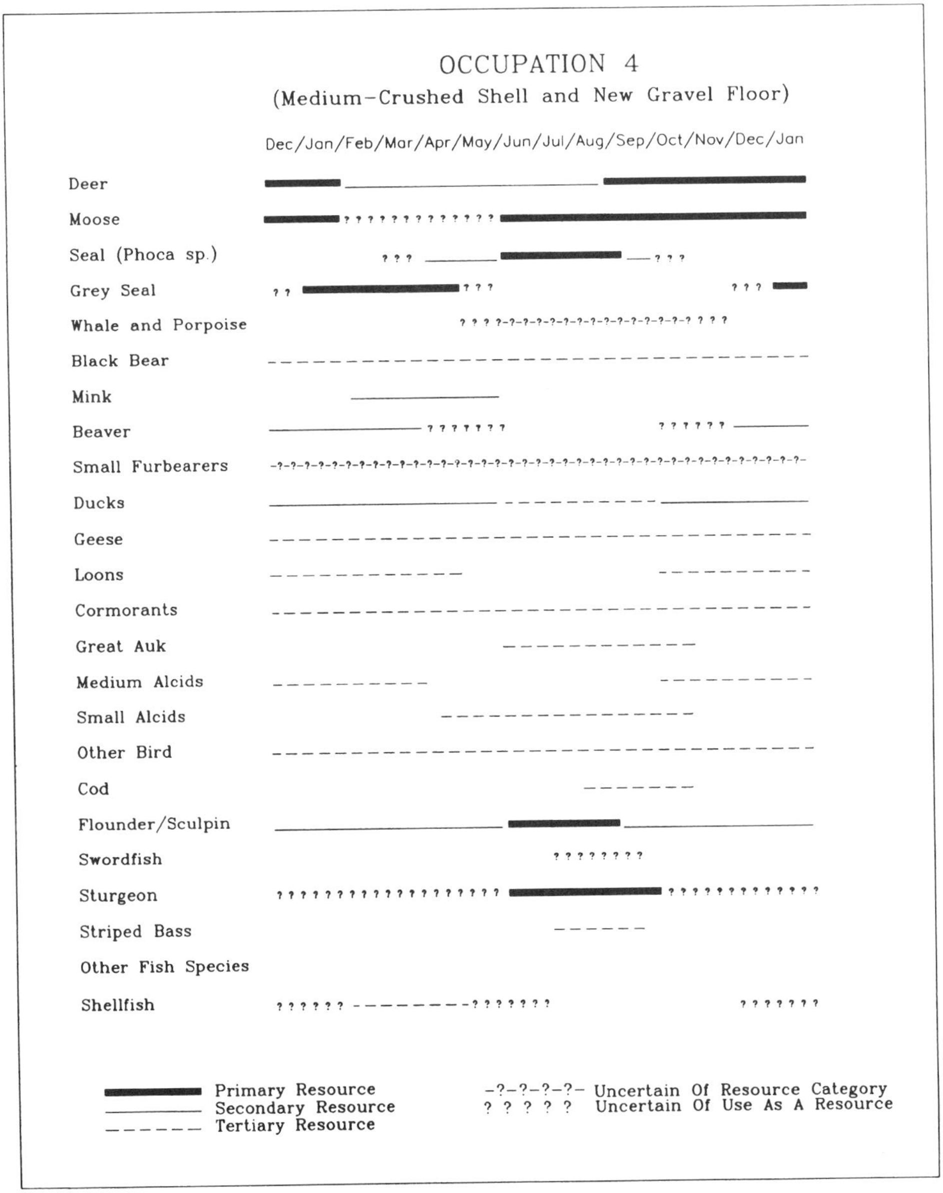

Figure 7.17. Faunal seasonality from Occupation 4: Moderately Crushed Shell, New Gravel Floor (Spiess and Lewis 1993).

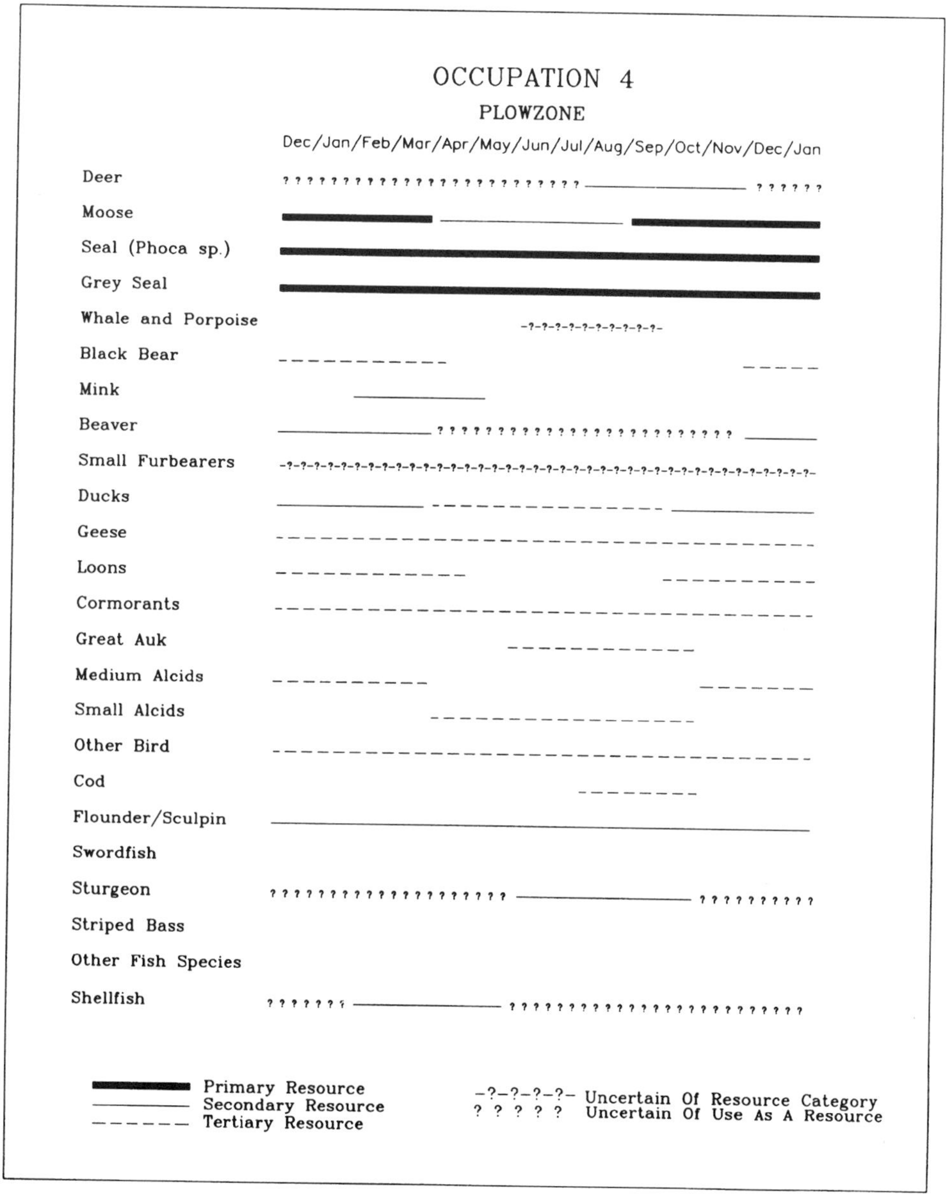

Figure 7.18. Faunal seasonality from Occupation 4: Plow Zone (Spiess and Lewis 1993).

indicators that the exploitation of faunal resources available in the site's catchment area intensified throughout the Ceramic period.

Seasonality of the deer hunt remained similar to that of Occupation 3. Data are available from eight sectioned teeth, 18 tooth eruption evaluations, and antler shedding from 56 male parietals. They indicate that deer were taken nearly year round, mainly during late fall and winter; probably few were taken during the warmest months.

Moose bone increased markedly in relative importance to deer, from about 1 percent in Occupations 2 and 3 to approximately 6 percent thereafter. This amounts to a 36 percent increase in reliance upon moose meat for Occupation 4 as a whole, but it is a trend that approaches an order of magnitude by late Occupation 4. Such a dramatic shift must reflect a significant increase in moose abundance in the area due, perhaps, to climatic cooling (Diaz et al. 1989;53–55; Zielinski et al. 1994). No data on the seasonality of the moose hunt are available.

Bear

Bear bone frequencies relative to deer show a modest increase in some Occupation 4 strata. Though they are not demonstrably a major contributor to the diet of any Turner Farm site occupants, their frequency in later strata is sufficient to demonstrate the existence of a bear population on the Fox Islands. Seasonality data from five sectioned teeth indicate a range of kills between late fall and spring, one probably after the bear emerged from winter dormancy.

Beaver

As in Occupation 2 strata, the evaluation of beaver remains from Occupation 4 is best attempted by omitting incisors because of their probable curation as tools. Ceramic levels show an average beaver-to-deer bone count ratio of about 13 percent, with a rise to 15 percent in the plow zone. These numbers represent an increase of about 40 percent and 60 percent, respectively, over Archaic levels, continuing a trend begun by a large increase in beaver between Occupations 2 and 3.

Seasonal data are scarce for beaver, primarily because dental cementum annuli do not form on molars until the root closes at two-and-a-half to three years of age (van Nostrand and Stephansen 1964:432). Two specimens with readable annuli sequences indicated death between late fall and winter, according well with their best pelt condition and greatest weight. Despite the upward trend in beaver predation, demographic data from Occupation 4 indicate no change from earlier times. Rather, all ages and both sexes were captured indiscriminately. Possibly this pattern reflects the historically recorded practice of killing entire lodge populations (Spiess and Lewis 1993).

Beaver present interpretive problems aside from incisor curation. Ethnographic data clearly indicate that this animal was used for both food and fur. All strata produced evidence for the breakage of forelimb bones in accord with widespread ethnographic beaver skinning practices, and we can assume that the meat would not have been wasted. However, given the increased importance in Occupation 4 of less edible fur bearers, discussed below, an increasing importance of fur may be what drove much of the increase in beaver capture rates. In this regard, it may be significant that eyed bone needles, which have been found in Archaic contexts in the Northeast, have been interpreted as indicators of tailored leather clothing. Such needles are not part of the Ceramic period bone tool inventory in this region, suggesting that an important shift to historically documented untailored fur garments may have occurred by Occupation 4 times.

Furthermore, the extent of beaver habitat on or near the Fox Islands is uncertain. No beaver live there today, but limited suitable habitat still exists around the Islands' freshwater ponds. Presumably, lower sea levels mean marginally more such habitat in the past. However, if we consider habitat versus capture rate trends since Occupation 2, clearly one is the inverse of the other. Therefore, the Fox Islands probably could not have produced the numbers of beaver in evidence during Occupation 4, and beaver hunting expeditions to the mainland are therefore likely to have occurred. Finally, it is possible that the relative increase in beaver in the uppermost strata indicates that European-induced demand for beaver pelts reached Penobscot Bay sometime during the late sixteenth century (Bourque and Whitehead 1985). Simple inferences regarding beaver hunting, however, are complicated by early historic accounts that beaver bones were ritually disposed of as a means of assuring their continuing abundance (LeClercq 1910:226).

Seal

Seals were an increasingly important resource during the Ceramic period. Gray and harbor seals were identified in a ratio of about 1 to 1.5, about the same as suggested by the sparse phocid samples from Occupations 2 and 3.

Seasonality data are available from six sectioned gray (plus three from the plow zone) and five (plus three from the plow zone) harbor seal teeth. These sections suggest that most gray seals were taken between January and March, during their pupping and molting seasons. Harbor seals also were generally taken during their molting season, which in the Northwest Atlantic falls between April and August. Thus, seals were apparently taken during their respective seasons of greatest vulnerability, in accordance with regional historical documentation (see, e.g., Thwaites 1896–1901, vol. 3:79).

The major change in seal hunting over Archaic patterns is in intensity. Seal bone frequencies undergo a two- to threefold increase in the earlier Ceramic period strata and an approximate doubling again in the MCS and plow zone levels. Its abundance in the plow zone probably is damped somewhat by the incorporation into it of older midden deposits that would have depressed the relative frequency of seal bone. Also worth mentioning is the fact that two harbor seal teeth from the plow zone suggest seasons of death outside the molting seasons, indicating a possible shift in or expansion of the seal hunting season. Moreover, the presence of immature seals, which in the north are ethnographically most often taken in open water by harpoon, also suggests that seal hunting had attained the importance of an economically primary activity. This evidence for increasing Ceramic period seal exploitation probably reflects Late Holocene climatic cooling and the historically documented importance of seal oil in this region (see, e.g., Thwaites, 1896–1909, vol. 3:79–83).

Other Marine Mammals

Five harbor porpoise (*Phocoena*) vertebrae probably represent two individuals. Because harbor porpoise probably had minimal value as beached carcasses and because they approach within harpoon distance of small boats, these may well represent live kills.

Fragments of a mandible and a rib from a large cetacean were recovered from separate

Occupation 4 contexts. Both show signs of cutting at their ends. Their size suggests that both came from right (*Eubalaena*) or humpback (*Megaptera*) whales. It remains unclear whether these bones represent live kills or scavenged carcasses. Whale bone has been recovered from other Maine shell heaps, though not commonly. James Rosier (Quinn and Quinn 1983:303–304) provided a detailed, if not an eye witness, account of Maine Indians hunting large whales from canoes, while Little and Andrews (1982) have reported the extensive use of beached whales on Nantucket Island.

Birds

The relative frequency of bird bones from the Occupation 4 midden is approximately double that of Occupation 3 and nearly four times that of Occupation 2. Frequencies fluctuate between adjacent strata, but no long-term trend is apparent. A significant drop in bird bone frequency in the plow zone is probably the result of differential bone destruction by plowing. Seasonality data are not abundant for the sample and no changes from Archaic seasonal patterns are evident. Modern data on bird availability suggest that they continued to be available as a secondary food resource year round. Furthermore, their use in other contexts—for example, for feathers—is likely.

Fish

Cod apparently continued to decline in importance throughout the site's history, from a peak in Occupation 2 to a nadir of 3.3 percent relative to deer bone in the plow zone. However, the reverse is true of flatfish species, which jump from a relative frequency of 9.1 percent compared to deer bone counts in Occupation 3 to an average of 66 percent in Occupation 4. The largest rise is in winter flounder (*Pseudopleuronectes americanus*), followed by dab (*Hippoglossoides plattessoides*) and yellowtail (*Limanda ferruginea*). For the first time, halibut (*Hippoglossus hippoglossus*) are also present.

Stripped bass, present only in trace amounts in Archaic strata (2 bones), rise slightly in importance (88 bones) in Occupation 4. The weight of sturgeon scutes jumps from about 32 g in Occupation 3 to 353 g in Ceramic period levels. Other species present in trace amounts include pollack, haddock, tomcod, spiny dogfish, and eel. Wolf fish (*Anarhichas lupus*), herring (*Culpea harengus*), and white shark (*Carcharodon carcharias*, one tooth) also appear for the first time in the sequence.

Except for cod, our efforts to determine fishing seasonality from hard tissue have been unsuccessful to date, in part because comparatively few specimens of known season of death have been collected. For the present we must rely upon modern behavioral analogues. Reference to these analogues suggest a general trend away from deep-water fishing toward shallow-water techniques during Occupation 4. Flatfish would have been available year round, while sturgeon would have been most available during the summer. A final caveat regarding marine food sources is that crustaceans were probably available in significant amounts during the Ceramic period, as they probably were earlier.

Shellfish

Soft-shell clam remained the predominant species throughout the Ceramic period sequence, comprising at least 99.5 percent of the sample for all strata. Other species represented include blue mussel, hen clam (*Spisula solidissima*), northern moon shell (*Lunatia heros*), sea urchin, and waved whelk (*Baccinum undatum*). The relative decline of shell weight versus large mammal live weight that began in Occupation 3 continues into Occupation 4. An anomalously high shell figure from the plow zone is attributed to the selective destruction of identifiable bone by plowing. Seasonality data from 23 sectioned chondrophores indicated no change from earlier strata; most harvesting took place between late February and early April.

SUMMARY BY STRATUM

As noted above, both the stratigraphy and horizontal patterning of Occupation 4 strata differ from those of earlier occupations. The general impression is of shorter but more frequent episodes of occupation. The expansion of seal and deer hunting over longer portions of the year, increasing hunting pressure on the deer herd, and the relative rise in the importance of seals all suggest intensification of mammal exploitation. The combination of these two trends implies that, while community size may have remained stable or increased somewhat, the available resources within the catchment area of a given base camp may have been more quickly exhausted during Occupation 4 than in earlier times. This, in turn, suggests that the number of such communities may have increased (because of a decrease in catchment area)—an observation that would seem obvious from the relatively much larger number of Ceramic period sites in the region were it not so difficult to account for the differential destruction of older coastal sites.

Below the Second Gravel Floor

The early post-Archaic period, represented by B2GF, is among the least understood throughout the Northeast, particularly in northern New England and the Maritime Provinces. Data from B2GF shed some new light on the post-Susquehanna period. Its technology seems clearly not to be derived from that of the Susquehanna tradition. Instead, it is similar to that found in later Occupation 4 levels, including lobate- and narrow-stemmed bifaces, scrapers, beaver incisor knives, and Vinette I pottery. Moreover, lithic use resembles later, rather than earlier, patterns at the site. Its faunal sample is small, but the relative importance of flounder seen in later levels is already apparent. In sum, perhaps as early as 3300 B.P., the Turner Farm site was resettled by people whose technology and subsistence patterns had shifted distinctly away from those apparent in Occupation 3 and toward the maritime-oriented patterns apparent in later times.

Second Gravel Floor and Coarsely Crushed Shell

The 2GF saw the full establishment of the Ceramic period artifact suite and faunal exploitation pattern. Despite the narrow temporal range suggested by the two radiocarbon dates for the stratum, the diversity of ceramic styles and the large number of features originating in it suggest extensive domestic activity over a considerable period. Most Vinette I pottery was recovered from this surface, but it also accumulated appreciable quantities of later pseudo-scallop-shell-stamped pottery and dentate-stamped. Lithics included numerous lobate- and narrow-stemmed points.

Shell lenses grouped under the label of CCS appear to represent trash accumulation on the 2GF. Both artifact and faunal remains are similar and horizontal patterns are roughly congruent as well.

First Gravel Floor and Moderately Crushed Shell

The 1GF appears to have been a long-exposed surface upon which MCS refuse accumulated. Artifact styles common in 2GF and CCS were encountered there, either because they remained in use or because of upward mixture. However, later styles, including cord-wrapped-stick-impressed pottery and side-notched, corner-notched, and even some triangular points also occurred, and in the MCS the earlier lobate- and narrow-stemmed point styles declined, perhaps to be replaced by side-notched forms.

New Gravel Floor

Our model for the midden deposition at the site suggests that the NGF probably developed over an area where shell refuse covered 1GF and, therefore, is probably actually contemporaneous with 1GF during its later stages. This interpretation is supported by the preponderance there of cord-wrapped-stick-impressed pottery.

Plow Zone

The plow zone includes materials from all occupations. However, it clearly reflects important changes during the terminal prehistoric and early historic periods. Faunal samples continue to reflect trends that first appeared in earlier Ceramic period strata: cod decline in frequency while flatfish increase; moose and, particularly, seal also increase in relative frequency. The general impression of increasingly intense faunal exploitation also persists. While this may reflect either regional population expansion or an increasing reliance throughout the region on marine resources, the two explanations are not mutually exclusive.

Both beaver incisor and bone point frequencies exhibit sharp drops. The decrease in incisor tools in the plow zone is particularly interesting in view of the increase in other beaver remains. This change, the presence of collared-incised ceramics, and three smelted sheet copper beads from the site's upper levels all point to the possible emergence of the historic beaver trade in the Penobscot Bay area before the site was abandoned for the last time (Bourque and Whitehead 1985).

Chapter 8

Implications of the Turner Farm Site for Eastern North American Prehistory

The previous chapters focused on relationships between Turner Farm and other sites in Maine and adjacent areas. Useful as these data have been for regional culture history, their relevance over a much broader range has become ever more apparent in recent years. This chapter, therefore, shifts focus from provincial issues to certain aspects of prehistory throughout much of eastern North America during the past 5,000 years (Figure 8.1; Table 8.1).

THE LATE ARCHAIC

In my first effort to untangle the confusion about the larger cultural provenience of the Red Paint people, I (Bourque 1992a:26–39, 119–122) found it useful to include them in a concept I named the Moorehead phase, using Willey and Phillips's concept of phase (see Chapter 1). Radiocarbon dates then available suggested that the Moorehead phase dated between about 4500 and 3800 B.P. A few habitation sites, including shell middens, were identified as having Moorehead phase components, and evidence for swordfish hunting was noted from some of these sites. I saw the Moorehead phase as characterized by discrete cemeteries of red ocher-filled graves—often richly furnished—a sophisticated heavy wood-working technology, ground slate bayonets, plummets, and nonutilitarian symbolic arti-facts. Because all bear more or less specific resemblance to assemblages from the north (especially the Port au Choix cemetery in northern Newfoundland) and, to a lesser extent, the west in assemblages attributed to the Laurentian tradition (Kennedy 1967; Tuck 1970), I was unsure about the ancestry of the Moorehead phase and suggested only that it origi-nated in "some widely established cultural tradition of the Canadian Maritimes and North-ern New England" (Bourque 1992a:43).

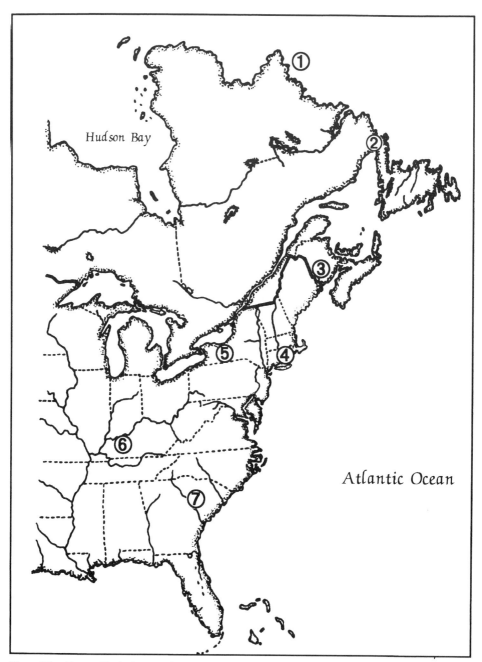

Figure 8.1.   Eastern North America showing important sites discussed in the text. 1, Ramah Bay; 2, Port au Choix; 3, Cow Point; 4, Griffin site; 5, Frontenac Island; 6, Indian Knoll; 7, Stallings Island.

Table 8.1. Comparison of Turner Farm Dates
and Regional Cultural Chronology

Occupation[a]	Turner Farm dates	Cultural affiliation	Temporal range[b]
Occ 1	c. 5000–4700 B.P.	Small Stemmed Point	c. 5000–4500 B.P.
Occ 2	c. 4400–4200 B.P.	Moorehead phase	c. 4500–3800 B.P.
Occ 3	c. 3800–3600 B.P.	Susquehanna tradition	c. 3800–3500 B.P.
Occ 4	c. 2700–350 B.P.	Ceramic period	c. 3000–350 B.P.
Historic (aboriginal)	c. 1600?	Contact	c. 1580–1759
Historic (European)	c. 1760 to present	Colonial to Recent	c. 1630–present

[a]Occupation dates: Occupations 1–4 based on radiocarbon dating. Historic based on artifact style.
[b]Temporal ranges: Occupations 1–4 based on dates from multiple related sites. Contact and Colonial to Recent based on historic records.

It was about this time, however, that Tuck was extending his concept of the Maritime Archaic tradition to include what I regarded as the Moorehead phase, while Sanger invoked another tradition—the Laurentian—to cover the same material. Moreover, Tuck, and Snow after him, adopted Goggin's notion of full cultural tradition, which Willey and Phillips regarded as "in effect, a self-sufficient archaeological unit more like a phase" (Willey and Phillips 1958:47–48).

It was Sanger's (1973) report on the Cow Point site that joined the debate. This monograph describes one of the best preserved, richest, and most carefully excavated Moorehead phase cemeteries ever found. Possibly because my thesis had not been published or widely circulated, Sanger did not address my Moorehead phase concept in his analysis but instead countered Tuck's Maritime Archaic tradition model by suggesting that the Maine Red Paint cemeteries were linked to the Laurentian and not to Tuck's Maritime Archaic tradition. Thus arose a stalemate about the significance of the Red Paint cemeteries that was to give special importance to the Turner Farm site.

The relevance of the site to this debate emerged slowly, becoming apparent during the mid-1970s as our analyses raised questions about the appropriateness of both Sanger's Laurentian and Tuck's Maritime Archaic hypotheses (Bourque 1975). Later, when the nature of Occupation 1 became evident, I (Bourque 1983) began to consider the possibility that the Moorehead phase arose from completely local antecedents, independent of either the Laurentian or the Maritime Archaic tradition. The analyses presented in Chapters 4 and 5, as well as data from other sites discussed below, reflect my increasing confidence that the historic roots of the Moorehead phase extend back to Middle Archaic populations in the Gulf of Maine region to the south of both the Gulf of St. Lawrence and the domain of the Laurentian tradition. What follows is a summary of the Moorehead phase origin debate.

The Debate

Tuck (1971:350) originally asserted that his Maritime Archaic tradition represents a distinct, coastally adapted population that occupied a "fairly homogeneous natural area," particularly with respect to the important game species caribou and seal. Archaeologically, the Maritime Archaic tradition was characterized by certain artifact styles known mainly from the Port au Choix cemetery in Newfoundland, and Moorehead phase cemeteries in

Maine, but also from Harp's (1951, 1964; Harp and Hughes 1968) work in the Strait of Belle Isle and to the north along the Labrador coast (Fitzhugh 1972, 1975a). These styles include ground slate points and bayonets, diverse marine hunting weaponry and other implements of bone, stone woodworking tools such as adzes and gouges, plummets, and items of decoration and personal adornment, some of which Tuck thought reflect a "magico-religious system well adjusted to the area" (Tuck 1971:353).

Tuck later somewhat revised his assessment of the ecological variability encompassed by his Maritime Archaic tradition, asserting that

> although the area transects several biotic provinces, there is considerable homogeneity in the resources important to man throughout this area. Caribou were the dominant cervid, with the possible exception of moose or elk in the south. Black bear, beaver, fox, and smaller mammals are also present over much of the area. (Tuck 1978a:32)

Tuck also listed seals, walrus, porpoise, and whales as "available throughout the area" but did not specifically mention white-tailed deer, by far the predominant large vertebrate in the Turner Farm faunal sample. He did later suggest that variations on the basic Maritime Archaic theme include "the harpooning of swordfish in the southern Maritimes" but regarded the practice as "perhaps a transference of an older sea mammal technique" (Tuck 1978a:32–33).[1]

Tuck further revised his definition of the Maritime Archaic in 1982, this time omitting reference to caribou and seals, which had been found to be scarce (seals) or absent (caribou) in Maine Archaic sites:

> I am still convinced that there is a strong Maritime Archaic element in the Maritimes, at least on the Atlantic coast. . . . The sea-hunting technology, ground slates, celts and gouges, and other objects from coastal Maine and Maritimes compare too closely with those from Port au Choix and other more northerly sites to deny the existence of a *common tradition throughout the entire area*. (Tuck 1982:207, emphasis added)

By this time, Tuck's model had become the controlling paradigm for interpreting the Late Archaic cultures of the coastal Northeast, and he had also greatly increased the temporal range covered by this concept to include both earlier and later cultures in a "Northeast Maritime Continuum," a broad technological tradition that was thought to have begun in Middle Archaic times, or earlier, and to have extended along much of the Atlantic coast of North America (Tuck 1975).

In his Cow Point report, Sanger rejected Tuck's extension of the Maritime Archaic concept to Maine:

> Tuck has used the Port au Choix site as a kind of "type site" for his Maritime Archaic Tradition which, by virtue of similarities with the Nevin site in Maine, he extends from Newfoundland to the central Maine coast. Recently, Fitzhugh (1972) and Tuck have applied the Maritime Archaic Tradition to non-cemetery components on the Labrador coast. On the basis of published data and examination of collections . . . I see very little relationship between the Labrador artifacts and those from similar-aged sites in Maine except on a very general level; a level of generality which typifies much of the middle to late Archaic from the Great Lakes east. A single exception would be the joint presence in Maine and in Newfoundland-Labrador of stemmed points [of] "Ramah chert" [Fitzhugh 1972]. (Sanger 1973:121)

---

[1]To date, no swordfish remains have been recovered from any site in the Maritime Provinces.

Sanger proposed a new concept—the "Moorehead burial tradition"—comprising the cemeteries I (Bourque 1992a:26–34) had included within the Moorehead phase but that he regarded as "a late cultic phenomenon of the Laurentian tradition as represented in Maine and the Maritimes" (Sanger 1973:130). Although Snow (1975:58) initially agreed with Sanger, he (Snow 1980:19–201) later supported Tuck's position that the cemeteries were a manifestation of the Maritime Archaic tradition.

In 1975, Sanger elaborated his view of the Laurentian tradition in the Maine-Maritimes region.

> There is very little evidence for man in the area between . . . 10,600 and 5000 B.P. . . . After 5000 B.P. the picture changes dramatically in the form of a culture whose closest affiliations are *not* with the Atlantic Coastal Plain [i.e., the Maritime Archaic Tradition of Newfoundland-Labrador] but rather with the Vergennes phase of the Laurentian Tradition.[2] (Sander 1975:72)

The first to posit a link between the Laurentian tradition and sites I include in the Moorehead phase, particularly the Nevin site, was Ritchie. His (Ritchie 1936) original definition of the Laurentian aspect included three foci in and around the state of New York and a fourth tentative focus in Maine.[3] Sanger's adoption of the idea was influenced by his discovery of Vergennes-like artifacts, mainly Otter Creek points, from east central Maine and southwestern New Brunswick (Sanger 1975:62–67). At the Hirundo site in Alton, Maine, for example, "Assemblage 2," which was attributed to stratigraphic Zones I and II, was described as "very reminiscent of the Vergennes phase of the Laurentian tradition in Vermont" (Sanger et al. 1977:465). Two radiocarbon dates of about 4300 B.P. from Zone II were thought "probably [to] apply to the final centuries of Assemblage 2" (Sanger et al. 1977:465).

When we encountered what came to be called Occupation 2 at the Turner Farm site in 1971 I, too, considered a Laurentian affiliation model plausible, in part because my thesis research (Bourque 1992a:119–122) had previously identified Otter Creek points and other Laurentian-like artifacts from a few Maine sites, and in part because no more likely local ancestor for the Moorehead phase was apparent at the time. My (Bourque 1975) first discussion of this issue was written in response to drafts of Sanger 1975 and Tuck 1975, all of which were prepared for a conference on Moorehead and Maritime Archaic issues held at the Smithsonian Institution in 1974 and published together. There, on the one hand, I agreed with Sanger that the Vergennes-like assemblage from the Hirundo site presented a plausible cultural ancestor to the later Moorehead phase because "the former is found locally just prior to the latter and bears obvious typological similarities to it" (Bourque 1975:40). On the other hand, I (Bourque 1975:37–38) pointed out that substantial morphological differences were also apparent. A few artifacts from the Hirundo site—especially the small plummet illustrated in Sanger et al. (1977:465, Figure 5, lower left)—closely resemble artifacts from Turner Farm Occupation 2, and the narrow ground slate bayonet tip illustrated in the same figure (top row, 2nd from the right) is typical of the longest and most distinctive style found in Moorehead phase cemeteries (see Figure 8.4, bottom row). Both might very well pertain to a component responsible for pit features at Hirundo being radiocarbon dated to about 4300 B.P. (Sanger et al. 1977:464). Most of the artifacts

---

[2]Much evidence for Archaic occupation predating 5000 B.P. has subsequently been found in Maine, particularly west of the Penobscot River, an area then little known to archaeologists.

[3]See Funk 1988 for a detailed analysis of the history of the Laurentian tradition.

attributed to Hirundo, Assemblage 2, however, seem more typical of the Vergennes phase, which recent data indicate was much earlier, ending by about 5000 B.P. (Funk 1993: 188–190).

The early age of the Vergennes phase in Maine has recently been confirmed at site 95.20 on the Grand Falls drainage in Indian Township, where Cox (1991) excavated what appears to be a single-component site with an assemblage including Otter Creek points, crude tabular choppers, and other artifacts closely resembling the Vergennes-like elements from the Hirundo site (Cox 1991:Figures 5–7; Sanger et al. 1977:Figures 5–6). Also recovered were fully grooved gouges, stone rods, quartz scrapers, and ulus. All of these styles are quite different from artifacts found in Moorehead phase cemeteries, Turner Farm Occupation 2, and other components in Maine of similar age, but are common in earlier contexts (see, e.g., Petersen 1991:59–124). Three radiocarbon dates from site 95.20 average 5073 ± 112 B.P., very close to dates from other Vergennes components in the Northeast.

Although I did not say so in 1975, I had concluded that the solution to the puzzling diversity of artifacts from Hirundo site, Assemblage 2, probably was the result of stratigraphic ambiguity there. Sanger and McKay (1973:24) stated that there is an "absence of clear-cut stratigraphy" at the site and Sanger et al. (1977:463) later described it as "actively washed" with stratigraphic zones having "no clearly recognizable boundaries." These conditions apparently had led to the conflation of artifacts from different components. Thus, despite the late dates from Zone II, which were not directly associated with artifacts, the Laurentian-like artifacts probably had originated in a significantly earlier occupation.

As the nature of Occupation 2 became clearer, and especially after dates averaging about 5000 B.P. were obtained from a very un-Laurentian-like Occupation 1, it became obvious that a Laurentian tradition affiliation with the Moorehead phase was untenable because their technologies were simply too divergent (Bourque 1975:40–41). Tuck's Maritime Archaic tradition thus became more attractive as a broad cultural context with which to affiliate the Moorehead phase on economic, technological, mortuary, and temporal grounds. In the first place, there was good reason to suspect that Archaic populations in Newfoundland and Labrador became dependent upon marine resources at least as early as in the Gulf of Maine (McGhee and Tuck 1975:42–49). Second, the technological similarities, especially those shared with Tuck's Port au Choix cemetery, include bone and antler weaponry designed for maritime hunting; wood-working tools such as gouges, adzes, and beaver incisors; long slate (and bone) points—truly "bayonets"—and stemmed (as opposed to side-notched) projectile points. Finally, concrete evidence for contact between the northern and southern ranges of the Maritime Archaic tradition was to be found in at least two artifact classes: stemmed points of Ramah chert from the north Labrador coast found in Maine cemeteries, and certain bayonet styles that occur mainly in mortuary contexts in both Maine and the Newfoundland Maritime Archaic. Because these forms are far more numerous in Maine, I now suspect that they probably originated there and moved northward through some form of exchange, possibly to reciprocate the southward movement of Ramah chert points (Bourque 1994:27).

Despite these points of similarity, significant problems in applying the Maritime Archaic tradition model to Maine and the Maritime Provinces have continued to emerge. Clearly, the "whole culture" sense of the tradition intended by Tuck stumbles on the lack of both cultural and ecological uniformity. But problems remain even if Willey and Phillips's sense of tradition is employed (that is, to imply some kind of long-term continuity in shared characteristics among the included cultures), for although the similarities shared by the Moorehead phase and sites like Port au Choix are quite specific, most are limited to only a brief period between about 4500 and 3800 B.P. Tuck's Maritime Archaic tradition in Newfoundland and Labrador actually does satisfy Willey and Phillips's definition by virtue of its purported long life history, beginning perhaps as early as about 9000 B.P. and lasting until at least 3800 B.P. (Fitzhugh 1987:147; Tuck 1978a:33–34). The problem with extending it south of the Gulf of St. Lawrence to include the Maritime Peninsula is that the sense of long temporal continuity of the tradition's salient traits cannot be demonstrated there.

Thus, using Willey and Phillips's terminology, I was, and still am, "inclined to view this period of close ties almost as a horizon, rather than a tradition, which resulted from shared technologies and ceremonial behavior rather than from long-term ethnic unity" (Bourque 1975:41). In a preliminary report on the Turner Farm site, I (Bourque 1976) once again invoked the concept of the Moorehead phase to emphasize the important similarities between Occupation 2 (and a handful of other coastal Archaic habitation components mentioned in Chapter 5) and the Red Paint cemeteries, as well as the distinctness of these sites from both the Laurentian and Maritime Archaic traditions.

In sum, Occupation 2 at the Turner Farm site demonstrated that the nonmortuary aspect of the Moorehead phase was neither historically derived from the Laurentian tradition, as Sanger had postulated, nor was it merely the southern limit of Tuck's Maritime Archaic tradition. Rather, it had become evident that the Moorehead phase, especially its nonmortuary aspects, arose from local antecedents.

Tuck's (1982:207–208) most recent discussion of the Maritime Archaic tradition overcomes still more of the difficulties present in earlier formulations. The sense of tradition is less holistic, the emphasis is shifted to shared technology (ground slate tools, celts, gouges, etc.), and the maritime food quest is broadened to "sea hunting," no longer suggesting that Maine cod and swordfish fisheries were derived from marine mammal hunting. Moreover, the geographic focus has been modified somewhat to include the Atlantic coastal zone rather than Maine and the Atlantic provinces. In the end, however, no unitary Maritime Archaic tradition can encompass the archaeological variability encountered over such a broad region.

There remain three problems. The first is that the purported thread of continuity between the northern and southern end of Tuck's Maritime Archaic tradition is based on his claim that artifact assemblages appropriate to the tradition are to be found in Nova Scotia. While the occurrence of plummets, adzes, gouges, and the like in southern Nova Scotia has long been recognized (Piers 1889, 1896, 1912), such artifacts are relatively few in number, often do not specifically resemble either Moorehead phase or Maritime Archaic analogues, and have uncertain origins. This is not the case, however, with bayonets, which have recently been reported, albeit from poorly documented contexts, at Tusket Falls near the southwestern tip of Nova Scotia, and from Cape North at the northeast tip of Cape Breton Island (Davis, personal communication, 1993). In both instances the bayonets are of the long-hexagonal form common in Maine Red Paint cemeteries. They may possibly have been from cemetery deposits although no association with grave furniture typical of the Moorehead phase (or the Maritime Archaic tradition) has been reported. Other artifacts that indicate contact between Nova Scotia and Maine much more strongly than with Newfoundland and Labrador are stemmed points that Sanger regards as "strikingly like" those from

Occupation 2 and other Moorehead phase components (Sanger 1991:58). No points of Ramah chert have been reported, however.

With the possible exceptions just noted, no burials typical of the Moorehead phase have been encountered east of the Cow Point cemetery, and even if some are eventually found it is unlikely that anything remotely approaching the Moorehead phase cemetery florescence of eastern Maine and southwestern New Brunswick will be discovered (Bourque 1994). A few red ocher deposits that have been found in Nova Scotia may pertain to a wide range of Archaic cultural contexts other than either the Moorehead phase or the Maritime Archaic traditions (see, e.g., Robinson 1992). Sanger interpreted the new data from Nova Scotia as evidence that Moorehead phase populations (and other Late Archaic populations as well) traveled by boat across the Bay of Fundy rather than along its shore, perhaps seasonally, to exploit alewife runs. This seems a more parsimonious explanation than positing the extension of a Maritime Archaic tradition from Newfoundland southward across the Gulf of St. Lawrence to the ecologically very different Maritime Peninsula.

Another remaining problem is the number of north–south differences in relative frequencies (and sometimes in artifact form as well) that remain among basic artifact classes. Gouges, plummets, and whetstones are very abundant in Moorehead phase cemeteries but relatively rare and different in form at Port au Choix. Moreover, although formal resemblances between the bone weaponry of the Moorehead phase and that of Port au Choix (e.g., bayonets, foreshafts, harpoons, etc.) are sometimes striking, their sizes are dramatically different. The remaining north–south resemblances are too generalized to allow detailed interpretation. Moreover, any assertion that they reflect a common cultural heritage must be weighed against the fact that the available samples are separated by great distance. Bone preservation in sites of this age throughout the Northeast is so limited that we have no clear idea how widely distributed marine hunting technology may actually have been during Late Archaic times there. Finally, as pointed out below, the most important remaining problem with the extension of the Maritime Archaic tradition to Maine is the fact that the Moorehead phase can now clearly be seen to have derived from something very akin to Ritchie's Small Stemmed Point tradition, which Tuck (1978a:29, 35), after Dincauze (1971:197–198), included in the Narrow Point tradition, and which may ultimately be related to cultures of the Piedmont (Funk 1993:223, 323–325).

In conclusion, the Moorehead phase remains a useful construct, appropriately scaled to the time range and stylistic similarities exhibited by Late Archaic sites in eastern Maine and southwestern New Brunswick and comparable in its explanatory power at least to the phases of the Laurentian tradition recently reified by Funk (1988). It cannot be explained by reference to earlier broad-scale patterns originating outside the region but, instead, seems to have been a dynamic, short-lived, in situ cultural development during which a maritime-oriented people based in the Gulf of Maine—known to us mainly because they practiced complex mortuary rituals—were in close contact with a similarly maritime culture in the far north. No comparable linkage with the Vergennes phase of the Laurentian tradition is demonstrable.

In his summary of the Holocene peopling of northern latitudes of North America, Workman (1980:50) pointed out that "maritime hunting appears on a worldwide basis to be another Holocene adaptation, depending on middle Holocene relative stabilization of the coasts, both for the full flowering of its possibilities and for the preservation of the evidence for its development." Fitzhugh (1975b:343) has noted, however, that true maritime adaptation occurs most commonly in the higher latitudes of both hemispheres (see also Mc-Cartney 1975). Such cultures, he argues, all conform to a "northern maritime adaptation type." His list for the northern hemisphere includes examples from Scandinavia, Labrador, the Northwest Coast, the Aleutians, Bering Strait and Northeast Asia (Fitzhugh 1975b:372). To this list must now be added the Moorehead phase in the Gulf of Maine.

Moorehead Phase Relationship to the Maritime Archaic Tradition

Although it is now apparent that the Moorehead phase arose independently of the Maritime Archaic tradition, undeniably close north–south resemblances exist that need to be explained. At a very general level, Dincauze (1976) noted the close resemblances shared by stemmed Early and Middle Archaic biface assemblages from North Carolina and the Neville site in New Hampshire and asserted that "there can be no denying the relatively direct derivation of the northern cultural expression from the southern one, since antecedents are well documented in the south" (Dincauze 1976:139). McGhee and Tuck noted similarities between the broad-stemmed points from the Barney site in L'Anse au Loup, Labrador, and Middle Archaic Neville Points from the Neville site. These similarities were basic to their formulation of a Northeast Maritime Continuum, which they regarded essentially as a northward extension of a "horizon or tradition . . . which may be broad indeed for Dincauze (1971) has related the Neville Complex to the still more southerly Kanawah level at the St. Albans site, West Virginia (Broyles 1971) and to Coe's (1964) Stanly Complex from the North Carolina Piedmont" (McGhee and Tuck 1975:104–105, see also pp. 32–41, and Plate 5 on p. 201). All these assemblages stand apart from the flaked biface technology of the Laurentian tradition, which is typified by the broad, side-notched points of the Vergennes and subsequent phases. These observations by Dincauze, McGhee, and Tuck continue to be born out by subsequent research and they provide a useful backdrop for evaluating the more specific resemblances between the Moorehead phase and the late Maritime Archaic tradition.

The basic stemmed biface technology noted by Dincauze, McGhee, and Tuck persisted for several millennia among Atlantic coastal peoples and probably reflects common Early Archaic ancestry in the mid-Atlantic Piedmont with subsequent spread and local divergence. The much later and more specific similarities between the Moorehead phase and the Late Maritime Archaic tradition, however, are not primarily manifest in stemmed biface technology, nor did they likely derive from common Early Archaic ancestry. Even the presence in both areas of richly furnished cemeteries and similar pecked and ground stone tools does not set them distinctly apart from other Late Archaic cultural entities, specifically the Laurentian tradition (Kennedy 1967; Ritchie 1945). Their bone technologies share considerably more similarities but, as pointed out above, the evidence for this kind of technology throughout the Northeast is currently too limited to justify detailed inferences based on the few available samples.

What does set them apart is their maritime economies, the importance of maritime animals reflected in their art, and clear evidence for contact found in the frequent occurrence of Ramah chert bifaces in Moorehead phase graves and what are probably Maine bayonets at Port au Choix and Twillingate (Figure 8.2; see also Fitzhugh 1975b:349). This combination of resemblances (some attributable to common maritime pursuits and others indicative of direct contact) most likely arose as the result of contact between populations

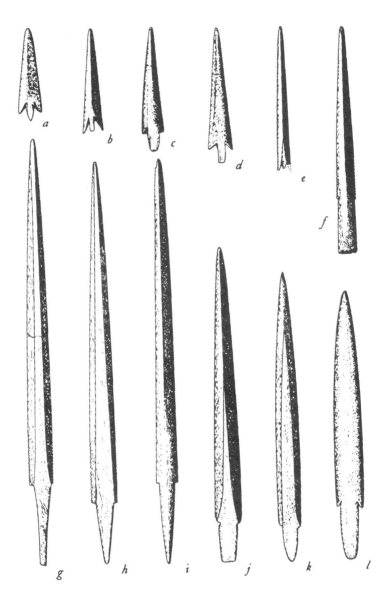

Slate Points. From Maine: a, Bucksport; b, d, e,
Warren; c, Orland; g, h, i, Ellsworth; f, j, k, l, Blue Hill; d, f, j, k, l, Andover Archaeological
Museum; a, c, g, h, i, Peabody Museum, Cambridge. (1:3.)

Figure 8.2. Slate bayonets of the narrow-hexagonal cross-section style from various Maine contexts (after Willoughby 1935/1973:Figure 34).

on both sides of the Gulf of St. Lawrence, each exploiting their own rich maritime environments and encountering the other in the process.

The notion that the Moorehead phase actively sought contact with neighboring cultures throughout the region is further supported by evidence for contact with the Lake Champlain Basin to the west. The evidence is in the form of eared-stem bifaces made of Cheshire quartzite and Lake Champlain Basin cherts—identical in form and raw material ratios to assemblages, apparently from caches, found near Lake Champlain in Vermont— that have been found in numerous Moorehead phase graves (University of Vermont Collections; Bourque 1992a:28–39). Our current understanding of the Late Archaic in Vermont provides no clear cultural context for these large, possibly ceremonial, bifaces. Their probable age, however, can be established on the basis of one cache from Colchester Point on Lake Champlain, which contained similar points along with Normanskill-like points. Ritchie included the latter style in the River phase, which he dated to about 4000 B.P., although more recent dates on Normanskill points from the Upper Susquehanna region suggest a slightly younger age (Funk 1993:195; Ritchie 1971b:37–38, 90–91, 1980: 129–140).

Tuck (1982:207–208) has asserted that ground slate lances, gouges, ulus, and plummets have greater antiquity on the Atlantic coast than in the St. Lawrence estuary and that the implied time depth of this technological complex, and thus of the Maritime Archaic, is greater to the north of the Gulf of St. Lawrence than to the south. Other intimations of Tuck's belief in the temporal priority of the north are evident in his suggestion that swordfishing in the Gulf of Maine is derived from earlier sea mammal hunting and in his description of burial mounds predating 7000 B.P. in the Strait of Belle Isle area as somehow ancestral to the later cemeteries of the south, including the Maine cemeteries and those of Newfoundland (Tuck 1978a:33, 1978b).

This impression has apparently become widespread, probably in part because the recently discovered and well-published Newfoundland cemetery data have overshadowed older, less well-published data from the Maritime Peninsula. Thus, to Snow (1980:215– 216), "it seems likely that ground slate points and the artifacts they mimic were introduced (to Maine) from farther northeast. The rich nonlithic tool industry includes toggling and barbed harpoons, needles, and awls as well, further evidence of a maritime orientation and links to the northeast."

Until the discovery of early swordfishing at Seabrook Marsh, and the publication of paleoenvironmental data summarized in Spiess et al. (1983:101–102), the notion that Moorehead phase swordfishing was inspired from the north was plausible. A northern origin for elaborate mortuary ceremonialism was also plausible until the discovery of elaborately furnished graves in 6000- to 7000-year-old cemetery components between the Merrimack and Penobscot Rivers (Robinson 1992). Of particular importance are three grave assemblages from a prominent sand knoll at the mouth of the Merrimack River on the northern Massachusetts coast (Robinson 1992:80–83, 93; Whittall 1982). Grave goods there included red ocher, serrated-blade points similar to Barney points from southern Labrador (McGhee and Tuck 1975:116), typical Middle Archaic fully grooved gouges, and rod-shaped whetstones. Dates on charcoal in the graves ranged from c. 7000 to 6500 B.P.

This new evidence strongly supports the inference that both maritime hunting and mortuary ceremonialism arose independently on opposite sides of the Gulf of St. Lawrence. However, even if there existed a greater degree of historic connectedness between the two regions than I have argued for here, the available dates hardly support the idea that the north had temporal priority over the south. In fact, the closest technological parallels appear somewhat later in northern sites, particularly Port au Choix, than at least some Moorehead phase sites, notably the Turner Farm site and the Bradley cemetery. A time slope in the opposite direction thus seems more plausible (Belcher et al. 1993; Tuck 1976: 162–163).

The Small Stemmed Point Tradition and the Moorehead Phase

Bourque (1976) offered no resolution to the impasse between those arguing for the Laurentian versus the Maritime Archaic traditions as potential ancestors to the Moorehead phase. During the late 1970s, however, we began to perceive that a more likely ancestor for the Moorehead phase lay literally beneath our feet as we excavated the Occupation 2 midden at the Turner Farm. Our focus on Occupation 1 intensified as it became apparent that the Vergennes phase had probably ended by about 5000 B.P. (see, e.g., Funk 1978:26), possibly even before Occupation 1 began, thus reinforcing the notion that a Vergennes-to-Moorehead phase transition was unlikely.

At about the same time, our research at the Davis-Tobie site (mentioned in Chapter 5) revealed a stratigraphic sequence similar to that at the Turner Farm site: a Moorehead phase component overlying a Small Stemmed Point tradition component dating to about 4500 B.P. Unlike the situation at the latter site, where the constituent elements of Occupation 1 technology were defined using somewhat equivocal stratigraphic evidence, stratigraphic associations between the Small Stemmed Point tradition and Moorehead phase components were clear at the Davis-Tobie site and we were surprised at the extent of the similarities between the two technologies. Both had pecking stones, plummets, and gouges of similar form, as well as narrow-stemmed points spanning the size range between those of Turner Farm Occupations 1 and 2. Also found in the earlier component were two classes of artifact that evoked Middle Archaic origins: a fully grooved cobble and a spheroidal atlatl weight.[4]

These discoveries were important for two reasons. First, Occupation 1 at the Turner Farm was no longer anomalous on the Maine coast, and its affinities to other Small Stemmed Point components, and possibly to even earlier assemblages to the west, became apparent. Second, artifact forms similar to those of (Moorehead phase) Occupation 2, but distinct from those of the Laurentian tradition, were in evidence.

Nevertheless, neither site had established an association of the Small Stemmed Point tradition in Maine with red ocher mortuary ceremonialism and with deep water maritime exploitation. No human burial features had been found at either site. Moreover, although a small faunal sample, including cod and swordfish, had been recovered from Turner Farm Feature 5-1972, and a few bones of cod and harbor seal had been found in early levels of the Davis-Tobie site, these data were weak in comparison to the abundant evidence for maritime exploitation available for the Moorehead phase.

---

[4]Another association of small stemmed points with atlatl weights, one winged and one spheroidal, has been reported from a probable mortuary feature at the Bear Swamp site in Berkeley, Massachusetts. This is the same feature referred to in Chapter 4. The age of grooved pebbles in the Penobscot drainage has recently been extended back to about 6000 B.P. at the Sharrow site in Milo (Petersen and Putnam 1992:39).

It was Brian Robinson's (1985:22–48) excavations at the Seabrook Marsh site in 1975 that suddenly made apparent the mortuary ceremonialism and maritime orientation of the Small Stemmed Point tradition. Once again, small stemmed points were found in association with plummets and gouges closely resembling those of the Moorehead phase sites, but there were also red ocher burials and the bones of cod and swordfish, including a cache of swordfish rostra. The burials lacked the elaborate furnishings found later in Moorehead phase cemeteries, and recent isotopic analysis of the skeletal material indicates a lower relative marine contribution to the protein diet than in the Moorehead phase Nevin population (Bourque and Krueger 1992). Nevertheless, the basic resemblance of the Seabrook Marsh assemblage to the Moorehead phase is unmistakable.

Robinson's discoveries came as our Turner Farm excavations were nearing an end and as intensive analysis was getting underway. The Seabrook data caused us to reexamine the attribution of all swordfish bone, plummets, gouges, and pecking stones previously assigned only to Occupation 2. Radiocarbon dates of basal features and the analysis of their contents soon revealed the presence of at least some additional swordfish and cod dating between c. 4500 and 5000 B.P., and, as mentioned above, we have concluded that some of the artifacts found near the subsoil surface and formerly attributed to Occupation 2 had, in fact, originated in Occupation 1.

The strong linkage between Small Stemmed Point tradition and Moorehead phase ceremonialism has recently become better established as a result of Robinson's (1992) analysis of the collection from the Godfrey cemetery in Old Town, Maine. There, during the early twentieth century, Frederick Godfrey and, later, Moorehead (1922:93–130) excavated Red Paint graves furnished with numerous large adzes and gouges closely resembling those from several Moorehead phase cemeteries along the Penobscot River in both form and raw material. From one grave came a quartz stemmed point, larger than most from Turner Farm Occupation 1 and the Davis-Tobie site, but reminiscent of them. Another grave yielded a spheroidal atlatl weight and a third produced three winged atlatl weights (Figure 8.3). All of the atlatl weights were made of two-tone green and dark gray slate or siltstone, which is visually identical to that used in the atlatl weight from the Davis-Tobie site. Winged atlatl weights have also been found in apparently early Red Paint cemetery contexts at the Hathaway and Emerson sites (Moorehead 1922:Figure 36, Figure 54; Snow 1969:94–95). The Emerson specimen also was made of the two-tone green and dark gray stone. Only the Hathaway specimen has a recorded association with a gouge and an adz, but the association of the rest with the Late Archaic burials among which they were found seems highly likely since there is no evidence of earlier or later burials at these particular sites.[5]

No radiocarbon dates are available for the Godfrey site, but some indication of its age can be gained from the Hathaway site, which yielded very similar artifacts, especially hemiconically grooved gouges made of metamorphosed volcanic rock. One ocher-filled feature at the Hathaway site has been dated at about 5100 B.P. (Snow 1969:39, 56–57; 1975:50). The fact that no small stemmed points were found at either the Hathaway or Emerson sites leaves their contemporaneity with the Godfrey, Davis-Tobie, and Turner Farm Occupation 1 components somewhat in doubt. It is worth pointing out, however, that projectile points, aside from exotic imports, are relatively scarce in many Red Paint ceme-

---

[5]A similar burial association of hemiconically grooved gouges and an ovoid atlatl weight was excavated by Moorehead on the Salmon Falls River in Dover, New Hampshire (Moorehead 1922:208, Figure 108).

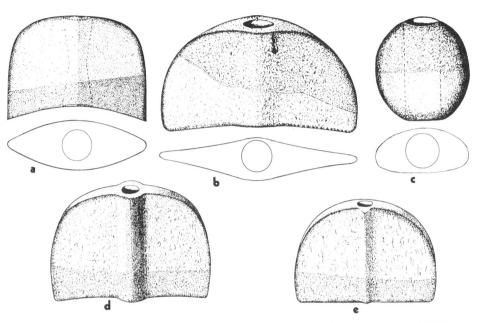

Figure 8.3. Atlatl weights of green and dark gray stone from the Godfrey site (after Smith 1948:51).

tery assemblages. Thus, it seems likely that the Godfrey assemblage and at least some features at the Hathaway and Emerson cemeteries, as well, represent a budding Moorehead phase-style burial regime deposited by a people very similar to those responsible for Occupation 1 and the basal stratum at the Davis-Tobie site.

Taken together, all these data suggest two important conclusions. First, the Small Stemmed Point tradition in Maine has roots in local Middle Archaic cultures. Second, its components provide evidence for both a maritime focus and a mortuary ceremonialism that emerge fully developed in the Moorehead phase.

Summary

Following Tuck's (1971) original definition of a Maritime Archaic tradition occupying a supposedly uniform ecological zone extending from Newfoundland and Labrador south of the Gulf of St. Lawrence to Maine, evidence has emerged that considerable ecological diversity has long existed within that broad region, and that a cod and swordfish based maritime hunting culture—the Moorehead phase—arose in the latter area independent of the marine mammal based one in the north. Under these circumstances, if we were to revise the three traditions defined in Tuck (1978a:30–37), the Moorehead phase would be dropped from the Maritime Archaic tradition to be included in the Narrow Point tradition, which, in turn, is probably derived from an Atlantic slope tradition stretching back to Early Archaic times. The Atlantic slope tradition probably also gave rise to the Maritime Archaic tradition in the north, via something like the Northeast Maritime Continuum (Tuck 1975).

Its specific resemblances to, and contacts with, the Moorehead phase, however, cannot be attributed to this ancient common ancestry.

Where the appropriate boundary between the two should be drawn remains unclear. The numerous artifact finds in New Brunswick and Nova Scotia discussed above suggest that both Tuck's Narrow Point and Maritime Archaic traditions may have occupied that region. The southernmost clear manifestation of the Maritime Archaic tradition is at the Beaches site in Bonavista Bay (Carignan 1975), Newfoundland, far to the north of the Maritimes, whereas components of both the Small Stemmed Point tradition and Moorehead phase lie nearby to the west in an ecologically similar area on the central Maine coast. Thus, the parsimonious inference is that these artifacts reflect a much closer linkage to Maine than to the Maritime Archaic tradition even though, so far, we have little evidence that people in the Maritimes were much involved in either maritime exploitation or in Moorehead phase-like mortuary ritualism.

The Ground Slate Point Problem Reconsidered

The remaining link between the Laurentian tradition and the Moorehead phase that is not demonstrably shared by the Small Stemmed Point tradition is the stemmed biface made of ground stone (usually slate). Past discussions of ground slate point origins have focused so heavily on the combination of a certain raw material (slate) and production technique (grinding) at the expense of other raw materials and morphology that two important points have often been overlooked. The first is stylistic variability. As Tuck (1976:116) has pointed out, this artifact class includes two major subclasses: relatively short, broad, barbed points predominantly associated with the Vergennes phase of the Laurentian tradition and long, narrow points, often referred to as "bayonets," and generally found in non-Laurentian contexts, primarily in Moorehead phase and Maritime Archaic cemeteries (cf., e.g., Ritchie 1980:88 and Willoughby 1935/1973:Figure 32 with Figure 8.4 this volume; Sanger 1973:Plates 6–12; Tuck 1976:Plates 16–22). These differences are frequently difficult to discern from the literature because they have been obscured by the long-established use of such terms as "slate point" to refer to both styles. They have sometimes been further obfuscated by the use of the term "ground slate," which also includes the semilunar knife, or ulu, a style common to several Middle and (early) Late Archaic complexes throughout northeastern North America.

Vergennes-related slate points, on the one hand, generally have distinctly excurvate blade margins, lenticular or lozenge-shaped cross sections, and are relatively broad (3–5 cm) and short (usually less than 12 cm); most have contracting stems, often with multiple notches (see, e.g., Moorehead 1900:114; Ritchie 1980:88; Willoughby 1935/1973:54). Their overall proportions and generally nonmortuary contexts suggest that these were functional weapon tips. Moorehead phase and Maritime Archaic slate forms, on the other hand, include a series of distinct styles, some of which are much longer and narrower and so susceptible to breakage that it is difficult to imagine them as functional weapons. One minority Moorehead phase form differs radically from the others, being the smallest of all northeastern slate points (Willoughby 1935/1973:Figure 34a–e). Because so many of these artifacts occur in highly standardized styles that could not be expected to withstand actual use in the hunt and because the great majority have been found in mortuary contexts, they may have served a mainly symbolic purpose. Close resemblances between the Laurentian

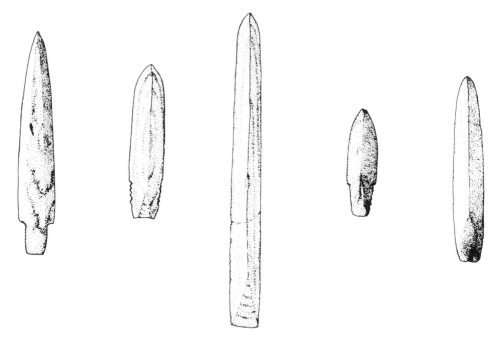

Figure 8.4.   Left: bayonet of broad-hexagonal cross section from Port au Choix (after Tuck 1976:208). Right: four bayonets of pie-wedge cross section; the two on the right are from the Cow Point cemetery in New Brunswick (after Sanger 1973:190); the two on the left are from Port au Choix (after Tuck 1976:213; drawings: Patricia Arey).

and these coastal Atlantic ground slate points do occasionally occur, but the similarities are confined to a minority of specimens that are atypical of both groups.

The second point overlooked or not addressed in the ground slate point debate is the presence in northeastern Archaic assemblages of long, ground points of both bone and stone (McGhee and Tuck 1975:91–92, 240–241; Ritchie 1962:99, Plate 2, 1980:93). The oversight may be because of Ritchie's assertion that the former were "prototypes, probably of Ancient Old World origin," for this was the last faint allusion to the outdated concept of a circumpolar cultural complex (Ritchie 1969:389). The idea was revisited once again, however, by Fitzhugh, who suggested that in the Mesolithic of northern Europe and, by implication, elsewhere as well, ground stone knives and points evolved "by transference of Mesolithic bone and antler grooving and honing techniques to a more durable medium" (Fitzhugh 1974:52).

Fitzhugh's argument may well apply to the Gulf of Maine and probably elsewhere in the Northeast, for forms made not of stone but of swordfish rostrum were recovered at three probably early Moorehead phase sites with bone preservation: Waterside, Nevin, and Turner Farm (Figure 8.5; Bourque 1992a:124; Byers 1979:48).Especially noteworthy is the fact that two of these, the Waterside and Nevin sites, also produced ground slate bayonets. A fourth contemporaneous component at Taft's Point produced swordfish bone, but only stone bayonet fragments (Bourque 1992a:23; Hadlock 1939). The close association of bayonets made of swordfish rostrum with those made of stone suggests that the ground stone forms may very well have been copied from bone prototypes.

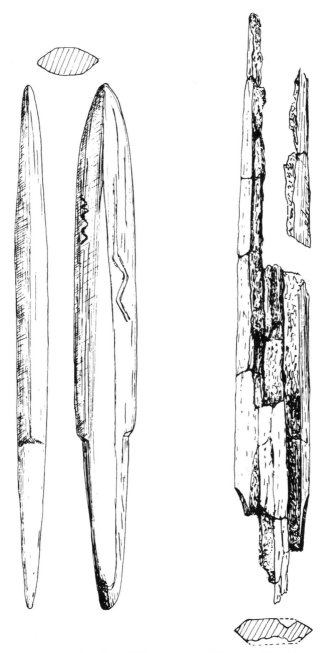

Figure 8.5. Bayonets of slate (left) and swordfish rostrum (right) from the Waterside site (after Rowe 1940: Figures VIII, IX).

Tuck has suggested that the slate points of the Laurentian tradition "are not indigenous to Laurentian culture but were adopted by Laurentian people after their eastward expansion brought them into contact with Maritime Archaic peoples" (Tuck 1982:208). While the earliest known slate points have, in fact, been found on or near the Atlantic coast, many of the closest analogues to Laurentian tradition forms are made of native copper from the Upper Great Lakes. As maritime hunting was presumably insignificant in the St. Lawrence east of Quebec, this western copper and slate point manifestation may instead have arisen independent of the Atlantic coast (cf., e.g., Ellis et al. 1990:89, Mason 1981:189, and Moorehead 1900:95 with Ellis et al. 1990:87, Ritchie 1980:88, and Willoughby 1935/1973:54). A small sample of bayonets in the collections of the Royal Ontario Museum, all apparently isolated finds from southern Ontario, bears very specific resemblance to forms known primarily from Moorehead phase and Maritime Archaic cemeteries. There is no evidence, however, that any of these was found in a Laurentian tradition context.

Where, then, do the origins of ground slate point technology lie? Despite the relatively large amount of attention given to Vergennes-like assemblages in Maine, very few Vergennes-style ground slate points have been found there. Furthermore, no Vergennes component has yet been reliably dated later than about 5000 B.P.—that is, at least half a millennium after very non-Vergennes-like slate bayonets began to appear in Moorehead phase contexts. Given the morphological, spatial, and temporal distances between the Laurentian tradition and the coastal Atlantic producers of slate points, it seems unlikely that the former is the source of the more easterly manifestation.

Nevertheless, Cox (1991:153) used data from the Sharrow site in Milo (Petersen 1991) to make that argument. There in Stratum III were found slate preforms and fragments of finished ground slate points that Petersen described as "elongate" and having "squarish [and] rounded shoulders." The Sharrow site slate points are rather generalized in form, lacking traits specific to those of the Vergennes phase. If anything, they more closely resemble forms later found in Moorehead phase contexts (Peterson 1991:107–109, Figures 77–82). Also from Stratum III were five side-notched biface fragments (Petersen 1991:108). Three of these resemble Otter Creek points, which led Cox to conclude that the Sharrow site data, combined with his Vergennes phase component, "certainly suggest that Vergennes or a closely related culture had a rather long temporal span within the region" (Cox 1991:153). Cox also noted that "many of the elements of the Vergennes artifact complex, including ground slate points, choppers, quartz end scrapers, gouges, celts, and stone rods were also found in Middle Archaic levels at Sharrow," apparently seeing in them further support for a long-term Vergennes phase presence in the area (Cox 1991:153).

There are two problems with Cox's inference. First, Stratum III, where were found the slate and other artifacts referred to by Cox, is actually a very complex microstratigraphic sequence, which yielded radiocarbon dates ranging from 7000 to 5000 B.P. Thus, there is good reason to question their association, as well as Cox's argument for a Vergennes component there, particularly one associated with the ground slate points.

In all, Petersen (1991:107–109) regards at least 9 of the 13 ground slate specimens in the Sharrow sample as 6,000 years old or older. In contrast, all five side-notched points referred to by Cox were found in contexts that Petersen (1991:61, 66) regarded as dating to about 5500 B.P. or younger. Other clues to the cultural origins of the Sharrow site slate points come from additional artifacts found in Stratum III that were not discussed by Cox: two probable Middle Archaic stemmed points (Petersen 1991:61, Figure 40, left and center).

Both of the stemmed points came from features dating to about 6000 B.P. or earlier (Petersen 1990:60). One of these features also produced a fragmentary ground slate point (Petersen 1990:108). The second problem with Cox's argument is that all of the elements he lists in support of a supposed Vergennes component at the Sharrow site, except the slate point, have been found in non-Vergennes Middle *and* Late Archaic contexts throughout much of the Northeast, including, as Cox notes elsewhere, the Small Stemmed Point tradition (Cox 1991:157, Ritchie 1980:215).

In sum, three conclusions can be drawn from the Sharrow site data. First, the evidence for a Vergennes component there is weak at best. Second, evidence for the association of ground slate points with possibly Vergennes-related side-notched points is essentially nonexistent. Third, the association of ground slate points with *stemmed* points and other typical Middle Archaic artifacts is much stronger. As we begin to look back into the early history of ground slate point technology, I suspect that we will find it firmly established in the repertoire of the stemmed point-making cultures of the putative Atlantic slope tradition that persisted from Early Archaic times. Because it is known to occur prior to 6000 B.P. both in the Gulf of Maine and in the Maritime Archaic of Newfoundland and Labrador, its ultimate origin remains unclear.

It is worth noting that no ground slate points have yet been reliably documented from Small Stemmed Point assemblages. Moorehead (1922:94) implied that some were recovered from the Small Stemmed Point-related Godfrey cemetery, but none survive in the collection from that site. Although this absence is puzzling, we should keep in mind that no slate points have been found in reliable Maine Vergennes-like contexts either.

Territorial Issues

Cox noted that the territory of the Small Stemmed Point tradition is not congruent with that of the Moorehead phase and queried, "If small stemmed point is ancestral to Moorehead, why does the Moorehead phase not extend south of the Kennebec River? Why is a pre-Moorehead small stemmed point complex apparently absent along the river systems of eastern Maine, over much of the Moorehead phase's range?" (Cox 1991:158).

The first of these rhetorical questions is probably best answered by simply restating the apparent fact that the Moorehead phase, as it is presently understood, has an unusually discrete geographic range and that, aside from some conjectures regarding differential marine productivity across the Gulf of Maine coast, the causes of that apparent discreteness are unknown. Nevertheless, in attempting to understand its likely origins, one cannot ignore the clear adaptational (swordfish hunting and cod fishing), mortuary (burials with red ocher), and technological (stemmed points, plummets, gouges) similarities it shares with a slightly earlier Late Archaic complex, the Small Stemmed Point tradition, which was more broadly distributed, as were most Late Archaic traditions, but which extends well into the territory of its putative cultural descendant, as demonstrated in two stratified contexts—the Davis-Tobie and Turner Farm sites—and elsewhere.

Cox's second question, concerning the absence of the Small Stemmed Point tradition along the eastern river systems of Maine, inaccurately characterized the distribution of both that tradition and the Moorehead phase, for neither is primarily a riverine phenomenon anywhere in its respective range. Only a very few Small Stemmed Point components have been found more than a few miles above the head-of-tide of Maine's rivers and, although their distances from tidal water has surely decreased over the past 5,000 to 4,500 years, this does not basically alter their characterization as near-coastal. Likewise, few significant Moorehead phase components have been found far above the present heads-of-tide on their respective drainages (Bourque 1994). A more useful question is why no evidence of the Small Stemmed Point tradition has been encountered in eastern coastal and near-coastal Maine and New Brunswick where the Moorehead phase—mainly evident in mortuary components—is present. Part of the answer may lie in the relatively greater extent of coastal submersion east of Penobscot Bay, which would have differentially destroyed evidence of the older Small Stemmed Point tradition. Part may also lie in the ecological differences, which are discussed below, between the central Maine coast and the Gulf of Maine coast farther east.

Moreover, it seems unlikely in the extreme that cultural traditions adapted to a dynamic Gulf of Maine would have remained microterritorially static. On the contrary, a far more likely scenario is that these cultures responded to changes in the abundance and distribution of marine resources and that this response included adjustments in their territorial range. In fact, it is unlikely that the Gulf of Maine has been uniformly productive of marine resources during the Holocene. In historic times, marine resources occurred in greater abundance off the coast between the Kennebec and St. John rivers than farther to the east or west. The apparent eastward extension of the Small Stemmed Point tradition range by the Moorehead phase may simply have been in order to exploit those resources.

The relative abundance of large offshore islands in this central area may also have encouraged eastward expansion. These islands seem to have provided ready access to the deep water cod and swordfisheries, as suggested by the Stanley site on Monhegan Island and the Candage site on Vinalhaven (Sanger 1975:62; Bourque 1992b). Similar sites may eventually be found on islands east of Penobscot Bay, although the higher rate of coastal submersion there has probably reduced their chances of survival (Turnbull 1985).

Finally, Cox has asserted that "the geographic range of Vergennes in Maine, from the Kennebec eastward, is suspiciously similar to that of Moorehead" (Cox 1991:158). A comparison of the distributions of Moorehead and Vergennes phase components, however, casts doubt on this assertion (Bourque 1994). Although both seem bounded by the Kennebec River on the west and St. John River on the east, what of the north–south axis? Admittedly the data are few, but Cox himself (1991:153) cites Vergennes-like material from the upper West Branch of the Penobscot, nearly 95 km from the coast and well to the north of any known Moorehead phase component. Other Laurentian-like artifacts have been identified farther up the Penobscot, and one of the very few typical Vergennes-style slate points from Maine comes from Eagle Lake in northern Aroostook County (Maine State Museum collection). The area between Eagle Lake and the St. Lawrence River, only about 110 km to the north, is little known archaeologically but, not surprisingly, significant Vergennes-related components have recently been reported there (Archambault 1987; Clermont 1987:24; Coté 1987).

The distribution of Vergennes-like artifacts from Maine, the Maritime Provinces, and Quebec, then, can be summarized much as Dincauze (1974:49) described Laurentian and earlier artifact distributions in southern New England: "The suggestion is that all these remains may reflect specialized interior-derived hunting patterns of small bands not adapted to the special ecological riches of [the coast]." For the present, therefore, Sanger's (1975:73) suggestion, offered almost two decades ago, that Vergennes-like material culture in Maine reflects only a southern extension of a St. Lawrence-based population seems still to describe the available data accurately (see also Tuck 1975:Figure 1, 30–32).

The End of the Moorehead Phase

Data from the Turner Farm and other sites in southern Maine suggest the emergence of the Moorehead phase from the Small Stemmed Point tradition after about 4500 B.P. between the Kennebec and St. John rivers, where an emphasis on deep water maritime exploitation fostered the development of elaborate technology and probably the elaborate mortuary ceremonialism of the Red Paint cemeteries. Parallel developments in Newfoundland and Labrador are probably due to a similar maritime emphasis and to concomitant close links maintained by boat travel across the Gulf of St. Lawrence.

Analyses of skeletal material from the Moorehead phase cemetery at the Nevin site suggest that the population was well adjusted to life on the Gulf of Maine coast, had a high protein diet, and enjoyed good health (Bourque and Krueger 1994; Shaw 1988). Why, then, did the Moorehead phase apparently suddenly disappear around 3800 B.P.? An examination of changes in the Gulf of Maine may provide the answer.

The Gulf of Maine is a marginal sea connected to the Atlantic Ocean by a deep channel known as the Northeast Channel. It is characterized by vigorous tidal mixing and surprisingly cool water. Its complex circulation patterns are controlled by basin topography, inflows from both the Atlantic and Scotian shelves, runoff from three major and several smaller river basins, tidal mixing, and the winds (Brooks and Brown 1985). Historically, these characteristics have made it a highly productive fishery, but the Gulf has undergone dramatic change during the Late Pleistocene and Holocene, much of it caused by fluctuation in relative sea level. After a low stand of about 60 m below its modern level (Belknap, Anderson et al. 1987) at about 11,000 B.P. (Kelley et al. 1992), sea level rose rapidly to −20 m at about 9500 B.P., slowed until 7000 B.P., resumed a rapid rate of rise to −5 m at 5000 B.P., then slowed progressively into the historical era, with a distinct deceleration at about 2000 B.P. (Figure 3.3; Belknap et al. 1989; Gehrels and Belknap 1983).

These sea-level changes have affected the composition and distribution of water in the Gulf, which in turn has determined its biological productivity. The rise allowed penetration of relatively warm and very salty offshore waters along with associated species from areas south of Cape Cod. About 5000 B.P., diatomaceous flora and benthic foraminifera became completely modern, with the species *Bolivina subaenariensis* dominating the foraminifera. This association of flora and fauna indicates the arrival of a very high tidal regime that caused upwelling of deep nutrient-rich waters to the surface, where photosynthetic algae consumed them to form the bottom of a highly productive food web that persists to the present. Associated with these changes were slight declines in temperature and salinity. Eventually, about 2000 B.P., the Gulf became too large for the perfect tidal resonance that had caused the extremely high tides, and attained its modern state (Schnitker 1986). In addition to sea-level change, Fillon (1976) has suggested that before about 3500 B.P. warm southern water penetrated northward along the Atlantic coast as far as Newfoundland, locally amplifying the effects of the climatic optimum.

In combination with apparently rapid climatic cooling after about 4500 B.P. (Zielinski et al. 1994:Fig. 1c), marine environmental changes of this magnitude must have had a noticeable impact on the human occupants of the Gulf shore. The clearest impact of these environmental changes is the sudden cessation of swordfishing around 3800 B.P. Swordfish are a warm-water species only occasionally seen along the Maine coast today (Bigelow and Schroeder 1953:355). The prevalence of their remains in Moorehead phase sites, however, suggests that formerly their populations were high. This abundance reinforces the hypothesis that the water temperatures in the Gulf were warmer, at least during the summer, before the advent of extreme tidal mixing. At the Turner Farm site, the discontinuity between Occupations 2 and 3 is accompanied by the disappearance of *Mercenaria mercenaria*, another indicator of warmer-than-modern seawater temperatures.

In any event, as Sanger (1975:70–71) originally suggested, and as recent human skeletal isotopic research confirms, the disappearance of swordfish would probably have had a distinctly negative impact on Moorehead phase populations and may have forced them to leave the region or radically to alter their lifestyle. As we shall see below, the former result currently seems the more likely hypothesis.

THE SUSQUEHANNA TRADITION

The Susquehanna Tradition North and South

Turner Farm Occupation 3 clearly demonstrates the extensive use of shellfish, as well as at least marginal use of other marine resources. Several additional Fox Islands middens also contain traces of Susquehanna occupation, although no in situ midden deposits have been found in association, probably because of erosion. Finally, although human bone isotope data suggest a smaller marine protein component in the diet of these people, the sample still falls well above the range exhibited by inland populations such as the Boucher site sample from Lake Champlain in Vermont (Figure 6.13). Unanimity of opinion regarding the intrusive nature of the Susquehanna tradition in Maine raises questions regarding the timing and extent of changes in lifestyle from patterns that prevailed in the more southerly portion of its range. Several researchers have stated or implied that south of New England there is little evidence for the use of marine fish or shellfish, or even of coastal occupation, by the Susquehanna tradition and related complexes (see, e.g., Funk and Rippeteau 1977; Pfeiffer 1992:91–95; Tuck 1978a:37–38). The Atlantic ledges site in Massachusetts, however, suggests at least occupation of the coast (Dincauze 1972), and Ritchie thought his early Susquehanna tradition data from Martha's Vineyard suggested a "primarily hunting economy . . . beginning to adjust to a littoral ecology" (Ritchie 1969a:55). Thus, it appears that marine resources increased in importance as the Susquehanna tradition penetrated Massachusetts, and continued to become more important northward into Maine and the Maritime Provinces.

Significant north–south differences also are apparent in technology. Two important differences between the Maine Susquehanna artifact inventory and that of southern New England are the total absence in Maine of winged atlatl weights and the scarcity of steatite bowls. The winged atlatl weight style associated with the early Atlantic phase in southern New England and with other related manifestations westward to southern Ontario and southward along the Atlantic slope to the Savannah River generally has a **D**-shaped profile, wing margins that are squared in cross section, and faceted septums (Plate 8.1, bottom; Claflin 1931:Plate 46; Dincauze 1972:51, 53; Ellis et al. 1990:104; Hawkes and Linton

Plate 8.1. Atlatl weights from Stallings Island (photo: Peabody Museum, Harvard University).

1917:Plate 14; Knoblock 1939:476–477; Kraft 1970:103; Ledbetter 1991:150–154; Regensberg 1971; Turnbaugh 1977:144). This form is absent from early broadpoint assemblages west of the Appalachians, where atlatl weights of other styles, often made from shell, predominate (see, e.g., Webb 1974:267–271).

Although similar to, and clearly derived from, Middle Archaic winged prototypes in the East, few demonstrably earlier atlatl weights there share this specific combination of morphological traits (see, e.g., Plate 8.1). In the Northeast, the winged atlatl weights of the Atlantic phase and its southern cognates are the last manifestation of this artifact form. That none have been reported from Maine contexts probably reflects its abandonment just before Susquehanna tradition populations entered that area.

Steatite vessels have been found in very small numbers in Maine and as far east as St. John, New Brunswick (Sanger 1973:123). The unique steatite gorget from the Turner family collection generally resembles Adena-related forms and may be contemporaneous with the exotic chert point also in the Turner family collection and the Adena blocked-end tube recovered from Occupation 4 deposits (Plate 7.8, Figure 7.5). It certainly is not comparable to the "heavy thick soapstone gorgets," listed in Witthoft's (1949:10–11) initial definition of the Transitional, which are probably perforated boiling stones such as those reported from Late Archaic sites on the Savannah River (Anderson and Joseph 1988:174–175; Sassaman and Lewis 1990:57–58). However, the gorget seems clearly to be made from a steatite bowl sherd and may, therefore, pertain to Occupation 3.

The scarcity of steatite bowls in Maine probably cannot be explained by the absence there of steatite outcrops. Steatite vessels found at sites of the closely related Frost Island phase in New York were imported from distant raw material source areas probably located in southeastern Pennsylvania, while those from southern Connecticut were also imported, possibly from eastern Maryland (Mason 1981:206; Pfeiffer 1992:203). The distances of transport in both cases are comparable to the distance between Penobscot Bay and steatite source areas in Connecticut, Massachusetts, and Rhode Island (Willoughby 1935/1973:157–158).

Rather, the scarcity probably reflects the relatively late emergence of steatite pots after the Susquehanna tradition had mostly come and gone from Maine. In the Middle Atlantic states, Pennsylvania, and New York, where the tradition underwent a developmental sequence spanning several centuries, the earliest dates on lithic assemblages resembling those from Turner Farm Occupation 3 generally predate 3600 B.P. (Funk 1993:196; Kinsey 1972b:352; Tuck 1978a:38–39). Steatite bowls from Susquehanna tradition contexts, by contrast, generally date to about 3500 B.P. or later (see, e.g., Funk 1993:198; Pfeiffer 1992:81–83, 88, 89a; Ritchie 1980:157; Ritchie and Funk 1973:85–91).

More difficult to explain are north–south differences in lithic procurement patterns for flaked and ground stone tools. Susquehanna tradition preference for fine-grained volcanics, often from exotic sources, has often been noted (see, e.g., Mason 1981:206; Pfeiffer 1992:203–204; Turnbaugh 1977:146; Witthoft 1953:9). In Connecticut, heavy woodworking tools made of basalt apparently were also obtained from sources as far away as western New Jersey (Pfeiffer 1992:203). To the north, in Massachusetts, the frequency of exotics apparently declines, although a number of flaked bifaces made of Maine lithics—including Vinalhaven banded-spherulitic rhyolite and Kineo-Traveler rhyolite—have been identified in several large collections there (Bourque 1994; Dincauze 1968:73, 94, 1972:41–42). In Maine, however, virtually no exotic lithics have been found in any of the several large assemblages currently available. That exotic raw materials became less frequent in the northern range of the Susquehanna tradition even though northern lithics moved southward suggests that the Susquehanna tradition in Maine retained close ties to the south. That exotic lithics did not move northward in comparable volumes, however, suggests some degree of asymmetry in social relations between north and south, with the northerners perhaps more anxious to maintain close ties with southern relatives.

In summary, the flaked lithics of the Susquehanna tradition in Maine indicate its derivation from the Atlantic phase of southern New England. Although the populations responsible for Occupation 3 inhabited the antipodes of the Susquehanna tradition, not to mention the Savannah River Archaic, continuing analysis of Occupation 3 has made it increasingly clear that it was a full participant in the early northward expansion of the tradition. The precise timing and the brief duration of the intrusion into Maine may be indicated by the absence of atlatl weights and the scarcity of steatite vessels there. That the immigration apparently failed to establish a new population, and the fact that lithic materials from Maine moved southward without apparent reciprocity, may indicate the tenuous and exploratory nature of the migration.

The Susquehanna Tradition in the Larger Broadpoint Context

In Maine, the sudden demise of the Moorehead phase and the virtually simultaneous appearance of large Susquehanna tradition components replete with striking differences from the Moorehead phase make it entirely likely that the latter represents the arrival in a depopulated area of a relatively large group of immigrants. Dincauze's minimalist interpretation of Susquehanna tradition immigration into Massachusetts is understandable in view of her assertion that another population was present in the area when they arrived. Farther south, as we have seen, from Pennsylvania to Massachusetts, the Susquehanna tradition has been regarded not as the result of a major population movement but rather as an in situ development from older Archaic cultures, perhaps influenced by the diffusion of southern technology, or, at most, as a slow influx of small groups that ultimately were absorbed by established populations. These contrasting perceptions of Susquehanna tradition origins, although not necessarily mutually exclusive, are certainly cause to examine related "broadpoint" cultures in a wider geographic context.

It is interesting to note that none of the participants in this debate has addressed several artifact classes that have broad distributions similar to broadpoints. Even using Cook's own highly select site sample (and terminology), aside from broadpoints, from Stallings Island northward, most assemblages also share characteristic "knife" forms— scrapers, drills, chipped-stone axes, celts and adzes, grooved axes, hammers, anvils, abraders, and hones (Plate 8.2, 8.3 bottom two rows; Cook 1976:346). Thus, Cook's stringent definition of technological linkages clearly transcends the broadpoint. Dincauze's somewhat more liberal characterization of the Susquehanna tradition as "a complex set of behavioral patterns related to the manufacture and use of a few distinct styles of stone tools" also underestimates the extent of technological similarities found throughout the broadpoint range (Dincauze 1975:23).

Cook (1976:345–347) places particular emphasis on the absence in his northern sample of carved, plain, and incised bone pins such as those found in his southern shell midden sites. The shell middens of Martha's Vineyard, the only sites in his sample where

Plate 8.2. Stemmed bifaces from Stallings Island (photo: Peabody Museum, Harvard University).

Plate 8.3. Modified discoidal stones from Stallings Island (photo: Peabody Museum, Harvard University).

bone was at all well preserved, were singled out for their lack of these artifacts. In this regard, two facts are worth noting. The first is that in the Southeast bone pins are not particularly numerous outside a limited number of cemeteries (Claflin 1931:23–24; Valerie Haskins, personal communication 1993). Given the small size of the Susquehanna tradition sample from the Martha's Vineyard sites (including, e.g., a total of only nine Snook Kill points), the absence of bone pins there is hardly surprising. Second, it is worth recalling that while complex bone artifacts were found in the Occupation 3 burials, none at all, except for some bone dice(?) (Plate 6.9), were found in the midden.[6] Since the Martha's Vineyard middens contained no Susquehanna tradition burials, the absence of bone pins there is even more understandable. Thus, the discovery of plain and decorated bone pins in Occupation 3 burials, the only context north of the Carolinas with an extensive bone artifact sample, clearly establishes their distribution to the northern limits of the broadpoint range.

Cook also cited as evidence against population movement the distributional incongruity between steatite bowls and early pottery versus broadpoint technology. However, if the scarcity of steatite vessels in Maine is the result of the early dates of Susquehanna tradition sites there, as I have argued above, then stone bowl making must be regarded as an innovation within the already developed tradition, not as one of its defining technologies. This view accords well with the relatively late emergence of steatite vessel use in the Savannah River Archaic, which occurred after the emergence of fiber-tempered pottery (Kenneth E. Sassaman, personal communication 1993). It is also worth noting in this regard that the earliest pottery style so far recognized in the Northeast was used by the late Susquehanna tradition Orient phase, although, as pointed out below, the style of this pottery cannot be specifically tied to the Southeast (Ritchie 1959).

Beyond the traits cited by Cook and Dincauze, other close similarities between Occupation 3 and such southeastern sites as Stallings Island, the Bilbo Mound, and Indian Knoll are apparent in antler rods, bone gouges/scrapers, flake gravers, the inclusion of dogs with human burials, human skull deformation,[7] the motifs found on decorated bone objects, socketed antler points, and turtle shell rattles with quartz pebbles. All of these traits, including those noted by Cook, are so far unknown from earlier Archaic contexts in the Northeast—except the grooved ax and drill, which made minor appearances during the Middle Archaic period, and burials accompanied by canid remains, which occurred at Port au Choix (Dincauze 1976:42, 73; Maymon and Bolian 1992:126–127; Tuck 1976:77–78). Some traits were encountered in the Frontenac Island cemetery in western New York that Ritchie (1945) regarded as a manifestation of the Frontenac phase dating prior to 4000 B.P. If Ritchie's interpretation is correct, then clearly the novelty of these traits in the Northeast predates the Susquehanna tradition. In light of several subsequent decades of research in the Northeast, however, reexamination of the Frontenac Island data strongly suggests that it was a multicomponent cemetery used over an extended period from about 5000 B.P. to at least 3700 B.P. by several archaeologically distinct groups (see, e.g., Ellis et al. 1990:106).

---

[6]Snow (1980:197, 199, 243, 246, 247) incorrectly included an illustration of these, as well as two ground slate pendants, in his Chapter 5, which does not concern the Susquehanna tradition. Those photos belong with others of Occupation 2 artifacts in his Chapter 6, a discussion of the Terminal Archaic.

[7]Noting the prevalence of skull deformation among Adena burials (dating about 2500–2000 B.P.), Willey (1966:273) suggested that the practice "could well have been derived from Mesoamerica." Given the presence of similar deformation at Indian Knoll, and now at the Turner Farm site, a more parsimonious explanation would be that it arose in late Archaic contexts in eastern North America.

Ritchie encountered several graves at Frontenac Island that were furnished with broadpoint-like artifacts, mostly clustered at the southern end of the Island. It is mainly these graves that exhibited the closest similarities to broadpoint burial assemblages elsewhere, especially to the Indian Knoll site (Webb 1974).

Recent research at Late Archaic sites in Georgia has refined the late Archaic sequence there, enabling Elliot et al. (1992) to define the Mill Branch phase of the Savannah River Archaic tradition. This phase, which dates between about 4200 and 3800 B.P., is of particular interest because it appears to distill from the broad range of the Savannah River Archaic those traits that are most commonly found in broadpoint complexes to the north. Aside from the characteristic flaked stone technology described above, they include the D-shaped faceted-winged atlatl weight. More importantly, however, the Mill Branch phase exhibits a variety of burial styles resembling those encountered at the Turner Farm site, including flexed and bundle burials—only cremation is absent from this mortuary system.

Some final observations concern points of difference between the Susquehanna tradition and its southeastern contemporaries. Broadpoint technology in the Southeast is not particularly sophisticated in comparison to earlier biface technologies there (see, e.g., Plate 8.2). The earliest Susquehanna biface technology—as represented by such named styles as the Atlantic, Coens-Krispin, Lehigh Broad, Snook Kill, and possibly Genessee (Funk 1993:196)—reflects, at best, only a marginal reduction in relative blade thickness and outline improvement over more southerly forms. Derived point styles postdating about 3800 B.P., however, with their expanding stems and very broad but exceedingly thin blades (typified in named styles such as Perkiomen, Susquehanna Broad, and Watertown), reflect a level of technical sophistication rarely, if ever, achieved by earlier Archaic or later post-Archaic technologies of eastern North America.

Tracing the broadpoint phenomenon northward along the Atlantic slope, this increased sophistication in flaked tool manufacture seems to appear first in eastern Pennsylvania and New Jersey, where extremely broad and thin bifaces with expanding stems are often found in mortuary contexts associated with the faceted and notched "abraders." Cross (1990:226–229) has argued convincingly that these water-worn cobbles with "abraded" and notched margins, which have frequently been found in Susquehanna tradition contexts, were long-curated hammerstones used to produce the unusual bifaces with which they are associated (see Chapter 6). Both the extremely broad and thin points and the hammerstones are known mainly from Susquehanna cremation cemetery contexts and the hammerstones have so far not been identified in broadpoint contexts outside the range of the Susquehanna tradition. It may be, however, that a prototype for this specialized hammerstone is to be found in the discoidal stones recovered from Savannah River Archaic sites, some of which have abraded and "polished" margins and facets (Plate 8.3; Claflin 1931:30–31, Plate 49; Sassaman and Lewis 1990:58–59; Stoltman 1974:103, Plate 33). Closer analogues may also be evident in a group of unillustrated artifacts described as abrading stones with "polishing over one or more faces or pronounced grooves" from Mill Branch phase sites in Georgia (Ledbetter 1991:150).

In sum, an impressive array of similarities connect contemporaneous cultures that produced large, broad-bladed, stemmed bifaces throughout much of eastern North America between about 4000 and 3600 B.P. In the lower Midwest and the Southeast, these cultures seem to have developed from a local Middle Archaic base. As stated above, there may be an emerging consensus that the ancestors of the late Archaic Mill Branch phase were immigrants to the Piedmont from across the Appalachians. In the Northeast, from Pennsylvania to Nova Scotia, the specific similarities to assemblages from farther south represent a distinct break with earlier local patterns. Over the whole broadpoint range, the strongest similarities appear to be between the Piedmont and the southern limit of the Susquehanna tradition, while the relationship between the latter and Occupation 3 seems slightly more derived, reflecting the passage of some brief interval as the technological system spread northward.

The Southern Origin of the Susquehanna Tradition

Given the extent of these connections among broadpoint-using cultures, let us turn to the question of whether the evidence is sufficient to invoke population movement on a larger geographic scale than that of a Susquehanna tradition intrusion into Maine. When American archaeologists consider the possibility of prehistoric migrations it has become customary to consult "Rouse's rules," five criteria that constitute a minimum level of evidence considered by Rouse to warrant the consideration of migration as a better explanation than in situ development for culture change in the archaeological record (Rouse 1958; Snow 1980:245–249). Rouse's five rules are:

1. Identify the migrating people as an intrusive unit in the region it has penetrated.
2. Trace this unit back to its homeland.
3. Determine that all occurrences of the unit are contemporaneous.
4. Establish the existence of favorable conditions for migration.
5. Demonstrate that some other hypothesis, such as independent invention or diffusion of traits, does not better fit the facts (Snow 1980:245).

To these five Sanger (1975:73) has added a sixth:

6. Establish the presence of all cultural subsystems and not an isolated one such as the mortuary subsystem.

Rouse's rules were, in effect, a gauntlet thrown down to those archaeologists who had too frequently and speculatively invoked migration to explain changes in the archaeological record. The rules effectively placed the burden of proof on those who would argue for population movements, thus allowing in situ development to become the default explanation, particularly where hunter-gatherers were involved. Indirect support for this stance came from two additional sources (Bourque 1994). First, North American native peoples, and hunter-gatherers in particular, have historically been perceived as tradition-bound and culturally static. Second, since the mid-1960s, the influence of the New Archaeology has fostered research designed to explain culture change as an adaptive response to local environmental conditions. The net effect of these factors on eastern North America has been, first, to minimize the degree of culture change invoked to explain changes in the archaeological record and, second, to downplay all but the closest neighboring regions as potential sources of explanatory factors.

It is in the context of this praxis that we must consider the Turner Farm cemetery and related data from elsewhere in Maine. The task is made more difficult by the fact that, except for a few classic early studies (e.g., Ritchie 1932, 1945; Webb 1974), the Late Archaic period in the eastern United States has only recently become the focus of concentrated professional attention.

Rouse's rules clearly suit data from Turner Farm Occupation 3 and contemporaneous Maine sites vis-à-vis the Susquehanna tradition in southern New England, but how well do they apply to the broadpoint phenomenon as a whole? A great deal better, I think, than Snow (1980) asserted, and certainly well enough to sustain a major northward migration as a viable hypothesis, perhaps along with more persuasive diffusionary models that have yet to be formulated.

It is now apparent that the long list of attributes, enumerated above, evokes assemblages found among contemporaneous or near-contemporaneous sites over a large area of eastern North America. It is also clear that all appear suddenly in the Northeast about 3800 B.P., constituting a whole cultural system called the Susquehanna tradition, which often completely broke with preceding cultural patterns. Thus, even adhering to Rouse's strict standards, the parsimonious inference appears to be that the tradition represents a population movement into an abandoned (or partially abandoned) region from somewhere to the south of New England, possibly as far south as the Carolinas or as far west as the Tennessee Basin. Given the relative inattention accorded the Late Archaic in the Southeast, it is not surprising that the chronology of all these obviously related manifestations has yet to be worked out. However, it is interesting to note that mass population movement is among the mechanisms suggested by Winters (1974:xii, xx–xxii) for explaining why certain Late Archaic Midwestern cultures, including Indian Knoll, "either met extinction or underwent changes of such amplitude that the derivative cultures are no longer recognizable in terms of their earlier patterns."

Finally, yet another potentially useful "rule" can be derived from linguistics, which often counters cases where linguistic diversity increases following the first emplacement of an ancestral tongue. Just such diversity has recently been at the crux of debates regarding the arrival dates of populations in North America. The diversification of the early Susquehanna tradition in the Northeast, with its large, straight-stemmed points and minimally developed cremation mortuary ceremonialism, resulted in clearly derived manifestations such as those referred to as the Frost Island, Perkiomen, Watertown, and Orient phases. It is thus tempting to interpret this diversification as evidence of elaboration upon a unified, intrusive ancestral culture (e.g., Funk 1993:196–197, 224–225; Dincauze 1968:71–83).

Resistance to this hypothesis can be anticipated from those who cling to the premise that culture change in prehistoric hunter-gatherer societies is primarily driven by in situ adaptation. The specific objection is likely to be that no causal environmental shift, such as that offered by Turnbaugh, has been demonstrated. As Anthony (1993:898) has pointed out, however, prehistoric migrations may have arisen from complex sets of circumstances that may be impossible to identify archaeologically and, moreover, are likely to have included motivations that are adaptive in some cultural—rather than any simple environmental—sense.

The End of the Susquehanna Tradition

A salient feature of the Susquehanna tradition in Maine is its brief duration. Appearing suddenly at about 3800 B.P., it suddenly disappeared sometime before 3500 B.P., possibly resulting in regional depopulation. Stemmed bifaces that resemble later Susquehanna forms have occasionally been reported from a few sites in southern Maine, but nothing remotely like the coherent sequence reported from southern New England and New York. In those areas, the tradition culminated in what some regard as a merger with a long-resident population using narrow-stemmed points that became the Orient phase, the first ceramic-using culture in that region (Dincauze 1974:49; Ritchie 1980:219–222; see also Pfeiffer 1992).

The causes of this brief tenure are unknown. From an adaptational perspective, it may be that the preference for terrestrial over marine resources proved to be a nonviable long-term strategy that led to cultural instability and a retreat southward. Given the ubiquity of its cultural remains throughout southern Maine, however, it certainly appears that the Susquehanna tradition enjoyed at least short-term success and, once again, no compelling environmental reason for its departure from the region has been identified.

Anthony (1990:904) has called attention to the phenomenon of return migration, in which migrant populations are frequently seen to return to their point of origin, sometimes transmitting materials obtained from the hinterland in the process. It is tempting, if speculative, to see all these data, including the asymmetric movement of Maine raw materials southward, as evidence for this kind of remigration. If this is the case, then the archaeological hiatus that follows the latest Susquehanna tradition dates and is ended by the appearance of ceramics about 2700 B.P. may represent dramatically lower population levels in Maine over several centuries.

Moorehead and Susquehanna Mortuary Ceremonialism

The juxtaposition of the elaborate but very different mortuary ceremonial patterns that characterize the Moorehead phase and Susquehanna tradition underscores the differences between the cultures that gave rise to them. Indeed, the desire to express cultural distinctiveness may have been the original intent of these practices. Dincauze (1973:31) has suggested that among the peoples of the Susquehanna tradition such ceremonialism served group validation functions that "could have been vitally important adaptive mechanisms in a complex social environment." Tuck amplified this theme:

> The florescence of this burial ceremonialism, coming as it does at a time of natural and social tension, suggests that these mortuary rituals . . . served as rites of intensification or group validation in addition to the disposal of the dead. In fact, the former may even have become more important than the latter. (Tuck 1978b:74–75)

He went on to point out that at both the southern (Moorehead phase) and northern limits of his Maritime Archaic range, elaboration of mortuary practice tends to occur late, at the end of the manifestation and just before each region is overrun by distinctly different populations. In the north, the immigrant group were Paleo-Eskimo peoples, while in the south it was the Susquehanna tradition.

Continuing in a speculative vein, the mortuary elaboration encountered in the expanding Susquehanna tradition of New England may likewise reflect a reaction to the presence of alien Narrow Point tradition populations nearby. In this regard it may be significant that the extensive manipulation of the dead encountered at the Turner Farm site would seem to have provided open-ended possibilities for group-validation ceremonialism.

THE CERAMIC PERIOD

Subsistence and Population Size

The long temporal span of the Turner Farm faunal sample provides a new perspective on the difficult question of population trends during the Ceramic period, which have, at least implicitly, been estimated on the basis of relative numbers of components through time. The great advantage of the Turner Farm sample in this regard is that, although the local and regional environment was not static throughout the site's history, the geographic factor as a variable affecting faunal exploitation remains constant. Changes in faunal patterns through time may thus reflect cultural factors more clearly than when comparing components from different localities.

Faunal trends at the Turner Farm site, especially the relatively energy-intensive pursuit of marine species during the Ceramic period, show a consistent increase in dietary breadth through time. Based on the premise stated above, therefore, the site's occupants appear to have been adding prey species of lower desirability throughout the site's history. The strong marine dietary component signaled by Ceramic period bone isotopic ratios supports such an interpretation. Both trends would be likely outcomes of increasing population size and attendant sedentism in the region throughout the site's history.

Temporal Discontinuities during the Ceramic Period

Unlike the Archaic, where stone and bone tools constitute most of the culturally diagnostic artifact classes, during the Ceramic period it is the ceramics themselves that are usually most informative. Judging from the ceramic data, there appear to be three outstanding events during the Ceramic period, all of which are in evidence at the Turner Farm site (see also Petersen and Sanger 1991). The first is the appearance of Vinette I-like pottery over much of New York and New England about 2700 B.P. Tuck (1978a:39) regarded Vinette I as introduced into the Northeast from the north, while Snow thought "its production in the Northeast was stimulated by prototypes to the south" (Snow 1980:242). Recent research suggests that both views may be incorrect. Originally defined at the Vinette site in central New York, Vinette I ware is now recognized over a broad region stretching from southwestern Ontario eastward to Maine (Ritchie 1946:13, 16; Ritchie and MacNeish 1949:100; Petersen and Sanger 1991:126–131; Spence et al. 1990:125–137). In the western portion of its range, Vinette I resembles various early wares of Michigan, Illinois, and Ohio rather than the flat-bottomed early wares of the south (Garland 1986:47–71; Harn 1986:256–268; Kraft 1970:138; Mason 1981:216; Spence et al. 1990:131). Thus, the available evidence suggests that Vinette I may have been introduced from the west and spread very rapidly into New England. Alternatively, it may have developed nearly simultaneously over larger portions of its range.

The fact that Vinette I is not demonstrably later in Maine than anywhere else in the Northeast is interesting in light of the fact that it heralds the return of a robust archaeological record following several centuries after the disappearance of the Susquehanna tradition—during which time, so far, we have only the most anemic evidence for human occupation (Sanger 1988a:90). The situation is quite different to the south and west, where an elaborating Susquehanna tradition is followed by the Meadowood complex and a sequence of other ceramic-using cultures. Furthermore, as the data from Occupation 4 indicate, although early Ceramic period populations were at least as fully marine adapted as Late Archaic ones, they did not simply resume Archaic subsistence patterns.

The second event is the replacement of Vinette I-like pottery with thin, relatively well-fired rocker-stamped ware sometime before the birth of Christ. In southwestern Ontario, pottery of the Saugeen Culture exhibits a variety of dentate-rocker-stamped and pseudo-scallop-shell-stamped decoration (Mason 1981:265–266). Farther east, on both sides of the St. Lawrence and into northern Vermont, better-made but similarly decorated pottery characterizes cultures locally referred to as Point Peninsula (Clermont and Chapdelaine 1982:74–84; Powers et al. 1980:45–49; Ritchie 1980:205–208). Around the northern Great Lakes, another cognate ceramic style, generally the thinnest and hardest of the period, was made by the Laurel Culture (Mason 1980:286–290).

Similar pottery makes a strong showing in Maine and the Maritimes. Petersen and Sanger (1991:131, Table 2) refer to it as representing "an early perceived peak in terms of technological proficiency and decorative elaboration," but they also regard it as an "evolutionary development." As Mason (1980:266) points out, however, the developmental sequence from Vinette I to later styles remains to be demonstrated. Although some evidence for such development in southern Ontario has recently been reported by Spence et al. (1990:125–137), no such evidence has been reported from Maine, and the available radiocarbon dates there would appear to provide little time indeed for evolutionary change.

The stamped pottery tradition in Maine and adjacent regions underwent a series of changes, including the decline of pseudo-scallop-shell stamping, an increase in vessel wall thickness, an overall decline in fabric quality, and the elaboration of rim forms (Bourque 1992a:93–98, 236–281; Petersen and Sanger 1991:137–140). About 1200 to 1000 B.P., however, stamped decoration was replaced altogether by cord-wrapped-stick-impressed decoration (Petersen and Sanger 1991:140–141). A few sherds from Maine appear to bear decoration made by both dentate stamps and cord-wrapped sticks, but their number is exceedingly small. Moreover, although coil construction was apparently used throughout the Maine ceramic sequence, the extent to which coils were fused together in smoothing vessel walls apparently changed at the time when cord-wrapped-stick decoration appeared. As described above, breaks in stamp-decorated vessels are jagged and irregular, rarely occurring along coil joins, and lamellar failure and spalling are common; both characteristics probably reflect extensive thinning by paddle and anvil. The joins on many cord-wrapped-stick-impressed vessels, by contrast, apparently are weaker and frequently are where breaks occurred, while lamellar failure and spalling are rare (cf., e.g., Bourque 1992a, p. 243 with p. 253; see also Sanger 1987:120).

A final distinct change in ceramic manufacture falls near the end of the prehistoric period, when there appeared a very thin ware (or series of related wares) that have globular bodies, sometimes with cord-maleated exteriors, and decorated collars (Petersen and Sanger 1991:157–160). The vessel shown in Plate 7.26 exhibits all these attributes. It remains unclear whether this late ceramic technology completely replaced cord-impressed ware on a regional basis or whether some more complex pattern of co-occurrence or replacement occurred.

Unlike the initial appearance of ceramics in the Northeast, changes in ceramic manufacture have routinely been regarded as aspects of a dynamic ceramic tradition developing and changing within a temporally continuous regional population, not as the result of extraneous factors. Such a perspective is generally apparent in Petersen and Sanger (1991) and is explicit in Sanger's (1987:122) detailed construction of the Quoddy tradition, which was "defined on the basis of changes in decoration of ceramic vessels." Although Sanger (1987:88–136) makes a point of stating that "there is general synchroneity with regards to major (ceramic) stylistic changes" in the tradition, to him it nevertheless "represents nearly 2000 years of cultural stability and continuity that existed without interruption until the coming of Europeans about A.D. 1600."

These observations are meant not to assert any specific claims for population discontinuity in Maine and the Maritime Provinces during the ceramic period, but rather to point out that the assumption of continuity has often been made in the face of significant archaeological evidence to the contrary. Other evidence for continuity may well offset the ceramic evidence. In the case of the Quoddy tradition, for example, Sanger (1987:122) has abundantly demonstrated the survival into the late Ceramic period of "a generalist pattern little changed from that of earlier periods." However, if the issue of population discontinuity is not explicitly considered at some point, no consideration can be given to the alternative possibility that environmental constraints might force a newly arrived population to adopt a subsistence strategy that is similar to that employed by earlier peoples. In sum, it is worth calling attention to the apparent suddenness with which ceramics first appeared in the Northeast, as well as the fact that the two latter ceramic changes noted above also seem to reflect rapid and apparently extensive overhauls of ceramic manufacture, from paste preparation to decoration. When viewed in the broader context of developing ceramic traditions elsewhere in eastern North America, these changes seem profound enough to suggest that they were accompanied by other important cultural changes, possibly including actual migrations and population replacements.

A PARTHIAN SHOT AT LINGUISTIC PREHISTORY

As pointed out above, the main exception to the current unpopularity of migration hypotheses in the Northeast pertains to early historic linguistic distributions, particularly a number of Iroquoian-speaking groups in New York, Ontario, and Quebec that were surrounded by Algonquian speakers (Trigger 1978:ix). Snow (1980:232) began the more recent of his discussions concerning linguistic prehistory by criticizing the view shared by Tuck (1978a:39), Wright (1972b:67), and Sanger (1975:73) that the emergence of the Vergennes phase in New York and New England heralded the appearance of Iroquoian speakers. Like his criticism of Turnbaugh's Susquehanna tradition hypothesis, Snow (1980:232) characterizes Tuck's hypothesis as relying on "the presumed movement of a single artifact class." And also like the Susquehanna case, as we have seen, whether one believes that the Vergennes phase is "real" or not, the debate is about far more than Otter Creek points.

Snow also claimed that Tuck's proposed date of entry is too early to fit the "highly respected" opinion of Lounsbury (1978) that 4000 B.P. is the earliest likely date of Iroquoian entry into New York. Snow (1980:232–233, 258–259) countered Tuck with the assertion that the Frost Island phase of the Susquehanna tradition was the harbinger of Iroquoian language; that the Meadowood complex was the cultural offspring of the Frost Island phase, which began a line of continuity leading to the historic Iroquoians; and that "there is a clear evolution in the direction of semipermanent sedentary settlement" during Meadowood times; and thus that "the origins of the historic Iroquoian clans lie in this period" (Snow 1980:265–266).

Snow's view of the Meadowood complex is not widely shared, however. Both Mason (1981:209) and Tuck (1978a:39–41), for example, saw it as the persistence of the Archaic life way, inherited from Laurentian forbears. Granger (1978) also regarded Meadowood as Archaic, although he argued that its cultural ancestor was the Lamoka phase. In a summary of data pertaining to the northwestern range of the Meadowood complex, Spence et al. (1990:136) state that "we still do not have a very clear picture of the Meadowood settlement-subsistence system in Ontario. Most non-mortuary sites are small fall camps for processing deer and nuts." Most recently, Funk (1993:225–226, 325) assessed its relatedness to earlier and later cultures, noting that the evidence was weak in either case.

The basic weakness in Snow's model, however, is that the Frost Island phase is only one manifestation of the Susquehanna tradition that may have begun a long developmental sequence; others occupied what was historically Algonquin territory. An obvious example is the line that led to the Orient phase of southern New York and New England and thence as plausibly to later cultures there as did the Meadowood complex to the west. Snow reasoned that the arrival of the Frost Island phase in the Susquehanna Valley around 3500 B.P. appears to fit the window of opportunity defined by Lounsbury's 4000 B.P. estimate and also Goddard's (1978:70) estimate that eastern and central Algonquian languages, presumably split by the Iroquoian intrusion, "must have been diverging from each other for something on the order of 2000 years."

The measurement of absolute chronology using recent linguistic data remains one of the more contested methodological issues in linguistics. Thus, even the 1,000-year discrepancy between Tuck's estimate of the age of the Vergennes phase and Lounsbury's estimate should not be regarded as a fatal flaw. Indeed, Lounsbury himself revised his estimate from 3800–3600 B.P. (Lounsbury 1961:11) to 4000 B.P. (Lounsbury 1978:336).

The issue here is not really whether either Snow or Tuck is more or less likely to have been correct. Rather, it is whether we yet have reliable standards for evaluating hypotheses about linguistic links to archaeological complexes. Snow's (1992) most recent effort at explaining Iroquoian linguistic distributions well illustrates the dilemma, for he has completely reversed his earlier position, arguing instead for a very recent northward migration of Iroquoian speakers on the basis of demographic reconstructions. The dilemma may not be unsolvable, and Snow's arguments are interesting, certainly suggesting at least the theoretical possibility of a recent migration. It remains to be seen, however, whether independent archaeological support is available to support his hypothesis. Given recent debate regarding correlation between language and other aspects of human history, and the considerable uncertainty that still surrounds our ability even to detect prehistoric migrations (particularly by small-scale societies such as those encountered in eastern North American prehistory), it seems to me that the addition of a linguistic dimension to these debates is overly speculative (see, e.g., Bateman et al. 1990a, 1990b, 1990c).

POSTSCRIPT: OUTLOOK FOR FUTURE RESEARCH IN PENOBSCOT BAY

The Turner Farm midden still has tremendous research potential, and many aspects of the extant sample from the site warrant further analysis. Nevertheless, because prospects for the site's long-term survival are relatively good, the time has come to move on to other coastal sites, many of which are being destroyed by unchecked erosion, construction, and vandalism.

The Turner Farm project will very likely remain the largest undertaken in the Gulf of Maine for some time to come. Few other sites in the Penobscot Bay area appear to warrant such extensive attention. Indeed, it appears that the most productive strategy in the near future will be briefly to explore numerous sites that fill gaps in the Turner Farm chronological sequence—a strategy that will allow us to explore the variability of the record for those periods represented at Turner Farm. The outlook for enhanced understanding of the issues addressed above is increasingly optimistic owing to the continued diversification of archaeological research on the Maritime Peninsula. Among many promising developments are the expansion of multidisciplinary coastal research, a resurgence of interest in recent sites, and, especially, new research at stratified interior sites where the cultural record extends far back to the early Holocene (Belcher and Sanger 1988; Sanger, Belcher, and Kellog, 1992). Most promising is the reemergence of a sense that Archaic and later prehistoric cultures of the East were not mere isolates dependent on local ecological adaptations but were, instead, societies in vital contact with other cultures over broad geographic ranges. These new perceptions are already beginning to generate new kinds of research that will no doubt force rethinking of current formulations, including those presented here. The purpose of this closing chapter will have been served if some of the issues northeastern archaeologists have struggled with for decades have been clarified or redefined in such a way as to fuel the next round of debate.

Appendix *1*

Turner Farm Midden Analysis

Statistics presented in Table A1.1 below compare the shell and nonshell components of the midden by occupation. Estimates of excavated volumes of both shell-free and shell-rich lenses (Total) were made from stratigraphic profiles on a section-by-section, stratum-by-stratum basis, and totaled for each stratigraphic unit except the plow zone.

Shell weight was determined from column samples using a two-step procedure. Large shell fragments were separated from nonshell and small shell fragments by screening (.4 cm mesh) and hand sorting. The fraction that passed through the screen was weighed and soaked overnight in an HCl solution to dissolve all small shell fragments. It was then dried, and weighed again and the weight loss was then added to shell weight. The ratio of shell (kg) to total volume (S/T), which was calculated only for shell-rich strata, indicates the weight of shell per cubic meter of midden. Note that it decreased through time. The significance of this trend is enhanced by the taphonomic loss of shell density through time. The weight of the nonshell fraction (N.S.) was calculated using the following formula:

$$\text{N.S.} = \text{wt of residue/vol of residue} \times \text{vol of stratum}$$

The ratios of nonshell volume to shell volume (NSV/SV) were established by screening and hand sorting a separate set of column samples—three per stratigraphic unit per section. They are not directly comparable, however, because of differential crushing of the shell fraction. Note also that the nonshell fraction has little impact on overall midden volume until it saturates the interstitial voids in the shell fraction.

Table A1.1. Turner Farm Midden Analysis

Stratum[a]	Total (m³)	Shell (kg)	S/T[b]	N.S.[c]	NSV/SV[d]
Occupation 1	.3	190			
Occupation 2					
Shell-free	15.1	779			
Shell-rich	25.5	12,747	500	45.8	.23
Occupation 3					
Shell-free	14.7	812			
Shell-rich	19.9	11,424	574	340.1	.34
B2GF					
Shell-free	1.4	14			
Shell-rich	8.9	5,097	573		.34
2GF	17.6	908			
CCS					
Shell-free	.2	8			
Shell-rich	42.7	22,292	522	72.2	.13
1GF	19.2	999			
MCS					
Shell-free	.1	2			
Shell-rich	12.1	7,929	655	9.6	.13
NGF	.7	42			
FCS	64.7	52,435	810	.7	
Sod[e]	24.5				

[a]B2GF, below the second gravel floor; 2GF, second gravel floor; CCS, coarsely crushed shell; 1GF, first gravel floor; MCS, moderately crushed shell; NGF, new gravel floor; FCS, finely crushed shell, or plow zone.
[b]Ratio of shell (kg) to total volume (m³) midden.
[c]Nonshell fraction.
[d]Ratio of nonshell volume to shell volume.
[e]No breakdown or shell analysis done.

Appendix *2*

Radiocarbon Dates

The following is a comprehensive list of all radiocarbon dates from the Turner Farm site. Dates from different occupations are discussed and listed separately in relevant chapters.

Dates	Stratum/ Occupation	Section	Sample number	Feature number	Material	Association	Lab number
115 ± 65	1GF	W35S90	147C		Charcoal		SI 4246
175 ± 70	MCS	W55S90	7C		Charcoal		SI 4239
875 ± 70	1GF	W60S85	4C		Charcoal		SI 4238
1200 ± 100	CCS	W55S110	197C		Charcoal		GX 2465
1955 ± 50	2GF	E20S75	37C	19-1973	Charcoal	Pipe	SI 4240
2105 ± 75	2GF	E15S75	120C		Charcoal		SI 4245
2275 ± 130	B2GF	W55S105	195C		Charcoal		GX 2463
2530 ± 65	B2GF	W55S105	44C		Sea urchin	Points and pottery	SI 2407
2575 ± 75	B2GF	W55S105	43C		*Mya*	Points and pottery	SI 2398
2660 ± 100	OCC3	W15S70-75	4362	39-1974	Human bone	Bundle burial	GX 14968
2705 ± 60	OCC2	W40S90		12-1972	Antler	Hearth	SI 1926a
2895 ± 170	2GF	W65S115	30C		Charcoal		GX 20369
2970 ± 65	OCC2	E0S75	62C	14-1974	Swordfish	Pit in subsoil	SI 2402
3080 ± 160	2GF	W25S115	48C		Charcoal		GX 20370
3105 ± 75	OCC3	W25S70	64C	30-1974	Human bone	Primary inhumation	SI 2399
3115 ± 65	OCC2	W40S90		12-1972	Antler	Hearth	SI 1926b
3185 ± 65	B2GF	E40S65	81C	21-1974	Charcoal		SI 4244
3205 ± 75	OCC3	W15S70-75	66C	39-1974	Human bone	Secondary inhumation	SI 2400
3270 ± 75	OCC3	W25S70	63C	30-1974	*Mya*	Primary inhumation	SI 2397
3280 ± 50	B2GF	E20S80	78C	12-1974	Charcoal		SI 4243
3280 ± 180	OCC3	W30S65		18-1975	Human bone	Primary inhumation	GX 15744-A
3445 ± 70	OCC2	E40S65-70	72C		Swordfish	Subsoil surface	SI 2401

(Continued)

Dates	Stratum/ Occupation	Section	Sample number	Feature number	Material	Association	Lab number
3450 ± 75	OCC3	E0S65-70	60C	28-1974	*Mya*	Pit in subsoil	SI 2396
3470 ± 60	OCC3	W10S50	124C	9-1975	Charcoal	Primary inhumation	GX 19997-AMS
3480 ± 90	OCC2	E10S80	57C	22-1973	Charcoal	Cache	B 6031
3480 ± 75	OCC3	W30S65	153C	18-1975	Charcoal	Cremation	SI 4248
3490 ± 235	OCC3	W10S50		9-1975	Human bone	Primary inhumation	GX 15745-A
3515 ± 80	OCC3	W15S105	194C	3-1973	Soil sample	House floor	SI 1924
3610 ± 90	OCC3	W15S70-75	65C	39-1974	Charcoal	Secondary inhumation	SI 2404
3630 ± 85	OCC3	W35S90-95	14C	7-1972	Charcoal	Pit	SI 1919
3650 ± 75	OCC3	W20S100	31C	19-1972	Charcoal	Hearth	SI 1922
3662 ± 59	OCC3	W10S50		9-1975	Bone	Primary inhumation	GX 15745-G-AMS
3665 ± 55	OCC2	W25S105	42C		*Mercenaria*	Basal midden level	SI 2403
3700 ± 220	OCC3	W30S70	148C	6-1975	Charcoal	Primary inhumation	GX 14806
3700 ± 85	OCC3	W30S65	152C	18-1975	Charcoal	Primary inhumation	SI 4247
3710 ± 80	OCC3	W5-10S70	68C	24-1974	Charcoal	House floor	SI 2390
3710 ± 60	OCC2	E5S85	63C	15-1973	*Mya*	Pit (top)	S1 4242
3745 ± 75	OCC2	W25S95	37C	15-1972	*Mya*	Pit (needle)	SI 2406
3770 ± 260	OCC3	W10S50		9-1975	Human bone	Primary inhumation	GX 15745-G
3785 ± 75	OCC2	E5S85	41C		*Mya*	Layer above Feature 15	SI 2408
3825 ± 65	OCC3	W30S65	154C	18-1975	Charcoal	Primary inhumation	SI 4249
3825 ± 76	OCC3	W30S65		18-1975	Bone	Primary inhumation	GX 15744-G-AMS
3855 ± 75	OCC3	W10S55	70C	41-1974	Charcoal	Cremation	SI 2405
3870 ± 115	OCC3	W30S70	6657	6-1975	Human bone	Primary inhumation	GX 14807
3920 ± 25	OCC2	E15S80			Ivory	Walrus tusk	OS 1832-AMS
3945 ± 230	OCC3	W30S65		18-1975	Human bone	Primary inhumation	GX 15744-G
4005 ± 55	OCC2	E5S85	44C	15-1973	Charcoal	Pit (upper)	SI 4241
4020 ± 80	OCC3	W10S55	71C	42-1974	Charcoal	Cremation	SI 2393
4050 ± 220	OCC2?	W60S90	196C		Charcoal	Midden base	GX 2464
4135 ± 85	OCC2	E0S70-75	69C	24a-1974	*Mya*	Foreshaft	SI 2395
4310 ± 140		Marsh			Peat	Base of marsh	SI 2216
4390 ± 55	OCC2	E10S80	53C	24-1973	Charcoal	Dog burial	SI 1921
4410 ± 80	OCC2	W25S105	2051		Swordfish		SI 1920
4555 ± 95	OCC1	E5S85	54C	15-1973	Charcoal	Pit	SI 1923
4970 ± 85	OCC1	E40S65	65C	22-1974	Charcoal	Pit (biface)	SI 2392
5210 ± 70	OCC1	W35S105	13C	5-1972	Charcoal	Pit	SI 2394
5290 ± 95	OCC1	E5S85	39C	15-1973	Charcoal	Pit (biface)	SI 1925
Too small	OCC2	E0S75	61C	24a-1974	Charcoal	Foreshaft	SI 2391

Appendix *3*

Summary of Occupation 3
Burial Features

Feature number	Burial style[a]	Number of individuals[b]	Lithics[c]	Bone artifacts	Vegetable remains	Bone counts
30-1974	—	1 sa			—	—
34-1974	—	1 a♀	2 St points 1 TSB, Ocher			1 Aves
38-1974	C	1 a♂ 1 a♀ 1 a? 1 sa	1 Preform 1 MI blades 1 Boats blade 10 TSBs 5 St points 1 Cn point 2 Drills 1 Small biface 2 Adzes 2 Gravers	1 Awl Tool frags: 2 Engraved 1 Notched 1 Perf. 7 Antler frags	1 Beechnut	2 Deer 1 Fox 1 Mustelid 14 Phocid 6 Mammal 26 Aves
39-1974	B	1 a♂ 1 a♂? 1 a♀? 1 a? 1 sa	1 Boats blade 1 Blade frag, ocher	—	—	
41a-1974	C	1 a♂ 3 a? 6 sa	3 Preforms 4 TSBs 13 St points ≥4 Drills 2 Biface frags	—	—	1 Med Aves 6 Deer 1 *Mustela macrodon* 1 Mustelid 44 Lg mammal 1 Fish
Fea. 41a or b:						
41b-1974			1 Preform 1 TSB 2 St points 1 Drill 1 Biface frag 1 Gouge	1 Painted turtle scute 1 Worked bone		

			Artifacts	Worked bone/other	Plant	Faunal
42-1974	C	2 a? 5 sa	8 Preforms 4 TSBs 15 St points 5 Drills 1 Adz 3 Gouges 1 Beveled cobble	1 Box turtle carapace	2 Beechnuts	7 Deer 5 Dog 71 Lg mammal 1 Phocid 1 Lg Aves 1 Med Aves
6-1975	I	1 a♀ 2 sa	2 Drills	—	—	1 Mammal
7-1975	C	1 a 4 sa	1 TSB 3 St points	—	1 Beechnut	≥1 Deer 1 *Felis* sp. 1 Goose
9-1975	I C	1 a♀ 5 sa	2 Preforms 1 MI blade 2 Boats blades 6 TSBs 6 St points ≥2 Drills 1 Adz 1 Gouge 1 Grooved axe 1 Beveled cobble 6 Pebbles, ocher	4 Toggling harpoons 4 Awls 1 Antler harpoon 1 Bodkin 1 Gouge 1 Painted turtle plastron 1 Wolf maxilla Many worked bone frags 16 Antler frags	2 Beechnuts	36 Deer 9 Dog 30 Mammal 1 Goose 7 Aves
12-1975	C	1 a♂ 1 a 3 sa	3 Preforms 2 MI blades 2 Boats blades 1 TSB 7 St points 2 Cn points 3 Drills 1 Adz 1 Gouge 3 Pendants 18 Pebbles 10 Copper beads, limonite frag	1 Awl 1 Harpoon 1 Box turtle scute 1 Painted turtle scute 15 Antler frags	1 Beechnut	2 Raptor talons

(Continued)

Feature number	Burial style[a]	Number of individuals[b]	Lithics[c]	Bone artifacts	Vegetable remains	Bone counts
18-1975	1	1 a♂	7 Boats blades 5 St points	10 Gaming pieces 27 Antler frags	≥2 Plum pits	
19-1975	C	4 a? 5 sa	6 Preforms 6 Ml blades 5 TSBs 39 St points 6 Cn points ≥4 Drills 1 Grooved axe 1 Beveled cobble 1 Grooved abrader 4 Limonite nodules	4 Gouges 1 Barbed bone spear 1 Needle 1 Bead 1 Porcupine incisor Many worked bone frags 26 Antler frags	—	155 Deer 1 Moose 1 Bear 1 Mustela macrodon 38 Mammal 1 Lg mammal 1 Turtle
24-1975	C	1 a? 1 sa	10 Preforms 23 Ml blades 3 Boats blades 5 TSBs 21 St points ≥3 Drills 3 Gravers 1 Wedge (?) 5 Gouges 5 Adzes 3 Whetstones 3 Beveled cobbles 1 Notched cobble 1 Anvil stone 1 Rod	2 Barbed spear frags 1 Toggling harpoon 5 Gouges 1 Needle 2 Beads 1 Engraved bone Several worked bone frags 46 Antler frags	—	1 Moose 4 Deer 17 Beaver 3 Dog 1 Porcupine 452 Mammal 379 Lg mammal 6 Aves
24a-1975	C	—	1 Boats blade 2 TSBs 6 Biface frags	—	—	

Feature	Burial style[a]	No. individuals[b]	Lithics[c]	Bone/antler	Plant	Faunal
28a-1975	C	1 a? 2 sa	1 St point 2 Drills 3 Biface frags 1 Stone rod frag	1 Bone gouge 18 Antler frags	—	7 Lg mammal
Fea. 28a or b			—			
28b-1975			1 TSB 1 Drill 1 Tip 4 St. points 1 Drill 3 Biface frags	1 Worked frag	—	—
30-1975	1	1 a♀	—	—	—	1 Dog 28 Mammal
33-1975	1	1 sa				
34-1975	1	1 a♀ 1 sa	2 St. points 1 Util. flake	—	—	2 Aves
35-1975	I?	?	5 Preforms 4 MI blades	—	2 Beechnuts	—

aBurial style: B, bundle; C, cremation; I, inhumation.
bNumber of individuals: a, adult; sa, subadult; in, infant.
cLithics: St point, stemmed point; TSB, tapered-stem blade; MI blade, Mansion Inn blade; cn point, corner-notched point.

Charcoal Identification

Dosia M. Laeyendecker

Twenty-eight charcoal samples were selected from a larger set submitted between 1978 and 1980 (Table A4.1). Some were single pieces, while others included multiple fragments. All were collected by hand during excavation from contexts ranging from about 5000 B.P. to 500 B.P. All told, they are remarkable for the diversity of species represented. In fact, one sample produced charcoal of two species.

METHOD

For identification the charcoal fragment is broken by hand along transverse, tangential, and radial sections. These surfaces are studied with a reflective light microscope under 50 to 300 power magnification. Wood and wood-slide collections from the Smithsonian Institution Department of Botany were used for comparisons. The wood structure is remarkably well preserved in charcoal, but even so, it can usually be identified only to genus or family. Identification to species level may be dependent on species diversity in the area of investigation. For instance, there is only one native species of beech in North America, thus *Fagus* sp. may reasonably be identified as *Fagus grandifolia*. The condition and the size of the charcoal fragment are important factors for identification and the fragments from the Turner Farm site were satisfactory in this respect. Other reference materials include photographs and descriptions (see, e.g., Core, Coté, and Day 1979; Panshin and de Zeeuw 1970; Schweingruber 1978).

DISCUSSION

The charcoal fragments from the Turner Farm site provide some information about paleoenvironments during the site's occupation. However, this material is not suitable for

DOSIA M. LAEYENDECKER • Department of Anthropology, Smithsonian Institution, Washington, DC 20560.

Table A4.1. Charcoal Samples

Catalog number	Occupation	Section	Feature	Species[a]	Comment[b]	Date
62c	1	E5 s85		*Pinus strobus*		
135c		W30s75		*Ostrya virginiana*	1	
168c	2	W95s80		*Tsuga canadensis*		
55c	2	W5s95		*Fagus grandifolia*		
56c	2/3	E20s75	21-1973	*Fagus grandifolia*		
95c	3	W10-10s70	38-1974	*Fagus grandifolia*		
104c	3	W10s55	41-1974	*Acer* sp.		
105c	3	W10s55	42-1974	*Franxinus* sp.		
24c	3	W35s100		*Fragus grandifolia*		
12c	3	W20s100		*Platanus occidentalis* or *Fagus grandifolia*	3	
1c	B2GF	W60s95		*Abies balsamea*		
43c	B2GF	W5s80		*Betula* sp.		
78c	B2GF	E20s80		Hardwood, maybe *Betula* sp., and softwood, probably *Abies* sp.		3820 ± 50 (SI 4243)
40c	2GF	W25s115		*Betula* sp.		
116c	2GF	E15s70-75		Hardwood		
35c	2GF	W15s90		*Ostrya virginiana*	1	
11c	2GF	W55s85		*Pinus strobus*		
48c	2GF	W25s115		*Fraxinus* sp.		
114c	CCS	E35s70		Hardwood, *Platanus occidentalis* or *Fagus grandifolia*		
60c	CCS	W15s95		Hardwood, *Platanus occidentalis* or *Fagus occidentalis*	2	
74c	CCS	E40s70		Hardwood, probably *Betula* sp.		
119c	CCS	E75s50		Hardwood, *Platanus occidentalis* or *Fagus grandifolia*	2	
130c	1GF	W30s85		*Fagus grandifolia*		
23c	1GF	W40s95		*Quercus* sp., oak		
142c	1GF	W15s55		*Fagus grandifolia*		
147c	1GF	W35s90		*Pinus strobus* and probably *Fagus grandifolia*		115 ± 65 (SI 4246)
6c	MCS	W55s85		*Fagus grandifolia*		

[a]*Pinus strobus*, white pine; *Ostrya virginiana*, eastern hophornbeam; *Tsuga canadensis*, eastern hemlock; *Fagus grandifolia*, American beech; *Acer* sp., maple; *Franxinus* sp., ash; *Platanus occidentalis*, sycamore; *Abies balsamea*, balsam fir; *Betula* sp., birch; *Quercus* sp., oak.

[b]1. Tentative identification; occurs in Maine today, but is more common to the south. 2. Sycamore occurs today in Maine, but is more common to the south; its similiarity to beech raises doubt about this identification.

analysis of quantitative trends in forest composition or environmental change through time (Smart and Hoffman 1988:191–192).

The vegetational history of the period covered by the Turner Farm site—about 5000 to 500 B.P.—can be reconstructed roughly with the help of pollen analysis. In northeastern North America in postglacial times, between 12,000 and 10,000 years ago, tundra and spruce woodland were replaced by pine forests (*Pinus strobus* mostly) mixed with oak and birch. Hemlock (*Tsuga canadensis*) spread into New England between 10,000 and 8,000 years ago and continued to become more abundant until around 6000 B.P., when beech populations expanded within the forests of the Northeast. Thus the modern hemlock-beech-birch forests of the East were formed during the mid-Holocene, largely replacing the white pine-dominated forests of earlier times (Jacobson et al. 1987:282). Pollen diagrams from Moulton Pond, Maine, register closed forest in the area from about 7,000 years ago. Around 5,000 years ago hemlock reached its maximum pollen values in these diagrams. Pine, birch, and oak were also important and at the same time there are indications of an increase in diversity of the forest. A major decline in conifers, especially of hemlock, is found around 4,700 years ago and this was followed by a maxima of hardwoods, mainly beech, maple (*Acer* sp.), and ash (*Fraxinus* sp.) at around 3,500 years ago. Hemlock reached a second maximum in the diagrams before decreasing again (together with the temperate hardwoods) around 2,000 years ago, when the diagrams indicate that spruce was on the increase, which suggests more severe environmental conditions (edaphic and/or climatic and/or anthropogenic; Davis et al. 1975:435, 453–455).

CONCLUSION

The wood types identified in the charcoal samples from the Turner Farm site all derive from mixed hardwood-dominated forests. This agrees with the data from pollen diagrams from the area. The regional change from conifer-dominated forests to hardwood-dominated forests around 4,700 years ago would presumably have taken place during Occupation 1. The sample from that time period is identified as pine. The samples from Occupations 2 and 3 and later strata represent hardwoods that were available in the area. The fact that no spruce shows up in the latter strata does not mean that is was not there. Archaeologically deposited charcoal is in itself an unnatural assemblage. Firewood was not collected at random nor in proportion to the species in the natural environment (Ford 1979:301). We can say, however, that the charcoal samples from the Turner Farm site indicate a great variety of available firewood for the people to choose from, and the availability of a variety of conifer and hardwood species with different characteristics for cultural use.

This diversity stands in contrast to the spruce-dominated growth that covers wooded areas of the Penobscot Bay islands today. This dichotomy was caused mainly by extensive deforestation during the late eighteenth and early nineteenth centuries and the mid-nineteenth century when virtually all wooded areas of the Maine coast were being cleared for agriculture and sheep raising. As sheep herds shrank during the early twentieth century, dense growths of spruce spread over old pastures. Today, older stands are increasing in species diversity.

Geoarchaeology in Central Coastal Maine

Daniel F. Belknap

INTRODUCTION

Archaeological sites along the coast of Maine demonstrate marine adaptation by the people who constructed them. Geology properties of the sites and their environs are important influences on the nature of the sites, the cultural record within them, and their preservation potential. This appendix is concerned primarily with the geologic setting and paleo-geographic evolution of two Maine coastal sites as determined from remote sensing and cores, and the use of these examples to develop a model of preservation potential on the Maine coast.

A primary control of coastal change, particularly in Maine, is relative sea-level change. Sea-level rise of approximately 60 m (Belknap, Anderson, et al. 1987) over the past 10–11 thousand years (Kelley et al. 1992) has resulted in coastal retreat in Maine and created a transgressive stratigraphy (Belknap, Shipp, Kelley et al. 1989). This setting results in shoreline destruction of a majority of sedimentary facies, along with any record of human occupation. Only a fraction of the record of sedimentary environments (and, potentially, the archaeological record) may be preserved in specialized settings.

Masters and Flemming (1983) summarized marine geoarchaeology, and Pearson et al. (1986) discuss specific examples of site preservation in the nearshore realm. Kraft et al. (1983) presented a particular model of site preservation potential in transgressive coastal settings. They emphasized that the depth of burial, composition and size of the site, and energy (depth of shoreface erosion) are critical variables. These general examples can be applied to the Maine coast.

Bourque (1976, 1983), Goldthwait (1935), Kellogg (1982, 1991), Myers (1965), Sanger (1975, 1981, 1988a, 1988b), Sanger and Belknap (1987, 1991), Sanger and Sanger (1986), Yesner (1980), and others have examined the geoarchaeology of Maine coastal sites. Oldale

---

DANIEL F. BELKNAP • Department of Geological Science, University of Maine, Orono, Maine 04473.

(1985), Kellogg (1988), Sanger and Kellogg (1983), and Snow (1972) have discussed sea-level change in regard to regional archaeology. Kellogg (1982) developed a model of site distribution based on intertidal energy environments within Maine's embayments, finding the majority of sites in protected mid- to upper-estuarine settings with southern exposures, beaches, moderate slopes, and access to food resources and travel routes. These sites represent human choices within the context of geologic environments and biological resources. Shipp et al. (1985, 1987), Belknap, Shipp et al. (1986), and Kelley (1987) developed this zonal concept geologically, demonstrating that Maine embayments have a high-energy outer zone of erosion, an intermediate zone of bluff erosion and sediment transfer, and an inner zone of sediment accumulation, with mudflats and marshes. Belknap (1986) and Belknap, Kellogg et al. (1986) discussed applications of the geologic model in archaeological sites. Recently, Young (1990), Young et al. (1992), and Davies (1992) have applied the specific preservation potential model of Kraft et al. (1983) and Belknap and Kraft (1985) in Pemaquid Beach and Damariscotta River geoarchaeological studies.

This appendix presents two case studies of archaeological sites and the geologic environments in which they are imbedded—at Turner Farm on North Haven Island, and Lazygut Island, off Deer Isle, both in central coastal Maine. The context of cultural and faunal remains is intimately related to this setting, and in particular reflects changes in coastal environments over time. The sites represent two extremes of preservation. Lazygut Island is completely eroded, and is represented by isolated dredge and scuba retrievals. Turner Farm is a deeply stratified site, with a record, stretching back over 5,000 years, that has been intensively studied by traditional archaeological techniques (Bourque, this volume). Its remains reflect coastal changes, climate change, rising sea level, and changes in human culture. It is presently undergoing erosion at a gravel beach and bluff front. A primary goal of this study is the evaluation of preservation potential for these two examples, and a prediction of preservation potential and optimal exploration schemes. Preservation potential in eroding coastal sites is very low, while discovery potential for hypothetical buried, protected sites may be equally low.

GEOLOGIC AND ARCHAEOLOGICAL SETTING

Maine's complex coastline results from drowning by the sea of a crystalline bedrock framework. These rocks were eroded by rivers and glaciers into hills and valleys because of their differential resistance. This topography was modified by glacial and glacial-marine deposits draped over the bedrock during retreat of the Wisconsin-age Laurentide ice sheet margin 14 to 12 ka (thousand years ago). Major glacial deposits include till and outwash. The glacial-marine Presumpscot Formation is a blue-gray mud containing ice-rafted drop-stones. Modern sedimentary environments are predominantly found within the peninsulas and embayments of the coast, such as tidal flats, marshes, and pocket beaches flanking bedrock ledges and bluffs of Quaternary sediment. Sandy barrier beaches are found predominantly in the southwestern part of the state.

The distribution of sedimentary environments is intimately linked with geomorphology of the coast. The Maine coast comprises four major coastal compartments (Kelley 1987; Shipp et al. 1985). They reflect primarily bedrock structure and composition, but also abundance of glacial sediment sources for modern littoral systems. The two study areas are located in the east-central compartment, typified by large islands and bays (Figure A5.1).

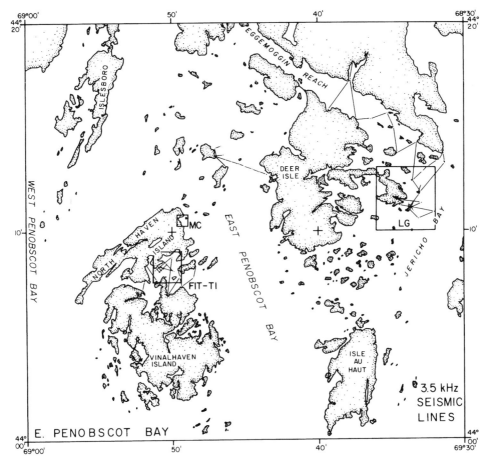

Figure A5.1. Location map of central coastal Maine, East Penobscot Bay, and Jericho Bay. Boxes refer to Marsh Cove (MC) and to detailed location maps of Turner Farm (FIT-TI) and Lazygut Island (LG).

Within the coastal compartments, Shipp et al. (1985, 1987), Belknap et al. (1986b), and Kelley (1987) have identified a three-zone embayment model of geomorphology and sedimentary environments. This model extends Kellogg's (1982) shoreline model to a fuller evaluation of embayment sedimentary lithosomes and establishes an evolutionary model, tested with quantitative sedimentary analyses (Duffy et al. 1989; Hay 1988; Kelley et al. 1988; R. Smith 1990; Walsh 1988; Whalen 1989; Wood 1991; Wood et al. 1989). The inner zone accumulates sediments temporarily. The middle zone contains eroding bluffs, and involves active transfer of sediment from a Pleistocene source to temporary storage in the inner zone or loss offshore. The outer zone is stripped of sediments except for small, coarse-grained pocket beaches in the intertidal level, and has smaller volumes of sediments preserved in the subtidal level. This geographic arrangement of zones reflects a geologic history of transgression. As shorelines move landward, transgression exposes more of the embayment to greater wave energy and increased tidal current activity, while at the same time bluff and subtidal sources of sediment are depleted. The zones of protection, transition, and stripping translate landward, with variable preservation of the transgressive record.

Within the embayments salt marshes and mudflats are important biological habitats. *Mya arenaria* (soft-shell clam) and *Mytilus edulis* (blue mussel) are abundant here today. Between 6 and 1.5 ka, *Crassostrea virginica* (eastern oyster) was abundant in the estuaries. Various anadromous fish migrate through the estuaries, while abundant fish and crustaceans are found in the productive Gulf of Maine offshore. All these resources are represented in shell middens in various proportions (although crustacean shells do not preserve well). Shellfish are particularly important to geoarchaeology because they are preserved both in geologic facies and the middens, and are indicators of the contemporary environmental conditions. Their importance in diet and culture is a separate issue, of course.

Processes that influence these sedimentary environments include sea-level change, wave activity, tidal currents, and slumping. Sea-level change is a long-term and slow process, but it has profound effects on coastal stratigraphy and evolution.

Postglacial sea-level changes have been complex, a result of global eustatic sea-level rise and local glacioisostatic effects. The Presumpscot Formation was laid down during a local submergence between 14 and 11 ka, when the coast was rebounding from profound glacioisostatic depression. Rebound caused emergence and local sea-level lowstand (Belknap, Andersen et al. 1987; Schnitker 1974; Shipp et al. 1989, 1991) about 60 m below present at 10–11 ka (Kelley et al. 1992). During this emergence the recently deposited sediments were eroded, with deep valleys continuing seaward of the present coast (Kelley et al. 1986). Sea level rose rapidly to −20 m between 9 and 8 ka, reached −15 m by 6.3 ka, and then rose at a decreasing rate over the past 5 ka until historic times, when a further acceleration appears to have begun (Belknap, Shipp, Stuckenrath et al. 1989; Figure A5.2).

Affecting productivity, tides are important in mixing of the Gulf of Maine and its coastal embayments (Schnitker 1975). Tidal range has changed through the late Holocene, increasing from about 1 m 6 ka to present variable ranges as sea-level rise changed tidal resonance within the Gulf of Maine-Bay of Fundy system (Grant 1970; Scott and Greenberg 1983). Variations in tidal mixing and regional climatic changes were responsible for a lower productivity but warmer Gulf of Maine prior to 6 ka, and cooling with higher productivity since that time, as determined from fossils of foraminifera and diatoms preserved in offshore cores (Schnitker 1975; Schnitker and Jorgensen 1990).

Most of the Maine coast has a low river input of water or sediment, with the result that the embayments are neutral embayments (Johnson 1925) rather than estuaries. Most have nearly normal marine salinity and are well mixed (Fefer and Schettig 1980). Only the Kennebec-Androscoggin and Saco rivers differ in transporting sand at their mouths, while they and the Penobscot have sufficient flow to have major freshwater dilution in their lower reaches. The Penobscot Bay region containing the present study areas has open-marine conditions.

Wave activity is controlled by fetch and coastal orientation. Outer portions of embayments are exposed to high wave energy, particularly during winter storms. Elsewhere, wave energy is fetch limited. Tides in eastern Penobscot Bay average 3.0 m mean range, 3.5 m spring range (NOAA-NOS 1992a). Tidal currents are effective where constricted in channels, and can reach 1 m/sec or greater, sufficient to move gravel, resulting in effective scour. Tidal currents in Fox Islands Thorofare, off Burnt Island 5 km east of the Turner Farm site,

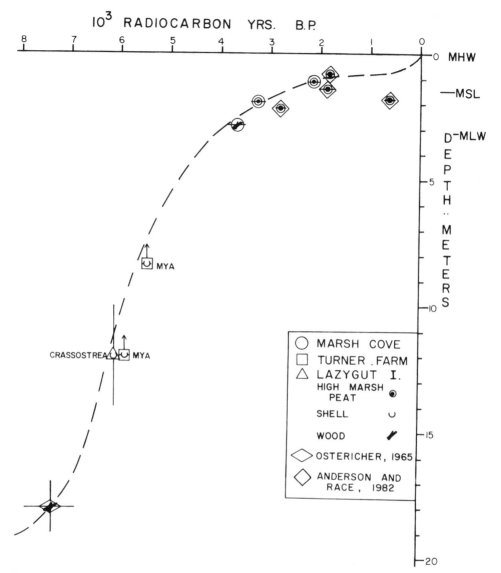

Figure A5.2. Sea-level curve for Penobscot Bay, Maine. Data are shown in Table A5.1. Sea-level trend is generalized from Kelley et al. (1992) and Belknap et al. (1989b).

reach 0.7 m/sec (NOAA-NOS 1992b). Currents off Lazygut are less constricted, and thus have lower velocity (0.15 m/sec). Ice is an effective mover of sediment, but also can act to dampen waves during the winter. Mass movements, especially slumps on bluffs of glacial-marine sediment, are important in destabilizing supratidal (and subtidal) sediments, emplacing them in areas where they can be redistributed by waves and tides (Kelley and Hay 1986; R. Smith 1990).

An increasingly important coastal geologic process is human intervention. Coastal development and larger-scale engineering threaten many shorelines (e.g., Kelley et al. 1989). Recent attention to geologic preservation (e.g., Maine Sand Dunes Regulations) and laws protecting archaeological sites are an important control, but private efforts are critical as well. For example, Maine Historic Preservation has recently protected sites on donated land on Dodge Point in the Damariscotta River, while the Glidden Midden in Damariscotta is protected by a private landowner.

Human occupation of the coast is not new, however. The archaeological record of coastal adaptation is at least 5,000 years in extent, and it is possible that there is a record between 10 and 5 ka submerged on the present inner shelf. Kellogg (1982, 1991) showed that site distribution is predictable, following a logic of access and utilization of resources, but also probably reflecting preservation potential. The majority of sites are found within the mid-inner zone of embayments. Middens record occupation and utilization of local resources, but require specialized analysis of stratigraphy (e.g., Bourque 1976; Sanger 1981; Skinas 1987).

METHODS

Submerged coastal environments were examined using two remote sensing techniques: seismic reflection profiling and side-scan sonar. These techniques have been discussed in detail by Belknap and colleagues (Kellogg et al. 1986; Kelley et al. 1987; Shipp, Kelley et al. 1989) and Kelley and Belknap (1988, 1989). The Raytheon RTT1000A high-resolution 3.5-kHz system can penetrate 50 m of Quaternary sediments and has a vertical resolution of 25 cm. We also used an ORE Geopulse "boomer" 1.5-kHz sonar at 125 joules to penetrate sediments as much as 150 m thick. This device has vertical resolution of about 0.5 m. Seismic reflection data were used to construct cross sections and maps of depth to reflector surfaces. The side-scan sonar, an EG&G SMS 260, is digital, providing rectified, dimensionally correct surficial images of the seafloor typically in 200-m-wide swaths. Depending on the scale, pixels of 0.5 m horizontal scale can be resolved.

Vibracores using an aluminum tube 7 cm in diameter and up to 10 m in length were taken using a cement-settler vibrator. We have modified the standard Lanesky et al. (1979) and Hoyt and Demarest (1981) technique for underwater work using a scuba diver and three-point mooring on our research vessels (Belknap, Kellogg et al. 1986). Core sites were chosen based on seismic data to sample representative facies and explore potential sites. Cores were continuous and penetrated all Holocene marine sediments easily, and up to a meter into the Pleistocene Presumpscot Formation. Cores were split and described for sediments and fossils. Subsamples were collected for radiocarbon dates. Dated samples from all sites are listed in Table A5.1.

The seismic, side-scan, core, and available bathymetric data were integrated into maps of depth to particular reflectors (structure contour) and thickness of sedimentary lithosomes (isopach). The most important map is a structure contour on the top of the Pleistocene and/or bedrock. This easily identifiable pre-Holocene reflector represents the upland erosional surface before transgression (the *basal unconformity*), modified in some cases by shoreface erosional processes (the *ravinement unconformity*; Belknap and Kraft 1985). The local relative sea-level curve (Belknap, Kelley et al. 1987; Belknap, Shipp,

Table A5.1. Radiocarbon Dates below Eastern Penobscot Bay

Lab number	Core number	Material[a]	Depth below MHW (m)	Corrected age (years B.P.)	δ^{13}C
Upper Penobscot Bay (Ostericher 1965)					
W-1306	211	W	20 ± 1	7390 ± 500[b]	
Holt Pond Marsh, Stonington (Anderson and Race 1982)					
SI-4596	HD-1	BM(?)	0.83–0.89	1825 ± 55	
SI-4595	HC-3	BM(?)	1.37–1.43	1880 ± 150	
SI-4767	HB-3	BM(?)	1.84–1.94	655 ± 75	
SI-4768	HA-3	BM(?)	2.94–2.29	2835 ± 70	
Fox Island Thorofare (Belknap, Kellogg et al. 1986)					
GX-11004	TF-VC-2	S–MA	11.96	5880 ± 105	2.0
GX-11005	TF-VC-3	S–MA	8.31	5430 ± 100	1.6
Marsh Cove, North Haven (Belknap, Kellogg et al. 1986)					
GX-11006	MC-VC-4	HM	1.12	2145 ± 125	−19.0
GX-11007	MC-VC-4	HM	1.87	3255 ± 150	−27.7
GX-11008	MC-VC-4	W	2.83	3700 ± 200	−26.3
Lazygut Island (Belknap, Kellogg et al., 1986)					
SI-4650	Dredge	S–CV	8–11	6100 ± 65	

[a]HM, high marsh (*Spartina patens, Juncus gerardi*); BM, basal marsh (± terrestrial and humic compounds); S, shells: MA, *Mya arenaria*, CV, *Crassostrea virginica*; W, wood.
[b]Date is uncorrected, raw age.

Stuckenrath et al. 1989; Kelley et al. 1992) was then used to guide construction of paleogeographic maps, by intersecting sea level and the pre-Holocene surface. Geologic experience resulted in modifications to this simplistic intersection, by restoring former coastal environments and accounting for losses at the shoreface ravinement. Thus, the paleogeographic reconstructions are somewhat subjective models.

Finally, this framework was used to constrain an interdisciplinary geoarchaeological interpretation of the two regions. Cultural and faunal remains in middens indicate human selection from available environments, and relate to natural fossils in cores. For example, the contemporary coexistence of *Mya arenaria* (soft-shell clam) in the Turner Farm midden and in situ in nearby vibracores suggests a local food source for the midden builders. The present environment does not provide immediately available *Mya*, because it is an open gravel beach. This suggests a more protected mudflat environment 5 ka.

TURNER FARM SITE

The Turner Farm site is in a protected location facing Fox Islands Thorofare (Figure A5.3). The site is on a terrace and eroding bluff at the northern end of a small gravel barrier beach between Fish Point and Kent Cove. Modern environments include a fresh-to-brackish back-barrier marsh, sand and gravel barrier, and eroding bluffs of glacial sediment sitting on a bedrock ledge. Tidal flats containing *Mya arenaria* exist within 1–2 km NW and N of the site today, but the immediate intertidal area is a relatively steep, coarse-grained beachface.

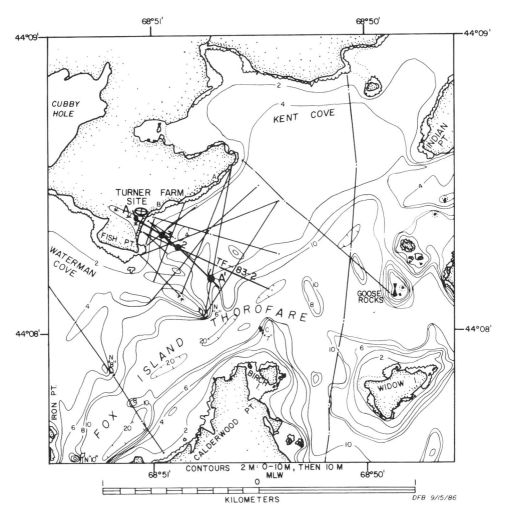

Figure A5.3. Turner Farm site, detailed location map. Seismic reflection tracklines are shown by dot-long-dash lines, while cores are shown by filled dots.

Results

Seismic profiles using the 3.5-kHz profiler were run in 1984. A total of 12 km was profiled (Figure A5.3) for general stratigraphy in the adjacent Fox Islands Thorofare, with a grid of closely spaced lines immediately offshore of the site. Seismic data reveal facies interpreted as bedrock, uppermost Pleistocene Presumpscot Formation, Holocene mud, and littoral sand and gravel units. Within the mud are pockets of natural gas that obscure deeper reflectors. These seismic facies and techniques of interpretation are described in detail by Belknap et al. (1989a) and Belknap and Shipp (1991). Seismic profile TF-83-2 (Figure A5.4) crosses a broad subtidal flat with more than 6 m of Holocene mud overlying Presumpscot Formation and bedrock. A strong gas signature suggests organic-rich mud at

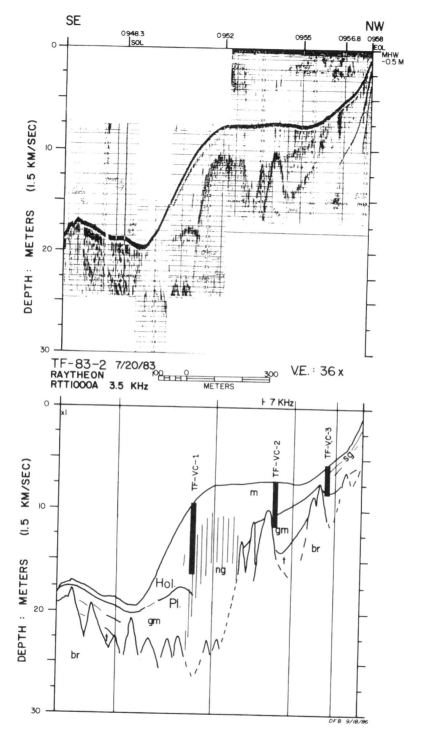

Figure A5.4. Example of 3.5-kHz data, raw and interpreted, along line TF-83-2 (see Figure A5.3 for location). Underwater vibracores (solid bars) are projected up to 100 m laterally to this line. Hol., Holocene; Pl., Pleistocene; m, mud; ng, natural gas; sg, sand and gravel; gm, glaciomarine mud; t, till; br, bedrock.

the base of the Holocene sediments. This profile runs normal to the barrier, and is the site of the three vibracores taken in this area. Spiky bedrock (including Fish Point Ledge) is evident, overlain by Presumpscot Formation and a landward-thinning wedge of Holocene estuarine mud. Coarse beachface sediments are not clearly resolved on profile TF-83-2 because of shallowness of the water, but visual observations confirm the coarse surficial sediments in depths less than 5 m on the profile.

Based on the seismic data, cores were sited in a shore-normal transect along TF-83-10, in a paleovalley thought to connect with the present back-barrier marsh. This protected environment was hypothesized to be a likely region of human occupation or resource supply. Three underwater vibracores (Figure A5.3) were taken in 5, 8, and 10 m depths below mean high water (MHW), and one hand auger (Dutch core) was taken in the back-barrier marsh. These cores and seismic profile were used to construct the cross section in Figure A5.5. Core TF-VC-1, farthest offshore, is subtidal embayment mud, containing fine sand lenses and fossils of *Macoma balthica* and *Yoldia* sp. Cores TF-VC-2 and TF-VC-3 are remarkably alike, with a thin upper unit of subtidal estuarine mud grading to intertidal embayment mud with scattered pebbles and sand, and fossils of *Mya arenaria*. Each core penetrates a distinct erosional unconformity on the Presumpscot Formation. At this contact, in situ *Mya arenaria* are found in growth position, burrowing into the underlying stiff Pleistocene mud. These shells provide a minimum estimate of sea level (Figure A5.2) at 5880 ± 105 and 5430 ± 100 B.P., respectively. There is no evidence for a barrier at that time. After 5000 B.P., as rate of sea-level rise slowed (Belknap et al. 1989b), a barrier formed across

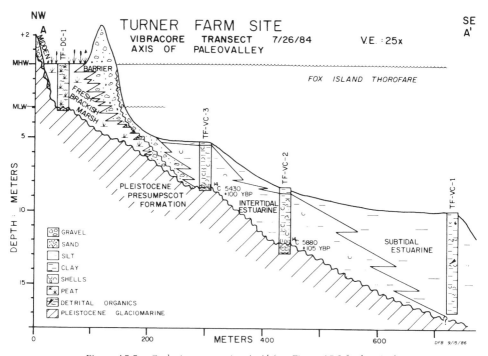

Figure A5.5.   Geologic cross section A–A' (see Figure A5.3 for location).

the upper reaches of the Fish Point paleovalley, enclosing a back-barrier marsh. This marsh is now 3 m thick, but its offshore extent and precise time of initial formation is unknown. Formation of the barrier may also be related to interception of new coarse-grained sediment sources, and increasing fetch as Fox Islands Thorofare widened with sea-level rise.

In Marsh Cove, 4.5 km to the northeast (Figure A5.1), more saline back-barrier marsh deposits were cored to aid in constructing the local sea-level curve. The stratigraphy of the Marsh Cove barrier/back-barrier demonstrates transgression, as at the Fish Point barrier, but contains back-barrier lagoonal muds and salt marsh peat.

Seismic data and absolute core control were used to devise structure contour maps of the area. The most useful (Figure A5.6) maps the base of the Holocene section (top of the

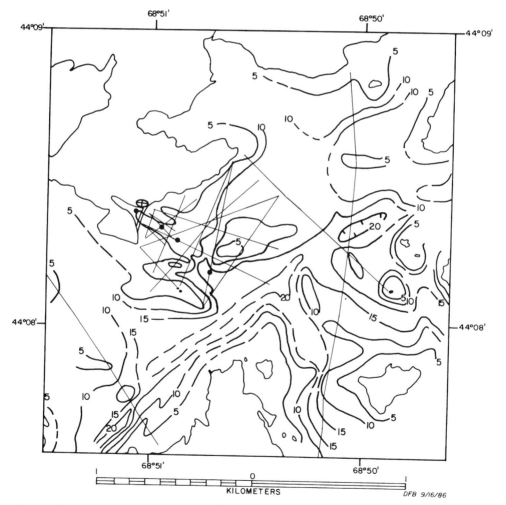

Figure A5.6.   Structure contour map of central Fox Island Thoroughfare, off Turner Farm Site, base of Holocene.

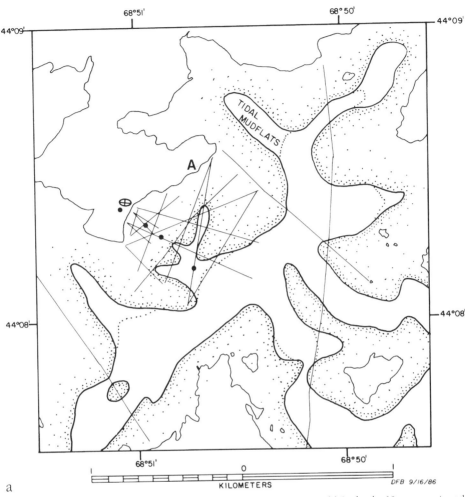

68°51'   68°50'

A

TIDAL
MUDFLATS

44°09'   44°09'

44°08'   44°08'

68°51'   68°50'

a

KILOMETERS   DFB 9/16/86

Figure A5.7. Paleogeographic reconstruction of the Turner Farm site region. (a) Sea level −10 m, approximately 6000 B.P. (b) Sea level −5 m, approximately 4500 B.P.

pre-Holocene, including bedrock, till, and Presumpscot Formation). The pattern of structure contours identifies a major bedrock-controlled paleochannel in the location of the present axis of Fox Islands Thorofare, with tributary paleovalleys into Kent Cove and the Turner Farm back-barrier marsh. A similar paleovalley probably exists in Waterman Cove as well. The surficial bathymetric expression does not always correspond to these paleovalley trends, as is seen in the smaller tributaries, indicating a thick Holocene valley fill. Another important feature is the broad flat between 10- and 5-m depth, located east of the site off point "A" in Figures A5.3 and A5.7a. Seismic profiles record thick Holocene mud with gas wipe-out, suggesting a relatively flat pre-Holocene surface and a possible former intertidal flat. Whether this flat was produced subsequent to retreat of an eroding bluff, or by

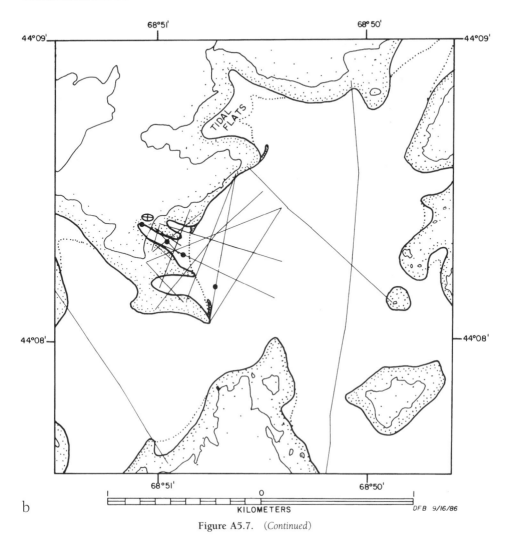

Figure A5.7. (*Continued*)

relatively passive flooding of a previously existing flat area, cannot be determined from the seismic data alone.

Discussion

Structure contour maps of the pre-Holocene surface and core and seismic information concerning facies distributions are combined to create paleogeographic reconstructions, which are more subjective interpretations of the whole data set. Figure A5.7a and b illustrates two reconstructions for the area, at sea levels of 10 and 5 m below present, respectively. These levels correspond to approximately 6000 and 4500 B.P., based on the

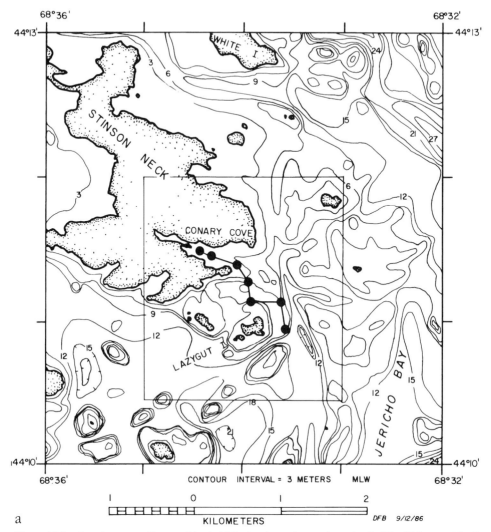

Figure A5.8. Location maps of Lazygut Island. (a) Regional map, box encloses detail of 8b. (b) Lazygut Island and Conary Cove, with tracklines (solid line) and underwater vibracores (filled dots). Thick line connecting vibracores is a synthetic cross section (Figure A5.11). Vibracore 2 is in the artifact producing area.

sea-level curve (Figure A5.2). At 6000 B.P. (Figure A5.7a) sea-level rise overtopped the narrow margins of the Fox Islands paleochannel, flooding the Fish Point paleovalley. A much broader area became available for development of tidal mudflats, including coloniza-tion by *Mya arenaria*. This was also the end of the hypsithermal in the Gulf of Maine (Schnitker 1975). Swordfish remains in Maine middens suggest deep-sea swordfish hunt-ing, from bases such as Turner Farm. The protected channel with the natural harbor of Fish Point paleovalley makes this a logical site for human occupation. In situ *Mya* in cores TF-VC-2 and TF-VC-3 clearly demonstrate an abundant mudflat resource between 5800 and

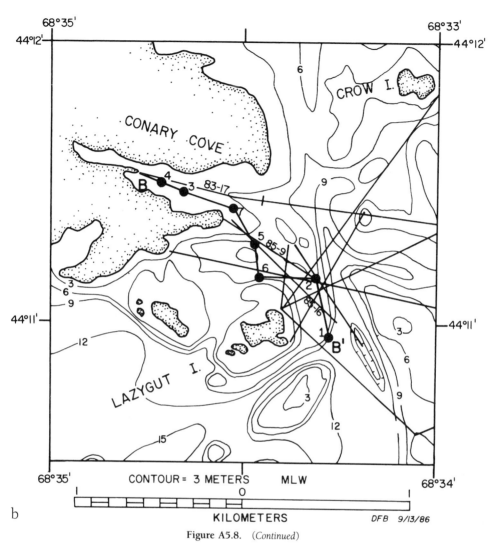

Figure A5.8. *(Continued)*

5300 B.P. By 4500 B.P. (Figure A5.7b), rising sea level and coastal retreat allowed intrusion of intertidal water to the present back-barrier of Turner Farm. Mudflat resources may have begun to wane immediately in front of the site, but northwestern Kent Cove and Waterman Cove may have been alternative sources of *Mya*. Barriers may have formed as fetch increased within Fox Island Thorofare, and then migrated landward to become the present beach.

It is difficult to reconstruct the original size of shell midden sites when affected by modern coastal erosion (e.g., Skinas 1987; Kellogg 1991; Young et al. 1992). Turner Farm is the oldest (5290 ± 95 B.P.) deeply stratified site on the Maine coast. Sea level rose from at least 8 m below the present over this period of occupation, suggesting either protection from erosion, or unusual placement with respect to the eroding coastline. The coastal evolution suggested in Figure A5.7 allows for a narrow tributary embayment very different from the modern setting, evolving to a barrier with back-barrier marsh. Present coastal erosion is thus attacking the *side* (SE), rather than the *front* (SW) of the site. Turner Farm presently represents zone 2 of the embayment sedimentary evolution model, with eroding bluffs and sediment redistribution. It has evolved from a more protected zone 1 setting within the past 5,000 years.

LAZYGUT ISLAND

The Lazygut Island site has yielded a set of isolated artifacts found near a bedrock knob submerged at 10-m depth 500 m NE of Lazygut Island at the intersection of Eggemoggin Reach and Jerico Bay (Figure A5.8a). This site is open embayment, stripped of intertidal sediment and exposed to normal and storm wave conditions from the Gulf of Maine.

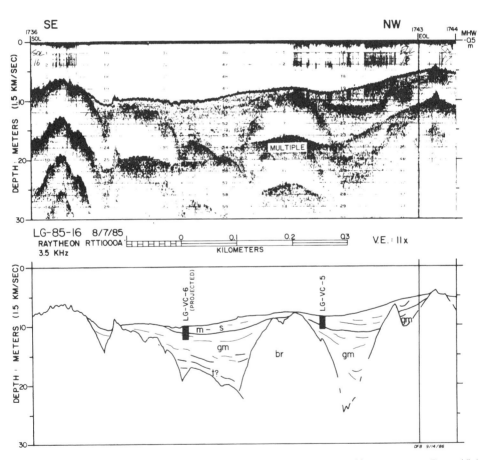

Figure A5.9. Seismic reflection profile LG-85-16, raw data and interpretation. Abbreviations as in Figure A5.4, except m-s, muddy sandy.

Conary Cove (Figure A5.8b), 800 m to the northwest, is contiguous with this site but contains more protected flats environments. Artifacts were recovered by fishermen in 1982, and systematic scuba exploration was performed in 1983. Only isolated flakes were found, and no coherent site was recognized on the seafloor.

Results

Seismic profiles totaling 13 km were run using the same techniques as off Turner Farm. Bedrock and glaciomarine mud are clearly identifiable (Figure A5.9) at the base of the section. Overlying the pre-Holocene erosional unconformity is a thin (< 2 m) section of

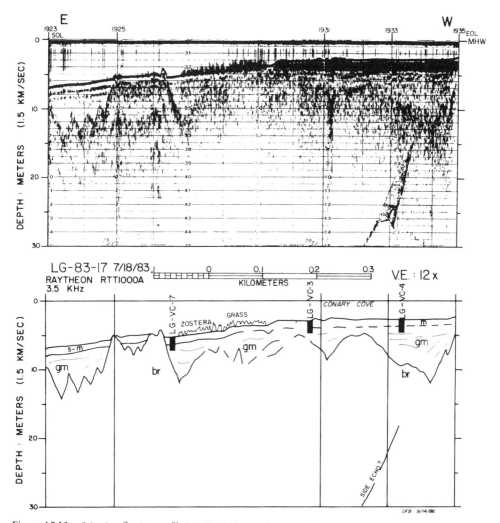

Figure A5.10. Seismic reflection profile LG-83-17, Conary Cove, raw data and interpretation. Abbreviations as in Figure A5.4, except s-m, sandy mud.

embayment mud. This is overlain in turn by an erosional ravinement surface, representing the present higher-energy open embayment, with a thin (< 0.5 m), coarse surficial lag. In Conary Cove, section LG-83-17 (Figure A5.10) shows thicker mud and no ravinement unconformity or coarse surficial lag. Profile LG-85-16 (Figure A5.9) runs over the flake discovery site and was used to site four vibracores.

Side-scan sonar mapping provided an alternative view of distribution of the site. There is an isolated granite knob at the site of the flake discovery, while the surrounding seafloor is relatively uniform, with a dark return typical of coarse surficial lag. There is no suggestion of an anomaly that might indicate a midden.

Cores were sited roughly along a SE–NW transect at approximately 2-m-depth intervals. Cores are arranged in a synthetic cross section (Figure A5.11) including Conary Cove. Cores LG-VC-1,2,6,5, and 7 contain a consistent stratigraphy of muddy, shelly gravel representing high-energy open embayment, overlying an erosional ravinement surface cut into subtidal embayment mud, gradually evolving from a shallower, lower-energy embayment or mud flats. The upper unit contains *Modiolus modiolus* (horse mussel), *Crepidula fornicata* (slipper shell), barnacles, and fragments of many other (probably reworked) shells. *Crassostrea virginica* were dredged up in this vicinity from this surface lag by fishermen. The deeper embayment is interpreted from fossils of *Modiolus* and articulated *Arctica islandica* (black quahog) in growth position, while the shallower embayment is interpreted from detrital organics, *Ilyanassa obsoleta* (periwinkle), *Argopecten irradians* (bay scallop), and *Mya arenaria*. The base of the Holocene is an erosional surface with burrows into the Pleistocene Presumpscot Formation. Articulated *Mya* were abundant, as at Turner Farm. Cores LG-VC-3

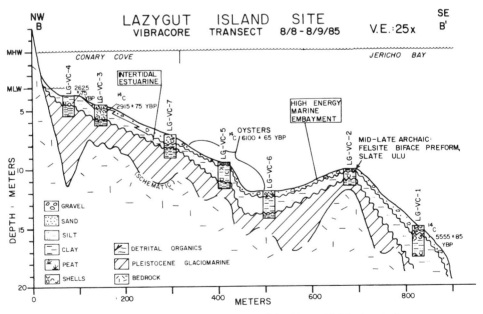

Figure A5.11.   Geologic cross section B–B' (see Figure A5.8 for location).

and 4 were within the more protected Conary Cove mudflats environments. Core 3 is similar to the outer cores, while core 4 contains a continuous Holocene mudflat section with no ravinement surface. *Mya* provide rough sea-level indicators for 2625 ± 75 and 2915 ± 75 B.P. in cores LG-VC-3 and 4, respectively. Radiocarbon dated *Arctica* in core LG-VC-1 are deeper-water shells, and can only provide a minimum sea level at -16 m 5555 ± 85 B.P.

Discussion

Seismic and core data were combined to construct a structure contour map of the pre-Holocene surface. As might be expected from the cores, the structure contour map parallels the present bathymetry closely. Paleogeographic reconstructions of the Lazygut Island area at -10 m and -5 m (Figures A5.12a and A5.12b) reveal a gradual isolation of the region into separate bedrock islands. The embayment presently framed by Stinson Neck and Lazygut Island was a likely site of a broad mudflat environment c. 5000 B.P. Continued transgression exposed the region to shoreline erosion and increasing wave energy. Any hypothetical coherent site at the bedrock knob would have been destroyed by littoral actions, redistributing sediments, shells, and artifacts into the surficial lag, from which a few scattered remnants have been recovered. Lazygut Island is a prime example of zone 3 of the embayment sedimentary evolution model (Belknap, Kellogg et al. 1986), with stripped shorelines and eroding subtidal zones.

Discovery of archaeological materials at this location was serendipitous, but hindsight allows an understanding of why this site was viable. The direct access to open Gulf of Maine environments is obvious, and would have changed little throughout the history of the location. Abundant *Mya* in nearby flats would have provided another resource. If a shell midden existed at this site, it was completely removed, due to lack of sheltering from open marine wave conditions.

CONCLUSION

Central Coastal Maine Sites

Two archaeological sites in central coastal Maine were investigated with seismic reflection profiling and coring to reconstruct paleogeography and sedimentary environments. Geologic data allow modeling of the geomorphology and geologic environments of the landscape at times of lower sea level, specifically -10 m (c. 6000 B.P.) and -5 m (c. 4500 B.P.). At Turner Farm, a stratified midden on North Haven Island, a restricted interisland channel gradually widened, and broad tidal flats developed nearby, containing abundant soft-shell clams. A paleovalley leading to the present site was gradually filled and cut off by changing shorelines. The present coastline configuration is steeper, with shellfish resources more than 1 km away. Lazygut Island is not a coherent site, simply scattered artifacts found on the seafloor. Reconstruction of paleoenvironments reveals a headland-embayment setting with protected tidal flat and abundant clams c. 5000 B.P. This evolved into the open high-energy embayment environments of the present, erasing much of the stratigraphic record. These two sites illustrate an evolutionary model of coastal sites, and provide evidence for a model of preservation potential.

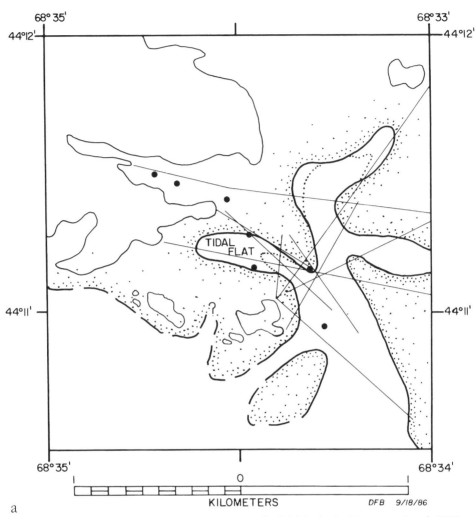

a

Figure A5.12. Paleogeographic reconstruction at Lazygut Island. (a) Sea level −10 m, approximately 6000 B.P.
(b) Sea level −5 m, approximately 4500 B.P.

Archaeological Preservation Potential

Kraft et al. (1983) discussed a model of preservation potential that emphasized the importance of depth of shoreface erosion versus depth of burial of back-barrier or estuarine sites during transgression. This concept can be applied to the Maine coast as well.

Exposed coastal sites typically stand on bluffs with eroding faces. The face may be simply the thickness of the midden itself, directly on top of Pleistocene sediments. Depth of erosion from a few meters to more than 10 removes the entire stratigraphic column, resulting in complete destruction of the site as a coherent, stratified unit. Scattered lithic artifacts might conceivably survive such a transgression. This model describes the Lazygut

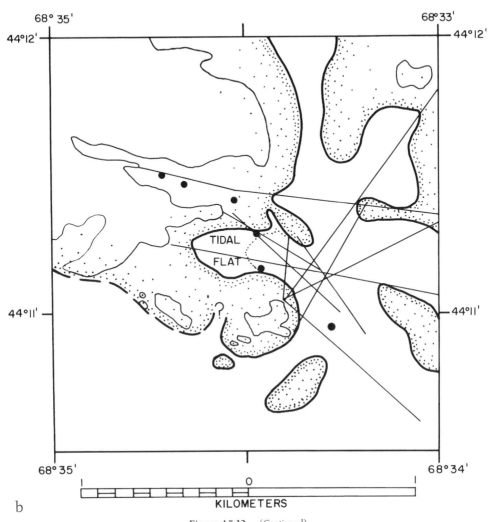

b

Figure A5.12. *(Continued)*

Island finds, and probably the majority of pre-Ceramic sites that may have existed on the now submerged inner shelf.

In contrast, sites that were situated in a tributary embayment, back-barrier, or similar sheltered setting have the potential to be preserved by delayed erosion, or by deep burial before the arrival of the eroding littoral zone. The Turner Farm site displays the delayed erosion model of preservation. The site buried in the Fish Point paleovalley has thus been partially preserved below the shoreface ravinement surface. Discovery potential of such sites is low, however, with present remote sensing devices. However, Shipp (1989) and Davies (1992) discuss discovery of buried natural shell bioherms (natural oyster mounds) within the Damariscotta River, a potential model for a buried midden. Chance sampling by vibracoring is the most likely mechanism for discovery potential at present. The likelihood of discovery is undoubtedly small, but modeling of most probable site locations increases this potential.

For the present, the most likely locations for preserved sites on the inner shelf are best modeled using archaeological and geoarchaeological criteria. Following Kellogg (1982, 1991), potential sites would be S or SE facing, near a headland, with access to a beach for landing boats and mudflats for food resources. Enhanced preservation potential occurs on the flank of a paleovalley, perhaps in a back-barrier setting. Shelter from open gulf marine conditions lessens the depth of shoreface erosion. A systematic search in the expanding database of seismic reflection profiles from the Maine coast could result in identification of such potential sites. Kellogg (1991) has in fact accomplished the goal in Muscongus Bay. Recent advances in Geographic Information System technology may make this task cost effective.

ACKNOWLEDGMENTS

Several University of Maine students and other professionals aided in gathering the information for this study. Dr. Bruce Bourque, Maine State Museum, was the principal investigator who requested geologic assistance. R. Craig Shipp and Stephanie Staples were primary field assistants for coring and seismic work at both localities. Robert Lewis, Maine State Museum, helped in the field. The University of Maine, Darling Marine Center and Center for Marine Studies provided equipment.

Appendix **6**

Analysis of Lithic Artifacts

The Identification, Petrologic Description,
and Statistical Analysis of the Lithic Artifacts
Recovered from the Turner Farm Site

ROBERT G. DOYLE

INTRODUCTION

The study of artifact lithology at the Turner Farm site began in the mid-1970s as a cooperative field project between the Maine State Museum and the Maine Geological Survey. Extensive bedrock mapping in Penobscot Bay (Figure A6.1) during the 1970s provided excellent geologic information that helped locate many nearby Turner Farm lithic source areas. In fact, one of the two most commonly used materials at the site—a banded-spherulitic rhyolite (BSR)—was located on the north end of Vinalhaven Island (Figure A6.1) by the author using data published in a 1968 report (Dow, 1965). This lithic represents at least 15 percent of all the artifacts found at the site. This discovery (Bourque et al. 1984; Doyle 1978) stimulated the systematic petrologic analysis of the entire Turner Farm artifact collection. A total of 1,920 artifacts, plus several hundred flakes and chips, were examined over a three-year period.

The results of this initial work were summarized in an internal memorandum to Bourque in 1978, and in two later unpublished reports. Two other lithic artifact source studies undertaken subsequent to the initial Turner Farm lithic research contributed greatly to an understanding of coastal Maine lithic materials.

OBJECTIVES

The objectives of the Turner Farm lithic study are threefold: (1) to identify and describe all the lithic artifact materials, (2) to locate the lithic source area for each lithic type, and

ROBERT G. DOYLE • Maine State Museum, Augusta, Maine 04333.

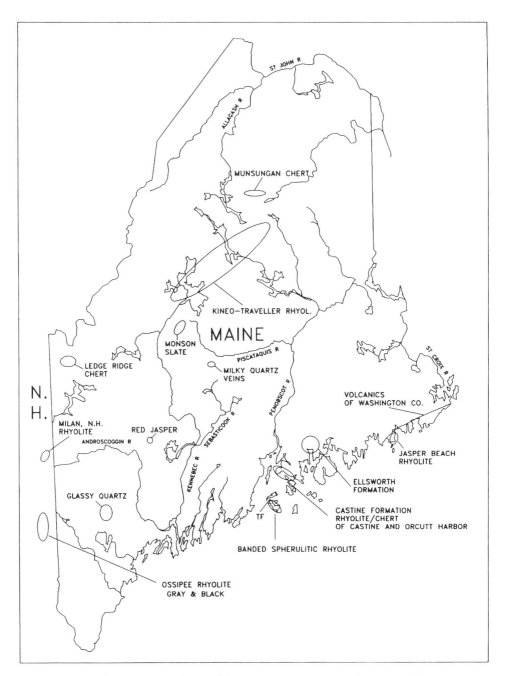

Figure A6.1. Location of principal lithic source areas in Maine and New Hampshire.

(3) to present these data in a way that would compare lithic preference through archaeological time. There are four sections in this study:

1. Research methods.
2. Petrologic description, provenience, and geologic setting of lithic materials.
3. Presentation of statistical data for the lithic materials.
4. Summary and conclusions.

METHODS

Petrologic Analysis

Artifacts were examined individually and their lithology described. Most were made from readily identifiable rock types with a confirmed source provenience. This allowed for rapid lithic identification. Certain exotic lithologies, highly weathered rocks, and undistinguished volcanic rocks received more careful petrologic examination. Identification, however, was mostly limited to hand-specimen and binocular analysis. Thin-section petroscopy was rarely employed. It is an expensive procedure, and for this project, not a critical consideration. There are a few instances, such as the Munsungan chert or banded-spherulitic rhyolite, where already-published petrographic analyses (see, e.g., Billings 1965; Pollock 1986) were useful.

Mineral composition, grain size, texture and fabric, color, luster, and hardness were the primary identifying parameters. Some lithologies were difficult to identify. These included very fine grained, dense, highly silicious rocks; strongly metamorphosed quartz-feldspathic layered rocks; and weathered rocks, particularly with the fine-grained silicious volcanics. The weathering process frequently masks the identity of certain rock types, although some lithologies such as the Castine volcanics, Kineo-Traveler volcanics, Trap rock, and the black variety of the Orcutt Harbor volcanics had diagnostic weathering characteristics. For other fine-grained silicious rocks, however, there was no easy identification, except to assume that they were probably volcanic. It is nearly impossible, by hand-specimen analysis, to differentiate between highly weathered cherty rocks and very fine grained volcanic rocks. Fortunately, the Turner Farm collection contained few cherty lithologies. About 30 artifacts of unique or rarely seen lithologies required special consideration. Some have been source provenienced, at least to a geographic region; others have not. The more common exotics were (1) white to buff-colored opaque cherts, usually mottled, spotted, or swirled in red, yellow, or brown; (2) a dense, slightly lustrous, and highly silicious massive rock (possibly mylonite, a resilicified fault gouge); (3) complex volcanic pyroclastic rocks, which occurred in spatter cones, volcanic breccias, and finely bedded, rippled, flow-banded ash beds; and (4) highly silicious rocks, with no genetic telltales, that appear to have been subjected to multiphase metamorphism. These are possibly from the Canadian Shield.

ARTIFACT AND LITHIC GROUPING

The artifacts themselves are separated into three topologies: bifaces, scrapers, and ground and pecked tools. Bifaces include all flaked tools that were formed as projectile points, blades, and large bifacial scrapers; scrapers include all end scrapers and smaller bifacial scrapers; ground and pecked tools include all tools—gouges, adzes, and plummets—that were fashioned by grinding or pecking stones.

About 30 individual lithologies were identified from lithic studies conducted during the 1980s on over 200 central coastal Maine artifact collections. Artifacts from the Turner Farm represent 18 of these 30 lithologies. These 18 lithic types were separated into five major lithic groups:

1. Rhyolites (lavas, tuffs, ash, and pyroclastics).
2. Other volcanic rocks (local andesite plus rhyolite varieties from eastern Washington County).
3. Quartz, plus five chert varieties.
4. Plutonic rocks (granite, gabbro, diabase, basalt, trap).
5. Metasedimentary and metavolcanic rocks of moderate to high metamorphic grade. These include Ellsworth Formation rocks, quartzite, and slate.

These data are summarized in four tables, presented and discussed in a later section. They offer a wide variety of statistical information that attempts to define lithic materials use, tool applications, and changes in lithic preference through time at the site.

LITHIC SOURCE AREAS

Lithic source areas are narrowly defined geographic areas where a specific lithology was present and available to prehistoric people. They occur as proximal sources, such as bedrock outcrops, from which fragments of the rock were extracted, or as distal sources, as cobbles or rock fragments in glacial drift or the bed load of streams and rivers. Munsungan chert is an example of a proximal source area. The Kineo-Traveler Mountain rhyolite is primarily a distal source area, because it is so common in the glacial drift.

The 30 specific lithic types that I have identified can be traced to individual source areas in the Northeast. They are distributed throughout New England, the Champlain Valley and eastern New York, the mid-Atlantic States, and the southern Canadian Maritimes. Ramah chert of coastal Labrador and possible Canadian Shield rocks are also included (Figure A6.2). These source areas contain either single lithologies, such as the banded-spherulitic rhyolite of Vinalhaven, or a petrologic group, such as "quartzite," which embraces all types of quartzite, defined by color and grain size. Unique and important lithologies within such groups, such as the Cheshire quartzite, are noted as a source-area subset.

The lithic data are organized in two formats. The first is a simple listing, by cultural period, of each artifact by its site number, tool type, and lithology. Though not published here, this large folio of artifact listings is available at the Maine State Museum. The second format is a series of biaxial matrices that match tool type against lithology for each cultural period. For the Turner Farm site this is a 40-page document.

PETROLOGIC DESCRIPTION AND PROVENIENCE OF THE LITHIC MATERIALS

This section presents a petrologic description of each of the 18 lithologies found at the Turner Farm site, and the geologic and geographic setting of each source lithology.

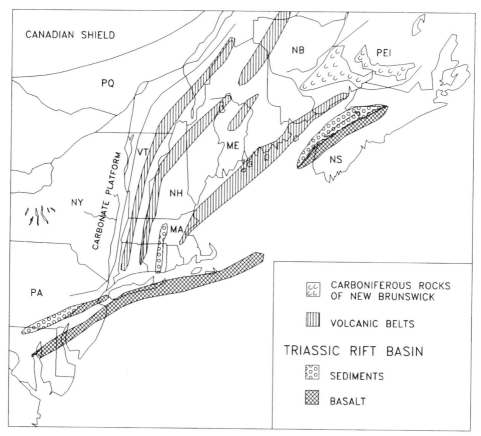

Figure A6.2. Generalized geologic map of the northeastern United States and adjacent Canada.

Regional Geology

It is important to present a brief picture of the geologic setting of the region within which the lithic materials were found. The region extends from Virginia to the eastern Maritime Provinces, westward to the Champlain Valley, and includes the rocks of the Canadian Shield and Labrador (Figure A6.2). It embraces a wide variety of regionally metamorphosed rocks, a multicomponent stratigraphy, and complex geologic structures, all of which have contributed to generation of a large number of lithic artifact materials.

The geology is characterized by a series of northeast-trending rock belts containing a variety of rock suites. They range in age from the Late Precambrian to Mid-Mesozoic, and are intruded by large masses of plutonic rocks, mostly granite, gabbro, and a number of extrusive basalt flows and related trap dikes. This rock sequence forms the Appalachian Geologic Province, about 350 miles wide and extending from the Maritimes to Georgia (Figure A6.2). It is bounded on the west by the weakly folded Paleozoic Carbonate Platform west of the Champlain Valley in New York and Ontario. These rocks contain many of the chert lithics found at the Turner Farm site. On the east the province is bounded by the Gulf of Maine and occasional exposures of younger cover rocks of Mesozoic and Tertiary age. This region is the very large hunting ground for lithics used by the Maine peoples.

Metamorphosed Rocks.   Within the region there are four clearly defined metavolcanic belts separated by metasedimentary rocks; they contain most of the rock types used for Maine coastal artifacts. The two eastern belts contain the largest number and greatest variety of source materials. Metasedimentary rock belts consist of two lithologic types. There is a weakly metamorphosed, fine-grained, platy, and brittle type (slate, metasiltstone, and phyllite) and a more strongly altered type that consists of granular, usually coarse-grained schist and gneiss. Much softer and not amenable to flaking, these were mostly used for ground and pecked tools. The most important source areas of slaty rocks used for ground stone tools are the northern and central Maine Clastic Basins, the western Maine-New Hampshire Clastic Basins, and the Vermont Slate Belt (Figure A6.2).

Quartzite, a metamorphosed sandstone, becomes tougher with increased metamorphism and is often used for flaked tools. It occurs in a great variety of localities, but flaking-quality quartzite is rarely found in Maine rocks.

Sedimentary Rocks.   The eastern side of the Paleozoic Carbonate Platform (Figure A6.2) contains several thousand feet of gently folded layers of limestone/dolomite, shale, and coarse to fine argillaceous sandstone. Beds and nodular layers of chert are scattered throughout this sequence, which extends from Niagara Falls and Ontario, eastward to Albany, where it bends south down into Virginia.

Igneous Rocks.   The Mesozoic rocks of the Minas Rift Basin of central New Brunswick are composed of terrestrial Red Bed sediments and a large, elongate mass of basalt—the North Mountain basalt. The basalt contains two varieties of chalcedonic material: bedded, nodular, and fracture-filling chalcedony, and agate/petrified wood. Both varieties are found at the Turner Farm site. The basalt also contains native copper, which was probably the source of copper bead specimens found at coastal Maine sites.

It is possible that a small amount of finer-grained, tough, hornfelsed argillites may be present in the Red Bed sequence and found its way to the Maine coast. However, such rock types were not of the excellent-quality argillite—the dark gray, very hard, compact, and silicious hornfels—that is present throughout northeastern collections. Those come from rift basin rocks of the eastern rift basin terrane (Figure A6.2), where the siltstone layers were contact metamorphosed by intruding basalts.

Petrologic Descriptions

The 1,920 artifacts from the Turner Farm represent, as noted above, 18 lithic types, separated into five major petrologic groups: rhyolites, varietal volcanics, quartz/chert, plutonic rocks, and metasediments/volcanics.

Rhyolite Group

This group contains four distinct rhyolitic lithologies.

1. Banded-spherulitic rhyolite from Vinalhaven.

2. Rhyolite lithologies from the Cape Rosier/Castine portion of the Castine Formation.
3. Orcutt Harbor dark-colored Castine Formation varieties from Brooksville.
4. Kineo-Traveler Mountain porphyry.

Banded-spherulitic rhyolite (BSR) is a finely banded rhyolite flow composed of quartz and plagioclase feldspar. In fresh rock, there are light-colored (light gray to lavender) bands of microcrystaline quartz and feldspar, and dark-colored (dark brown to black) bands of intergrown smoky quartz (Billings 1965). The bands occur in two distinct habits, and both are found in artifacts. In one, the bands are nearly flat, planar features; in the other, the bands are contorted into whorls, spherules, or wavy streamers. Surface weathering changes the color of the bands to buff and very dark gray, with occasional patches of deep rose red. Heat treating will also develop this red coloration.

BSR is exposed on the northern end of Vinalhaven in a one-half-mile-wide band from Perry Cove to Crockett Cove (Figure A6.1), with the layered BSR variety best exposed in Perry Cove, and the spherulitic variety on Crockett Point. (Thin-banded, often spherulitic rhyolite is fairly common in felsic volcanic environments of the northern Appalachians, but the BSR of the Crockett Cove member is a very unique lithology). There are two other nearby exposure areas of the Vinalhaven Formation that include banded rhyolite (Figure A6.1). Mapped by Stewart and Wones (1974) and Dow (1965), one is on the southwest side of Isle au Haut, and the other on Great Spruce Island, but these are lithologically quite distinct from the BSR. Two other banded rhyolite localities are found in New England. They are the rhyolite vein fillings at Milan, New Hampshire, and the banded rhyolite in the Blue Hills south of Boston (Figure A6.2). These two are common lithic materials in the Northeast, but distinctive from the BSR.

Castine volcanics (CAS) underlie a very large part of eastern Penobscot Bay. They are rhyolitic rocks of the Siluro-Devonian age Castine Formation (Brookins, Berdan, and Stewart 1973). The Formation is broken into segments by plutons and the waters of the Bay (Figure A6.1), but the segments are all of the same geologic age and petrology. Two distinct lithologies were used for Turner Farm artifacts: (1) the typical Castine Formation gray-green rhyolite that underlies the Cape Rosier and Castine peninsulas (CAS), and (2) the Orcutt Harbor varieties, dark gray to black-colored rhyolite found at Orcutt Harbor (OHB). The lithology of the typical CAS is first described, followed by the description of the OHB varieties.

There are three kinds of CAS used for artifacts:

1. A dark gray, slightly lustrous, fine-grained, tough rock, occasionally micro-porphyritic in texture. It appears chalky to buff-colored when weathered. It is the most common variety of CAS.
2. A slightly vitreous gray-green tuff (?), with occasional pyrite crystals present. It commonly has a wavy mottled texture. When weathered, it has a dull gray color and powdery surface texture.
3. A gray to gray-green, slightly granular pyroclastic (?) rock that weathers to a chalky surface texture.

The Orcutt Harbor varieties occur in the south corner of Brooksville Township in central Hancock County (Figure A6.1) as scattered exposures all around the Harbor. There are four varieties used for artifacts:

1. OHB, a dark gray, vitreous to slightly dull rock, very fine-grained to nearly aphanitic. It contains ± 15 percent submillimeter, glassy, white feldspar phenocrysts.

Larger (up to 1.0 mm) feldspar phenocrysts are also seen. It has a very dark gray to black chertlike lithology, but its volcanic texture and the presence of phenocrysts define its volcanic origin.

2. OHW, a dark gray to black rhyolite that contains irregularly shaped, subrounded spots and mottles of gray to white feldspar that appears to have undergone chemical alteration before induration. Artifacts of this material vary from very slightly spotted to a nearly all white.

3. OHM is a mottled and wavy-textured rhyolite, dark gray to gray-brown and brick red in color. It is slightly coarser grained and moderately vitreous.

4. OHC, a very dark gray to black chert, with moderate to dull luster, and excellent conchoidal fracture. Some specimens have a very slightly granular, "flinty" texture.

The Orcutt Harbor varieties do not develop a strong weathering patina. For the Turner Farm study, these four varieties are included under the name *Orcutt Harbor Black* (OHB).

Kineo-Traveler Mountain Porphyry (KTM) is the most common rock type used in artifacts in coastal and southern Maine sites. At the Turner Farm it represents 25 percent of all artifacts. The type KTM is commonly a green-gray, glassy, porphyritic rhyolite containing rectangular phenocrysts of feldspar, tiny glass beads of quartz, plus several accessory minerals. Its source area is the Traveler Mountain-Kineo Mountain rhyolite belt, described by Rankin (1968) as the Piscatiquis Volcanic Belt. It is a belt of caldera centers that extends for over 100 miles from Flagstaff Lake northeast to Grand Lake Matagamon (Figure A6.1). Three calderas—Traveler Mountain, Big Spencer Mountain, and Kineo Mountain—were the major contributors of artifact material. Each center has its peculiar petrologic character, and artifacts may commonly be tied back to an individual caldera.

The Traveler Mountain center is composed of a dark-colored, quite glassy, welded ash flow tuff containing phenocrysts of clear quartz and white to buff (plagioclase) feldspar. Quartz is rare, but does occur both in euhedral grains and in clear glass beads. Magnetite and hornblende phenocrysts are present in the upper part of the volcanic mass. The Big Spencer caldera rhyolite has a dark green to blue-green, quite glassy groundmass that contains phenocrysts of prismatic-shaped feldspar (occasionally cross-twinned), clear quartz glass beads, almandite (red) garnet, plus occasional pink apatite. The Kineo Mountain rhyolite is lighter colored than that from the other centers, with a gray-green to light green and wavy-banded gray-green color and texture. Feldspar phenocrysts are much larger, and quartz glass beads and garnet are very common. Rankin (1968) provides an excellent petrologic description of all varieties of KTM. KTM lithologies have, for a long time, been identified in the archaeological literature as Kineo felsite, presumably because of the presence of a large prehistoric quarry waste dump at the base of the mountain (see, e.g., Moorehead 1922:215–219). However, in lithic samples from coastal sites there does not seem to be a statistically greater number of artifacts from the Kineo caldera. Although not inappropriate, the name Kineo felsite or rhyolite should not be used to identify all KTM lithics. It should be used only for material from the Kineo caldera.

Volcanic Varieties Group—Andesite (AND)

There are two source areas of andesite used for artifacts at the Turner Farm. One is an outcrop exposure located a few hundred yards west of the site. The other is a series of random exposures of andesitic rocks intercalated with the Washington County portion of the Coastal Volcanic Belt.

Andesite (AND). The artifact lithics from both sources are fine-grained, silicious, and similar to those in the rhyolite group. They are separated from that group on the basis of either an andesitic composition or because they have petrologic characteristics that tie them to the Washington County Volcanics. They are also present at some other small outcrop areas along the Washington County coast. Turner Farm is one of the few coastal sites that contains a significant number of andesite specimens (89, or 6 percent of the total artifacts). The other coastal sites examined contained less than one-half percent andesite specimens. This is probably due to the proximity of andesite exposures. It was acceptable as a local source, but perhaps not fine enough or in sufficient quantity for export. Artifacts are dark gray-green or rose-violet to dull gray in color, moderately to slightly vitreous, with a swirled and mottled, flow-banded texture. Specimens are usually coarser grained than the average rhyolitic artifact.

Washington County Volcanics (WCV)

A large section of the Washington County coast and part of New Brunswick is underlain by weakly metamorphosed volcanic and associated sedimentary rocks—the *Washington County volcanics* (WCV). The sequence was very carefully mapped by Gates (1978), and much of the descriptive petrology and locality information comes from his work.

WCV source rocks range from a silicious mudstone to fine-grained, vitreous rhyolite lava flows. They contain significant amounts of the richly textured and brightly colored felsic volcanic lithologies found in many coastal collections. Pyroclastic rocks, commonly from explosive volcanic activity, are a common petrology of WCV lithics. They include tuff, tuff breccia, autobreccia, and lapilli piles. Lava fountain spatter-cone-textured rocks are also present in both outcrop and artifact. Mixtures of tuff, ash beds, and shallow-water mud deposits provide a mottled, swirly bedded, multicolored silicious mudstone lithology. Silicious mudstone is fairly common in this terrain, where the intermixing of pyroclastic particles and sea-bottom mud generated a very fine, tough silicious rock with an almost cherty texture. Jasper Beach, a small cove in Machiasport (Figure A6.1), contains large numbers of brick red, purple, brown, and pink cobbles of silicious mudstone. It has a dull luster, and colors often have a faded hue. Jasper Beach cobbles were commonly used for artifacts at coastal Maine sites. Another silicious mudstone source area is the pelagic sediment portion of the various chert facies of the Munsungan Formation at Munsungan Lake in northern Piscatiquis County.

The rhyolite and volcanic varieties groups together comprise the more silicious (felsic to intermediate) volcanic lithic suite at the Turner Farm site. They form more than three quarters of the total number of artifacts, and most of the bifacial tools.

Quartz/Chert Group

The quartz/chert group includes all the pure silica (SiO_2) lithologies found at the site. It contains the mineral quartz class and four classes of chert—one from Maine, one from Nova Scotia, and two from New York. *Quartz* (QZ) occurs randomly in the glacial drift, and in veins and cavities in bedrock. It has such a ubiquitous distribution that a single source area attribution is impossible. However, one Maine bedrock source of quartz crystal and one of milky quartz are well known and may have been lithic source areas. These are the extensive milky quartz fracture filling (in places up to two feet wide) that occurs in the Vassalboro Formation near Albion in central Maine, and pegmatitic glassy quartz from Sagadahoc and Oxford counties, Maine. Several kinds of quartz appear in the collection, including glassy crystal, rose, smoky, milky, and dull, massive, gray bull quartz. Small stemmed points were commonly made from glassy or milky quartz; small end scrapers of fairly glassy varietal and rose quartz are also common.

The four chert classes are Munsungan chert, Nova Scotia chalcedony, eastern New York chert, and varietal chert, which includes varicolored jasper, gray-brown chert, and exotic chert, much of which may have a Canadian Shield provenience.

Munsungan chert (MUN) is a commonly occurring lithology at many coastal sites, with the largest number found in Ceramic-age collections. There are statistically fewer MUN chert specimens found at the Turner Farm site (about 3.5 percent of the total artifacts) than at many coastal sites. The Goddard site a few miles to the east has about 10 percent Munsungan material.

The chert occurs as interbeds in the Munsungan Lake Formation, a dacitic (intermediate composition) submarine volcanic and volcanoclastic rock of Ordovician age (Figure A6.1) located in northwestern Maine (Hall 1970; Pollock 1986). The dacite flows, and accompanying pyroclastics, appear to have been deposited in repetitive cycles with the chert beds near the top of each cycle. The chert beds range in thickness from a few centimeters to tens of meters, thus providing good quarrying ground. Bonnichsen et al. (1980) reported extensive quarry and debitage evidence in the area. The geologic environment for the chert deposits at Ledge Ridge, in northern Oxford County (Figure A6.1), is similar to the Munsungan chert; however, the "host" rock at Ledge Ridge is a basalt.

In artifacts, MUN chert occurs in a variety of colors, with deep wine red, dark green, and mottled red and green the most popular. Gray, dark gray, and occasional black specimens are also present. The gray shades are the most commonly occurring in outcrop. It is a moderately fine-grained, massive textured chert, weakly translucent on thin edges, with excellent conchoidal fracture. Stress fractures are nearly absent. Most artifact specimens contain up to 15 percent dark gray diatom spheres. Pyrite has not been seen in outcrop or artifact specimens. Munsungan chert cobbles have not been reported in the glacial debris deposits along the coast, nor to any extent down the glacial travelway as is the case with ubiquitous KTM material. Even around the shore of adjacent Munsungan Lake, there is not a large amount of MUN chert cobbles. Early people must have obtained MUN chert from its proximal outcrop source.

The *Nova Scotia chalcedony* (NSC) lithic class is composed of varicolored and textured chalcedony and agate. Both varieties were deposited from slow-cooling, late magmatic stage, silicious exhalates that filled veins, fractures, and cavities in a Triassic-age rift basalt. Artifact-quality masses of chalcedony and agate are present throughout much of the length of the flow—a steep-sided, 300-foot-high ridge (North Mountain) that forms the southern shore of the Minas Basin from Digby Cove to Parrsboro, Nova Scotia (Figure A6.3). Native copper is also present in small veinlets, often in close association with chalcedony.

Both in outcrop and artifact the chalcedony/agate specimens are brightly colored, translucent to transparent, generally have a glassy luster, and show both a brittle and weakly

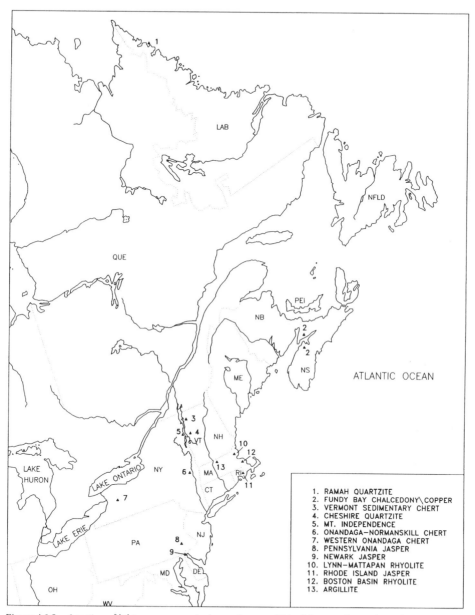

Figure A6.3. Location of lithic source areas in the northeastern United States and Canada, exclusive of Maine and New Hampshire.

conchoidal fracture pattern. The glassy varieties occur in a wide range of colors: pink, rose, deep wine red, light and dark purple, as well as red-brown and dark red-brown. Textural habits include wavy banded, swirled, mottled, spotted, and layered. The chalcedony of Blomidon Point is different from the rest of the localities along the mountain. It has a dull luster, is opaque, and is often massive textured. Colors include pale pink, rose, and buff-violet. It looks more like a porcelainite than a chalcedony, but was quite popular as an artifact material, perhaps because it occurs in thicker beds and is quite accessible, with a lot of material in one place.

The mottled, swirled, dark wine red and purple, glassy chalcedony is quite common near and northeast of Digby. A yellow to pale orange-yellow moss agate was found on Moose Island, just east of Parrsboro.

There is also a weakly banded, dull to bright red to purple variety found in a few coastal artifacts that has been traced to Scotts Cove, a small fish-hook-shaped cove across the Bay from Parrsboro. The base of the basalt flow at this locality is in contact with a thin limestone bed deposited as lacustrine limy mud at the margin of a large lake that formed sometime after the basalt was extruded and chilled. Thompson (1974) postulates that the chalcedony occurs as silica replacement of organic material (such as tree trunks and limbs), and of clay nodules and thin silty beds in the limestone. Some of the tree trunk chalcedony masses have amethyst tube cores.

Genetically equivalent Triassic basalt flows are also present on Grand Manan Island about 50 miles to the southwest (Figure A6.2). However, only a few fracture-filling patches of dull white chalcedony have been observed. It was of very poor quality and size for artifacts, and is not seen in the Turner Farm collection.

New York cherts (NYC) include a variety of bedded and nodular deposits contained within the carbonate and clastic sedimentary rocks of the Carbonate Platform west and northwest of the Appalachian folded belt (Figure A6.2). They have been a major lithic source for the prehistoric peoples of New England.

These Carbonate Platform cherts are not common at coastal Maine sites, but even the Turner Farm site contained at least 30 Platform chert artifacts. Most of the NYC artifacts are light- to dark-colored, dull gray, sometimes gray-brown or pale green, mottled cherts, of varying grain size and texture. There are three specimens of the gray-brown, mottled Onandaga chert and four of the lustrous, diatom-rich green Normanskill chert, plus a dull gray, massive chert artifact of presumed Helderberg provenience.

Varietal chert (VAR CHE) is represented by a number of chert artifacts that may have a New York source area, but no provenience can be determined. These include common vitreous and dull-luster gray and black chert, and a red jasper of possible central Maine provenience. There are also six "exotic" varieties with no recognizable provenience. Varietal chert was much more commonly used during the Ceramic period.

Plutonic Group

The Plutonic group includes three major igneous rock types: granite, gabbro and diabase, and basalt and trap rock. Though of different genesis and petrology, they form a common lithic material for many of the ground and pecked artifacts. A few flaked arti-facts of trap rock and basalt are present. Most of the plutonic lithics in the Turner Farm collection can be found in outcrop or in drift cobbles on the Island.

Granite (GRA) is composed of orthoclase (K-feldspar) and some sodic plagioclase feldspar, quartz (± 5 percent), micas, and accessory minerals such as garnet and tourmaline. Such rocks are coarse grained, fairly soft, with a texture that is easily pecked. They are light colored, often with rich color patterns, which may have led to their use as ornamental pecking stones or plummets. Locally available granite is red, pink, whitish, light green, or gray colored.

Grabbo and *diabase* (GAB/DIA) are the darker-colored, more iron-rich equivalents of granite. They are usually green-gray, dark green, or almost black. Gabbro is composed of calcic plagioclase, hornblende, biotite, and olivine. There is a small gabbro body exposed at the north end of North Haven Island that may have been a local source. Some artifacts were presumably derived from beach cobbles. Diabase is the porphyritic variety of gabbro, found throughout Maine, but more commonly along the eastern coast. Like common gabbro, it is composed of dark gray to black, fine- to medium-grained mafic minerals, but it also contains fairly large (1.0–3.0 mm) laths of white to buff Ca-rich plagioclase that give the rock a spotted appearance. It is rarely found in artifacts, usually as poorly formed bifaces and occasional hammerstones.

Basalt and *trap* (BAS/TRA) rock types are the extrusive (lava flow) equivalents of gabbro. Both are found in outcrop and in the beach drift on North Haven. Basalt is very fine grained, almost aphanitic, massive, and rarely textured. Colors range from dark greenish black to black and very dark gray. Disseminated pyrite is fairly common. Many basalt flows on the East Coast occur in Triassic rift basins such as the Palisades in New Jersey and North Mountain in Nova Scotia.

An older basalt flow that crops out conveniently to the Turner Farm at Mullins Head on North Haven (Figure A6.1) may have been a source rock. Its primary use was for ground and pecked tools, but some varieties are sufficiently tough and brittle for making bifacial tools.

Trap rock is an ultra fine-grained variety of basalt that occurs in dike and sill swarms, part of the Triassic lava intrusions associated with Atlantic rifting. The fine texture is caused by very rapid cooling (quenching) as lava came in contact with the cold country rock it invaded. It is very dark gray to black in color, very brittle, with fair conchoidal fracture, and has a characteristic orange to orange-yellow weathering rime. Trap was used for bifaces and scrapers. Dikes and sills of trap rock are quite common along the coast, and on islands in Penobscot Bay.

Metamorphic Group

The metamorphic group includes rocks of both low- and high-grade metamorphism. Low-intensity metamorphism, such as that which alters shale to slate or devitrifies glass particles in volcanic rocks, had little impact on, or sometimes improved, the flaking quality of a rock. High-intensity metamorphism, however, completely alters the fabric, grain size, and composition of rocks, often rendering them nearly useless for flaked artifacts. Quartzite is an exception; its flaking properties were often improved by intense metamorphism. Four individual lithologies are included here: metamorphosed sediments and volcanics, Ellsworth Formation lithologies, quartzite, and slate.

Metamorphosed sediments and volcanics (MSV) includes phyllite, schist, gneiss, granulitic rocks, and magmatite. They are usually coarse, granular, soft, and contain much mica.

Phyllite is a micaceous, often chlorite-rich metamorphic rock with a shiny, platy texture, often rippled in appearance. It is soft and easily scraped into shape, with colors of green to dark gray to black. Phyllite was used for ornaments or plummets. Ellsworth Formation phyllite was commonly used for that purpose.

Schist, gneiss, and granulite are varieties of coarsely recrystallized, granular rocks composed of quartz-feldspar-biotite + muscovite + calcareous minerals. They have a banded to massive texture and tend to be coarse-grained. Source areas for these lithologies were probably from the Kearsarge-Central Maine Synclinorium of central Maine (Osberg et al. 1985). Cobbles of these lithologies are common in the drift on North Haven, which provided a plentiful local supply. The granulite and schist/gneiss cobbles are occasionally found on North Haven, but gabbro and granite are more common.

The *Ellsworth Formation* (ELS) crops out from Castine to Gouldsboro, concentrated around Ellsworth Falls (Figure A6.1). It consists of a number of strongly metamorphosed igneous and sedimentary rocks of early Paleozoic age (?). The rocks are characterized by a green to dark green color, intense shearing and microfolding (often with a chevron pattern), and the presence of large amounts of chlorite. Nearly every central coastal site contains ELS artifacts. The rock is quite soft, and weathers quickly. It is not often found in the drift, and thus outcrop quarrying was probable. Ellsworth Formation rock occurs in four characteristic lithologies:

1. Green- and gray-banded schist with chlorite > hornblende green bands and feldspar > mica > quartz gray bands. Band thickness is variable, but averages 0.5 cm.
2. Folded and strongly foliated green chlorite-rich phyllite, often containing thin lenses of "greenstone."
3. Massive, highly sheared and foliated greenstone, composed of chlorite, calcic feldspar, hornblende, and mica.
4. Fine-grained gabbro, usually dark gray-green in color.

Their distribution is random, although the banded schist is more common at the northern boundary of the Ellsworth Formation. Bright green, subglassy crystalline chlorite was used for finely carved and ornamented plummets.

Only 2 of the 16 *quartzite* (QZT) artifacts have a confirmed source provenience. These are from the Cheshire Quartzite of northwestern Vermont. The remaining 14 are from unknown source areas, although the Canadian Shield, eastern New Brunswick, and possibly far northwestern Maine are suspected source areas. Many of the other 15 specimens are fine-grained, massive, weakly lustrous to glassy, with good conchoidal fracture. Magnetite and tourmaline impurities are common. Color ranges from black to blue-gray to gray and brown. The flaking quality varied from excellent to moderate, with the Cheshire Quartzite having the best quality. Ramah chert from Labrador, another high-quality material, was not found at the Turner Farm site, though it is present in many coastal Maine sites. Cheshire Quartzite is a Paleozoic rock unit that occurs in a narrow, arcuate outcrop band in northern and western Vermont (Doll et al. 1961; Figure A6.3). It is medium brown to honey brown in color, with occasional faint gray mottling, very fine grained, and with a subglassy luster. Most pieces are translucent on thin edges. It displays a strong mineral grain lineation and a slight "nubbly" grain texture. These characteristics and its particular brown color are diagnostic. One confirmed source of high-quality Cheshire Quartzite is a series of outcrops near Otter Creek, a few miles east of Vergennes, Vermont.

Slate (SLT) is a very common rock type in the Appalachian folded belt, occurring in nearly every geologic terrain. With rare exceptions, slate did not survive glacial drift transport. I suspect that it is a proximal source area that required direct quarrying. Slate is the product of strong compression (at fairly low temperature) of shale that formed a tough, strongly cleaved rock. Slaty cleavage allows it to be split into very thin plates. Slate with a high percentage of adulterating minerals is classed petrologically as a metasiltstone. It too is found at the site and has a variety of source areas, largely in the mid-Maine sedimentary basin. The few ground stone tools from the Turner Farm were made from slate or, less commonly, from metasiltstone. Those of highest quality are almost surely made from Monson slate, a thin lens of highest-quality slate from a still-operating quarry in Monson, northern Franklin County, Maine (Figure A6.1).

STATISTICAL DATA ON THE LITHIC MATERIALS

This section summarizes the lithic identification data of artifacts from the Turner Farm site according to their lithic class, tool type, and cultural period. The data are presented in four tables.

There were 1,920 lithic artifacts in the collection analyzed, comprising 1,242 bifaces, 388 scrapers, and 290 pecked and ground tools (Table A6.1). These recoveries are about normal for coastal Maine sites. Bifaces represent 65 percent of the total, with nearly 90 percent of them made from two of the three silicious lithologic groups—rhyolite, volcanic varieties, and quartz/chert. Most of the other bifaces were of basalt, trap, and quartzite. Scrapers represent about 22 percent of the tools, and, like the bifaces, were made mostly (+90 percent) from the silicious lithologic groups. Local Penobscot Bay sources and distant sources are about equally represented, with about 4 percent each. The percentage of KTM scrapers (8.39 percent), as usual, was twice that of local or distant sources. This is also a common statistic in coastal Maine. The largest percentage of pecked and ground tools were made from KTM, CAS, and EPB, mostly from beach drift cobbles.

There were 1,292 rhyolite group artifacts recovered, representing 67 percent of the total tools. This is the most common lithologic group used. When we add the 166 tools of the volcanic varieties group, they together total 1,458 artifacts—about three-fourths (76 percent) of all tools studied. The silicious volcanic lithologies are, by a wide margin, the most commonly used rock type at the Turner Farm site. Except for WCV, their source areas are local, within 25 miles of the site. I have included cobble-derived KTM as a locally derived, distal-source lithic. This decision is based on extensive coastal beach surveying where up to 15 percent of the beach cobbles are of KTM.

The quartz/chert group contains 224 tools (12 percent of all tools), most of them bifaces. There were 84 scrapers (4.38 percent of the total), mostly OTZ, MUN and NSC, consistent with other coastal sites. The absence of NYC scrapers is due in part to a cautious identification of chert lithologies. It is possible that some scrapers (and some bifaces as well) may well have a Hudson Valley provenience. There were nine pecked and ground tools, most of them probably reused cores, or irregular chunks of quartz.

Plutonic Group lithologies include granite (GRA), basalt (BAS) and trap (TRA), and gabbro (GAB) and diabase (DIA). All these rock types except diabase are common to Penobscot Bay, both in outcrop and glacial drift. There were 144 tools in this group. Of

Table A6.1. Artifact Summary by Tool Type

| | Tool type | | | | | | Total tools | |
| | Bifaces | | Scrapers | | Ground and pecked | | | |
Lithology[a]	Number of tools	Percent of tools	Number of tools	Percent of tools	Number of tools	Percent of tools	Total number	Total percent
Rhyolite group								
BSR	414	21.43	24	1.25	8	0.42	446	23.25
CAS	59	3.08	56	2.92	35	1.82	150	7.82
OHB	160	8.36	22	1.15	25	1.29	207	10.79
KTM	261	13.74	161	8.39	67	3.52	489	25.49
Total rhyolite	894	46.61	263	13.75	135	7.05	1,292	67.36
Volcanic varieties group								
AND	73	3.81	5	0.26	11	0.57	89	4.64
WCV	57	2.97	13	0.68	7	0.36	77	4.01
Total volcanic varieties	130	6.78	18	0.94	18	0.93	166	8.65
Quartz/Chert group								
QZ	27	1.41	14	0.74	4	0.21	45	2.35
MUN	26	1.36	37	1.93	0	0	63	3.28
NSC	10	0.52	12	0.63	0	0	22	1.14
NYC	7	0.36	1	0.05	0	0	8	0.42
VAR CHE	61	3.18	20	1.04	5	0.26	86	4.48
Total Quartz/Chert	131	6.83	84	4.38	9	0.47	224	11.68
Plutonic group								
GRA	0	0	0	0	11	0.57	11	0.58
BAS/TRA	58	3.02	14	0.73	10	0.79	82	4.27
GAB/DIA	3	0.16	2	0.10	46	2.36	51	2.66
Total plutonic	61	3.18	16	0.83	67	3.49	144	7.51
Metamorphic group								
MSV	12	0.62	5	0.26	41	2.13	58	3.02
ELS	0	0	0	0	12	0.63	12	0.63
QZT	12	0.62	2	0.10	2	0.11	16	0.83
SLT	0	0	0	0	3	0.15	6	0.31
Total metamorphic	24	1.25	7	0.36	61	3.18	92	4.80
All totals	1,240	64.65	388	20.23	290	15.12	1,918	100.0

[a]Reader is referred to text for definitions of abbreviations.

these, 72 bifaces and scrapers were made from trap or basalt. There were three weathered, flaked tools made with unusually tough gabbro and diabase. There were 57 ground and pecked tools of coarse-grained plutonic rocks, plus 10 made from basalt.

Metamorphic group lithologies include 92 artifacts, two-thirds of them ground and pecked. The bifaces and scrapers are made with a fine-grained granulite lithology, a possible Bangor-area source rock that may have come from the beach drift. In the quartzite class there were 14 flaked artifacts and 2 pecking stones. Twelve ELS artifacts were identified, mostly formed into plummets. Quartzite artifacts are not as common in the collection as at other coastal sites, but there is considerable evidence from chip recovery that quartzite was probably commonly used at Turner Farm, although identifiable artifacts are rare. Unlike most other of the metamorphic class lithics, quartzite has no local provenience. Drift cobbles of possible Canadian Shield quartzite were a potential source. Only six slate ground-stone tools were found, although I had noted considerable slate debris from the screenings. Slate tools at the Turner Farm did not seem to survive well.

Summarizing the data from Table A6.1, there is evidence of heavy dependence on two very local materials—BSR and the nearby outcrops of AND. Their rate of use was at least twice the average of most other central coastal sites, some of which were not very distant from these source areas. The rhyolite group, as expected, represents the most numerous lithologic type for all tools. WCV, MUN, and varietal chert are next most numerous of the silicious lithologies. There is the usual correlation with the metamorphic and plutonic lithic groups as the commonly used lithology for pecked and ground tools. The use of KTM for these nonflaked tools is slightly above average for coastal sites. The chert lithologies have the highest percentage of use for scrapers, with MUN the most commonly used chert. The few GRA tools probably represent a poorly selected sample; I identified many of the granite pecking stones as noncultural cobbles. In general, the pattern of use for each tool type and lithology follows the pattern for most coastal Maine sites.

The Archaic period is represented by 974 tools and the Ceramic by 944 (Table A6.2). The rhyolite group was the most common lithic group in both periods, with 75 percent and 57 percent, respectively, for the Archaic and Ceramic. The preferential use of fairly local silicious volcanic material remained fairly constant between Archaic and Ceramic times, with a slight lessening of the percentage of use of rhyolitic tools by the Late Ceramic period. Quartz/chert group lithologies were more common in the Ceramic than the Archaic by a more than 2 to 1 margin, the largest difference being the high scraper use of MUN and NSC in the Ceramic. The lithologies in this group generally have distal source areas, indicating the possibility of more extensive travel and outside contact by Ceramic period people. The use percentage for plutonic group lithologies in the Ceramic period was somewhat greater than that for the Archaic, although the use pattern for each lithology in the plutonic group did not change much over time. There was merely a slightly increased use percentage of plutonic lithologies in the Ceramic. Metamorphic group lithics, as a group, show a marked decline in use percentage and total numbers from Archaic to Ceramic. There were 92 artifacts, in all, representing about 5 percent of all tools at the site. Of these, 41 were from the Archaic. The 12 ELS artifacts were recovered from both Moorehead and Susquehanna deposits.

There were 16 QZT artifacts found, largely from the Archaic. Two Cheshire Quartzite bifaces, however, were from Late Ceramic features. Although the quartzites are generally

Table A6.2. Artifact Summary by Culture

Lithology[a]	Archaic		Ceramic		Total tools	
	Number of tools	Percent of tools	Number of tools	Percent of tools	Number of tools	Percent of tools
Rhyolite group						
BSR	295	30.28	151	16.50	446	23.25
CAS	99	10.16	51	5.40	150	7.82
OHB	108	11.09	99	10.49	207	10.79
KTM	232	25.82	257	27.22	489	25.48
Total rhyolite	734	75.36	558	59.11	1,292	67.36
Volcanic varieties group						
AND	34	3.49	55	5.83	89	4.64
WCV	16	1.64	61	6.46	77	4.01
Total volcanic varieties	50	5.37	116	12.29	166	8.65
Quartz/Chert group						
QZ	18	1.84	27	2.86	45	2.35
MUN	5	0.51	58	6.14	63	3.28
NSC	1	0.10	21	2.22	22	1.14
NYC	3	0.31	5	0.53	8	0.42
VAR CHE	41	4.21	45	4.77	86	4.48
Total quartz/chert	68	6.98	156	16.53	224	11.68
Plutonic group						
GRA	5	0.51	6	0.63	11	0.58
BAS/TRA	43	4.41	39	4.13	82	4.27
GAB/DIA	33	3.37	18	1.91	51	2.66
Total plutonic	81	8.32	63	6.67	144	7.51
Metamorphic group						
MSV	26	2.67	32	3.39	58	3.02
ELS	12	1.23	0	0	12	0.63
QZT	0	0	16	1.69	16	0.83
SLT	3	0.32	3	0.31	6	0.31
Total metamorphic	41	4.21	51	5.70	92	4.80
All totals	974	100.00	944	100.00	1,918	100.00

[a]Reader is referred to text for definitions of abbreviations.

considered to have distant source areas, the tough nature of this rock allows for its survival in the glacial drift train. Except for the known source area of the Cheshire material, the quartzites are not a good indicator of a wider area of contact.

Summarizing the data from Table A6.2, there is an increase in the use of more distantly sourced lithics by Ceramic period people. The percentage of use of locally derived lithologies—like the rhyolite group, AND, and plutonic rock cobble material—stays roughly equal in both major cultural periods. However, most distant source area lithologies like the WCV and the quartz/chert group show an increase from Archaic to Ceramic times.

The distribution of nearby and distantly derived lithologies is shown in Table A6.3, a comparative listing of many of the 18 rock types by source distance and number of artifacts for each lithology and cultural period. Nearby source areas are defined as within a few miles of the site. Distant source areas are more than 25 miles away. Because of its extensive distribution pattern in the coastal drift, the KTM numbers are arbitrarily divided in half; for

Table A6.3. Preferential Use of Nearby versus
Distant Sources of Lithic Materials

	Nearby			Distant	
Lithic type[a]	Archaic	Ceramic	Lithic type[a]	Archaic	Ceramic
BSR	295	151	KTM(½)	116	129
CAS	99	51	WCV	16	61
OHB	108	99	MUN	5	58
KTM(½)	116	128	NSC	1	21
AND	34	55	NYC	3	5
QZ(¾)	13	20	VAR CHE	41	45
BAS/TRA	43	39	QZT	0	16
GAB/DIA	33	18	SLT	3	3
MSV(¾)	21	24	QZ(¼)	5	7
ELS	12	0	MSV(¼)	6	8
Totals	774	585		206	353
All totals	1,359			559	

[a]Reader is referred to text for definitions of abbreviations.

the same reason, quartz (QZ) and MSV have been split 3:1, for nearby and distant sources, respectively.

Nearby lithologies were used far more than distant sources, and much more extensively in the Archaic than in the Ceramic. It appears that these Archaic people preferred not to travel for distant lithologies as much as those who lived later on. The largest percentage increases between the Ceramic and Archaic in use of distantly sourced lithics were for WCV (16 to 61), MUN (5 to 58), and NSC (1 to 21). There was a marked decrease in use of the BSR from Archaic to Ceramic. It appears that Ceramic period people developed a preference for distantly sourced cherts, more exotic rhyolite, and quartzite, thus reducing their use of the excellent BSR source only one mile away.

CONCLUSIONS

The conclusions of this study are largely defined in Table A6.4, a summary of the distribution of lithic materials through the five major cultural traditions uncovered at the site. Table A6.4 is a summary document. It presents, in both tabular and graphic form, the complete range of numbers of lithic artifacts used in turn by each of the five major cultural levels, thus indicating how use preference changed through time. The stratigraphic units are those used elsewhere in this volume (see Chapters 4–8).

Table A6.4 is quite straightforward, although two numbers bear emphasis. They are the very high frequency of BSR in Occupation 3 and its high frequency in the late Ceramic. Other traditions certainly knew BSR was nearby, but seemed to prefer other materials for their tools. Occupation 2 stone workers definitely preferred KTM to BSR. There appears to have been no Archaic period quartzite artifacts identified. Likewise, ELS artifacts are not present in the Ceramic period recoveries. These anomalies have been checked and seem valid. There are no lithic source data that would explain this strange relationship.

Table A6.4. Distribution of Lithic Materials

Lithic materials[a]	Culture						
	Archaic				Ceramic		
	Occupation 1	Occupation 2	Occupation 3	Total Archaic	Early Ceramic	Late Ceramic	Total Ceramic
BSR	3	27	265	295	38	113	151
CAS	0	28	71	99	15	36	51
OHB	0	42	66	108	9	90	99
KTM	11	133	88	232	74	183	257
AND	1	12	21	34	12	43	55
WCV	3	7	6	16	11	50	61
QZ	10	6	2	18	4	23	27
MUN	0	2	3	5	6	52	58
NSC	0	1	0	1	5	16	21
NYC	0	0	3	3	3	2	5
VAR CHE	2	29	10	41	6	39	45
GRA	0	3	2	5	5	1	6
BAS/TRA	5	13	25	43	0	39	39
GAB/DIA	0	25	8	33	0	18	18
MSV	0	14	12	26	11	21	32
ELS	0	7	5	12	0	0	0
QZT	0	1	1	2	3	13	16
SLT	0	0	3	3	1	2	3
Total	35	349	590	974	203	741	944

[a]Reader is referred to text for definitions of abbreviations.

The scant recoveries from Occupation 1 suggest an almost complete dependence on nearby source areas. With the exception of two fairly well confirmed brown and gray cherts, all the other tools could have been recovered right on the Islands. I still have the impression that there was probably a much larger use of granite and slate for hand tools, but the fragile nature and fire cracking of these rock types have lost many tools in the ground.

In a general way, however, the pattern of lithic preference is quite typical of the Maritime cultural evidence I have examined during the past decade. Archaic populations seem to have stayed close to home and used native material. Later traditions began to expand their travel and distant contacts, culminating in the greatly expanded use of "exotic" cherts and other distant silicious lithologies during the Late Ceramic. This pattern, as noted, is common to the majority of Maritime occupations. It is interesting to observe that when we add the lithic preferences of the Paleoindian tradition to the Archaic and Ceramic, we see an expansive trade and travel style in the oldest people, a drawing in during the middle period, and another expansion in the later traditions.

Appendix 7

The Human Burials
from the Turner Farm Site

Lenore T. Barbian and Ann L. Magennis

INTRODUCTION

The rise of the population-based approach to skeletal analyses is a landmark event in the field of skeletal biology. Not only did this approach greatly contribute to our understanding of skeletal pathology (Buikstra and Cook 1980), it provided the framework with which to address issues of wider anthropological interest. Skeletal analysis need no longer be viewed solely in a typological perspective. Now skeletally derived data (including age, sex, and pathology) can be used to address questions of social complexity, social organization, and population adaptational success. While this approach has proven useful in the analysis of a wide number of temporally and spatially distinct prehistoric populations (see Cohen and Armelagos 1984), its application has been largely lacking in the Northeast. The blame for this situation cannot be placed entirely on the research interests of past scholars. New England generally lacks the large, homogeneous skeletal series that is essential for population-based studies. As a way around this problem, Schindler and coworkers (1981) have advocated a regional approach to questions of biocultural adaptation and suggest ways in which data generated from small samples can be combined to address questions of larger regional concern. It is precisely this suggestion for using small samples that guided Shaw's (1988) study of the Late Archaic Moorehead phase skeletal series from the Nevin site. Given the current issue of reburial and the uncertainty regarding the continued availability of skeletal material, it is essential that we continue to integrate analyses of these small samples into studies of larger regional interest.

It is in the light of these concerns that the analysis of the Turner Farm Late Archaic skeletal series was undertaken. The purpose of the study presented here is to characterize the size and demographic composition of the sample and to present detailed descriptions of

LENORE T. BARBIAN • Department of Anthropology, University of Florida, Gainesville, Florida 32608.
ANN L. MAGENNIS • Department of Anthropology, Colorado State University, Fort Collins, Colorado 80523.

both the unburned and cremated interments that will focus on the age, sex, and pathologies associated with each interment feature. Although the process of cremation results in the destruction of most aging, sexing, and pathology indicators that are crucial for studies of biocultural adaptation, the analysis of burned bone can provide important information on the condition of the corpse at the time of incineration. Bodies can be burned soon after death, curated for a period, or dismembered and/or defleshed prior to burning. Since this information is an important component of biocultural studies, we will present descriptions of the burning patterns associated with each cremation feature. More detailed discussion of the mortuary activities associated with the cremation features is available elsewhere (Barbian and Magennis 1994). The information presented here is an attempt to contribute to the regional database, which can be used by other researchers to address a variety of questions concerning prehistoric biocultural adaptation. More synthetic summaries of the Turner Farm skeletal series are available elsewhere (Barbian and Magennis 1994; Magennis and Barbian 1995).

METHODS

Minimum Number of Individuals

The first step in generating a profile of the Turner Farm series is to determine the minimum number of individuals (MNI) present. This was fairly straightforward for the primary inhumation features. All features were inventoried, and no duplication of body parts was noted that would suggest the presence of another individual (Table A7.1).

Table A7.1. Minimum Number of Individuals by Feature

Feature type	Feature number	MNI[a]
Primary unburned inhumations	6-1975	3
	9-1975	1
	18-1975	1
	30-1974	1
	34-1974	1
Secondary unburned inhumations	30-1975	2
	39-1974	5
Cremations	7-1975	5
	9-1975	6
	12-1975	5
	19-1975	9
	24-1975	2
	28-1975	3
	30-1975	2
	34-1975	2
	38-1975	5
	41-1974	10
	42-1974	7
Total		70

[a]MNI, minimum number of individuals.

MNI counts for the secondarily deposited features were determined by sorting the skeletal remains by bone type and size and counting the most commonly represented feature or element (Table A7.1). Subadults were identified by lack of epiphyseal closure on the long bones or presence of deciduous dentition. All individuals given the designation subadult represent individuals most likely less than 18 years of age at the time of death. However, it should be noted that many skeletal elements achieve developmental maturity before the age of 18, including the vertebrae, temporal, and the bones of the hands and feet. It is possible, therefore, that at least some of the subadult elements are included in the adult category. This is unlikely to inflate the MNI counts artificially since we adopted a conservative approach to determining the number of individuals. If the bony landmark used to establish the MNI count was not diagnostic of either adult or subadult status, the number of subadults, based on identifiable immature elements, was subtracted from this MNI estimate in order to determine the number of adults present.

Sex Determination

Accurate assessment of the sex of a skeleton is important to the development of reliable measures of sex-specific rates of mortality or morbidity. Such measures can prove to be useful tools for the investigation of environmental or cultural factors that influence the adaptive success of prehistoric populations. Two factors influence the accuracy of the sex determination of skeletal material: (1) age at death and (2) completeness of the skeleton. In general, the skeleton shows a marked lack of sexual dimorphism until puberty, at which time the structural constraints associated with childbirth for females and the bony landmarks associated with the increased muscle mass of adult males begin to be manifest. However, dental (Ditch and Rose 1972; Hunt and Gleiser 1955) and osseous (Boucher 1955; Hunt and Gleiser 1955; Reynolds 1945) observations and measures have been developed in order to sex prepubescent skeletons. While the success of these studies has varied, they all require a large sample of complete individuals. Since the Turner Farm site does not meet this criterion, none of the subadult material was assigned a sex.

Even though assessment of subadult sex remains problematical, sexing of adult skeletons is well established and known to have a high degree of accuracy (e.g., Bass 1971; Brothwell 1981; Krogman 1962; Ubelaker 1978; Workshop of European Anthropologists 1980). The two bony elements used most often to assign sex are the pelvis and the cranium. In general, sex is determined based on a set of visual criteria, although metric measures do exist. When utilizing visual inspection of the pelvis and cranium together to determine sex, accurate determination has been reported in 98 percent (Krogman 1962) and 97 percent (Meindl et al. 1985) of the cases studied. Using solely the pelvis, researchers have reported 96 percent (Meindl et al. 1985; Phenice 1969) and 95 percent (Krogman 1962) accuracy. Investigations of the accuracy of sex determination based solely on cranial morphology have reported 92 percent (Meindl et al. 1985) and 90 percent (Krogman 1962) success rates. Metric measures of the cranium and/or mandible have been developed to determine sex (Giles 1964, 1970; Giles and Elliot 1963), but the question of population-specific differences in the male–female dividing point has limited their application. In a recent study, Meindl and coworkers (1985) found that cranial metric determinations of sex are less accurate than subjective sex assessments. They attribute the failure of metric techniques to accurately determine sex to the age-related increase in dimensions experienced by the cranium.

While most studies to determine the accuracy of sexing techniques rely on complete pelves and crania, archaeologically derived skeletal series are often characterized by a fair to high degree of fragmentation. In a study in which only the pubis was available for the assessment, a lower but still substantial accuracy (83 percent) in sex determination was reported (Lovell 1989). In addition, techniques have been developed to estimate sex for those remains that lack either pelvic or cranial elements. Although less reliable than visual cranial or pelvic inspection, the diameter of the humeral or femoral head and circumference of the femoral midshaft have been used to metrically determine sex (Black 1978; DiBennardo and Taylor 1979; Krogman 1962; MacLaughlin and Bruce 1985). While caution needs to be used when applying these methods to small samples since sex-related size differences tend to be population specific, DiBennardo and Taylor (1979) suggest that femoral circumference may represent a fairly plastic measure perhaps due to functional demands associated with bipedalism. They have reported a substantial degree of accuracy (82 percent) in their study of modern autopsy specimens utilizing the regression techniques developed by Black (1978).

The sexing of the primary inhumations at the Turner Farm site was fairly straightforward, and visual observation of the pelvis and cranium was utilized. However, sex determination of the secondarily deposited inhumations and cremations was made more difficult by the lack of complete skeletons and the differential representation of the bony elements used in determining sex. Feature 39-1974 and all the cremations represented features in which a large degree of comingling of individuals' body parts occurred. While the most accurate assessments of sex are based on both the cranium and pelvis, this was not possible for these features. However, Feature 30-1975 appears to represent a fairly discrete bundle based on field notes and photographs, and we were, therefore, able to assign cranial and pelvic elements to this individual.

Accurate sexing of the cremated material is further complicated by the fragmentation bone experiences when burned. It should be noted that the fragment size of the cremated material at Turner Farm was generally small, resulting in the destruction of most of the bony landmarks used to establish sex. Even where adequate portions of the cranium or pelvis were present, the burning process can further complicate accurate sex determination. First, it should be remembered that sex determination based on a single landmark appears to have accuracy rates similar to those associated with metric techniques. Second, the twisting, warping, and shrinkage bone experiences when burned may confound both visual observation of sex characteristics as well as metric techniques. Studies investigating the effects of burning upon bone reduction have found bone shrinkage rates to be variable and highly dependent on the temperature at which the bones were burned (Buikstra and Swegle 1989; Burns 1987; Herrmann 1977; Shipman et al. 1984). Shipman and colleagues (1984) suggest that a sliding-scale correction factor can be applied to control for bone shrinkage if the temperature at which the bones were incinerated can be independently determined. Until such independent techniques are forthcoming, metric determinations of the sex of cremated osseous material appear unwise.

The sex determination of the secondary interments was based on a variety of criteria. Visual observation of any available complete or partial pelvis, cranium, or mandible was used to determine the sex of the individuals. In addition, femoral midshaft circumference was used to aid in the determination of the sex of the individuals in the comingled secondary unburned inhumation. Due to the problems of bone shrinkage already discussed, metric analyses were not used for the cremation features. It should be noted that it was not possible to distinguish individuals due to the comingling of the remains of the secondary interments. In addition, many of the adult individuals contained within the cremation features could not be assigned a sex due to the lack of appropriate skeletal elements. The sex, and criteria used to establish sex, of the adult interments are presented in the feature descriptions below.

Age Determination

Adult Age at Death

Numerous criteria exist for establishing adult age at death, including degenerative changes of the symphyseal face of the pubis, cranial suture closure, dental wear, and long-bone microstructure. While often one indicator (usually the pubic symphysis) is used, Lovejoy, Meindl, Mensforth, and Barton (1985) advocate a multifactorial approach to determining age at death. Their rigorous approach includes seriation of the sample based on five different age indicators: pubic symphysis and auricular surface metamorphosis, dental wear, cranial suture closure, and trabecular involution of the proximal femur. Although Lovejoy and coworkers present a convincing argument for such a multifactorial approach, constraints exist that may limit its applicability to archaeologically derived populations. Most notable are skeletal completeness and amount of time available for the analysis. While it was not possible to employ all the age indicators advocated by Lovejoy and colleagues, we did attempt to incorporate as many as possible. Seriation was used to reduce observer error and, where possible, two or more aging criteria were employed to determine adult age at death.

Perhaps the most commonly used and widely studied indicator of adult age at death is the metamorphosis of the pubic symphyseal face. One result of this intensive scrutiny has been the development of several different aging standards (see Gilbert and McKern 1973; Katz and Suchey 1986; McKern and Stewart 1957; Todd 1920, 1921). While the availability of so many aging standards may make the choice difficult, Meindl and colleagues (1985), in a blind test of three aging standards, found that the Todd (1920, 1921) 10-phase system yielded the most reliable estimates, although all methods tended to underage the oldest individuals.

A less utilized, though potentially more accurate (see Lovejoy 1985), means of aging skeletal material is dental attrition. Although dental wear is highly variable between populations due to differences in diet, food preparation techniques, and nondietary tooth use, Lovejoy (1985) argues that it is the most reliable indicator for establishing age at death for archeological skeletal series and is useful even in studies of contemporary skeletal populations. Since rates of tooth wear are population specific, a universal standard cannot be applied. Rather, attrition rates must be developed for each population in question based on functional wear gradients (see Brothwell 1981; Lovejoy 1985; Miles 1963, 1978).

For small skeletal samples such as Turner Farm, establishing attrition rates is often difficult, since a series of both subadults and adults of all ages is needed. Due to the paucity of individuals in the 6- to 18-year age range, functional wear gradients could not be constructed for the Turner Farm series. However, since dental attrition represented the only criterion available for aging some individuals, the Turner Farm dentitions were seriated by degree of wear. The dentitions were then grouped into 10-year age intervals based on the dentitions of individuals whose age was determined by other methods.

Aging criteria used in our assessment of the Turner Farm adult sample included Todd's (1920, 1921) stages of the pubic symphysis as modified by Meindl and colleagues (1985), dental wear, and auricular surface metamorphosis (Lovejoy, Meindl, Mensforth, and Barton 1985). Cranial suture closure was not recorded due to the extreme age of many of the adult skeletons, as well as the presence of artificial cranial deformation (Features 6-1975 and 18-1975) and severe craniofacial pathology (Feature 30-1975).

For the primary unburned inhumations and Feature 34-1975, we assessed the skeletons for as many of the above criteria as possible. Due to the comingling of Feature 39-1974, crania and pelves were aged independently. The size of the fragments associated with the secondary cremation features resulted in the preservation of few aging criteria. In instances where the dentitions or the appropriate pelvic elements were preserved, the standard aging techniques were used.

Subadult Age at Death

Unlike sex, age determination of subadult remains can be firmly established by several developmental standards using both osseous and dental remains. Age estimates based on the dentition can use either dental developmental standards of the deciduous and permanent dentition (Moorrees et al. 1963a, 1963b) or dental eruption rates (Schour and Massler 1941; Ubelaker 1978). The maturation of the skeleton involves the fusion of the epiphyses on the long bones and vertebrae. Since maturation does not occur uniformly across the skeleton, the pattern of epiphyseal closure can be used to determine age at death within a fairly narrow range (Brothwell 1981; Goss 1977; Krogman 1962; McKern and Stewart 1957; Modi 1957; Ubelaker 1978). Standards also exist that utilize long-bone length to determine subadult age at death (Johnston 1962; Merchant and Ubelaker 1977; Ubelaker 1978). Similarly, a series of regression equations can be used to estimate fetal age based on the length and width of fetal bones (Fazekas and Kosa 1978).

All subadult aging standards are based on the developmental and maturation rates of the skeleton. It is known that both development and maturation are influenced by a wide variety of factors, including but not limited to nutrition, genetics, and sex. Aging standards that utilize long-bone length appear to be particularly sensitive to population differences since adult stature is known to be determined by both environmental and genetic factors. On the other hand, dental development appears to yield the most accurate estimate of subadult skeletal age. However, due to the burning of the majority of the subadults, few teeth are available for analysis. Due to the paucity of other aging criteria, the long-bone length standards presented by Ubelaker (1978) were often utilized to determine subadult age at death.

In the determination of age for the Turner Farm subadults, multiple indicators were used where possible. Where dentitions were preserved, the dental development standards of Moorrees and colleagues (1963a, 1963b) were assumed to offer the most accurate estimate of age. Since discrete individuals were lacking in the cremation features, the appropriate bony elements were aged by the relevant standards and the results were compared and pooled to determine the ages of the subadults in each feature. Often epiphyses remained the sole indicator of the presence of subadults in the cremation features. In these cases, the epiphyses were seriated according to size and the subadults were placed into large age categories (less than 1, 1–10, 10–18) based on the size of the epiphysis. Table A7.2 presents the age distribution of the Turner Farm unburned and cremated interment features.

Incineration of Bone

Patterns of fractures of cremated bone can be analyzed for information regarding whether the body was burned fresh or curated for a period of time prior to incineration. Burning of fresh individuals may not always signify a lack of preincineration manipulation of the corpse since individuals or parts of individuals can be "green" when burned. Green-bone burning refers to the incineration of recently defleshed but still fresh bones. Bones in which much of the organic component has been allowed to decompose are referred to as dry. When attempting to distinguish between in-flesh, green-, or dry-bone burning, it is also necessary to control for the degree of incineration. Bones can be completely incinerated (calcined), incompletely incinerated (smoked), or unburned. The degree to which a bone is burned obviously depends on a wide variety of factors, including length of the burning, type of wood burned, and proximity of the bone to the center of the fire. All these factors can affect the nature and fracturing pattern of cremated bone (Thurman and Willmore 1980).

Due to the large number of variables that contribute to the fracture patterns of cremated bone, it is not surprising that contradictory and conflicting results have been found by researchers. In general, it is easier to distinguish dry-bone burning, while the distinction between fleshed and green specimens is more difficult. Calcined bone fragments that demonstrated no warpage, deep longitudinal or vertical fractures, and superficial checking most likely represent bone that was dry at the time of incineration (Baby 1954; Binford 1972; Buikstra and Swegle n.d.). Calcined fragments characterized by diagonal fracturing, deep checking, warping, and cracks extending nearly the length of the bone may be indicative of either fleshed or green-bone burning (Baby 1954; Binford 1972; Buikstra and Swegle n.d.; Thurman and Willmore 1980–81). While Thurman and Willmore (1980–81) were able to distinguish those bones which were green from those which were fleshed at the time of burning, their criterion is primarily one of degree of warping and checking. Buikstra and Swegle (1989) were unable to duplicate their results and, in fact, suggest that the only feature distinctive of in-flesh burning of calcined material is a pattern of concentric curved cracks in the popliteal region of the femur.

Buikstra and Swegle (1989) were able to distinguish dry, green, and fleshed bone in smoked specimens. Bones that exhibit a uniform smoked appearance are indicative of green-bone burning. Bones that were dry at the time of incineration fail to achieve a uniform black color and retain areas of unburned bone. Those areas that fail to burn apparently reflect the lack of organic material within the bone for combustion. In fleshed burning, some areas calcined before others became smoked. It has been suggested that this characteristic of in-flesh cremation—variation in the degree of burning due to differential protection of the bone by the surrounding soft tissue—is the best means to distinguish in-flesh from green-bone burning (Buikstra and Goldstein 1973). However, care must be exercised when evaluating these characteristics since a similar pattern can result from dismemberment prior to burning or may reflect the position of the bone in the fire.

Table A7.2. Age Distribution of the Inhumation Features

Burial type	Feature number	Subadult age category				Adult age category					
		<1	1–10	10–18	Subadult	Adult	18–25	25–35	35–45	45–55	55+
Unburned inhumations	6-1975	1									1
	9-1975										1
	18-1975										
	30-1974			1					1		
	30-1975					1					
	34-1974							1			1
	39-1974		1					3	1		
Cremations	7-1975	1	1	2		1					
	9-1975	2	2	1							
	12-1975	2	1			2					
	19-1975	2	1		2	4					
	24-1975				1	1					
	28-1975		2			1					
	30-1975			1		1					
	34-1975		1			1					
	38-1974		1			1		1	1	1	
	41-1974	1	4	1		2		1	1		
	42-1974	1	3	1		1			1		
Totals		10	18	7	3	16	0	6	6	1	3

FEATURE DESCRIPTIONS

Primary Unburned Inhumations

Four of the primary unburned inhumations recovered at Turner Farm represent the interment of single individuals (Features 9-1975, 18-1975, 30-1974, and 34-1974). In addition, Feature 6-1975 represents the inhumation of three individuals: an adult female, a newborn or infant less than 0.5 years of age, and an infant aged 1–1.5 years. While the adult female clearly represents a primary inhumation, it is not clear whether the subadults associated with her were intact or partially decomposed at the time of their burial. Although body part representation can be an indictor of secondary interment, it is not possible to determine the degree of body part loss due to vagaries of preservation. Age, sex, and the criteria used to establish them, as well as the pathologies associated with each of the primary unburned inhumations, are detailed in Table A7.3.

Secondary Unburned Inhumations

Feature 30-1975

A complete but disarticulated skeleton of a female aged 55+ years was recovered in this feature. The degree of disarticulation and position of the remains suggest that there was little or no soft tissue remaining on the bones at the time this individual was buried. At least one more individual was identified on the basis of an additional patella and a fragment of a femoral condyle. Detailed descriptions of these individuals are included in Table A7.3.

Feature 39-1974

A minimum of five individuals were interred in Feature 39-1974 based on left zygomatic processes. At least one of these individuals was a subadult based on the presence of a mandible with deciduous dentition as well as immature long-bone, innominate, scapula, vertebral, and sacral elements. Based on the degree of epiphyseal union/nonunion (Modi 1957; McKern and Stewart 1957; Ubelaker 1978) and dental formation of a first mandibular molar and a mandibular canine (Moorrees 1963b), this individual was between 8 and 10 years of age at the time of his or her death. The remaining four individuals were classified as adults based on the complete union of all long-bone epiphyses. Based on the morphology of four reconstructed skulls and two partial innominates, one adult is male, one is a probable male, one is a probable female, and the other is of indeterminate sex. Only a modest amount of osseous material was recovered from this feature, suggesting that complete individuals were not buried.

Based on the metamorphosis of the pubic symphysis (Meindl et al. 1985; Todd 1920, 1921) and auricular surfaces (Lovejoy, Meindl, Pryzbec, & Mensforth 1985) of the two male os coxae, one individual is 35–40 years of age and the other is 20–26 years of age. This correlates well with the age ranges generated from the degree of dental wear. The two male skulls were aged at 20–30 years and 30–40 years. The cranium of indeterminate sex was aged at 20–30 years, and the female cranium was 25–35 years of age. Therefore, Feature 39-1974 contains the remains of an 8- to 10-year-old subadult, a male aged 30–40 years,

Table A7.3. Skeletal Inventories and Descriptions of the Unburned Inhumations

Feature	Sex[a]	Age (years)[b]	Skeletal completeness	Pathology
6-1975 Sk 1	F (C)	50+ (AS)	Incomplete: mandible missing, all maxillary teeth lost antemortem, right radius missing, pelves incomplete.	Porotic hyperostosis on occipital and both parietals; remodeled periostitis on left femur, right and left tibia; unremodeled periostitis on left tibia; osteoarthritis of glenoid fossa of right scapula, sternal articular surfaces of right and left clavicles, and cervical, thoracic, and lumbar vertebrae. Note: cranial deformation with parietal flattening, entire vault compressed superior/inferior resulting extreme parietal bossing; occiput rounded and protrudes posteriorly; frontal flattened and slopes posteriorly.
6-1975 Sk 2	S	1–1.5 (DE, LBL)	Fragmentary and incomplete: incomplete cranium; sternum, left clavicle, right ulna, innominates, and most of the bones of the hands and feet missing; left femur and the vertebrae very fragmentary.	Slight, active periotic hyperostosis over frontal, occipital, both parietals, and temporals; slight, active periostitis on right femur and right tibia; hypocalcification, hypoplasias, and circular caries on maxillary and mandibular deciduous dentition.
6-1975 Sk 3	S	0–0.5 (LBL)	Incomplete: few cranial fragments, right scapula, both humeri, right ulna, right ischium and pubis, both femurs, tibiae, fibulae, some ribs, and thoracic vertebrae present.	All bones show moderate to severe, active periostitis; medullary cavities of all long bones are restricted in width.
9-1975	F (C)	55+ (AS, DA)	Nearly complete but fragmentary: cranium, hands, and feet incompletely represented.	Slight, remodeled periostitis on left tibia; osteoarthritis on distal articular surface of right fibula, both patellar articular surfaces, and cervical, lumbar and S1 vertebral fragments; a mid-thoracic vertebral body collapsing; all long-bone cortices are very thin suggesting advanced osteoporosis.

Burial	Sex[a]	Age[b]	Completeness	Pathology
18-1975	M (C, P)	35–40 (PS, AS)	Basically complete	Slight remodeled porotic hyperostosis on frontal and both parietals; osteoarthritis on L5. Note: cranial deformation.
30-1974	S	10–12 (EU, DE, DF)	Incomplete: right and left femurs, right innominate, sternum, sacrum, and bones of both hands and the right foot missing.	Slight, remodeled porotic hyperostosis in both orbits and on parietals and occipital; slight, remodeled periostitis on right tibia, root of I^1 is resorbing; healed fracture of the trochlea of the right humerus resulting in the formation of a pseudo-facets on the radius and ulna; healed fracture of the left 1st and 2nd metatarsals.
30-1975 Sk 1	F (C, P)	55+ (AS, PS)	Fragmentary and incomplete: both scapulae, right radius, left clavicle, left humerus, and both hands missing; vertebrae, ribs, and both feet poorly represented.	Slight, remodeled porotic hyperostosis in right orbit and on parietals, temporals, and the occipital; osteoarthritis on right distal femur and proximal tibia, left femur fovea, cervical, lumbar, and sacral vertebrae; internal sagittal sulcus does not run along the midline but from the frontal runs right of midline; mandible has large abscess at midline; the body of the left mandible appears foreshortened in the ventral-dorsal aspect.
30-1975 Sk 2	?	?	Incomplete: one patella and one fragment of a femoral condyle.	None.
34-1974	F? (C)	25–35 (AS, DA, EU)	Incomplete: both femurs, both patellae, left tibia, left innominate, sacrum, and coccyx missing; remaining bones are fragmentary and incompletely represented.	Slight, remodeled porotic hyperostosis on frontal, parietals, and occipital; highly porotic olecranon process of right ulna, lesser sigmoid cavity appears abnormally small; anconeus attachment is pronounced and brachialis attachment area is porotic; insertion for subscapularis on right humerus is porotic.

[a]C, Cranial morphology; P, Pelvic morphology.
[b]AS, auricular surface (Lovejoy et al. 1985); DA, dental attrition (Lovejoy 1985; Miles 1963, 1978); DE, dental eruption (Schour and Massler 1941; Ubelaker 1978); DF, dental formation (Moorrees et al. 1963a, 1963b); EU, epiphyseal union (Brothwell 1981; Goss 1977; Krogman 1962; McKern and Stewart 1957; Modi 1957; Ubelaker 1978); LBL, long-bone length (Johnston 1962; Merchant and Ubelaker 1977; Ubelaker 1978); PS, pubic symphysis (Meindl et al. 1985; Todd 1920, 1921).

a probable male 20–30 years of age, a probable female 25–35 years of age, and an adult of indeterminate sex aged 20–30 years.

The pathologies associated with the adult individuals interred in Feature 39-1974 are minor. A well-healed fracture occurred on one left clavicle. A fracture to a right vertebral arch resulted in the formation of a pseudo-arthrosis on L4. Osteophytosis is present on the vertebrae of at least two individuals, on the glenoid fossa of one left scapula, and four right and three left ribs.

Cremations

Feature 7-1975

There is a minimum of five individuals represented in this feature, each very poorly represented. This is especially evident in the paucity of recovered cranial fragments and in the lack of symmetrical representation of body parts. With the possible exception of ulnar shafts, none of the five individuals is represented by both a left and a right side of the same bone or element. Long-bone fragments are overrepresented in comparison to the total amount of bone in the feature.

Of the five individuals, four are subadults and one is an adult. The youngest individual is aged at birth to 6 months based on the degree of development of the basioccipital (Redfield 1970) and the size of the ilium. The second subadult is approximately 2–6 years of age based on crown development of an incomplete mandibular first molar (Moorrees et al. 1963b). The third subadult is at least 6 but less than 15 years of age. This rough age determination is based on bone size and the degree of epiphyseal union/nonunion of the distal humerus, distal radius, and the acromion and coracoid processes of the scapula (Brothwell 1981; Krogman 1962; McKern and Stewart 1957; Modi 1957; Ubelaker 1978). The fourth subadult is approximately 14–18 years of age based on the degree of epiphyseal union/nonunion of the proximal humerus (Brothwell 1981; Krogman 1962; McKern and Stewart 1957; Modi 1957; Ubelaker 1978). Adult age estimation for the fifth individual is based on the complete epiphyseal union of a proximal tibia fragment. Sex of the adult could not be determined.

The majority of the bone in this feature is calcined, but some fragments are only smoked. There is evidence of some red-ocher staining, and it is most apparent on the subadult remains. The majority of the bones show color and cracking patterns indicative of dry-bone burning. A number of fragments, however, suggest they were burned when the bones were fairly fresh. This is especially evident on the vertebrae and the large limb bone fragments. Overall, it appears that both fresh and dry bones were burned.

Feature 9-1975

The minimum number of individuals represented in this feature is six, of which one is an adult and the remaining five are subadults. At least two newborns are represented by temporal, sphenoid, and long-bone fragments. Age is estimated on the basis of length of the tibiae (Johnston 1962; Merchant and Ubelaker 1977; Ubelaker 1978). A subadult is represented by a right-mandibular permanent second molar, proximal humeral epiphysis, and scapula fragments. Development of the molar crown suggests an approximate age of 5 years (Moorrees et al. 1963b). A subadult of 5–10 years of age is represented by the proximal humeral epiphysis and scapula fragments. This age estimate is based on the relative size of this individual compared to individual number three. A 16- to 20-year-old subadult is represented by a radius and humerus. The age estimate is based on the recent fusion of the distal radial epiphysis and initial union of the proximal humeral epiphysis (McKern and Stewart 1957; Modi 1957; Ubelaker 1978). Based on morphology of an incomplete pubic symphysis (Meindl et al. 1985; Todd 1920, 1921), an adult 30–40 years of age is present in this feature. Sex could not be determined for this individual. The counts of adult elements suggest that at least two adults are contained in this feature. However, it is likely that the individual aged 16–20 years was included in those adult categories. While it is possible that there is at least one additional adult in this feature, this individual would be represented by only two cuneiforms and a fifth metatarsal.

Nearly all of the bones in this feature are completely calcined. Only a few fragments exhibit evidence of being both smoked and calcined. The color of the calcined fragments ranges from white to gray to buff, but gray predominates. It would appear that both fresh and dry bones were burned. At least one individual was burned green. Characteristics of green-bone burning (twisting, extreme warping and cracking, as well as checking) are most evident on those bones representing the 16- to 20-year-old individual. Further, cranial fragments representing one of the younger subadults (excluding either of the newborns) appear to have been burned green. The adult appears to have been burned dry.

Feature 12-1975

The minimum number of individuals represented in this feature is five: two adults and three subadults. The minimum number of adults was determined on the basis of maxilla, mandible, and petrous portions of the temporal fragments. Of these two adults, at least one is a male as determined on the basis of pubic bone morphology. It was not possible to determine the sex of the other adult, and age could not be estimated. Despite the fact that portions of a pubis were preserved, symphyseal morphology was sufficiently distorted due to burning such that no age estimate could be made with confidence.

There are at least three subadults of distinctly different ages represented in this feature. One is a fetus, approximately 6 to 7 lunar months of age based on the breadth of a distal humerus and the length of the petrous temporal (Fazekas and Kosa 1978). The second subadult is aged at newborn to 1 year based on the long-bone size and the lack of fusion of the vertebral arches to the bodies (Goss 1977; Ubelaker 1978). The third subadult is estimated as older than the other two (4–7 years of age), primarily on the basis of tooth crown formation of the unerupted permanent canine, premolar, and first molar (Moorrees et al. 1963b). These three teeth survived the cremation episode due to the protection offered by the surrounding bone of the maxilla.

Although there were at least five individuals represented in this feature, the total quantity of bone was relatively small. This suggests that complete bodies were likely not included. In general, all skeletal elements were poorly represented, but this is particularly striking with regard to the cranium, of which only a few vault fragments were recovered. It should be noted that one cranial fragment from this feature conjoined with a cranial fragment from Feature 19.

The majority of the bone in this feature was calcined, indicating rather complete burning for an extended period. Fragment size was very small, suggesting that the bones were subject to significant amounts of manipulation, perhaps either by stirring during the burning process or due to some unknown postburning treatment.

Based on patterns of cracking, checking, and amount of warping, it appears that a continuum of dry- to green-bone burning is represented among these individuals. Neither the fetus nor newborn provided clear evidence of bone state at the time of burning. The vault and long-bone fragments of the 4- to 7-year-old subadult appear to have been more green than dry. At least one of the adults appears to represent dry-bone burning. The other adult was too poorly represented to determine whether the bone was green or dry.

Feature 19-1975

At least nine individuals are represented in this feature. This MNI is based upon eight left temporals and eight proximal right ulnae as well as one tibia of a newborn that is not represented by either of the other two elements. Among the five subadults, there is at least one aged at birth to 6 months based on the size of the tibia (Johnston 1962; Ubelaker 1978), and one aged at 6 months to 1 year based on deciduous canine crown development (Moorrees et al. 1963a). Based on the eruption of the maxillary deciduous dentition (Schour and Massler 1941) and the formation of a permanent central incisor crown (Moorrees et al. 1963b), a third individual is aged at 2–5 years. Reasonable age estimates could not be made for the other two subadults since they were represented only by femoral epiphyses. Due to differences in their size, however, it is clear that they are of distinctly different ages, ranging from 2 to 15 years. In addition, there are four adults, based on the mandibular third molar sockets and complete epiphyseal union of the long bones.

In general, the skeletal elements of these nine individuals are not evenly represented in this feature. In particular, cranial fragments are relatively overrepresented, while postcranial elements are greatly underrepresented, despite the fact that there were at least eight proximal ulnae recovered. Long bones were particularly poorly represented. Cranial fragments from this feature conjoined with one of those included in Feature 12.

The majority of the bones in this feature are completely calcined. There is a fair amount of smoked bone represented as well, however. Burning, warping, cracking, and checking suggests that the burning was largely of dry bone. Differential burning patterns on internal and external portions of some of the cranial fragments suggest that bones were fragmented prior to burning or that the fragmentation occurred soon after the burning started and portions of the skull(s) were scattered and turned. In some cases, the outer table was calcined and the inner table only smoked, while the exact opposite pattern was evident on an immediately adjacent vault fragment.

Feature 24-1975

There are two individuals represented in this feature: one adult and one subadult. Mature adult status is determined on the basis of bone size and complete epiphyseal union. The subadult is represented only by a distal femoral epiphysis fragment and a few cranial vault fragments. The adult is nearly as poorly represented as the subadult. There are only about 15 cranial fragments, a few fragments of the femur, tibia, and fibula all from the area of the knees, five vertebrae fragments, nine rib fragments, a small number of foot bones, and a number of unidentifiable long-bone fragments. By far, the majority of bone recovered from this feature is animal, there being at least eight times as much faunal bone as human bone. There were fragments that could not easily be assigned to the human or faunal category and were kept separate for analytical purposes.

The human bones in this feature largely were smoked, although a few fragments were calcined. The animal bone was both smoked and calcined. There is no evidence to suggest that the human and animal bone were not burned simultaneously, despite the fact the human bone appears to be burned to a slightly lesser degree than the animal bone. It is quite clear that a large quantity of faunal remains were burned with the scanty remains of these two individuals. In fact, the human remains are so poorly represented as to be potentially interpretable as an incidental inclusion.

Feature 28-1975

There are at least three individuals represented in this feature: one adult and two subadults. The adult is represented only by the left patella and a few fragments of a femur. The subadults are not well represented either. The most common elements from the subadults are vertebrae. Age estimates for these two subadults were based on the degree of vertebral development and union of the arches with the bodies (Goss 1977). The older subadult is likely between the ages of 6 and 12. The other subadult is approximately 3–8 years of age.

While degree of burning in this feature ranges from calcined to unburned, it stands in contrast to the others by virtue of the large quantity of bone that is not burned. While the remains of the adult are smoked or calcined, the subadults are incompletely burned or unburned. The older of the two subadults appears to be represented by unburned remains (at least vertebrae), while the bones of the younger individual are smoked. It appears that the fire was not especially hot or of long duration because so many bones were not burned.

Feature 30-1975

There are at least two individuals represented in this feature: one adult and one subadult. The subadult is approximately 12–16 years of age based on initial union of the first metacarpal epiphysis (Modi 1957; Ubelaker 1978). A precise age estimate of the adult is not possible. This small amount of cremated bone was recovered in association with Feature 30-1975, an unburned inhumation. Observations recorded in the field suggest that this feature may extend into an unexcavated area. Therefore, the remains reported here may only represent a small portion of the entire feature.

These two individuals are very poorly represented. There are about 30 adult and subadult cranial vault fragments. The adult is also represented by a few fragments of the ilium, ribs, vertebrae, feet, and long bones. The subadult is represented by fragments of ribs, innominate, first metacarpal, vertebrae, and ulna. There is also a distal tibia epiphysis and the neck and trochanter areas of both right and left femora demonstrating lack of epiphyseal union. Bone size and lack of epiphyseal union suggest that this subadult is between the ages of 5 and 15. It is quite possible that the subadult fragments represent two individuals of different ages. The distal tibia epiphysis is much larger relative to the size of the proximal femora. The first metacarpal showing initial union of the epiphysis also does not appear to represent the same individual as that of the femora. The cranial vault fragments are quite thin and are not in keeping with a subadult near the age of 12–15. None of the individuals is well represented and the total number of fragments is quite small.

All of the bone fragments in this feature are completely calcined white with the exception of two fragments that are smoked. The morphology of the smoked fragments suggests that they likely are animal bone. Warping and splitting of some of the cranial fragments suggests that they were burned fresh.

Feature 34-1975

There are two individuals represented in this feature: one adult and one subadult. The subadult identification is based on the presence of fragments of the mandible, ulna, cranial vault, and ribs. Based on crown formation of the mandibular left permanent canine and first premolar (unerupted), age is estimated to be 4–6 years (Moorrees et al. 1963b). The adult is represented only by a fragment of the atlas and at least two long-bone fragments. A precise adult age estimate could not be obtained. Overall, neither of these individuals is well represented.

The degree of burning observed on the bone from this feature varies from smoked to calcined. Approximately half of the fragments are completely calcined, while the rest are both smoked and calcined. It appears that two of the fragments are unburned. Whether the bones were burned when they were still fresh or dry is not clear.

Feature 38-1974

There are at least five individuals represented in this feature: four adults and one subadult. The subadult is represented by only a few elements, including a fragment of the temporal, occipital, distal humerus, axis, a fragment of the ischium, and a thoracic vertebra centrum. That the centrum was not fused to the vertebral arch suggests this individual is probably less than 6 years of age (Goss 1977). Although five adults are indicated by the temporal, mandible, and scapula, those portions on which the MNI was based are not readily distinguished on the basis of age. Therefore, the count for these three elements may include bones that are, in fact, the subadult.

Among the adults, relatively well-preserved portions of the innominate allowed broad age estimates for three of the four individuals. Two adults of indeterminate sex are 20–30 and 40–50 years of age based on pubic symphysis morphology (Meindl et al. 1985; Todd 1920, 1921). The third adult is 35–45 years of age based on characteristics of the auricular surface (Lovejoy, Meindl, Pryzbec, and Mensforth 1985). Age could not be estimated for the fourth adult. Of these four individuals, at least one is female and one is male. Sex of the female was determined on the basis of morphology of the pubis. There is at least one very large, robust male included in this feature who is represented by a number of elements including femora, innominate, and fragments of the face.

This feature was distinct from the rest of those at the site in several regards. First, the bone fragments are relatively large. Second, representation of body parts is quite even, suggesting that complete, or nearly complete, individuals (except the subadult) were cremated. Third, the relative representation of calcined bone is slightly less than in other features. It appears that these five individuals were relatively complete and represent a single burning event followed by interment in the pit. This feature is also notable since it appears that the bones of at least some of the individuals were stained with red ocher prior to burning.

Feature 41-1974

There are at least 10 individuals represented in this feature. Six are subadults under the age of 18. The age of one subadult is between birth and 1 year based on dental crown formation (Moorrees et al. 1963a) and the development of the bassi-occipital (Redfield 1970). Age of three of the subadults is between 3 and 10 years. This broad age estimate is based on the maximum diameter of the proximal femoral epiphysis. While there are no standards in print that show the age-related size differences of subadult long-bone epiphyses, these age assignments are based on measurements of maximum diameter of a small sample of subadult epiphyses of known age. Obviously, a large margin of error was placed around those measures we obtained. The fifth subadult is between 3 and 10 years of age based on vertebral development (Goss 1977). The sixth subadult is 14–18 years old based on degree of metacarpal epiphyseal union (Ubelaker 1978). Among the four adults, one is a 35- to 45-year-old male as judged by the pubic symphysis (Meindl et al. 1985; Todd 1920, 1921). Another of the adults is young (20–35) based on lack of alveolar recession exhibited on the maxilla. More precise age estimates for the other two adults could not be determined.

The anomalous aspect of this feature is that a right and left femur and ischium most likely representing one individual (likely a male based on the large size and robustness of the bones) are largely unburned or smoked. One other proximal right femur of an adult is also largely unburned or smoked. For a minimum of 10 individuals included in this feature, they are poorly represented across body parts. Only three of the subadults and three of the adults are consistently represented.

The vast majority of the bones in this feature are calcined with some showing calcined cortex and smoked trabeculae. Further, most of the bones appear to be burned dry. At least one subadult, however, and likely one adult appear to have been fairly fresh at the time of burning.

Feature 42-1974

There are at least seven individuals represented in this feature. Of these, five are subadults ranging in age from a late-term fetus/newborn to approximately 2–14 years of age. The late-term fetus/newborn was identified on the basis of humerus length (Johnston 1962; Ubelaker 1978). The measure is approximate because the humerus is quite warped due to burning. This individual is represented at least by a tibia, an ilium, and two femur fragments. One subadult is approximately 10–14 years of age based on the recent eruption of the second mandibular molar (Schour and Massler 1941). The remaining three subadults, based on counts of the glenoid fossa of the scapula, are younger than this individual, and are aged from 2 to 10 years. This assertion is based on size of the bones of these individuals relative to the 10- to 14-year-old. There are also at least two adults represented. A portion of an adult left maxilla with second premolar through third molar was preserved. Those teeth present exhibited wear to at least the middle third of the crowns, while the first molar showed wear to the root on the lingual surface. This degree of dental attrition suggests that this individual was at least 40 years of age. No elements indicative of sex were sufficiently well preserved to allow sex determination. The minimum individual counts for the frontal, temporal, occipital, zygomatic, and maxilla would indicate that there are more than two adults represented here. The elevated counts on these bones can be explained as an inability to distinguish between subadults and adults based on size and developmental characteristics of these elements.

Most of the bones in this feature are completely calcined, although a few are both smoked and calcined. Further, the majority of the fragments, especially those that are obviously adult, appear to be burned dry. There are a few fragments (one cranial fragment and a few long-bone fragments likely representing a single subadult) that exhibit characteristics indicative of fresh-bone burning. Whether this individual was articulated or disarticulated at the time of burning could not be determined.

Like that demonstrated in all other features with the exception of Feature 38-1974, the distribution of fragments across elements indicates that complete individuals are not represented in this feature, and cranial and long-bone fragments are especially underrepresented.

CONCLUSIONS

A minimum of 70 individuals was recovered from Turner Farm, including subadults and adults of both sexes. Of the 38 subadults recovered, there is at least one fetus, nine individuals less than 1 year of age, 20 infants and children between the ages of 1 and 10, and eight subadults greater than 10 but less than 18 years of age. Similar to the broad age distribution of the subadults, each decade of the adult life span is represented in this series. Of the 32 adults, six are less than 35 years of age. Of these six, at least two females and one male are present. Ten adults are greater than 35 years of age with at least three females and two males represented. The remaining 16 adults were too fragmentary to further estimate age at death.

The Turner Farm skeletal series represents one of the largest skeletal samples yet recovered in the Northeast. However, the size of total burial population at Turner Farm is unknown. It seems likely that many more individuals were interred at Turner Farm since only a portion of the mortuary component was excavated (Bourque, Chapter 6 this volume). In addition, complete features were not consistently excavated at Turner Farm. For these features, at least, the true number of individuals interred is unknowable. On the other hand, there is evidence suggesting that some individuals may have been interred in more than one cremation feature for, as mentioned above, a cranial fragment from Feature 12-1975 was found to fit a partially reconstructed calvarium from Feature 19-1975. If this phenomenon was a common occurrence, the MNI counts associated with the cremation features may be inflated.

In absolute terms, the 70 individuals are a small sample, and care must be exercised not to overinterpret the results reported here. Rather, this report should be viewed as a contribution to the regional database that is needed to test hypotheses regarding prehistoric mortuary activity as well as human adaptive dynamics in the Northeast. The challenge remains for other investigators to add to this important database. The publication of both recently excavated and museum-curated inhumations and cremations will greatly contribute to our understanding of regional prehistory. Until then our understanding of northeastern Late Archaic cultural strategies and their biological consequences will remain as fragmentary and incomplete as the skeletal series associated with it.

Features and Activity Areas
The Spatial Analysis of Faunal Remains

ARTHUR E. SPIESS AND ROBERT A. LEWIS

INTRODUCTION

Bourque's excavation at the Turner Farm site is certainly the largest contiguous excavation using modern techniques of recovery and recording in a complex stratified shell midden in the Northeast. It may, in fact, be the largest area excavated in a shell midden in the Northeast since before World War II, when excavation comprised a rapid "turning over" of midden matrix for artifacts (Spiess 1985). Despite earlier basal dates on some middens in the Hudson Valley (Brennan 1977; Claassen 1991), the Turner Farm site also contains the longest and most detailed stratified series of separate occupations, beginning c. 5200 B.P. and ending with the Contact period.

These attributes of largest and longest, coupled with an intensive faunal analysis by the authors, allow two related lines of research that can be better addressed at this site than at others. First, Turner Farm provides a record of changes in hunting and fishing focus and seasonality across five millennia. The details of this chronological record, along with the faunal analysis techniques used to develop the data, are presented elsewhere (Spiess and Lewis 1993), although the techniques used are summarized in this appendix and the results are summarized in the main body of the book.

This appendix primarily addresses the faunal content of features, and the horizontal distribution of faunal remains within each occupation. The horizontal distribution of faunal remains is markedly nonrandom. Data from horizontal groups of features are scrutinized in an attempt to characterize the feature "association." Particularly in Occupation 3, fauna from the evident association of house floors, hearths, and pits contain significant behavioral data on seasonal length of occupation, and on faunal processing and disposal. Faunal remains recovered from contexts outside defined features were also nonrandomly distributed horizontally within a given occupation level. Often, concentrations of faunal remains

ARTHUR E. SPIESS • Maine Historic Preservation Commission, Augusta, Maine 04333. ROBERT A. LEWIS • Maine State Museum, Augusta, Maine 04333.

from outside the physical boundaries of the features seem to be associated with feature complexes. Coupled with information on feature distribution and form, we have detected several discrete activity areas across the site, especially within the Moorehead phase (Occupation 2) and Susquehanna tradition (Occupation 3). There is a repetitive sequence of Moorehead phase activity areas along what is now the seaward edge of the site, which for the first time gives some evidence for the size of Moorehead phase domestic activity areas. We think we have detected "dog yards" behind the human focus of habitation. The faunal content of pit and hearth features, in particular a detailed season-of-death analysis and minimum-numbers-of-individuals counts, provides information about whether the feature was used for one short season or multiple seasons. In particular, a complex of domestic features from Occupation 3 seems to provide support for a hypothesis of year-round, or nearly year-round, occupation of the site during the Susquehanna tradition. Also for the Susquehanna tradition, faunal contents of grave features provide additional information on how the deceased were treated.

The Turner Farm faunal analysis is not the only modern faunal analysis of a shell midden in New England and the Maritime Provinces; we do, however, believe that it is the most detailed, and may eventually form a comparative basis for regional reconstructions. Although much shell midden faunal analysis has been done recently, relatively little of it has been published in detail. The reader is referred to Barber 1982, Bernstein 1993, Spiess and Hedden 1983, Sanger 1987, and Stewart 1986, as well as to Spiess and Lewis (1993) for a more complete review of unpublished work.

METHODS: RECOVERY AND STATISTICS

The faunal sample from each feature at the Turner Farm site was saved and processed as a unit. In several cases, stratigraphic divisions were recognized within features, and the faunal remains were recovered and processed separately for each division. For example, some of the Occupation 3 grave pits contained a different quality of fill in their uppermost levels than lower in the pit. The upper pit fill contained mostly "noncalcined" bone, while the lower pit fill was characterized by a high percentage of calcined human and animal bone. The upper pit fill may represent midden material washed or moved into the depression from the surrounding matrix; so, in such cases the faunal remains are reported as separate samples from the two kinds of pit fill. Unless such stratigraphic evidence indicated reason for separation, we assume that the fill of each pit is an "association" reflecting a single depositional event, or deposition over limited time.

The faunal data from the features are searched for several types of patterns. Species counts (and for some species, body parts counts) are compared with the suite of faunal data from the rest of the (relevant) occupation in a search for significant differences (Spiess and Lewis 1993). Different types of features (e.g., hearths or pits) are compared for significant faunal differences. Finally, the seasonality data are carefully scrutinized to test the hypothesis that all fauna associated with a given feature may be of limited seasonality (the null hypothesis) versus the alternative that the features accumulated faunal material from animals killed during many seasons. The provenience unit for faunal remains from outside of individual, defined features was either a 5 × 5 foot section (and appropriate stratum), or a balk between squares.

An extensive literature has developed around the statistical search for horizontal distribution patterning in archaeological samples (Berry et al. 1980; Dacey 1973; Hietala and Stevens 1977; Whallon 1973, 1974). This literature was reviewed for potential applicability to this study. The variance–mean ratio test was considered for use in detection of spatial patterning, but its use was rejected as being too insensitive to some types of nonrandom patterning (Hietala and Stevens 1977). Hietala and Stevens's recommendation of a "balance between induction and deduction" characterizes the Turner Farm study. We have relied on scanning by the human eye to detect patterning, backed by contingency table analysis (chi square), and Fisher's exact test where borderline statistical significance is suspected.

One crucial step in this visual analysis was deciding on the categories of bone to plot on a site plan. Various categories of deer bone were plotted to test for differential distribution of deer skeletal parts. Distal metapodial, proximal metapodial, metapodial diaphysis, astragalus, and first phalange were plotted separately in a search for skeletal parts reduction patterns similar to those reported by Binford (1978). Codfish vertebrae were plotted separately from codfish skull parts. Visual comparisons were made between seal distribution and deer, *Mustela* and deer, and so on. Only a few such comparisons produced visually differentiable (significant) patterns, although in Occupation 2 the total faunal sample shows evident nonrandom patterning.

METHODS: FAUNAL ANALYSIS

Faunal analysis techniques used in the Turner Farm study were chosen or developed to produce a variety of information on taxonomic identification, age (in years) or sex identification, and season of death. We paid relatively less attention to bone breakage patterns and bone cut marks, which form the focus of some faunal studies. This section summarizes the types of methods used. A complete and detailed description of methods can be found in Chapter 2 of Spiess and Lewis (1993). Some specific techniques and modern comparative data samples have been published elsewhere already: tooth sectioning, mounting, and grinding (Bourque, Morris, and Spiess 1978), seasonal change in Maine white-tailed deer tooth cementum layer thickness (Spiess 1990), measurement schemes for deer and seal skeletons (Spiess and Hedden 1983:188–199), and some modern comparative samples for clam (*Mya*) growth layer seasonality analysis (Spiess and Hedden 1983:203–206).

Identifications, especially of small mammals, birds, and fish, were made whenever possible with comparative skeletal collections—especially those at the Maine State Museum; Maine Historic Preservation Commission; Department of Anthropology, University of Maine—Orono; and the Museum of Comparative Zoology, Harvard University. The senior author had extensive experience with large mammal identifications from northeastern North America before the project began, but specific elements were often checked against comparative collections. Taxonomic identifications were recorded to the lowest possible taxonomic level, making certain assumptions about species distributions. For example, we assumed only one species of the deer genus *Odocoileus*—*O. virginianus*, the white-tailed deer—was present, and did not attempt to differentiate bone fragments between *O. virginianus* and *O. hemionus*. Sometimes taxonomic differentiation was possible only to the genus level (reported by just the genus name), or to a higher taxonomic level—for example, "seal." In the case of ducks we found that we could sort certain postcrania by size only, and one bone element by several morphological and size groupings, although each grouping may be multigeneric.

Various bone length and width measurements were recorded during the study, bone sizes being useful for a variety of analyses. In specific cases they can be used to separate closely related taxa—for example, harbor seal versus gray seal for some postcrania, or deer versus moose. Jaw measurements particularly were used to separate sea mink (*Mustela macrodon*) from common mink (*M. vison*). Some species, such as gray seal and *Mustela*, are sexually dimorphic, and bone measurements could differentiate some males from some females. Given a large enough sample (such as with deer bone at this site), we used bone widths to track the change in average size of deer over time. A decrease in the frequency of the very largest deer toward the present indicates either (deer) environmental degradation or intensification of hunting pressure and the decreasing frequency of very old age in the population. Finally, bone size measurements for a large sample of modern white-tailed deer were used to produce a pair-wise regression analysis and confidence limits of one bone fragment coming from the same (sized) deer as another bone fragment.

Bone length, coupled with epiphyseal union state, is a useful age determinant in many species. For example, in seals (genus *Phoca*), a humerus with unfused epiphyses with a length measurement below a certain value is indicative of a fetal or newborn seal. This is also true for deer. In some cases, these attributes convey season-of-death information. In many cases, epiphyseal fusion states can be used to construct age demographies by arbitrarily established age groupings, which provide some information on human hunting techniques.

Tooth wear and eruption states provided both age and season-of-death information. A tooth wear scheme for deer, developed by wildlife biologists, provided an adequate age demography. The eruption of some deer teeth are seasonal markers. Tooth eruption in seals, where the deciduous teeth are replaced shortly after birth, provides another age and seasonality tool.

In an attempt to detect season of death and, secondarily, age at death, tooth sectioning and observation of optical layers in dentin and cementum was attempted on many mammal species. The state and width of the last growth year was recorded and measured if applicable, and compared with the state and width of preceding growth layers. It was particularly successful on deer and seal species, especially after we corrected the deer data for deceleration of the growth rate throughout the growth season (Spiess 1990). A similar technique was used on soft-shell clam (*Mya arenaria*) hinges (chondrophores), although there is a high frequency of irregular layers in this species. Some fish otoliths (ear ossicles) were sectioned to determine season of death, and we made regular observations on the status of the last growth layer on the vertebral centrum. This vertebral centrum layer, however, can be misleading in certain fish species.

Some bird species are in themselves season-of death indicators. For example, the red-throated loon is a common fall migrant, absent most of the year. Other species, such as the common loon and Canada goose, tend to nest much more frequently on fresh water than along the marine coast. The vast majority of the population is resident along the coast only during the nonbreeding season. Thus, large numbers of these species are indicative of nonbreeding season hunting. Moreover, we examined fragmentary bird long bones that could be identified to species for the presence of medullary bone, a calcium reserve deposit inside the bone cavity in female birds just before nesting. Not only did the presence of medullary bone in certain species indicate season of death, but it also indicates the nearness of a breeding colony (rookery) in certain species.

Most of the raw data were recorded on an NISP (number of identified specimens) basis, as simple bone counts, and were manipulated as such for basic statistical tests. Only in rare circumstances were we interested in MNI (minimum numbers of individuals), most often during the analysis of the contents of features from which all feature fill had been recovered. The types of age, sex, and size information mentioned above were used occasionally to identify more individuals in feature fill samples than would have been identified by a simple right–left element comparison. For example, a 3- to 4-year-old deer molar and a deer metapodial with a fused distal epiphysis cannot come from the same deer, ergo MNI = 2. Thus, when we attempted an MNI analysis, it was a "maximal" MNI, using all sources of information available to differentiate individuals.

Now we proceed to an examination of the faunal content of features, and the horizontal distribution of faunal remains within each occupation.

OCCUPATION 1

A single feature, designated "Feature 5 and 6-1972," contains uncontaminated Occupation 1 faunal material. This shell- and soil-filled pit has yielded swordfish, cod (*Gadus*), deer, and *M. macrodon* (Table A8.1). Swordfish presence probably indicates summertime hunting. The deer-swordfish-codfish orientation presages a similar subsistence in Occupation 2, but because of the small sample there is little more we can say about Occupation 1.

OCCUPATION 2

Features

Three kinds of features occur in Occupation 2: hearths, pits, and dog burials (Tables A8.2–A8.4). Faunal samples from the hearths are too small to be informative. Faunal suites associated with the dog burials are small, but they are unusual. Feature 22-1973, which is a cache pit associated with a dog burial, contains two cervid distal tarsal bones (naviculo-cuboid), one each from a deer and a moose, as well as a *Mustela macrodon* skull. Moose are rare in Occupation 2, and inclusion of the same moose skeletal element with one of deer, the only cervid bones in the feature, is odd. The *Mustela macrodon* cranium is much more complete than those from the rest of the midden, adding to the impression that these bones

---

Table A8.1. Occupation 1 Faunal Remains

Odocoileus. 1 bone. Right P_2, 5–7 years of age by wear pattern.

Swordfish. 21 bone fragments. Postcranial.

Cod. 56 bones. Dentary, atlas, 24 caudal vertebrae, 29 precaudal vertebrae, basioccipital, parasphenoid. MNI = 4 based upon vertebrae exhibiting 5, 6, 7, and 8 annuli.

Duck, species indeterminate. Tibiotarsus diaphysis.

Flounder, species indeterminate. 10 caudal vertebrae.

Mustela macrodon. 1 right radius.

Table A8.2. Faunal Contents of Occupation 2 Hearths

Feature 3-1972. W50S90. Cooking pit.
    Odocoileus. 1 bone. Phalange 1, epiphysis fused. Heavy muscle markings.
    Castor. 1 bone. Upper-right molar, root open.
Feature 9-1972. W30S90. Hearth (possible mixture of bone from Occupation 3).
    Odocoileus. 9 bones, MNI = 2. Skull fragments, pelvis fragment, 3 scapula
        fragments, calcaneus.
Duck. 1 bone.
Feature 27-1972. W15S90. Hearth, brown soil floor.
    Odocoileus. 1 bone. Right scapula.
Feature 12-1972. W40S90. Hearth in low pit.
    Odocoileus. Antler basal fragment, shed. Large individual.

were placed especially in the cache. Feature 26-1974 evidently included a whole vertebral column from a sculpin possibly caught in late summer or fall.

The Occupation 2 pits (Table A8.4) contain relatively small identifiable bone samples. Feature 15-1972 and Feature 32-1975 contain both winter and "warm-season" catch remains. If these pits contain fill generated by one occupancy (rather than, say, material accumulated over a few years, swept up and dumped in one episode), then there is good evidence for multiseasonal use of the Turner Farm within each annual cycle during Occupation 2.

There are three feature associations for Occupation 2 that can be made on the basis of horizontal proximity. One association consists of Feature 15-1972, Feature 16-1972, and Feature 20-1972 (all pits), and possibly Feature 9-1972. There is no striking idiosyncrasy of the faunal assemblage within these four features. A minimum of four deer are represented: a fetus or newborn, a calf, and two adults. The other two associations—Feature 3-1972 (hearth/pit) with Feature 12-1972 (hearth), and Feature 27-1975 with Feature 32-1975 (both pits)—are without idiosyncracies in faunal representation.

Table A8.5 compares bone counts in the pits (excluding dog burials) and hearths with

Table A8.3. Faunal Contents of Occupation 2 Cache Pit Near Dog Burial

Odocoileus. 1 bone. Distal tarsal bone, left.
Alces. 1 bone. Distal tarsal bone, right.
Mustela macrodon. Anterior cranium with incisors and premolars, plus two probably associated canines. Sectioned
    canine showed very thin, light line forming; seasonality late winter or early spring.
Birds. Two vertebrae of large duck and/or other bird.
    Note. Interesting inclusion of skeletal element in this feature from one deer and one moose. Moose are rare in
    Occupation 2. Inclusion of almost complete cranium of *M. macrodon* is also rare, since this is the most
    complete cranium in the whole site. It is possible that each bone represents economically valuable prey of the
    associated dog.
Feature 26-1974. E0S70. Dog burial.
    Sculpin, short-horn. 9 vertebrae, probably one individual. 3-years-old, summer or fall catch.
    Ducks. 5 bones, MNI = 2. All forearm limb bones.
    Small alcid. 1 bone.

Table A8.4. Faunal Contents of Occupation 2

Feature 15-1972. W25S95. Pit.

   Odocoileus. 9 bones, MNI = 3.

      DM_3 with moderate wear—November to March kill, calf.

      Diastema and symphysis, term fetus or newborn, March to July kill.

      Adult: 2 metatarsal fragments, phalange, calcaneus, astragalus, axis vertebra, distal tibia; measurements indicate possibly one individual of modest size.

   Duck. 4 bones, MNI = 1. One identified as scaup, which are a winter duck in Maine.

   Alcid, small. 1 bone.

   Note. Could be a "two season" feature with winter and early spring kills represented.

Feature 16-1972. W20S95. Pit.

   Odocoileus. 6 bones, MNI = 3.

      DM_3 with moderate wear—November to March kill.

      2 adults represented by humerus and 4 tarsal bones.

   Swordfish. Bone fragment.

   Castor. Incisor fragment.

   Note. Swordfish probably indicates summer fishing, so this feature contains summer and winter garbage.

Feature 20-1972. W20S90. Pit in floor.

   Odocoileus. 1 bone. Mandible fragment.

Feature 20-1975. W35S80/W40S80. Larger shell-filled pit.

   Odocoileus. 1 bone. Proximal radius.

Feature 28-1974. W5S70. Pit.

   Mustela macrodon. Right mandible, female.

Feature 27-1975. W40S70. Pit, filled with rock and brown soil.

   Odocoileus. 1 bone. Very large astragalus.

   Swordfish. Blade fragments.

Feature 32-1975. W45S65. Whole-clam filled pit.

   Odocoileus. 3 bones, MNI = 1. Metatarsal fragments; calcaneus, deciduous M_2 with modest wear: November to March kills.

   Sturgeon. 2 scute fragments.

   Note. Sturgeon have been interpreted as warm-season fishing evidence, the deer as a winter kill.

Feature 5-1975. W30S80. Pit, filled with dark soil and crushed shell.

   Odocoileus. 3 bones, MNI = 1. Condyle fragment, left $M_{1/2}$ 3–4 years, distal phalange 1.

---

the nonfeature (i.e., midden) bone count from Occupation 2. There are no striking inclusions or exclusions of any particular taxon. There is only one detectable difference—a significantly different distribution of deer axial (e.g., skull, vertebra, pelvis, ribs) versus appendicular (e.g., limb) elements. Hearths contain 11 axial and two appendicular deer skeleton fragments, while the pits contain eight axial and 16 appendicular elements, respectively. By Fisher's exact test, the probability of this distribution being drawn from identical original samples by chance alone is 0.0035. Thus, although neither appendicular nor axial body parts are exclusively distributed in either category, axial body parts tend to be found in hearth debris, while pit debris tends to contain more appendicular elements. Material deposited in hearths may have been the "first discard" from the use of a carcass, while the pits accumulated refuse processed further, or curated longer.

Table A8.5. Occupation 2 Bone Frequencies
in Pits and Hearths

Taxon	Pits	Hearths	Rest of Occupation 2
Odocoileus	24	12	1,031
Alces	0	0	7
Castor	1	1	39
M. macrodon	1	0	87
Duck	4	1	41
Small alcid	1	0	4
Other bird	0	0	109
Swordfish	2	0	218
Sturgeon	2	0	12
Sculpin	0	0	14
Totals	35	14	1,562

Horizontal Distribution

The search for horizontal patterning within Occupation 2 began by indicating the number of bone elements appearing in each 5 × 5 foot section for several taxa, and various skeletal parts from some taxa (Table A8.6). These distributions were analyzed for patterning on three scales. First, bone concentrations of less than 5 × 5 dimension—very high concentrations of one taxon confined within one section—define small-scale patterning. Second, bone distribution patterns were scanned on a "whole-site" basis. Third, a compilation of feature location data and bone concentration data allowed the definition of three separate activity areas within Occupation 2.

Within Occupation 2 there is a stratigraphic dichotomy between the shell layer (soil containing shell) and dark shell-free soil (essentially the darkly stained subsoil upon which much of Occupation 2 lies directly). In all cases examined, the bone distributions of the two stratigraphic layers were congruent. This fact strengthens the hypothesis that material in the shell-free horizon was "trodden" into it, or otherwise closely mirrors the material still contained in the overlying shell-and-soil-deposition layer. For the rest of the analysis we have ignored this apparently "derived" stratigraphic subdivision.

Small-Scale Patterning

In the case of two taxonomic groups there is patterning on a scale smaller than the 5 × 5 section provenience unit. This patterning is evidenced by high concentrations of bone totally contained in one square, with much lower or no distribution outside that section. A high number of duck and "Aves: species indeterminant" (which is probably mostly duck) bones occur in two sections: W30S105 (30 bones), and W10S100 (27 bones). The W30S105 concentration contains eider, scaup, and black duck-sized *Anas* axial and appendicular skeletal parts, as well as bones of a few other bird species. The W10S100 bird bones cannot be identified beyond "duck" and some species larger than duck. No seasonality inferences can be made. Two sections contain high concentrations of codfish vertebra: W35S100 contains 7 vertebrae, and W25S105 contains 68. The codfish in W25S105 come

Table A8.6. Occupation 2 Taxa and Skeletal Body Parts Investigated for Horizontal Distribution Patterns

Deer: Metapodial shaft, metapodial proximal end, vertebrae, scapula, isolated teeth, skull parts, astragalus, distal tibia, first phalange, second phalange.

Bird: Bird, not further identified; duck; cormorants; loon; alcid, small and medium; geese; great auk.

Other taxa: Swordfish, sword; swordfish, other (includes postcrania); mink, skull, teeth and jaws; mink, postcrania; cod, skull fragments; cod, vertebra; seals, all elements.

from at least three individuals of ages 6, 7, and 8 years. These concentrations may represent highly localized processing or discard events, such as dumping the contents of a soup pot.

Whole Site Features

Search for distributional patterns on a "whole-site" basis consisted of comparing mapped representations of the number of bones per section for various taxonomic and skeletal parts categories. The distributions are highly nonrandom, as best exemplified in the distribution of a common bone type, isolated deer teeth (Figure A8.1). The teeth are grouped in three concentrations, one in the northeast corner of the main excavation, one in the northwest corner, and one in the south central portion of the excavation. Comparison of the deer teeth distribution with other taxa showed that the same concentrations appeared on all other bone maps (Figure A8.2). Thus, on the whole-site level there was a nonrandom bone distribution into three activity areas (areas 1, 2, and 3 on Figure A8.3), but all taxa and

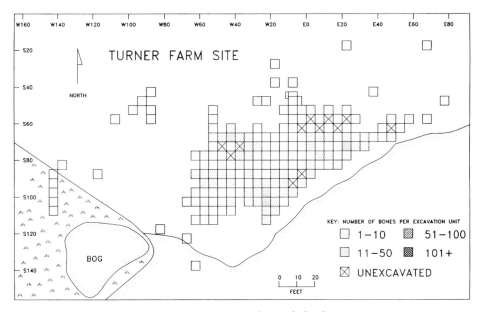

Figure A8.1. Occupation 2 deer tooth distribution.

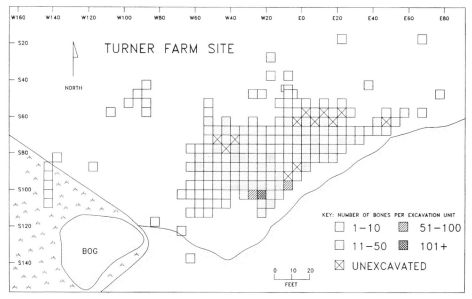

Figure A8.2. Occupation 2 bone refuse density.

body parts follow the same tripartite distribution pattern. A fourth area inland from Area 3 was defined in Chapter 5 (pp. 80–85), on the basis of artifact distribution.

The three sharply defined concentrations become clearer when all bone is considered on one map, and when the bone densities are mapped with hearth and pit features (Figure A8.3). Discrete groups of features correspond with the three faunal concentrations. The congruence of feature groups with bone concentrations, and the low density of bone between each concentration, allowed definition of three activity areas.

Activity Areas

Area 1 consists of a dense group of features (including hearths) associated with a dense bone scatter on the south central portion of the site. The highest bone density is immediately shoreward (south) of the features, suggesting a refuse dumping area peripheral to the hearth activity area. Area 2 consists of a group of pits roughly congruent with a moderately dense scatter of bone. Area 2 is immediately adjacent to Area 1, but further inland. Area 3 consists of a group of features (including hearths) and a moderate density of faunal remains among the features. If there is an area of high bone density adjacent to and associated with Area 3, it exists in the unexcavated portion of the site shoreward, and may be mostly eroded away.

Faunal remains were tabulated by activity area (Table A8.7). In many cases the distribution was found to be nonrandom. Swordfish sword, commonly used as a raw material for tool manufacturing, is more common relative to other swordfish bone in Area 3 than it is in Area 1. Conversely, swordfish bone that would have been attached to meaty

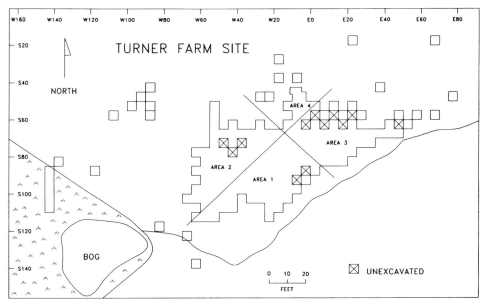

Figure A8.3.   Occupation 2 activity areas.

swordfish parts is more common in Area 1. This distribution is statistically significant (chi-square = 10.4, $DF = 2$, p less than 0.01). There is a higher proportion of mink postcrania to teeth and jaw fragments in Areas 1 and 3 than in Area 2. However, the distribution is not significantly different than chance ($p = 0.25$). The relative frequency of codfish bone, compared with all plotted bone, is lower in Area 2 (4 percent) compared with Areas 1 and 3 (15 to 16 percent). The differential distribution of cod vertebrae versus cod skull parts is marginally significant ($p \approx 0.10$). Note that the high cod vertebra count is caused in part by the location of the two concentrations of cod vertebra that are smaller than a 5×5 section in dimension. Seal bone is infrequent in Occupation 2, but that which is present is not randomly distributed. Seal bones are most relatively common compared with other bone in Area 2 (5.5 percent), more than twice as common as in the samples from Areas 1 and 2 (2.0 percent and 1.5 percent, respectively). Bird bone, as a proportion of total bone, is 4 to 5 times greater in Areas 1 and 3 (18 to 19 percent) than in Area 2 (4 percent).

Table A8.7 also examines the counts of deer skeletal parts that were horizontally plotted. Isolated teeth are relatively most common in Area 2. However, aside from the teeth, deer bone elements do not appear to be differentially sorted between these three concentrations. Even the appendicular and axial bone counts (other than teeth) exhibit the same pattern of relative proportion between activity areas.

Thus, except for the proportion of swordfish sword to other bone, the attributes of Areas 1 and 3 appear similar (Table A8.8), exhibiting hearth presence, high codfish count, low seal bone count, high bird bone count, and low isolated deer tooth count. Differences between the activity areas do not appear to be related to differential processing of deer carcasses, the primary terrestrial meat source in Occupation 2. Thus, we cannot easily

Table A8.7. Faunal Distribution in Occupation 2 Activity Areas[a]

	Activity area		
	1	2	3
Total bone count plotted	562	283	245
Swordfish: sword	15	16	26
Swordfish: other bone	28	19	14
Mink: teeth, jaw, skull	16	6	6
Mink: postcrania	25	5	18
Cod: skull fragments	13	3	10
Cod: vertebrae	87	8	23
Seals: cranial	8	8	2
Seals: postcranial	3	7	1
Seals (total elements)	11	15	3
Birds: all species, elements	101	11	36
Deer: skull elements	22	20	10
Deer: scapula	23	12	13
Deer: vertebrae	25	6	3
Deer: isolated teeth	69	84	43
Deer (total axial)	139	122	69
Deer (total axial less teeth)	70	38	26
Deer: metapodial shaft	15	13	6
Deer: metapodial, proximal	28	23	8
Deer: astragalus	23	16	5
Deer: tibia, distal	30	13	7
Deer: 1st and 2nd phalanges	31	13	14
Deer (total appendicular)	127	78	40
Deer (total elements)	266	200	109

[a]Note that some of the data are subtotals.

Table A8.8. Occupation 2 Activity Area Relative Attributes

Area 1	Area 2	Area 3
Hearths and pits	Pits	Pits and hearths
Adjacent, shoreward, high density bone concentration	Moderate bone density congruent with features	Moderate bone density congruent with features
High swordfish "meat" bone	Intermediate	High swordfish sword
High codfish proportion, especially high vertebra count	Low codfish proportion	High codfish proportion
Low seal bone	High seal bone, and high postcranial count	Low seal bone
High bird bone	Low bird bone	High bird bone
Low isolated deer tooth count	High deer teeth, isolated	Low isolated deer tooth count

account for these distributions in terms of Nunamuit-style cervid carcass processing activities (Binford 1978).

We have already commented on the multiseasonal content of some Occupation 2 features. Deer and seal tooth sectioning and eruption provides the following specific seasonality associated with Area 1: January–February, February–March, March–April, March–July, October–January. Thus, Area 1 contains multiseasonal data. The other two areas have smaller, and therefore less complete, seasonal indicator samples, but each exhibits multiple seasonality as well.

We hypothesize that the hearth and feature portion of Area 1 represents a focus of domestic activity (centered on the hearths), and that the heavy bone concentration extending seaward represents a "dump" that was "in front" of the domestic area. Some sort of structure associated with the hearth–feature complex is implied, although the only evidence for one is the boundedness of the rear of the bone distribution.

Area 2 clearly contrasts with Area 1: lack of hearths, a scatter of pits, no definite bone concentration, low codfish and bird bone proportion, high seal bone count (especially postcrania), and high count of isolated deer teeth. Area 2 lies "behind" Area 1 and is clearly not associated with hearth-focused activities. The Occupation 2 people made much of their dogs, according them special treatment upon death. In arctic and subarctic cultures that use "working" dogs, the dogs are often tied up adjacent to human living quarters. There is no hearth or other focus of obvious human activity in Area 2. The pits tend to be shallow and irregularly spaced. The suite of bones from Area 2 suggests some human selection of what was deposited in the area: low proportion of fish bone and bird bone and high proportion of seal bone, especially postcrania. While whole fish can be fed to dogs, other evidence suggests that human dependence on codfish was high, and that what was left after human use was discarded, often in discrete piles, in the dump of Area 1. Fish bone, especially the size of codfish bone (and bird bone as well), are notorious for choking dogs. Most owners of working dogs would avoid feeding them fish bone (defleshed fish "racks") or bird carcasses. In the arctic, pinniped meat is often used preferentially to cervid meat for dog food, because it has a lower human preference value. Since seals were not killed often during Occupation 2, it is even more likely that such (strange?) meat "went to the dogs." Moreover, many of the seal bones from this site exhibit ragged epiphyseal ends, a classic mark of dog chewing. We would expect seal skull fragments to end up in the dump of Area 1, and most of the postcrania to end up as dog food, as the data indicate. The high proportion of isolated deer teeth in Area 2 possibly results from human discard of the jaws, followed by canid chewing, which destroys the bone holding the teeth, freeing the isolated teeth for deposition into archaeological context. It is, therefore, possible that Areas 1 (human) and 2 (dog) represent a human–dog occupation unit of some kind.

Area 3 is similar in all respects to Area 1 except for its high proportion of swordfish bill to other swordfish bone. Inspection of the distribution of swordfish bone within Area 1 reveals a dichotomy between the sections in the feature area (S95 and northward) and the dump. In the Area 1 dump, other swordfish bone outnumbers swordfish sword 22:4, while the ratio of other bone to sword is 6:7 in and around the features. If Area 3 (as excavated) is associated with an unexcavated dump area rich in nonsword swordfish bone, then the faunal assemblages from Areas 1 and 3 would resemble each other very closely. We hypothesize that Area 3 is an incompletely excavated domestic activity area, and that a "dump" area that may be partially eroded remains unexcavated to shoreward.

OCCUPATION 3

Features

Three types of features that contain bone are found in Occupation 3: pits, cobble hearths and floors, and graves. The hearths tend to be extensive cobble or boulder structures that merge with cobble pavements to form hearth–floor complexes. The graves contain cremated, noncremated secondary burial, and noncremated articulated human remains. In many cases the grave pits contain cremated (calcined) animal bone, and some fresh animal bone. In some graves a stratigraphic division was clearly visible, separating a cremation from deposition of noncremated material. Such cases will be noted. The human remains from these graves are described in Appendix 7.

Hearths, Floors, and Pits

By far the largest faunal collection comes from Feature 19-1972, a hearth complex (Table A8.9). Deer bone from a minimum of eight individuals dominates the collection. The feature contains faunal remains taken during all seasons of the year, with the possible exception of March-April-May. Swordfish bone is included in the sample. Its presence is attributed to some mixture from underlying Occupation 2.

**Table A8.9. Occupation 3 Faunal Remains
from Hearth–Floor Complex Feature 19-1972 (W25S100)**

Odocoileus. 113 bones, MNI = 8; 2 calves (less than 1 year), 1 at 2 years, 3 at 3–4 years, 1 at 5–7 years, 2 at 8+ years.
    Skeletal parts: 34 teeth and jaw parts, 3 skull fragments, 6 scapula, 2 pelvis, 2 vertebrae, 7 tibia, 4 radius, 6
    phalanges, 6 auxiliary/dewclaw parts, 23 carpals/tarsals/sesamoids, 6 metapodials, proximal, 10 metapodials,
    distal, 1 metapodial, shaft fragment, whole circumference but broken transversely.
    Note on body parts: All sections of body represented. One striking difference from Occupation 3 body parts
        distribution is lack of broken metapodial shaft fragments.
Phocid. 4 bones. Canine, humerus, metacarpal/tarsal, acetabulum fragment; MNI = 1.
Mustela sp. 2 bones, MNI = 1. A tibia and vertebra.
Castor. 5 upper postcanines, MNI = 1.
Canis. 6 bones, MNI = 1.
Bird. 2 bones. 1 black guillemot coracoid, one unidentified bird skull fragment.
Swordfish. 21 bones, including vertebral fragments, and mandible fragment, MNI = 1.
Codfish. 2 vertebrae, MNI = 2.

Seasonality of the above sample:
   a. *Odocoileus*, parietal with shed antler. January to June kill.
   b. *Odocoileus*, left lower M_1 and M_2: M_1 erupted, M_2 3/4 erupted, 6–8 months of age. December to February kill.
   c. *Odocoileus*, right lower DM_3 and M_1; wear on DM_3 indicates 5–9 months of age. November to March kill.
   d. *Odocoileus*, right lower DM_2, DM_3 and M_1; wear and eruption pattern: 5–9 months of age. November to
       March kill.
   e. *Odocoileus*, right M_1; 3–4 years of age, sectioning indicates 1/4 thickness width of growth layer. August to
       September kill.
   f. *Phoca*, canine; rest (translucent) layer forming. June to July kill.

Summary: Deer hunting during summer (August–September) and winter (December–February) confirmed.
    Fall and spring possibly represented. Seal hunting during hauling-out period confirmed (June–July). Overall
    confirmed seasonality: June–July, August–September, December–February. Springtime is also possible.

**Table A8.10. Occupation 3 Faunal Remains
from Hearth–Floor Complex Feature 24-1974 (W20S70)**

Odocoileus. 37 bones, MNI = 5. One ≤ 2 years, two 3–4 years, one 5–7 years, one 8+ years.
  Left $M_{1/2}$, 2–4 years of age; 3 isolated teeth 3–4 years; right and left mandibles 3–4 years of age; lower molar 5–7 years, upper molar 8+ years.
Mustela. 5 bones, MNI = 2. 3 mandibles (2r, one 1l), talus, lumbar vertebra.
Castor. 6 bones. 2 incisors, 1 molar, 2 metacarpal/metatarsals, ulna.
Phocid. Bulla and phalange.
Halichoerus. Postcanine tooth.
Ursus. Phalange.
Great auk. Humerus, femur.
Ducks. 1 bone each: scaup (probable winter kill); *Anas*, coracoid.
Cod. 3 bones. Caudal vertebra, articular, precaudal vertebra with 4 annuli.

  Note: Scaup confirms winter, probably cod, indicates fall use of this living floor.

Feature 24-1974 (Table A8.10) is another hearth–floor complex, again dominated by deer, but containing a diversity of other species and of multiple seasonality. The collections from the smaller hearths (Table A8.11) are dominated by deer but contain a diversity of species. The inclusion of swordfish again (Feature 3-1973) is probably caused by upward mixture by excavation for the houses.

The collections from Occupation 3 pits (Table A8.12) are generally small and unremarkable. Feature 35-1974, a pit with shell in the fill, contains a variety of furbearers, a seal, and probably one tomcod, which is a late fall or winter catch. Feature 19-1975 is a stratigraphically distinct collection of uncalcined bone associated with a cremation feature; its faunal contents should probably be considered equivalent to other pit fill.

Two major associations between groups of hearths and pits can be postulated on the basis of contiguity or proximity. Association 1 consists of Feature 24-1974 (hearth and floor), Feature 19-1972 (hearth complex), Feature 2-1973 (hearth), Feature 3-1973 (hearth), and Feature 25-1972 (hearth). Together these features form a functional complex exhibiting multiple faunal seasonality, greatly strengthening the hypothesis that year-round or near year-round use of the site occurred during Occupation 3. The alternative hypothesis—a series of short occupations at random with respect to season—is seemingly contradicted by the association of these features into one activity complex.

Association 2 consists of Feature 12-1974 (hearth), Feature 7-1974 (pit), Feature 27-1974 (pit), and Feature 19-1974 (pit). Feature 12-1974 contains a few bones from at least two deer individuals: a calf killed in October-November, and an adult. The pits add cod and *Phoca* to the list of fauna in this association, without providing more seasonality data.

Burial Features

Collections of nonhuman faunal remains from Susquehanna burials are dominated by calcined bone fragments (Table A8.13). Unburned bone is also included within these features, as is some burned (black, but not calcined white) bone. Burned (black) bone has been in a fire, but not heated enough (600 °C) for calcination. The presence of a few pieces of burned (black, not calcined) faunal bone does indicate incomplete or partial combustion of some faunal inclusions. Since the human bone in Susquehanna burials included calcined,

Table A8.11. Faunal Remains from Occupation 3 Hearths

Feature 18-1972. W30S100. Hearth?
  Odocoileus. Proximal radius
Feature 1-1973. W10S90. Hearth.
  Odocoileus. Phalange/proximal.
  Flounder. 1 bone
Feature 2-1973. W15S100. Hearth.
  Odocoileus. 6 bones. Left M$_{1/2}$ 2 years, carpus radial, metapodial fragment, 2 phalanges, scapula fragment.
  Mustela. Right pelvis.
Feature 3-1973. W15S105. Hearth.
  Odocoileus. 4 bones. Antler tine, proximal radius, astragalus (charred), phalange.
  Mustela macrodon. Female. Right mandible.
  Castor. Incisor and 6 molars.
  Ursus americanus. Canine.
  Swordfish. 23 blade fragments (upward mixture Occupation 2).
  Duck. Ulna.
  Ardeid (heron), large Carpometacarpal.
  Bird, unidentified. Tibiotarsus.
    Note: Heron indicates warm-season occupation.
Feature 12-1974. E20S80. Hearth.
  Odocoileus. 10 bones, MNI = 2. Left lower mandible with M$_1$ 3/4 erupted (October–November), 3 phalanges,
    astragalus, 2 right calcaneus, 2 vertebrae, distal tibia epiphysis closed.
Feature 25-1972. W15S90. Hearth or shallow pit.
  Odocoileus. 2 bones. 2 metapodial fragments.
  Eider. Coracoid.

burned, and unburned bone, we assume that faunal material (as food for the deceased perhaps) might also include all three types of bone.

Unfortunately, however, some unburned bone could have been mixed with the feature fill as grave pits were dug in preexisting midden matrix. Therefore, we can only state with certainty that the calcined and burned faunal material was included in the grave fill with the human interment. Unburned bone may or may not be deliberate inclusions in the grave fill.

Primarily looking at data derived from the calcined bone inclusions, therefore, there are some patterns that emerge. The volume of calcined faunal bone in these features varies tremendously, from nil in several cases to approximately 800 fragments and 1-kg mass in the case of Feature 24-1975. The large volume is primarily dependent on the amount of large mammal bone (probable deer) and identified deer bone in the feature.

There is no "standard" set of faunal inclusions—that is, no evidence of a "deer cult," "bear cult," or similar pattern. However, the faunal sample from each feature may be dominated by the bones of one taxon, and usually the minimum number of individuals represented by that taxon is one or two. The most common "dominant" species inclusion is deer (*Odocoileus*). In several cases deer antler and jaw fragments are present along with postcrania, so that we can reasonably conclude that whole deer were cremated. In Feature 24-1975 beaver bone is dominant. Based on an examination of epiphyseal fusion states, it is likely that only one beaver was cremated. In cases where deer (or moose) bone is not the dominant inclusion in a cremation, the deer or moose are represented most often by

Table A8.12. Faunal Remains from Occupation 3 Pits

Feature 13-1975. W35S90. Hearth or pit.
  Odocoileus. 1 bone. Upper left premolar, 3–4 years.
Feature 2-1971. W55S80. Pit with black soil and some shell.
  Odocoileus. 2 bones. Phalange I and mandible symphysis.
Feature 32-1974 and 33-1974. W15S65. Shell- and dark-soil-filled pit.
  Odocoileus. 1 bone. Carpus intermedial cuneiform.
Feature 32-1974. W15S65. Shell-filled pit.
  Cod. Caudal vertebra.
Feature 7-1974. E25S75. Pit.
  Cod. 2 skull bones.
Feature 27-1974. E15S70. Pit.
  Odocoileus. 5 bones. 3 phalanges, cervical vertebra, antler tip.
  Phoca. 2 bones. Canine and scapula.
Feature 19-1974. E15S75. Pit, dark soil and shell fill.
  Odocoileus. 1 bone. Phalange II.
Feature 35-1974. W20S70. Pit with shell.
  Lutra. 1 bone. Ulna distal.
  Castor. Incisor.
  Phocid. Tibia, right, proximal fragment.
  Mustela macrodon. Left proximal femur.
  Tomcod. 8 vertebrae, MNI = 1. 2 annuli, all exhibit full growth layer. Late fall or winter.
Feature 26-1975. W30S70. Pit.
  Odocoileus. 5 bones, MNI = 2. 3 teeth: 2 upper molars, 3–4 years of age, upper molar, 2 years of age; distal
    metapodial, male parietal with shed antler (January to May kill).
  M. macrodon. Lower right M_2.
  Phoca. Canine.
Feature 19-1975. W5S55. (Part of Feature 11-1975.) Uncalcined bone stratigraphically separated from cremation
    feature.
  Odocoileus. 3 bones. Lower right mandible, 3–4 years, ulna fragment, sesamoid.
  Phoca vitulina. Bulla.
  Branta canadensis. Right humerus, proximal.
Feature 16-1975. W15S55. Pit filled with brown soil and shell.
  Cod. Premaxillary bone.
  Mustela macrodon. Ulna.
Feature 7-1972. W35S95. Shell-filled pit.
  Odocoileus. Right proximal radius.
Feature 26-1972. W20S75. Pit.
  Odocoileus. 2 bones. Astragalus, parietal with mature antler still attached (September to January kill).

metapodials or other leg bones. These may represent marrow bones (metapodials with no meat on them) or small "packages" of meat.

In addition to whole deer and beaver, or deer and/or moose parts, there are other common inclusions. Canids, sometimes identifiable by size as probable domestic dogs, are commonly represented by skull parts (five cremations), although postcranial canid parts are present in two of these cremations. The most commonly identifiable bird inclusions are wing bones of large geese, presumably Canada goose. Furbearers, such as bobcat, mink (species indeterminant), and fox are represented by a few bones, as are one or more seal species.

Table A8.13. Detailed Bone Identifications of Occupation 3 Cremation Burial Features

Feature 6-1975. W30S70.
  Tomcod. 2 individuals, one 2 years of age, one 4 years; late fall to early winter catch.
  Mustela macrodon. 1 bone. Left mandible, probably male.
  *Mammal bone fragment, unidentified.
      Note. This feature contained a flexed human adult female and infant burial, with some red ocher present.
Feature 7-1975. W15S55.
  *Felis sp. (probably bobcat). Left maxilla without preserved teeth.
  Odocoileus. Right proximal radius fragment, epiphysis fused.
  *Canada goose. Proximal right humerus.
  *39 unidentified mammal bone fragments.
  4 unidentified mammal bone fragments.
Feature 9-1975. W10S45 and W10S50.
  *Large mammal (probably *Odocoileus*), 36 long-bone fragments.
  *Aves, medium-sized. One long-bone fragment.
  Uncalcined tomcod. One 2-year-old individual; spring catch.
  *Canada goose. Proximal left humerus.
  *Aves, unidentified. 6 fragments.
  *Mammal, unidentified. 30 fragments.
  *Dog. 8 skull fragments including zygomatic, occipital, sagittal crest and maxilla, and one rib fragment.
      Note: Feature includes burial of an uncalcined human skeleton with cremated material placed on the gut
      cavity.
Feature 18-1975. W30S65. (Uncalcined burial of an adult male.)
  Odocoileus. 2 bones, MNI = 2. An upper left molar exhibiting wear in 5–7 year range, and distal metapodial
      fragment, unfused epiphysis. Both uncalcined.
Feature 12-1975. W10S50.
  *Large mammal. 41 small long-bone fragments.
  Odocoileus. Distal metapodial condyle, epiphysis unfused.
  *Aves, large. 28 long-bone fragments.
  *American eel. Caudal vertebra.
  *Fish, very small. Jaw fragment, 2 spines or fin rays.
  *Aves, large. 4 phalanges.
  *Aves, large. Proximal carpometacarpus fragment.
  *Canada goose. 2 humerus fragments, a right proximal and a right distal, which may or may not be from the
      same bone.
  Odocoileus. Right astragalus fragment.
  *Mammal, unidentified. 88 fragments.
  *Small mammal. Tooth root, probably incisor or canine.
  Odocoileus. 9 antler fragments.
  *Seal, probably gray seal. Phalange fragment.
  *Dog. Maxilla with incisors and two premolars, left and right zygomatic arches.
  *Moose. Proximal left metatarsal fragment.
  *Turtle, probably a box turtle. 3 marginal scute fragments.
  *Turtle, unidentified. 1 scute fragment.
  *Beaver. Anterior mandible fragment.
  Odocoileus. MNI = 2. Lower right M_1 and M_2.
  Odocoileus. Upper left deciduous molar with moderate–heavy wear.
  Odocoileus. Proximal metacarpal.
  Odocoileus. Two metapodial diaphysis fragments.
  Odocoileus. Phalange I, distal.
  Duck. Left femur, distal.

(Continued)

Table A8.13. (*Continued*)

Loon. Right tarsometatarsus.

Codfish. Precaudal vertebra, 8 years, L_5 growth state (late fall catch).

Castor. Molar.

> Note: There are multiple layers of deposition of cremated material in Feature 12. It is possible that the uncalcined material was accidentally in the feature fill during feature construction.

Feature 19-1975 (and Feature 11). W10S50.

*Large mammal long-bone fragments, all deer-sized. 16 large fragments, 133 small fragments.

**Odocoileus*. Auxiliary second phalange, epiphysis unfused, calf.

Odocoileus. Phalange II, distal fragment.

Odocoileus. Phalange I, epiphysis fused, uncharred. Length of phalange indicates a modest buck or large doe.

Odocoileus. Left lower $P_{3/4}$. 2 years of age, uncharred.

Odocoileus. Left astragalus, complete, size matches Phalange I length individual.

Odocoileus. Antler and parietal, fused, uncharred.

Odocoileus. Phalange III.

**Odocoileus*. Astragalus fragment.

**Odocoileus*. 4 fragments radius shaft.

Odocoileus. 40 long-bone diaphysis fragments.

Odocoileus. Metatarsal fragment.

M. macrodon. Right humerus shaft, uncharred.

**M. macrodon*. Right humerus shaft, charred (second individual).

Alces. Proximal end of auxiliary metacarpal, head fusing, charred.

*Bear. Right ulna, fragment of semi-lunar notch.

*Turtle, painted (?). Marginal scute.

*Mammal, unidentified. 37 fragments.

Fish. Vertebral fragment, perforated and slightlly ground.

Longhorn sculpin. Preoperculum.

> Note: Two right humeri from two *M. macrodon* present poor probability of chance occurrence. Assemblage is dominated by deer, which does not exhibit evidence of more than one individual being involved. If one individual, it is a 2-year-old buck in the 200-pound weight range, killed between September and March or April.

Feature 24-1975. W10S40.

*Large mammal (could be *Odocoileus*). 37 large and small calcined long-bone fragments.

**Odocoileus*. Distal metapodial condyle fragment.

**Odocoileus*. 4th carpus.

**Odocoileus*. 3 anterior metacarpal diaphysis fragments.

**Odocoileus*. Metatarsal, right, proximal fragment.

**Moose*. Femoral head fragment.

*Mammal, small or medium. 425 fragments.

*Aves, medium size. Edge of sternum fragment.

**Castor*. Scapula, distal 1/3.

**Castor*. Pelvis, acetabulum.

**Castor*. Incisor fragment.

**Castor*. Left and right femoral heads with epiphyses fusing; three lumbar/sacral vertebrae with unfused epiphyses.

**Castor*. 3 tibial diaphysis fragments.

**Castor*. Caudal vertebra, epiphyses unfused.

**Castor*. Proximal left scapula fragment.

**Castor*. Third metacarpal.

**Castor*. Left radius, distal fragment, epiphyses unfused.

**Castor*. Clavicle, one proximal and one distal fragment.

(*Continued*)

Table A8.13. (*Continued*)

Castor. Acetabulum of pelvis, left, fragment.

*Canid, probable dog. 2 skull fragments. Maxilla and squamous temporal portion.

*Canid, probable dog. Metatarsal or metacarpal, proximal fragment.

*Porcupine. Fragment of right mandible.

*Aves, unidentified. 5 long-bone fragments.

Fish. 3 vertebrae identified as longhorn sculpin, tomcod, and American eel. May or may not be part of feature fill.

   Note: The assemblage is dominated by what appears to be the recognizable components of one complete beaver.

Feature 28. W20S40.

*Large mammal. 7 unidentified bone fragments.

Feature 30-1975. W15S55.

*Mammal, unidentified. 26 bone fragments.

*Canid, possible dog. Right maxillary fragment with alveolus for P^2/P^3.

*Odocoileus. 13 antler fragments.

*Odocoileus. One first phalange distal fragment.

Mammal. 3 longbone diaphysis fragments.

Feature 34. W11.5S46.

*Aves. Two long-bone fragments.

Feature 38-1975. W10S70-75.

*Odocoileus. 2 metacarpal fragments.

*Large mammal. 5 small long-bone fragments.

*Fox (species?). Fragments of left maxilla, no teeth preserved.

*Small mammal. Rib fragment (could be fox).

Phoca. Left pelvis, acetabulum area.

*Phoca. 14 rib fragments.

*Aves, medium-sized. A distal radius and humerus shaft.

*Aves, 84 long-bone fragments.

*Odocoileus, tooth fragment, probable lower P^2.

*Odocoileus, 2 antler fragments.

*Mustela sp., possible M. macrodon. Right pelvis, acetabulum, rim fragment.

   Note: This sample is "dominated" by a medium-sized bird, possibly a duck. Portions of a fox and seal also were included, as were portions of at least one leg bone of a deer.

Feature 41-1974 (Feature 3 and Feature 14). W10S55

*Large mammal (Odocoileus?). 20 large and 24 small long-bone fragments.

*Odocoileus. Left jaw symphysis.

*Odocoileus. Metatarsal shaft fragment, distal, epiphysis fusing.

*Odocoileus. 2 metapodial distal condyles, fused to shaft.

*Mustela macrodon. Right mandible.

*Small mustelid. Right humerus shaft (could be M. macrodon).

*Aves, medium-sized. A distal radius and humerus shaft.

*Aves, medium-sized. 7 long-bone fragments.

*Fish, Flounder (?). Opercular fragments.

   Note: Feature 41 is dominated by deer, with at least two individuals represented by lower leg bones.

Feature 42-1974 (and Feature 22). W10S55.

*Large mammal. 71 fragments.

*Odocoileus. Metapodial, distal condyle fragment.

*Odocoileus. Metatarsal, 5 diaphysis fragments.

*Odocoileus. Metacarpal diaphysis fragment.

*Odocoileus. Left mandible alveoli from M_2 and M_3.

(*Continued*)

Table A8.13. (*Continued*)

---

*Canid, possible dog. 4 fragments of right zygomatic bone, and one maxilla fragment with M^1 alveolus.
*Aves. Medium phalange.
Large mammal. Bone fragment, charred, not completely burnt.
Canid. Tibia, left, proximal end, epiphysis fused, unburnt.
Odocoileus. Vertebra, anterior articular process.
Cod. Right premaxilla.
*Phocid. Maxillary fragment.
*Aves. Large (goose-sized), long-bone diaphysis fragment.
*Aves. 36 long-bone diaphysis fragments, mostly from medium-sized species, some from large species.

---

*Denotes calcined bone.

Horizontal Distribution

Here we consider the distribution of bone outside of the features discussed above. The methodology is analogous to that used on Occupation 2. A substantial amount of horizontal patterning of Occupation 3 faunal remains exists at a scale below the size of the 5 × 5 foot excavation unit. This scale of patterning manifests itself as sections with high bone concentration adjacent to sections almost devoid of bone. For example, E25S70 contains 36 bones, only one adjacent section contains more than 5 bones. In this square, most of the bone is deer and nondeer mammal. Section W35S100 contains 54 bones, 35 of which are bird (ducks and unidentified medium-sized birds) and 10 of which are flounder. Thus, even apart from recognized features, there are faunal-deposition episodes that covered very small areas of the site.

The features of Occupation 3 are distributed as shown in Figure A8.4. A plot of total bone counts is superimposed on the features in Figure A8.5. We began to differentiate activity areas by arbitrarily blocking off the cremation and burial area as Area 1. Bone outside of feature fill in this area is uncommon. A tier of sections nearer the shore, adjacent to Area 1, is characterized by modest bone concentrations associated with pits, post holes, and a depression. The depression itself is nearly devoid of faunal remains. This area is designated Activity Area 2.

East of Area 2 we have designated Area 3a and Area 3b, while south of Area 2 is Area 4. The bone concentration in Area 4 is partially congruent with a distribution of hearths and cobble floors, although the southernmost sections contain a heavy bone concentration and lack features. Area 3a may be another partially excavated hearth–cobble floor series along its inland margin. Area 3b is not demonstrably associated with hearth–cobble floor features, but it may be an inland satellite activity area analogous to 3b, with the hearths unexcavated (eroded from the front of the site?). Area 5 appears to stand by itself as a separate bone concentration, associated with few features. Area 6 is a diffuse scatter of bone that may or may not be associated with a concentration in section W45S110 (see Figure A8.6, all taxa).

Table A8.14 presents comparisons of these areas divided among major faunal components. (Note: this comparison is only for bones outside of the features examined above.) The following attributes for these activity areas can be observed from the figures and Table A8.14:

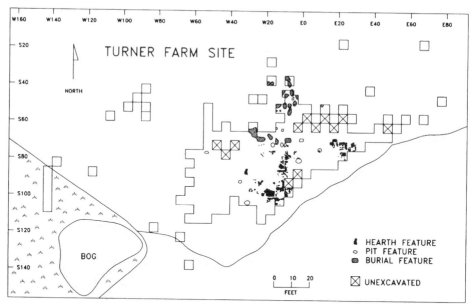

Figure A8.4. Occupation 3 features.

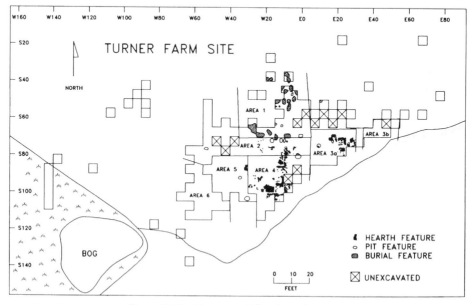

Figure A8.5. Occupation 3 faunal activity areas.

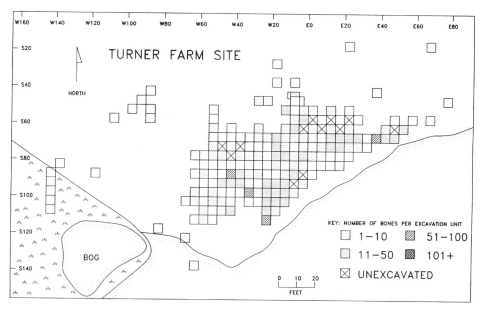

Figure A8.6. Occupation 3 bone refuse density.

Area 1—Cremation feature area.
- a. Moderate bone concentration and frequency.
- b. Distinguished only by high fishbone frequency due to a concentration of 11 codfish bones in W15S55. Other fish species do not exhibit higher concentrations.
- c. Overall, the suite of fauna from outside the features is "average."

Area 2—Concentration of pits, and a large depression, immediately shoreward of Area 1.
- a. Moderate bone concentration and frequency.
- b. Distinguished only by an especially low fishbone frequency.

Area 3a—A concentration of extrafeature bones to the inland and west of an area of hearths and pits.
- a. A dense concentration of bone.
- b. Characterized only by a moderately low fishbone frequency.

Table A8.14. Faunal Remains of Occupation 3 Activity Areas[a]

	Area 1	Area 2	Area 3a	Area 3b	Area 4	Area 5	Area 6
Deer	62	57	116	79	125	32	12
Other mammal	22 (0.35)	23 (0.40)	55 (0.47)	18 (0.23)	76 (0.62)	40 (1.25)	22 (1.83)
Fish	29 (0.47)	5 (0.09)	19 (0.16)	6 (0.08)	35 (0.26)	34 (1.05)	22 (0.29)
Bird	7 (0.11)	5 (0.09)	15 (0.13)	9 (0.11)	139 (0.11)	71 (2.22)	33 (0.29)
Total identified bone	120	90	205	112	392	160	70

[a]Numbers in parentheses denote frequencies relative to deer bone.

Area 3b—A dense bone concentration, seemingly distinct horizontally from Area 3a and perhaps only partially excavated. Same characteristics as Area 3a. These data suggest that Area 3b is adjacent to an unexcavated hearth–pit area (shoreward).

Area 4—A dense concentration of hearth and cobble floor–hearth complexes. Extrafeature bone distribution overlaps the feature distribution, although the greatest bone concentration lies shoreward (south and west) of the feature-filled area. Characterized by:

    a. A distinctly bounded, heavy concentration of bone, which may have extended shoreward of the excavated area.

    b. Low in deer bone frequency, since all other taxa are relatively high in frequency.

    c. There is an especially noteworthy concentration of bird bone in the most shoreward extension of this area.

Area 5—A definitively bounded, dense concentration of bone contiguous on the west of the hearth complex distribution in Area 4. Reflecting a pattern similar to Area 4, deer parts are underrepresented; all others overrepresented (in particular nondeer mammal and fish).

Area 6—A diffuse, light scatter of bone, except for a concentration of bone in W45S110. Overall this area is characterized by a very low concentration of fishbone and a high concentration of nondeer mammal. Except for W45S110, bird bone concentration is low. There are no hearths or pits in the area. The relatively high nondeer mammal count is caused principally by a concentration of mink postcranial bones, and a relative paucity of deer bone. Perhaps Area 6 can best be characterized as low in deer and exceptionally low in fishbone frequency.

A sample of deer cranial, axial, and appendicular skeletal parts was selected for distributional analysis within the seven activity areas (Table A8.15). Surprisingly, there is no evident patterning of deer skeletal parts among these activity areas despite the evident patterning of the other taxa described above. Thus, whatever were the processing patterns of deer body parts, that processing was not correlated with the activities that deposited differing proportions of fish, bird, and nondeer mammal bone across Occupation 3.

Table A8.15. Deer Postcranial Bone in Occupation 3 Activity Areas[a]

	Area 1	Area 2	Area 3a	Area 3b	Area 4	Area 5	Area 6
Teeth	15 (0.26)	22 (0.42)	46 (0.42)	25 (0.40)	49 (0.45)	12 (0.41)	1 (0.20)
Scapula	5 (0.07)	5 (0.10)	16 (0.15)	9 (0.14)	11 (0.10)	1 (0.03)	2 (0.40)
Tibia	2 (0.03)	1 (0.02)	1 (0.01)	0	4 (0.04)	0	0
Astragalus	4 (0.07)	7 (0.13)	4 (0.04)	6 (0.10)	3 (0.03)	5 (0.17)	1 (0.20)
Metapodial, proximal	8 (0.14)	4 (0.08)	14 (0.13)	3 (0.05)	7 (0.06)	5 (0.17)	0
Metapodial shaft fragment	4 (0.07)	5 (0.10)	8 (0.07)	7 (0.11)	9 (0.08)	2 (0.07)	1 (0.20)
Metapodial, distal	8 (0.14)	1 (0.02)	8 (0.07)	4 (0.06)	4 (0.04)	2 (0.07)	0
Phalanges 1 and 2	12 (0.21)	7 (0.13)	21 (0.19)	8 (0.13)	22 (0.20)	2 (0.07)	0
Totals	58	52	109	62	109	29	5

[a]Numbers in parentheses denote frequencies relative to column totals.

OCCUPATION 4

Occupation 4 is subdivided into six stratigraphic levels, from uppermost to lowermost as follows: New Gravel Floor, Moderately Crushed Shell, First Gravel Floor, Coarsely Crushed Shell, Second Gravel Floor, and Below Second Gravel Floor. All these subdivisions are represented over a wide area of the site, except for the New Gravel Floor, which is localized in the eastern end of the main excavation. In keeping with the chronological ordering of data from earliest to latest, this discussion begins at the bottom of the list.

Below Second Gravel Floor

It is possible that up to five activity areas are represented by the faunal remains (Table A8.16, Figure A8.7), although each was sampled by only one or two excavated sections each. Most taxa and all deer element categories appear to be distributed at random with respect to the rest of the bone sample. Exceptions are duck bone, unidentified bird bone, and flounder. Ducks and unidentified bird bone represent 10 to 21 percent of the bone sample in some squares, but are absent from others. Swordfish are represented by three bones, coming from the areas of densest bone concentration. They probably represent upward mixture from an Occupation 2 swordfish bone concentration.

Second Gravel Floor

The Second Gravel Floor exhibits a concentration of features at the eastern end of the excavated area, with only a single feature (Feature 1-1972) west of E0S100. Four of these features, including Feature 1-1972, have yielded identifiable faunal samples (Table A8.17). The collection from Feature 16-1974 is notable by its all-cervid composition—two adult deer and parts of a moose. Also notable is the house floor, Feature 8-1973, which contained a proximal rib end of a large whale, probably *Eubalaena* (right whale).

Our inspection of bone distribution failed to detect any significant horizontal distribution shifts among deer body part categories. The map of deer postcranial elements (Figure A8.8) is, therefore, representative of all deer skeletal part distribution (including teeth and cranial parts), and can be used for comparison with other taxa. Deer bone distribution within the main excavation area is divided into northeastern (Area 1) and southwestern (Area 2) distributions. The distribution patterns of several other mammal taxa mimic the deer bone distribution: moose, beaver, phocids (with gray and harbor seal being evidently inseparable).

Table A8.16. Faunal Distribution from Occupation 4
Below Second Gravel Floor Activity Areas

	Area 1	Area 2	Area 3	Area 4	Area 5
Total bones	15	43	71	29	195
Ducks and unidentified birds	0	0	8	3	41
Flounder, cod, sculpin, swordfish[a]	0	11	0	11	26

[a]Regarded as displaced from Occupation 2.

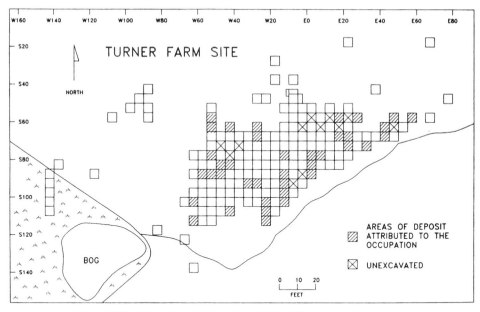

Figure A8.7. Occupation 4, Below Second Gravel Floor, areas of occurrence.

Table A8.17. Faunal Remains from Occupation 4 Second Gravel Floor Features

Feature 16-1974. E45S70. Hearth or floor.

Odocoileus. 25 bones, MNI = 2.

　7 teeth and fragments, 5–7 years of age (Individual 1?).

　2 teeth, 3–4 years of age (Individual 2?).

　3 phalanges, distal humerus, 2 scapula fragments, 2 carpals, atlas and axis vertebra fragments, left femoral head, 2 mandible fragments, 4 metatarsal shaft fragments, all adult when possible to age.

　Note: Very strong impression from measurements and complementary bone elements that only two fully adult deer are represented.

Alces. 2 bones. Lumbar vertebra fragment and 3rd phalange fragment.

Note: This feature is unusual in containing 100 percent cervid remains. No concrete seasonality indicators.

Feature 11-1973. E5S75. Hearth, in shell-free floor.

Odocoileus. 1 bone. Right 1st or 2nd molar, 2 or 3 years.

Sculpin. 1 bone. Cheek spine.

Striped bass. 1 bone. Caudal vertebra.

Birds. 2 bones.

Note: Striped bass indicates summer fishing.

Feature 8-1973. E5S85. House floor in N 1/2 of section.

Odocoileus. 1 bone. Metapodial shaft fragment.

Gavia immer (loon). Coracoid.

Whale of Balaenid family, possibly *Eubalaena.* Proximal end of rib.

Note: Inclusion of rare whalebone on house floor notable.

Feature 1-1972. W50S95. Hearth?

Odocoileus. 3 bones, MNI = 1. Scapula, ulna, distal humerus fragment.

Mustela marodon. 2 bones, MNI = 1. Right proximal femur, right proximal humerus, both epiphyses fused.

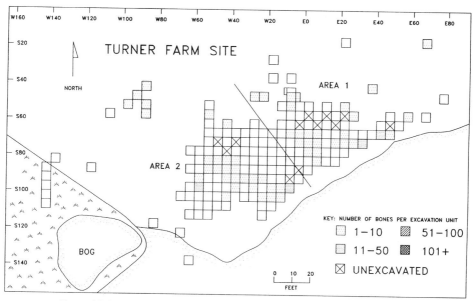

Figure A8.8. Occupation 4, Second Gravel Floor, distribution of deer postcranial.

Distributions of two mammal taxa (mink and bear) seem heavily weighted toward Area 2. In the case of mink, both cranial and postcranial fragments are involved. The skewed distribution favoring Area 2 is even more marked in the birds and fishes. The distribution of all bird taxa, as exemplified by the ducks, is almost exclusively in Area 2. (One partial exception is *Gavia immer* [common loon], with 4 of 31 bones in Area 1. The 4 loon bones from Area 1 are appendicular long-bone elements from a minimum of one individual.) Moreover, three bird species exhibit localized distributions within Area 2. Six cormorant bones are found in the western half, while 7 goose and 10 great auk bones are in the eastern half of Area 2. In the case of all three species, the minimum number of individuals is two, so the distributions are not caused by the localized spread of the carcass of a single individual. Fishbone exhibits almost exclusive distribution in Area 2 as well. Flounder occurs in two localized patches within Area 2, a pattern congruent with sculpin and swordfish. Sturgeon, however, occur only in one patch in Area 2.

The most obvious hypothesis to test is that Areas 1 and 2 represent different seasons of habitation (Table A8.18). Area 2, which essentially lacks features and has a great diversity of fauna, contains evidence of multiple seasonal use. Area 1 is full of features, but contains almost solely deer, moose, bear, and seal bones. Unfortunately, there is no tooth sectioning or tooth eruption data nor any immature seal bones that might indicate seasonality of Area 1. So we lack comparative seasonality data from these two areas to test the hypothesis.

Coarsely Crushed Shell

The coarsely crushed shell (CCS) layer essentially covers the entire excavated area of the Turner Farm. There are four features found in the CCS layer, of which two are

Table A8.18. Seasonality Data from Occupation 4 Second Gravel Floor, Area 2

1. *Halichoerus* (B572). W35S95. Mid-February through May kill.
2. *Ursus.* No sectioned teeth from Second Gravel Floor, but all bear kills of known seasonality at the site are late fall or winter kill.
3. *Mustela* (mink). No sectioned teeth from Second Gravel Floor, but all *Mustela* kills of known seasonality are winter or early spring kills.
4. Duck. A tibiotarsus with medullary bone deposits, indicating a spring kill before/during egg laying.
5. Loon. Tibiotarsus with medullary bone deposits, indicating a spring kill before/during April.
6. Ducks. Identification of scaup bone in duck sample indicates hunting between October and April.
7. *Gavia stellata.* A fall migrant.
8. Flounder vertebrae exhibit the following growth states: annulus (one individual), 1/4 or 1/2 growth (three individuals), 3/4 growth (two individuals), full growth (one individual).
9. Swordfish and striped bass confirm warm-season fishing as well.
10. Deer (E1776). Tooth section, June through December possible kill based upon growth layer of unknown width.

disturbances of uncertain origin truncated by the plow zone. Three of the four have yielded identifiable faunal samples (Table A8.19). Feature 11-1972, a hearth located toward the shoreline/midpoint of the site, contains bone from a deer killed sometime during December through February. Feature 10-1974, located toward the northeast end of the excavation, is a hearth or pit containing bone from a variety of bird species and from at least three deer. One of the deer was killed in late summer or fall. The suite of birds, especially the merganser and loon, are much more common along the coast during cold weather, suggesting winter seasonality as well.

The distribution of deer postcranial remains is widespread in the CCS level (Figure A8.9). The largest concentration occurs in five sections, W20S70 to E0S70, which are located between Feature 4-1974 and Feature 10-1974. Deer cranial bones and deer teeth

Table A8.19. Occupation 4 Coarsely Crushed Shell Feature Faunal Contents

Feature 4-1975. W30S70. Pit, contains fire-burned cobbles.
 Odocoileus. 3 bones, MNI = 2. Phalange III, auxiliary metacarpal, adult; distal metapodial, epiphyses unfused.
Feature 11-1972. W25S95 and W20S95. Hearth.
 Odocoileus. 1 bone. Left mandible with P_4, M_1, M_2; 3–4 years of age by tooth wear. M_2 successfully sectioned: 2nd full thickness growth layer formed. Killed in December–January–February.
Feature 10-1974. E15S75 (NW) and E10S75 (NE). Pit.
 Odocoileus. 16 bones, MNI = 3. Left $M_{1/2}$ 5–7 years of age; upper molar 3–4 years of age. Left DM_1, DM_2, DM_3, very light wear (August through November kill).
  13 postcrania: 2 left condyles, 3 carpal/tarsals, 2 scapula fragments, femoral head unfused, 5 metapodial fragments (proximal, shaft, and distal).
Phoca. Cervical vertebra fragment.
Bird, unidentified. 2 bones.
Duck, unidentified. 2 bones. Coracoid and humerus. (probably winter kill).
Merganser. Coracoid.
Gavia immer (loon). Humerus fragment (probably winter kill).
Branta canadensis (goose). Scapula.
 Note: Definite late-summer or fall deer kill. Suite of birds suggests cold-season hunting of birds.

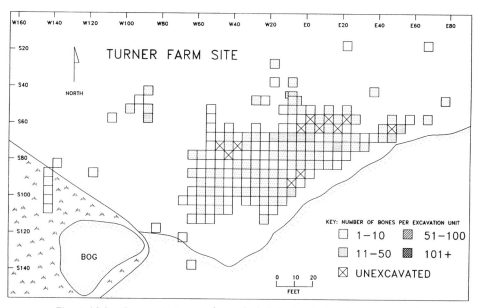

Figure A8.9. Occupation 4, Coarsely Crushed Shell, distribution of deer postcranial.

show very similar distributions, but without quite such a concentration of bone in W20S70 to E0S70. Beaver and phocid bone also show a nonfocused pattern. In contrast, the distribution of bear, moose, and mink (both postcranial [Figure A8.10] and cranial fragments) shows a concentration on the south-central and southwestern portions of the excavation. All bird species bones, as exemplified by the ducks (Figure A8.11), are concentrated in the south-central and southwestern portions of the site. Flounder also concentrate in the south-central and southwestern portions of the site with the notable addition of about 160 bones, including 136 vertebra, in W45S85. The general flounder–bird distribution pattern is similar to the swordfish, codfish, and sculpin bone distribution. Two fish species, striped bass and sturgeon, exhibit localized distributions of their own. Curiously, the most striking parallel in horizontal distribution patterns exists between mink bone distribution (Figure A8.10) and flounder distribution (Figure A8.12), even in such details as the W35S85 concentration, and a diffuse scatter of bone in the northeast corner of the site.

It is impossible to delimit activity areas of internally uniform faunal content larger than a few contiguous squares in this palimpsest of overlapping patterns. However, as in the Second Gravel Floor, there is an area of the site in the northeast corner that contains primarily deer and seal bone, while those taxa are joined by the majority of bird and fishbone in the south-central and southwestern portions of the site. A comparison of season of deer death (from tooth sectioning and tooth eruption data) with horizontal location within the coarsely crushed shell showed that there is no apparent seasonal difference in the deer bone reflected in the horizontal distribution pattern.

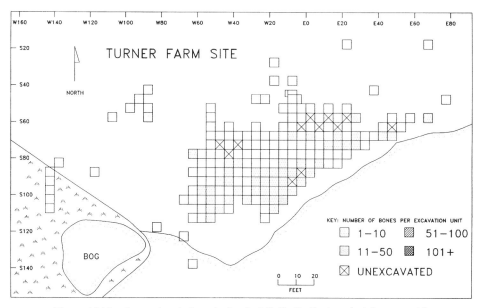

Figure A8.10.   Occupation 4, Coarsely Crushed Shell, distribution of mink postcranial.

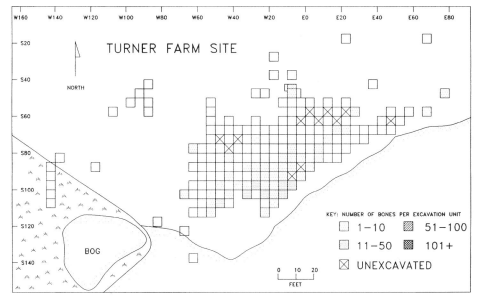

Figure A8.11.   Occupation 4, Coarsely Crushed Shell, distribution of duck.

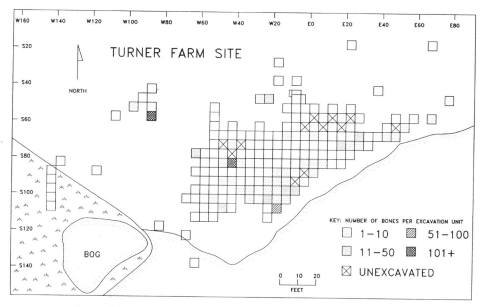

Figure A8.12. Occupation 4, Coarsely Crushed Shell, distribution of flounder.

First Gravel Floor

As with the underlying levels, deposits assigned to the First Gravel Floor are widespread. Two features associated with the First Gravel Floor have yielded identifiable faunal remains (Table A8.20). Both contain a variety of taxa. Feature 2-1975 is of at least summer seasonality, while Feature 3-1974 is of at least summer and early fall seasonality.

Deer postcrania (Figure A8.13) and deer tooth distribution is again widespread, and is closely paralleled by phocid, moose, and beaver distributions. As in antecedent ceramic levels, bear bones and mink crania and postcrania concentrate in the south-central–southwest areas of the main excavation.

Most fishbone is concentrated at the western edge of the excavation: flounder (Figure A8.14), sturgeon, and sculpin. There is an additional concentration of 100 flounder bones in W20S100. Two fish species, striped bass and swordfish, show distributions independent of this pattern. Bird bones, best represented by ducks (Figure A8.15), concentrate in the south-central and southwestern portions of the excavation. Again, we cannot explain these differential species distributions with concrete season-of-death information.

Moderately Crushed Shell

Deposits assignable to the Moderately Crushed Shell (MCS) level are widespread across the site, but with large lacunae. Feature 12-1973, a dense scatter of fire-cracked rock, has yielded a diversity of fauna (Table A8.21). Deer postcrania are essentially distributed evenly over the areas where MCS deposits have been identified (Figure A8.16). For the first time, however, there is a disparity between the distribution of deer teeth/cranial parts and

Table A8.20. Occupation 4 First Gravel Floor Fauna

Feature 2-1975. E5S60. Cluster of fire-burned rock resting on or in fire-burned floor.

Odocoileus. 5 bones, MNI = 2, one adult, one less than 3 years. 2 phalanges, one metatarsal distal condyle fragment, upper molar 3–4 years of age, left radius, distal epiphysis unfused.

Alces. 1 bone. Proximal metacarpal fragment.

Phocid. 1 phalange. One *Phoca* radius proximal end (2 bones).

Mustela macrodon. Left mandible, male.

Flounder. 2 bones, MNI = 1. 2 vertebrae, both with 3 annuli. Last layer forming L_3 (growth 1/4 formed). Late spring–early summer.

Note: At least summer seasonality, possibly more. Lack of evidence.

Feature 3-1974. E10S75. Hearth.

Odocoileus. 6 bones, MNI = 1. Femur, metapodial shaft fragment, phalange, 2 calcaneus fragments, incisor.

Castor. 1 bone. Incisor fragment.

Mustela sp. Canine.

Bird, smaller than duck. 1 bone.

Sculpin. 11 bones, MNI = 8. 2 vertebra, one L_3 (1/4 growth layer), one L_4 (1/2 growth layer). Late spring and summer.

Flounder. 22 vertebrae, MNI = 3. 3 exhibit L_6 (fully formed). Summer and fall flounder fishing.

Note: At a minimum, summer and early fall seasonality, probably late spring, summer, and early fall seasonality represented by fish remains.

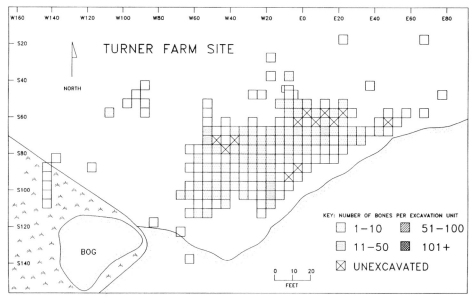

Figure A8.13. Occupation 4, First Gravel Floor, distribution of deer postcranial.

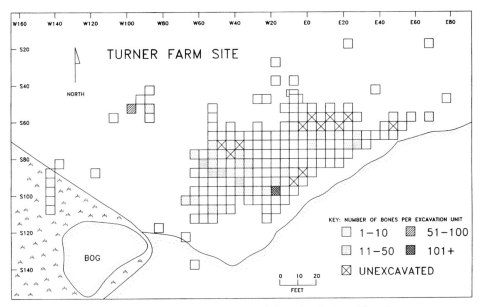

Figure A8.14.   Occupation 4, First Gravel Floor, distribution of flounder.

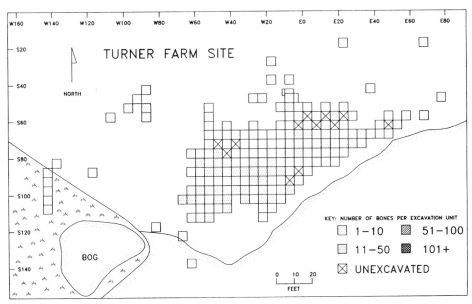

Figure A8.15.   Occupation 4, First Gravel Floor, distribution of duck.

Table A8.21. Occupation 4 Moderately Crushed Shell Feature Fauna

Feature 12/1973. W10S100. Dense scatter of fire-cracked rock.
Castor. Incisor.
Mustela and *M. macrodon*. 12 bones, MNI = 3. 4 mandible, 2
    maxilla fragments, cervical vertebra, pelvis, 2 ulna, 2 radius.
Flounder. 7 bones, MNI = 2. 1 American dab, 1 winter flounder.
Cod. Dentary.
Black guillemot. Humerus.
Alcid, medium-sized. Ulna.
Great auk. Tibiotarsus.
Duck. 7 bones, MNI= 2.
Bird, unidentified. 23 bones.

deer postcrania: deer teeth are much less frequent in the western and southern areas of the excavation (Figure A8.17). Moose, seal, and beaver distribution patterns follow that of deer postcrania. For the first time, there is a recognizable contrast between the distributions of mink crania and postcrania. The cranial parts concentrate in the north and south-central corners of the excavation (Figure A8.18), while the postcrania concentrate in the south-central and southwest corners (Figure A8.19). Bird bones concentrate in the northeast and south-central areas of the excavation, but are virtually absent from the western edges. All other bird taxa follow this pattern. Flounder bones (Figure A8.20) concentrate in the northeast corner of the excavation, with a small concentration at section W50S80. Cod,

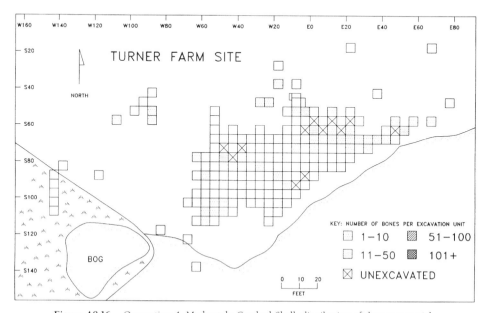

Figure A8.16.   Occupation 4, Moderately Crushed Shell, distribution of deer postcranial.

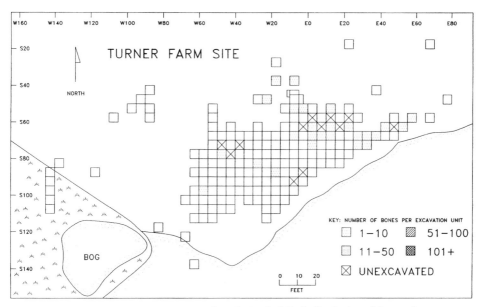

Figure A8.17.   Occupation 4, Moderately Crushed Shell, distribution of deer teeth.

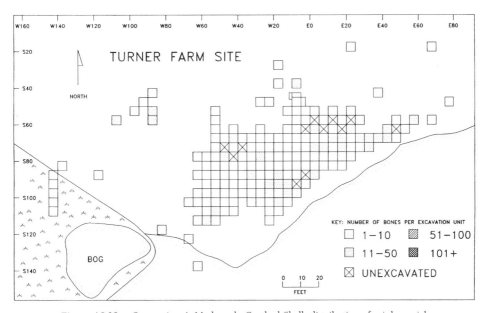

Figure A8.18.   Occupation 4, Moderately Crushed Shell, distribution of mink cranial.

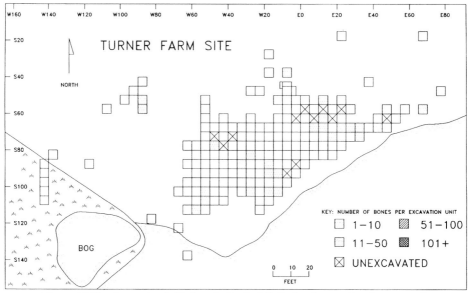

Figure A8.19. Occupation 4, Moderately Crushed Shell, distribution of mink postcranial.

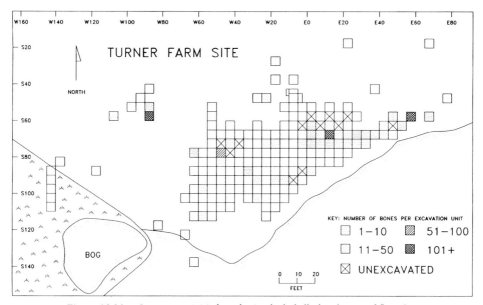

Figure A8.20. Occupation 4, Moderately Crushed Shell, distribution of flounder.

sturgeon, sculpin, and striped bass follow this pattern. Again, we are at a loss to explain these very large scale distribution patterns.

New Gravel Floor

Deposits assignable to the New Gravel Floor are concentrated in the northeast corner of the excavation. Because of the small bone sample size, and limited horizontal distribution, little can be said about horizontal distribution within the New Gravel Floor.

CONCLUSION

The dog burials in Occupation 2 and the human burials in Occupation 3 include "special" faunal inclusions that had meaning to the deceased or their survivors. The cache pit (Feature 22-1973) probably associated with dog burial Feature 24-1973 in Occupation 2 included, among several unusual artifacts, the same hoof element from a deer and a moose, the latter being rare at the time. There is no standard set of faunal inclusions in the human interments—no "bear cult," for example. Usually a limited number of species and specimens were included in a burial, such as one beaver in one feature. Dogs were evidently buried with humans during Occupation 3. Some bone assemblages, such as the hind limb of a deer, represent probable food stores added to the graves. Whether some of the species, such as furbearers, represented resources for the deceased, or whether they had special meaning beyond simple resources, is difficult to discern without further comparative data from other sites.

The horizontal distribution of bone and features is easily divided into three activity areas in Occupation 2. The addition of artifacts to the analysis defines an additional area—Area 4 (see pp. 80–85). Two seem to be human occupations near the shore, the easternmost one eroded. A possible dog yard has been identified behind the human occupation area. In Occupation 3, there are more evident activity areas, some associated with fire hearth and rock pavement complexes that must represent domestic structures. The scale of horizontal faunal patterning seems to change between the Archaic occupations (2 and 3) and subsequent Ceramic period levels. Part of the difficulty in interpreting these patterns may be the paucity of Ceramic period features with which to associate the faunal distributions. However, the whole site seems to be differentiated into only two or three major faunal deposition areas in each of the Ceramic period occupations. While it seems most likely that we are looking at major seasonal differences in use of the large area involved, we cannot prove that hypothesis despite the plethora of seasonality data available. At least we can say that the nature of occupation and deposition at the site changed significantly between the Archaic and Ceramic occupations.

References

Abbott, Charles C., 1881, *Primitive Industry*, The Salem Press, Salem, MA.

Ahler, Stanley A., 1971, Projectile Point Form and Function at Rodgers Shelter, Missouri, *Missouri Archaeological Society Research Series*, No. 8.

Allen, Patricia M., 1981, The Oxbow Site: An Archaeological Framework for Northeastern New Brunswick, in: *Proceedings of the 1980 Conference on the Future of Archaeology in the Maritime Provinces* (D. M. Shimabaku, ed.), Department of Anthropology, Saint Mary's University, Halifax, pp. 132–146.

Anderson, David G., and J. W. Joseph, 1988, *Prehistory and History along the Upper Savannah River: Technical Synthesis of Cultural Investigations, Richard B. Russel Multiple Resource Area*, National Park Service Interagency Archaeological Services, Atlanta, Georgia.

Anderson, R. Scott, and Charles D. Race, 1982, Evidence for Late Holocene and Recent Sea-Level Rise along Coastal Maine Utilizing Salt Marsh Data, in: *New England Seismotectonic Study Activities in Maine during Fiscal Year 1981* (Woodrow B. Thompson, ed.), Maine Geological Survey, Augusta, pp. 79–96.

Anonymous, 1943, Report on the First Archaeological Conference on the Woodland Pattern, *American Antiquity* 8(4):393–400.

Anthony, David W., 1993, Migration in Archaeology: The Baby and the Bathwater, *American Anthropologist* 92(4):895–914.

Archambault, Marie-France, 1987, L'Archaïque sur la Haute Côte du Nord du Saint-Laurent, *Recherches Amériennes au Québec* 17(1–2):101–114.

Baby, Raymond S., 1954, *Hopewell Cremation Practices*, Papers in Archaeology 1, Ohio Historical Society, Columbus.

Barber, Russel, 1982, *The Wheeler's Site: A Specialized Shellfish Processing Station on the Merrimack River*, Peabody Museum Monographs Number 7, Cambridge, Massachusetts.

Barbian, Lenore T., and Ann L. Magennis, 1994, Variability in Late Archaic Human Burials at Turner Farm, Maine, *Northeast Anthropology* 47:1–19.

Bass, William M., 1971, *Human Osteology: A Laboratory and Field Manual of the Human Skeleton* (2nd Edition), Missouri Archaeological Society, Columbia.

Bateman, Richard M., Ives Goddard, Richard O'Grady, V. A. Funk, Rich Mooi, W. John Kress, and Peter Cannel, 1990a, Speaking of Forked Tongues: The Feasibility of Reconciling Human Phylogeny and the History of Language, *Current Anthropology* 31(1):1–24.

Bateman, Richard M., Ives Goddard, Richard O'Grady, V. A. Funk, Rich Mooi, W. John Kress, and Peter Cannel, 1990b, On Human Phylogeny and Linguistic History: Reply to Comments, *Current Anthropology* 31(2): 177–183.

Bateman, Richard M., Ives Goddard, Richard O'Grady, V. A. Funk, Rich Mooi, W. John Kress, and Peter Cannel, 1990c, More on Human Phylogeny and Linguistic History, *Current Anthropology* 31(3):315–316.

Bates, Arlo, 1911, Fieldnotes. Manuscript on file, accession no. 19-22, Peabody Museum, Harvard University, Cambridge, Massachusetts.

Bates, Oric, and Herbert E. Winlock, 1912, *Archaeological Material from the Maine Littoral*, Bachelors thesis, Department of Anthropology, Harvard University, Cambridge, Massachusetts.

Belcher, William R., 1989, Prehistoric Fish Exploitation in East Penobscot Bay, Maine: The Knox Site and Sea-Level Rise. *Archaeology of Eastern North America* 17(fall):175–191.

Belcher, William R., and David Sanger, 1988, *Phase 2 Report on the Archaeology of the Basin Mills Project*. Manuscript on file at the Archaeology Laboratory, University of Maine, Orono.

Belcher, William R., David Sanger, and Bruce J. Bourque, 1993, The Bradley Cemetery. Manuscript on file at the University of Maine, Orono.

Belknap, Daniel F., 1986, Addison Marsh; Damariscotta River; Glidden Point Shell Middens; Sherman Lake; Cod Cove, North Edgecomb, in: *Coastal Processes and Quaternary Stratigraphy in Northern and Central Coastal Maine* (Joseph T. Kelley and Alice R. Kelley, eds.), Society of Economic Paleontologists and Mineralogists Eastern Section Field Trip Guidebook, Orono, Maine, pp. 46–49, 59–67.

Belknap, Daniel F., Bjorn G. Andersen, R. Scott Anderson, Walter A. Anderson, Harold W. Borns, Jr., George L. Jacobson, Jr., Joseph T. Kelley, R. Craig Shipp, David C. Smith, Robert Stuckenrath, Jr., Woodrow B. Thompson, and David A. Tyler, 1987, Late Quaternary Sea-Level Changes in Maine, in: *Sea-Level Fluctuation and Coastal Evolution* (D. Numendal, Orvin H. Pilkey, Jr., and J. D. Howard, eds.), Society of Economic Paleontologists and Mineralogists Special Pub. 41, pp. 71–85.

Belknap, Daniel F., Joseph T. Kelley, and R. Craig Shipp, 1987, Quaternary Stratigraphy of Representative Maine Estuaries: Initial Examination by High-Resolution Seismic Reflection Profiling, in: *Glaciated Coasts* (Duncan M. Fitzgerald and Peter Rosen, eds.), Academic Press, San Diego, pp. 177–207.

Belknap, Daniel F., Douglas C. Kellogg, Bruce J. Bourque, and Steven L. Cox, 1986, Paleogeographic Reconstructions at 3 Coastal Archaeological Sites in Maine from Seismic Profiling and Vibracoring, *SEPM Annual Midyear Management Abstracts* 3:8.

Belknap, D. F., and J. C. Kraft, 1985, Influence of Antecedent Geology on Evolution of Barrier Systems, in: *Barrier Islands* (G. Oertel and S. P. Leatherman, eds.), Special Issue, *Marine Geology* 63:235–262.

Belknap, Daniel F., and R. Craig Shipp, 1991, Seismic Stratigraphy of Glacial-Marine Units, Maine Inner Shelf, in: *Glacial-Marine Sedimentation, Paleoclimatic Significance* (John B. Anderson and Gail M. Ashley, eds.), Geological Society of America Special Paper 261, pp. 137–157.

Belknap, Daniel F., R. Craig Shipp, and Joseph T. Kelley, 1986, Depositional Setting and Quaternary Stratigraphy of the Sheepscot Estuary, Maine: A Preliminary Report. *Geographie Physique et Quaternaire* 40:55–69.

Belknap, Daniel F., R. Craig Shipp, Joseph T. Kelley, and Detmar Schnitker, 1989, Depositional Sequence Modeling of Late Quaternary Geologic History, West-Central Maine Coast, in: *Studies in Maine Geology*, vol. 5 (Robert D. Tucker and Robert G. Marvinney, eds.), Maine Geological Survey, Augusta, pp. 29–46.

Belknap, Daniel F., R. Craig Shipp, Robert Stuckenrath, Jr., Joseph T. Kelley, and Harold W. Borns, Jr., 1989, Holocene Sea-Level Change in Coastal Maine, in: *Neotectonics of Maine* (Walter A. Anderson and Harold W. Bornes, eds.), Maine Geological Survey, August, pp. 85–105.

Bernstein, David J., 1993, *Prehistoric Subsistence on the Southern New England Coast: The Record from Narragansett Bay*, Academic Press, San Diego.

Berry, Kenneth, Kenneth L. Kvamme, and Paul W. Mielke, Jr., 1980, A Permutation Technique for the Spatial Analyses of the Distribution of Artifacts into Classes, *American Antiquity* 45:55–59.

Bigelow, Henry B., and William C. Schroeder, 1953, *Fishes of the Gulf of Maine*, Fishery Bulletin of the Fish and Wildlife Service, vol. 53.

Biggar, Henry P. (editor), 1922–1926, *The Works of Samuel de Champlain* (6 vols.), The Champlain Society, Toronto.

Billings, Marland P., 1965, Quote in George M. Dow, *Petrology and Structure of North Haven Island and Vicinity*, Ph.D. dissertation, University of Illinois, Urbana.

Binford, Lewis R., 1972, *An Archaeological Perspective*, Seminar Press, New York, pp. 373–382.

Binford, Lewis R., 1978, *Nunamiut Ethnoarchaeology*, Academic Press, New York.

Black, David W. (editor), 1988, *Bliss Revisited: Preliminary Accounts of the Bliss Islands Archaeology Project Phase II*, Manuscripts in Archaeology, Department of Tourism, Recreation, and Heritage No. 24E, Fredericton, New Brunswick.

Black, David W., 1992, *Living Close to the Edge: Prehistoric Human Ecology of the Bliss Islands, Quoddy Region, New Brunswick, Canada*, Occasional Papers in Northeastern Archaeology No. 6, Dundas, Ontario, Copetown Press.

Black, Thomas K., III, 1978, A New Method for Assessing the Sex of Fragmentary Skeletal Remains in Femoral Shaft Circumference, *American Journal of Physical Anthropology* 48:227–231.

Bonnichsen, Robson T., Victor Konrad, Vickie Clay, Terry Gibson, and Douglas Schnorrenberger, 1980, *Archae-*

ological Research at Munsungun Lake: 1980 Preliminary Technical Report of Activities, Institute for Quaternary Studies, University of Maine, Orono.

Borstel, Christopher L., 1982, *Archaeology Investigations at the Young Site, Alton, Maine*, Occasional Publications in Maine Archaeology No. 2, Maine Historic Preservation Commission, Augusta.

Boucher, B. F., 1955, Sex Differences in the Foetal Sciatic Notch, *Journal of Forensic Medicine* 2:51–59.

Boulva, Jean, and Ian A. McLaren, 1979, *Biology of the Harbor Seal, Phoca Vitulina in Eastern Canada*, Fisheries Research Board of Canada Bulletin No. 200.

Bourque, Bruce J., 1975, Comments on the Late Archaic Populations of Central Maine: The View from the Turner Farm, *Arctic Anthropology* 12(2):35–45.

Bourque, Bruce J., 1976, The Turner Farm Site: A Preliminary Report, *Man in the Northeast* 11:21–30.

Bourque, Bruce J., 1983, The Turner Farm Archaeological Project, *National Geographic Society Reports* vol. 15, pp. 59–65.

Bourque, Bruce J., 1989, Ethnicity on the Maritime Peninsula, 1600–1759, *Ethnohistory* 36(3):257–284.

Bourque, Bruce J., 1992a, *Prehistory of the Central Maine Coast* (Ph.D. dissertation, Harvard University, 1971), Garland Publications, New York.

Bourque, Bruce J., 1992b, *Archaeological Investigations at the Candage Site (29-178), Vinalhaven Maine*, Ms. on file, Maine State Museum, Augusta.

Bourque, Bruce J., 1992c, Excavations at Cobbosseecontee Dam South, *Bulletin of the Maine Archaeological Society* 32(2):15–29.

Bourque, Bruce J., 1994, Evidence for Prehistoric Exchange on the Maritime Peninsula, in: *Prehistoric Exchange Systems in North America* (John E. Ericson and Timothy Baugh, eds.), Plenum, New York, pp. 17–46.

Bourque, Bruce J., and Steven L. Cox, 1981, The Maine State Museum Investigation of the Goddard site, 1979, *Man in the Northeast no. 22*:3–27.

Bourque, Bruce J., Robert G. Doyle, and Steven L. White, 1984, The Archaeological Distribution of Banded Spherulitic Rhyolite in Maine, *Man in the Northeast no. 28*:111–119.

Bourque, Bruce J., and Harold W. Krueger, 1991, *Dietary Reconstruction of Prehistoric Maritime Peoples of Northeastern North America: Faunal vs. Stable Isotopic Approaches*, Paper presented at the 24th annual meeting of the Canadian Archaeological Association, St. John's Newfoundland.

Bourque, Bruce J., and Harold W. Krueger, 1994, Dietary Reconstruction from Human Bone Isotopes for Five Coastal New England Populations, in: *Paleonutrition: The Diet and Health of Prehistoric Americans* (Kristen D. Sobolik, ed.), Southern Illinois University Center for Archaeological Investigations Occasional Paper No. 22, pp. 195–209.

Bourque, Bruce J., and Ruth H. Whitehead, 1985, Tarrentines and the Introduction of European Trade Goods in the Gulf of Maine, *Ethnohistory* 32(4):327–341.

Braun, David P., 1974, Explanatory Models for the Evolution of Coastal Adaptation in Prehistoric Eastern New England, *American Antiquity* 39(4):582–596.

Brennan, Louis A., 1977, The Lower Hudson: The Archaic, in: *Amerinds and Their Paleoenvironments in Northeastern North America* (Walter S. Newman and Bert Salwen, eds.), Annals of the New York Academy of Sciences 288, pp. 411–430.

Brennon, Branford, 1960, A Possible Secondary Cremation, *The New Hampshire Archaeologist* 10:2–5.

Brookins, Douglas G., Jean M. Berdan, and David B. Stewart, 1973, Isotopic and Paleontologic Evidence for Correlating Three Volcanic Sequences in the Maine Coastal Volcanic Belt, *Geological Society of America Bulletin* 84:1619–1628.

Brooks, David A., and Wendell S. Brown, 1985, An Overview of the Physical Oceanography of the Gulf of Maine, *Summaries of Plenary Session Talks by the Invited Speakers*, Gulf of Maine Workshop, 20–22 August, 1985, Portland.

Brothwell, Donald R., 1981, *Digging up Bones*, Cornell University Press, Ithaca, New York.

Broyles, Bettye J., 1971, Second Preliminary Report: The St. Albans Site, Kanawah County, West Virginia, 1964–1968, *West Virginia Geological and Economic Survey, Report of Archaeological Investigations* 3, Morgantown.

Bryan, Alan L., 1957, Results and Interpretations of Recent Archaeological Research in Western Washington with Circum-Boreal Implications, *Davidson Journal of Anthropology* 3(1), Seattle.

Buikstra, Jane E., and D. C. Cook, 1980, Paleopathology: An American Account, *Annual Reviews of Anthropology* 9:433–470.

Buikstra, Jane E., and Lynne Goldstein, 1973, *The Perrins Ledge Crematory*, Report of Investigations 28, Illinois State Museum, Springfield.

Buikstra, Jane E., and Mark Swegle, 1989, Cremated Human Bone: Experimental Evidence, Manuscript on file at the Department of Anthropology, University of Chicago.

Bullen, Ripley P., and William J. Bryant, 1965, Three Archaic Sites in the Ocala National Forest, Florida, *The William J. Bryant Foundation, American Studies*, vol. 6, Orlando.

Bullen, Ripley P., and H. Bruce Green, 1970, Stratigraphic Testing at Stallings Island, Georgia, *Florida Anthropologist* 23:8–28.

Bullen, Ripley P., and Arthur M. Hoffmann, 1947, The Hoffmann Site, *American Antiquity* 10(2):187–197.

Burns, Karen R., 1987, *Effects of Drying and Burning on Human Bones*. Ph.D. dissertation, University of Florida, Gainesville, University Microfilms, Ann Arbor.

Byers, Douglas S., 1959, The Eastern Archaic: Some Problems and Hypotheses, *American Antiquity* 24(3):233–256.

Byers, Douglas S., 1962, New England and the Arctic, in: *Prehistoric Cultural Relations between the Arctic and Temperate Zones of North America* (John M. Campbell, ed.), Arctic Institute of North America Technical Paper No. 11, Montreal, pp. 143–153.

Byers, Douglas S., 1979, *The Nevin Shellheap: Burials and Observations*, Papers of the Robert S. Peabody Foundation for Archaeology No. 9, Andover, Massachusetts.

Cameron, Austin W., 1970, Seasonal Movements and Diurnal Activity Rhythms of the Grey Seal (*Halichoerus grypus*), *Journal of Zoology* 161:15–23.

Carignan, Paul, 1975, *The Beaches: A Multi-Component Habitation Site in Bonavista Bay*, National Museums of Canada Mercury Series Paper No. 39, Ottawa.

Carlson, Catherine, 1988, "Where's the Salmon?": An Evaluation of the Role of Anadromous Fisheries in Aboriginal New England, in: *Holocene Human Ecology in Northeastern North America* (George P. Nicholas, ed.), Plenum, New York, pp. 47–80.

Charles, Douglas K., and Jane E. Buikstra, 1983, Archaic Mortuary Sites in the Central Mississippi Drainage: Distribution, Structure, and Behavioral Implications, in: *Archaic Hunters and Gatherers in the American Midwest* (James L. Phillips and James A. Brown, eds.), Academic Press, New York, pp. 117–146.

Claassen, Cheryl P., 1986, Shellfishing Seasons in the Prehistoric Southeastern United States, *American Antiquity* 51(1):21–37.

Claassen, Cheryl, 1991, New Excavations at Dogan Point, Westchester County, New York, in: *The Archaeology and Ethnohistory of the Lower Hudson Valley and Neighboring Regions: Essays in Honor of Louis A. Brennan* (Herbert C. Kraft, ed.), Occasional Publications in Northeast Anthropology 11, Bethlehem, Connecticut.

Claflin, William H., Jr., 1931, The Stallings Island Mound, Columbia County, Georgia, *Papers of the Peabody Museum of American Archaeology and Ethnology, Harvard University*, vol. 14, no. 1.

Clermont, Norman, 1987, Les Énigmatiques Objets Piriformes de L'Archaïque, *Recherches Amérindiennes au Québec* 17(1–2):37–46.

Clermont, Norman, and Claude Chapdelaine, 1982, Pointe-du-Buisson 4:Quarante Siècles d'Archives Oubliées, *Recherches Amérindiennes au Québec*.

Clermont, Norman, Claude Chapdelaine, and Georges Barré, 1983, *Le Site Iroquoien de Lanoraie: Téoignage d'une Maison-Longue, Recherches Amérindiennes au Québec*, Montreal.

Coe, Joffre L., 1964, The Formative Cultures of the Carolina Piedmont, *Transactions of the American Philosophical Society* n.s., vol. 54, no. 5, Philadelphia.

Cohen, Mark N., and George J. Armelagos (editors), 1984, *Paleopathology at the Origins of Agriculture*, Academic Press, Orlando.

Cook, Thomas G., 1976, Broadpoint: Culture, Phase, Horizon, or Knife, *Journal of Anthropological Research* 32(4):337–357.

Core, Harold A., Wilfred A. Côté, and Arnold C. Day, 1979, *Wood Structure and Identification* (2nd ed.), Syracuse University Press, Syracuse, New York.

Côté, Marc, 1987, Les Manifestations Archaïques de la Station 1 du Site Hamel, *Recherches Amérindiennes au Québec* 17(1–2):133–136.

Cox, Steven L., 1991, Site 95.20 and the Vergennes Phase in Maine, *Archaeology of Eastern North America* 19(fall):135–161.

Cox, Steven L., 1995, The Goddard Site, Report in preparation.

Cox, Steven L., and Deborah B. Wilson, 1991, 4500 Years on the Lower Androscoggin: Archaeological Investigation of the Rosie-Mugford Site Complex, *Maine Archaeological Society Bulletin* 31(1):15–40.

Cresson, Jack, 1990, Broadspear Lithic Technology: Some Aspects of Biface Manufacture, Form, and Use History with Insights towards Understanding Assemblage Diversity, in: *Experiments and Observations on the Terminal*

Archaic of the Middle Atlantic Region (Roger W. Moeller, ed.), Archaeological Services, Bethlehem, Connecticut, pp. 105–130.

Cross, John, 1990, *Specialized Production in Non-Stratified Society: An Example from the Late Archaic in the Northeast*, Ph.D. dissertation, Department of Anthropology, University of Massachusetts, Amherst.

Culin, Stewart, 1975, *Games of the North American Indians*, Dover, New York (Originally published 1902–3, Bureau of American Ethnology, Washington, D.C.).

Custer, Jay F., 1989, Prehistoric Cultures of the Delmarva Peninsula, University of Delaware Press, Newark.

Custer, Jay F., 1991, Notes on Broadspear Functions, *Archaeology of Eastern North America* 19(fall):51–73.

Dacey, Michael, 1973, Statistical Tests of Spatial Association in the Location of Tool Types, American Antiquity 38:320–328.

David, Steven A., 1978, *Teacher's Cove: A Prehistoric Site on Passamaquoddy Bay*, New Brunswick Archaeology Series No. 1, Saint Mary's University, Halifax, Nova Scotia.

Davies, C. P., 1992, *Estuarine Preservation Potential Model for Archaeological Sites in Coastal Maine*, Unpublished M.S. thesis, Institute of Quaternary Studies, University of Maine, Orono.

Davis, Ronald B., Theodore E. Bradstreet, Robert Stuckenrath, Jr., and Harold W. Borns, 1975, Vegetation and Associated Environments during the Past 14,000 Years Near Moulton Pond, Maine, *Quaternary Research* 5:435–465.

Deal, Michael, 1986, Late Archaic and Ceramic Period Utilization of the Mud Lake Stream Site, Southwestern New Brunswick, *Man in the Northeast no. 32*:67–94.

de Laguna, Frederica, 1946, The Importance of the Eskimo in Northeastern Archaeology, in: *Man in Northeastern North America* (Frederick Johnson, ed.), Papers of the Robert S. Peabody Foundation for Archaeology, vol. 3, Andover, Massachusetts, pp. 106–142.

de Laguna, Frederica, 1962, Intemperate Reflections on Arctic and Subarctic Archaeology, in: *Prehistoric Cultural Relations between the Arctic and Temperate Zones of North America* (John M. Campbell, ed.), Arctic Institute of North America Technical Paper No. 11, Montreal, pp. 164–169.

Denys, Nicholas, 1908, *Geographic and Historic Description of the Coasts of North America*, The Champlain Society, Toronto. (Original work published 1677.)

Diaz, Henry F., John T. Andrews, and Susan K. Short, 1989, Climate Variations in Northern North America (6000 B.P. to Present) Reconstructed from Pollen and Tree-Ring Data, *Arctic and Alpine Research* 22(1):45–59.

DiBennardo, Robert, and James V. Taylor, 1979, Sex Assessment of the Femur: A Test of a New Method, *American Journal of Physical Anthropology* 50:635–637.

Dincauze, Dena F., 1968, *Cremation Cemeteries in Eastern Massachusetts*, Papers of the Peabody Museum of Archaeology and Ethnology, vol. 59, no. 2, Harvard University, Cambridge, Massachusetts.

Dincauze, Dena F., 1971, An Archaic Sequence for Southern New England, *American Antiquity* 36(2):194–198.

Dincauze, Dena F., 1972, The Atlantic Phase: A Late Archaic Culture in Massachusetts, *Man in the Northeast no. 4*:40–61.

Dincauze, Dena F., 1974, An Introduction to Archaeology in the Greater Boston Area, *Archaeology of Eastern North America* 2(1):39–66.

Dincauze, Dena F., 1975, The Late Archaic Period in Southern New England, *Arctic Anthropology* 12(2): 23–34.

Dincauze, Dena F., 1976, *The Neville Site: 8,000 Years at Amoskeag, Manchester, New Hampshire*, Peabody Museum Monographs no. 4, Cambridge, Massachusetts.

Ditch, Larry E., and Jerome C. Rose, 1972, A Multivariate Dental Sexing Technique, *American Journal of Physical Anthropology* 37:61–64.

Doll, Charles G., William Kady, James B. Thompson, and Marland P. Billings (compilers and editors), 1961, *Centennial Map of Vermont*, Vermont Geological Survey, Montpelier, Vermont.

Dow, Garrett M., 1965, *Petrology and Structure of North Haven Island and Vicinity, Maine*, Ph.D. dissertation, Department of Geology, University of Illinois, Urbana.

Doyle, Robert G., 1978, Preliminary Report on Research into Banded Spherulitic Rhyolite, Manuscript on file, Maine State Museum, Augusta.

Dragoo, Don W., 1976, Archaic Man in the Ohio Valley, in: *Foundations of Pennsylvania Prehistory* (Barry C. Kent, Ira F. Smith III, and Catherine McCann, eds.), The Pennsylvania Historical and Museum Commission Anthropological Series, No. 1, pp. 109–118.

Duffy, William, Daniel F. Belknap, and Joseph T. Kelley, 1989, Morphology and Stratigraphy of Small Barrier-Lagoon Systems in Maine, *Marine Geology* 88:243–262.

Dumais, Pierre, 1978, Le Bas Saint-Laurent, in: *Images de la Préhistoire du Québec* (C. Chapdelaine, ed.), Recherches Amérindiennes au Québec, Montreal, pp. 63–74.

Dunn, Robert A., 1984, Form and Function of the Perkiomen Broadpoint, *Pennsylvania Archaeologist 54(3–4):* 11–19.

Elliot, Dan T., R. Jerald Ledbetter, and Elizabeth A. Gordon, 1992, *Golf, Transportation and the Archaic Period: Archaeology for the Bobby Jones Extension Project*, Report Prepared for the Georgia Department of Transportation, Southeast Archaeological Services, Athens.

Ellis, Christopher J., Ian T. Kenyou, and Michael W. Spence, 1990, The Archaic, in: *The Archaeology of Southern Ontario to A.D. 1650* (Christopher J. Ellis and Neal Ferris, eds.), Occasional Publication of the London Chapter, Ontario Archaeological Society, no. 5, pp. 125–171.

Fazekas, Istvan G., and F. Kosa, 1978, *Forensic Fetal Osteology*, Akademiai Kiado, Budapest.

Fefer, Stewart I., and Patricia A. Schettig, 1980, *An Ecological Characterization of Coastal Maine*, U.S. Fish and Wildlife Service Report FWS/OBS-80/29.

Fillon, Richard H., 1976, Hamilton Bank, Labrador Shelf: Postglacial Sediment Dynamics and Paleo-oceanography, *Marine Geology* 20:7–25.

Finch, Eugene, 1971, The Litchfield Site, *The New Hampshire Archaeologist* 16:1–15.

Fitzhugh, William W., 1972, *Environmental Archaeology and Cultural Systems in Hamilton Inlet, Labrador*, Smithsonian Contributions to Anthropology, vol. 16.

Fitzhugh, William W., 1974, Ground Slates in the Scandinavian Younger Stone Age with Reference to Circumpolar Maritime Adaptations, *Proceedings of the Prehistoric Society* 40:45–58.

Fitzhugh, William W., 1975a, A Maritime Archaic Sequence from Hamilton Inlet, Labrador, *Arctic Anthropology* 12(2):117–138.

Fitzhugh, William W., 1975b, A Comparative Approach to Northern Maritime Adaptations, in: *Prehistoric Maritime Adaptations of the Circumpolar Zone* (William W. Fitzhugh, ed.), Mouton, the Hague (Aldine, Chicago), pp. 337–386.

Fitzhugh, William W., 1978, Population Movement and Cultural Change on the Central Labrador Coast, in: *Amerindians and Their Paleoenvironments in Northeastern North America* (Walter S. Newman and Bert Salwen, eds.), Annals of the New York Academy of Sciences, vol. 288, New York, pp. 481–497.

Fitzhugh, William W., 1985, The Nulliak Pendants and Their Relation to Spiritual Traditions in Northeast Prehistory, *Arctic Anthropology* 22(2):87–109.

Fitzhugh, William W., 1987, Archaeological Ethnicity and the Prehistory of Labrador, in: *Ethnicity and Culture* (Réginald Auger, Margaret Glass, Scott MacEachern, and Peter H. McCartney, eds.), University of Calgary Archaeological Association, Calgary, pp. 141–153.

Ford, Richard I., 1979, Paleoethnobotany in American Archaeology, in: *Advances in Archaeological Method and Theory*, vol. 2 (Michael B. Schiffer, ed.), Academic Press, New York, pp. 286–336.

Ford, T. Latimer, Jr., 1976, Adena Sites on Chesapeake Bay, *Archaeology of Eastern North America* 4:63–89,

Funk, Robert E., 1976, *Recent Contributions to Hudson Valley Prehistory*, New York State Museum Memoir 22.

Funk, Robert E., 1978, Post-Pleistocene Adaptations, in: *Northeast* (Bruce G. Trigger, ed.), Handbook of the North American Indians, vol. 15, Smithsonian Institution, Washington, D.C., pp. 16–27.

Funk, Robert E., 1988, The Laurentian Concept: A Review, *Archaeology of Eastern North America* 18:1–42.

Funk, Robert E., 1993, *Archaeological Investigations in the Upper Susquehanna Valley, New York State, Volume 1*, Persimmon Press, Buffalo.

Funk, Robert E., and Bruce E. Rippeteau, 1977, Adaptation, Continuity, and Change in Upper Susquehanna Prehistory, *Occasional Publications in Northeastern Anthropology* No. 3, Franklin Pierce College, Rindge, New Hampshire.

Garland, Elizabeth B., 1986, Early Woodland Occupations in Michigan: A Lower St. Joseph Valley Prospective, in: *Early Woodland Archaeology* (Kenneth B. Farnsworth and Thomas E. Emerson, eds.), Center for American Archaeology Kampsville Seminars in Archaeology, vol., 2, pp. 4–46.

Gates, Olcott, 1978, The Silurian Lower Devonian Marine Volcanic Rocks of the Eastport Quadrangle, Maine, in: *New England Intercollegiate Field Conference Guidebook, Southeastern Maine and Southern New Brunswick* (Alan Ludman, ed.), Queens College, Queens, New York, pp. 1–16.

Gehrels, W. Roland, and Belknap, Daniel K., 1983, Neotectonic History of Eastern Maine: Evaluation from Historic Sea-Level Data, *Geology* 21:165–618.

Geological Survey, New York State Museum, 1986, *Bedrock Geology of New York*, Geological Survey Staff, Albany, New York.

Gilbert, B. Miles, and Thomas W. McKern, 1973, A Method for Aging the Female Os Pubis, *American Journal of Physical Anthropology* 38:31–38.

Giles, Eugene, 1964, Sex Determination by Discriminant Function Analysis of the Mandible, *American Journal of Physical Anthropology* 22:129–135.

Giles, Eugene, 1970, Sexing Crania by Discriminant Function Analysis: Analysis Effects of Age and Number of Variables, *Proceedings VIIIth International Congress of Anthropological and Ethnological Sciences* I:59–61.

Giles, Eugene, and Orville Elliot, 1963, Sex Determination by Discriminante Function Analysis of Crania, *American Journal of Physical Anthropology* 21:53–68.

Gjessing, Gutorm, 1944, Circumpolar Stone Age, *Acta Arctica* 2. Copenhagen.

Gjessing, Gutorm, 1948, Some Problems in Northeastern Archaeology. *American Antiquity* 13(3):298–302.

Goddard, Ives, 1978, The Eastern Algonkian Languages, in: *Northeast* (Bruce G. Trigger, ed.), Handbook of the North American Indians, vol. 15. Smithsonian Institution, Washington, D.C., pp. 70–77.

Goggin, John M., 1949, Cultural Traditions in Florida Prehistory, in: *The Florida Indian and His Neighbors: Papers Delivered at an Anthropological Conference Held at Rollins College, April 9 and 10, 1949* (John W. Griffin, ed.), Rollins College, Inter-American Center, Winter Park, Florida, pp. 13–44.

Goldstein, Lynne G., 1980, Mississippian Mortuary Practices: A Case Study of Two Cemeteries in the Lower Illinois Valley. *Northwestern University Archaeological Program Scientific Papers* 4.

Goldthwait, Richard P., 1935, The Damariscotta Shell Heaps and Coastal Stability, *American Journal of Sciences* 30:1–13.

Goss, Charles M. (editor), 1977, *Gray's Anatomy* 28th edition, Lea and Febiger, Philadelphia.

Granger, Joseph E., Jr., 1978, *Meadowood Phase Settlement Patterns in the Niagara Frontier Region of Western New York State*, Anthropological Papers, no. 65, Museum of Anthropology, University of Michigan, Ann Arbor.

Grant, D. R., 1970, Recent Coastal Submergence of the Maritime Provinces, *Canadian Journal of Earth Sciences* 7:676–689.

Hadlock, Wendall S., 1939, *The Tafts Point Shell Mound at West Gouldsboro, Maine*, Robert Abbe Museum, Bulletin 5.

Hall, Bradford A., 1970, *Stratigraphy of the Southern End of the Munsungan Anticlinorium, Maine*, Maine Geological Survey Bulletin 22.

Harn, Alan D., 1986, The Marion Phase Occupation of the Larson Site in the Central Illinois River Valley, in: *Early Woodland Archaeology* (Kenneth B. Farnsworth and Thomas E. Emerson, eds.), Center for American Archaeology Kampsville Seminars in Archaeology, vol., 2, pp. 4–46.

Harp, Elmer, Jr., 1951, An Archaeological Survey in the Strait of Bell Isle Area, *American Antiquity* 16: 203–220.

Harp, Elmer, Jr., 1964, Evidence of Boreal Archaic Culture in Southern Labrador and Newfoundland, *National Museums of Canada Bulletin* 193, pt. 1, pp. 184–261.

Harp, Elmer, Jr., and David Hughes, 1968, Five Prehistoric Burials from Port au Choix, Newfoundland, *Polar Notes* 8.

Hawkes, E. W., and Ralph Linton, 1917, A Pre-Lenape Culture in New Jersey, *American Anthropologist, n.s., 19*: 487–494.

Hay, Bradley B., 1988, *The Role of Varying Rates of Local Relative Sea-Level Change in Controlling the Holocene Sedimentologic Evolution of Northern Casco Bay, Maine*, Masters thesis, Department of Geological Sciences, University of Maine, Orono.

Herrmann, B., 1977, On Histological Investigations of Cremated Human Remains, *Journal of Human Evolution* 6:101–103.

Hietala, H., and D. Stevens, 1977, Spatial Analysis: Multiple Procedures in Pattern Recognition Studies, *American Antiquity* 42:539–559.

Holmes, William H., 1919, *Handbook of Aboriginal American Antiquities, Part 1, Introductory, The Lithic Industries*, Bureau of American Ethnology Bulletin 60, Washington, D.C.

Howe, Dennis E., 1988, The Beaver Meadow Brook Site: Prehistory on the West Bank at Sewall's Falls, Concord, New Hampshire, *The New Hampshire Archaeologist* 29(1):48–81.

Hoyt, William, and James M. Demarest, II, 1981, A Versatile Twin-Hull Barge for Shallow-Water Vibracoring, *Journal of Sedimentary Petrology* 5:656–657.

Hulton, Paul, 1984, *America 1585:The Complete Drawings of John White*, University of North Carolina Press, Chapel Hill, North Carolina.

Hunt, Edward E., and Izaac Gleiser, 1955, The Estimation of Age and Sex of Preadolescent Children from Bones and Teeth, *American Journal of Physical Anthropology* 13:479–487.

Jacobson, George L., Thomas Webb III, and Eric C. Grimm, 1987, Patterns and Rates of Vegetation Change during the Deglaciation of Eastern North America, in: *The Geology of North America*, vol. K-3, North America and Adjacent Oceans during the Last Glaciation, The Geological Society of America.

Jeffries, Richard W., 1987, *The Archaeology of Carrier Mills: 10,000 Years in the Saline Valley of Illinois*, Southern Illinois University Press, Carbondale.

Jeffries, Richard W., and Brian M. Butler (editors), 1982, *The Carrier Mills Archaeological Project: Human Adaptation in the Saline Valley, Illinois*, Southern Illinois University at Carbondale, Center for Archaeological Studies Research Paper no. 33.

Johnson, Douglas W., 1925, *The New England-Acadian Shoreline*, Facsimile ed., Hafner Publication Company, New York, 1967.

Johnston, Francis E., 1962, Growth of the Long Bones of Infants and Young Children at Indian Knoll, *American Journal of Physical Anthropology* 20:249–254.

Katz, Darryl L., 1989, Race Differences in Pubic Symphyseal Aging Patterns in the Male, *American Journal of Physical Anthropology* 80:167–172.

Katz, Darryl L., and Judy M. Suchey, 1986, Age Determination of the Male Os Pubis, *American Journal of Physical Anthropology* 69:427–435.

Kelley, Joseph T., 1987, An Inventory of Coastal Environments and Classification of Maine's Glaciated Shoreline, in: *Glaciated Coasts* (David M. Fitzgerald and Peter S. Rosen, eds.), Academic Press, San Diego, pp. 151–176.

Kelley, Joseph T., and Daniel F. Belknap, 1988, *Geomorphology and Sedimentary Framework of the Inner Continental Shelf of Central Maine*, Open File Report 88-6, Maine Geological Survey, Augusta.

Kelley, Joseph T., and Daniel F. Belknap, 1989, *Geomorphology and Sedimentary Framework of Penobscot Bay and Adjacent Inner Continental Shelf*, Open File Report 89-3, Maine Geological Survey, Augusta.

Kelley, Joseph T., Daniel F. Belknap, George L. Jacobson, Jr., and Heather A. Jacobson, 1988, The Morphology and Origin of Salt Marshes along the Glaciated Coastline of Maine, USA, *Journal of Coastal Research* 4:649–665.

Kelley, Joseph T., Stephen M. Dickson, Daniel F. Belknap, and Robert Stuckenrath, Jr., 1992, Sea-Level Change and the Introduction of Late Quaternary Sediment to Southern Maine Inner Continental Shelf, in: *Quaternary Coastal Systems of the United States* (Charles H. Fletcher and John F. Wehmiller, eds.), special pub., International Geological Correlation Programme/Society of Economic Paleontologists and Mineralogists.

Kelley, Joseph T., and Bradley W. B. Hay, 1986, Marine Geology of Casco Bay and Its Margin, in: *Guidebook for Field Trips in Southwestern Maine, NEIGC 78th Annual Meeting, Trip B-5:184–201* (Donald W. Newberg, ed.), Bates College, Lewiston, Maine.

Kelley, Joseph T., Alice R. Kelley, Daniel F. Belknap, and R. Craig Shipp, 1986, Variability in the Evolution of Two Adjacent Bedrock-Framed Estuaries in Maine, in: *Estuarine Variability* (Douglas A. Wolfe, ed.), Academic Press, Orlando, pp. 21–44.

Kelley, Joseph T., Alice R. Kelley, Orvin H. Pilkey, Sr., 1989, *Living with the Coast of Maine*, Duke University Press, Durham, North Carolina.

Kellogg, Douglas C., 1982, *Environmental Factors in Archaeological Site Location for the Boothbay, Maine Region with an Assessment of the Impact of Coastal Erosion on the Archaeological Record*, Unpublished M.S. thesis, Institute of Quaternary Studies, University of Maine, Orono.

Kellogg, Douglas C., 1988, Problems in the Use of Sea-Level Data for Archaeological Reconstructions, in: *Holocene Human Ecology in Northeastern North America* (George P. Nicholas, ed.), Plenum, New York, pp. 81–104.

Kellogg, Douglas C., 1991, *Prehistoric Landscapes, Paleoenvironments and Archaeology of Muscongus Bay, Maine*, Ph.D. dissertation, Institute for Quaternary Studies, University of Maine, Orono.

Kennedy, Clyde C., 1967, Preliminary Report on the Morrison's Island-6 Site, *Anthropological Series 72, National Museum of Canada Bulletin* 206:100–125, Ottawa.

Kent, Barry, Ira F. Smith III, and Catherine McCann, 1976, Archaic and Transitional Periods, in: *Foundations of Pennsylvania Prehistory* (Barry C. Kent, Ira F. Smith III, and Catherine McCann, eds.), The Pennsylvania Historical and Museum Commission Anthropological Series, no. 1., pp. 85–96.

Kenyon, Ian T., 1980, The George Davidson Site: An Archaic "Broadpoint" Component in Southwestern Ontario, *Archaeology of Eastern North America* 8:11–28.

King, Philip B., 1977, *The Evolution of North America*, Princeton University Press, Princeton, New Jersey.

Kingsbury, Isaac W., and Wendell S. Hadlock, 1951, An Early Occupation Site, Eastport, Maine, *Bulletin of the Massachusetts Archaeological Society* 12(2):22–26.

Kinsey, W. Fred, III, 1972a, The Brodhead-Heller Site, 36-Pi-12, in: *Archaeology in the Upper Delaware Valley* (W. Fred Kinsey III, ed.), Pennsylvania Historical and Museum Commission, Anthropological Series Number 2, pp. 199–224.

Kinsey, W. Fred, III, 1972b, Summary, in: *Archaeology in the Upper Delaware Valley* (W. Fred Kinsey III, ed.), Pennsylvania Historical and Museum Commission, Anthropological Series Number 2, pp. 327–398.

Knoblock, Byron W., 1939, *Bannerstones of the North American Indian*, Published by the author, LaGrande, Illinois.

Kraft, Herbert C., 1970, *The Miller Field Site, Warren County, New Jersey: A Study in Prehistoric Archaeology, Part I*, Seton Hall University Press, South Orange, New Jersey.

Kraft, Herbert C., 1972, The Miller Field Site, Warren County, New Jersey, in: *Archaeology in the Upper Delaware Valley* (W. Fred Kinsey III, ed.), Pennsylvania Historical and Museum Commission, Anthropological Series Number 2, pp. 1–54.

Kraft, Herbert C., 1990, The Terminal Archaic in the Upper Delaware Valley: A Broad and Narrow Perspective, in: *Experiments and Observations on the Terminal Archaic of the Middle Atlantic Region* (Roger W. Moeller, ed.), Archaeological Services, Bethlehem, Connecticut, pp. 63–83.

Kraft, John C., Daniel F. Belknap, and I. Kayan, 1983, Potentials of Discovery of Human Occupation Sites on the Continental Shelves and Coastal Zone, in: *Quaternary Coastlines and Marine Archaeology* (P. M. Masters and Nicholas C. Fleming, eds.), Academic Press, London, pp. 87–120.

Krigbaum, John S., 1989, *Subsistence and Health in an Early Woodland Skeletal Population from Vermont*, paper presented at the 54th Annual Meeting of the Society for American Archaeology, Atlanta.

Krogman, Wilton M., 1962, *The Human Skeleton in Forensic Medicine*, Charles C. Thomas, Springfield, Illinois.

Lanesky, Douglas E., Brian W. Logan, Raymond G. Brown, and Albert C. Hine, 1979, A New Approach to Portable Vibracoring Underwater and on Land, *Journal of Sedimentary Petrology* 49:654–657.

LeClercq, Christien, 1910, *New Relation of Gaspesia*, The Champlain Society, Toronto.

Ledbetter, R. Jerald, 1991, *Archaeological Investigations at Mill Branch Sites 9WR4 and 9WR11, Warren County, Georgia*, Prepared for J. M. Huber Corporation, Southeastern Archaeological Services, Inc., Athens, Georgia.

Little, Elizabeth, and J. Clinton Andrews, 1982, Drift Whales at Nantucket: The Kindness of Moshup, *Man in the Northeast no. 23*:17–38.

Loomis, Frederick B., and D. B. Young, 1912, On the Shell Heaps of Maine, *American Journal of Science* 34:17–42.

Loring, Steven, 1985, Boundary Maintenance, Mortuary Ceremonialism and Resource Control in the Early Woodland: Three Cemetery Sites in Vermont, *Archaeology of Eastern North America* 13(fall):93–127.

Lounsbury, Floyd, 1961, Iroquois-Cherokee Linguistic Relations, in: Symposium on Cherokee and Iroquois Culture (William N. Fenton and J. Gulik, eds.), *Bureau of American Ethnology Bulletin* 180, pp. 9–17.

Lounsbury, Floyd, 1978, Iroquoian Languages, in: *Handbook of North American Indians*, vol. 15 (Bruce G. Trigger, ed.), Smithsonian Institution, Washington, D.C., pp. 334–343.

Lovejoy, C. Owen, 1985, Dental Wear in the Libben Populations: Its Functional Pattern and Role in the Determination of Adult Skeletal Age at Death, *American Journal of Physical Anthropology* 68:47–56.

Lovejoy, C. Owen, Richard S. Meindl, Robert P. Mensforth, and T. J. Barton, 1985, Multifactorial Determination of Skeletal Age at Death: A Method and Blind Tests of Its Accuracy, *American Journal of Physical Anthropology* 68:1–14.

Lovejoy, C. Owen, Richard C. Meindl, Thomas R. Pryzbec, and Robert P. Mensforth, 1985, Chronological Metamorphosis of the Auricular Surface of the Ilium: A New Method for the Determination of Adult Skeletal Age at Death, *American Journal of Physical Anthropology* 68:15–28.

Lovell, Nancy C., 1989, Test of Phenice's Technique for Determining Sex from the Os Pubis, *American Journal of Physical Anthropology* 79:117–120.

MacLaughlin, S. M., and M. F. Bruce, 1985, A Simple Univariate Technique for Determining Sex from Fragmented Femora: Its Application to a Scottish Short Cist Population, *American Journal of Physical Anthropology* 67:413–417.

Magennis, Ann L., and Lenore T. Barbian, 1993, Diet, Health and Subsistence at the Late Archaic Turner Farm Site, Maine, *Northeast Anthropologist*, in press.

Mason, Ronald J., 1981, *Great Lakes Archaeology*, Academic Press, New York.

Masters, Patricia M., and Nicholas C. Flemming (editors), 1983, *Quaternary Coastlines and Marine Archaeology: Towards the Prehistory of Land Bridges and Continental Shelves*, Academic Press, London.

Maymon, Jeffrey H., and Charles E. Bolian, 1992, The Wadleigh Falls Site: An Early and Middle Archaic Period Site in Southeastern New Hampshire, in: *Early Holocene Occupation in Northern New England* (Brian S. Robinson, James B. Petersen, and Ann K. Robinson, eds.), Occasional Publications in Maine Archaeology, Number 9, pp. 117–134.

McCartney, Allen P., 1975, Maritime Adaptations in Cold Archipelagoes: An Analysis of Environment and Culture in Aleutian and Other Island Chains, in: *Prehistoric Maritime Adaptations of the Circumpolar Zone* (William W. Fitzhugh, ed.), Mouton, the Hague (Aldine, Chicago), pp. 281–338.

McElrath, Dale L., 1993, Mule Road: A Newly Define Late Archaic Phase in the American Bottom, in: *Highways in the Past: Essays in Honor of Charles J. Bareis* (Thomas E. Emerson, Andrew C. Fortier, and Dale L. McElrath, eds.), Illinois Archaeological Survey, Springfield, pp. 148–157.

McGhee, Robert, and James A. Tuck, 1975, *An Archaic Sequence from the Strait of Belle Isle, Labrador,* National Museums of Canada Mercury Series Paper No. 34, Ottawa.

McKern, Thomas W., and T. Dale Stewart, 1957, *Skeletal Age Changes in Young American Males,* Technical Report EP-45, Quartermaster Research and Development Center, Environmental Protection Research Division, Natick, Massachusetts.

McKern, William C., 1939, The Midwestern Taxonomic System as an Aid to Archaeological Culture Study, *American Antiquity* 4(4):301–313.

McLane, Charles B., 1982, *Islands of the Mid-Maine Coast,* The Kennebec River Press, Woolwich, Maine.

Medaglia, Christian C., E. A. Little, and M. J. Shoeninger, 1990, Late Woodland Diet on Nantucket Island: A Study Using Stable Isotope Ratios, *Bulletin of the Massachusetts Archaeological Society* 51(2):49–60.

Meindl, Richard S., C. Owen Lovejoy, Robert P. Mensforth, and R. A. Walker, 1985, A Revised Method of Age Determination Using the Os Pubis, with a Review and Tests of Accuracy of Other Current Methods of Pubic Symphyseal Aging, *American Journal of Physical Anthropology* 68:29–45.

Meldgaard, Jørgen, 1960, Prehistoric Culture Sequences in the Eastern Arctic as Elucidated by Stratified Sites at Igloolik, *Selected Papers of the Fifth International Congress of Anthropological and Ethnographical Sciences* (Anthony F. C. Wallace, ed.), Philadelphia, pp. 588–595.

Meldgaard, Jørgen, 1962, On the Formative Period of the Dorset Culture, in: *Prehistoric Cultural Relations between the Arctic and Temperate Zones of North America,* (John M. Campbell, ed.), Arctic Institute of North America Technical Paper No. 11, Montreal, pp. 92–94.

Mellgren, Guy, 1974, *The Goddard Site Reviewed,* Paper presented at the 41st annual meeting of the Eastern States Archaeological Federation, Bangor, Maine.

Mellgren, Guy, and Edward Runge, 1958, Goddard's, *Bulletin of the Massachusetts Archaeological Society* 19(3):41–43.

Merchant, V. L., and Douglas H. Ubelaker, 1977, Skeletal Growth of the Protohistoric Arikara, *American Journal of Physical Anthropology* 46:61–72.

Milanich, Jerald T., 1994, *Archaeology of Precolumbian Florida,* University Press of Florida, Gainesville.

Miles, A. E. W., 1963, Dentition in the Assessment of Individual Age in Skeletal Material, in: *Dental Anthropology* (D. R. Brothwell, ed.), Pergamon, Oxford, pp. 191–209.

Miles, A. E. W., 1978, Teeth as an Indicator of Age in Man, in: *Development, Function, and Evolution of Teeth* (P. M. Butler and K. A. Josey, eds.), Academic Press, New York, pp. 455–464.

Modi, J. P., 1957, *Medical Jurisprudence and Toxicology* (12th edition), Tripathi Private, Ltd., Bombay.

Moorehead, Warren K., 1900, *Prehistoric Implements: A Reference Book,* Robert Clark, Cincinnati, Ohio.

Moorehead, Warren K., 1922, *A Report on the Archaeology of Maine,* The Andover Press, Andover, Massachusetts.

Moorrees, Coenraad F. A., Elizabeth A. Fanning, and Edward E. Hunt, Jr., 1963a, Formation and Resorption of Three Deciduous Teeth in Children, *American Journal of Physical Anthropology* 21:205–213.

Moorrees, Coenraad F. A., Elizabeth A. Fanning, and Edward E. Hunt, Jr., 1963b, Age Variation of Formation Stages of Ten Permanent Teeth, *Journal of Dental Research* 42:1490–1502.

Myers, Allen C., 1965, *The Damariscotta Oyster Shell Heaps: Some Further Considerations,* unpublished Bachelor's thesis, Department of Geology, Princeton University, Princeton, New Jersey.

NOAA-NOS, 1992a, *Tide Tables 1992, High and Low Water Predictions East Coast of North and South America,* National Oceanic and Atmospheric Administration National Ocean Service, Riverdale, Maryland.

NOAA-NOS, 1992b, *Tidal Current Tables 1992, Atlantic Coast of North and South America,* National Oceanic and Atmospheric Administration National Ocean Service, Riverdale, Maryland.

Oldale, Robert N., 1985, Rapid Postglacial Shoreline Changes in the Western Gulf of Maine and the Paleo-Indian Environment, *American Antiquity* 50(2):145–150.

Oliver, Billy L., 1985a, Refinement of the North Carolina Chronological Sequence, in: *Piedmont Archaeology: Recent Research Results* (J. Mark Wittkofski and Lyle E. Browning, eds.), Archaeology Society of Virginia Special Publication No. 10, pp. 125–147

Oliver, Billy L., 1985b, Tradition and Typology: Basic Elements of the Carolina Projectile Point Sequence, in: *Structure and Process in Southeastern Archaeology* (Roy S. Dickens, Jr., and H. Trawick Ward, eds.), University of Alabama Press, Tuscaloosa, Alabama, pp. 195–211.

Osberg, Philip H., Arthur M. Hussey II, and Gary M. Boone, 1985, *Bedrock Geologic Map of Maine,* Maine Geological Survey, Augusta.

O'Shea, John M., 1984, *Mortuary Variability: An Archaeological Investigation*. Academic Press, New York.

Ostericher, Charles, 1965, *Bottom and Subbottom Investigations of Penobscot Bay, Maine, 1959*, U.S. Naval Oceanographic Office Technical Report 173.

Panshin, Alexis J., and Carl de Zeeuw, 1970, *Textbook of Wood Technology*, vol. 1, McGraw-Hill, New York.

Pearson, C. E., D. B. Kelley, R. A. Weinstein, S. M. Gagliano, 1986, *Archaeological Investigations on the Outer Continental Shelf: A Study within the Sabine River Valley, Offshore Louisiana and Texas*, OCS Study MMS 86-0119, U.S. Minerals Management Service.

Pendergast, James F., and Bruce G. Trigger, 1972, *Cartier's Hochelaga and the Dawson Site*, McGill-Queen's University Press, Montreal.

Petersen, James B., 1985, Ceramic Analysis in the Northeast: Resume and Prospect. *Occasional Publications in Northeastern Anthropology* no. 9, part 4 (James B. Petersen, ed.), Franklin Pierce College, Rindge, New Hampshire, pp. 5–25.

Petersen, James B., 1990, Evidence of the Saint Lawrence Iroquoians in Northern New England: Population Movement, Trade, or Stylistic Borrowing? *Man in the Northeast* 40:31–39.

Petersen, James B., 1991, *Archaeological Testing at the Sharrow Site: A Deeply Stratified Early to Late Holocene Cultural Sequence in Central Maine*, Occasional Publications in Maine Archaeology Number 8, Maine Archaeological Society and Maine Historic Preservation Commission, Augusta.

Petersen, James B., and David E. Putnam, 1992, Early Holocene Occupation in the Central Gulf of Maine Region, in: *Early Holocene Occupation in Northern New England* (Brian S. Robinson, James B. Petersen, and Ann K. Robinson, eds.), Occasional Papers in Maine Archaeology No. 9, Augusta, pp. 13–61.

Petersen, James B., and David Sanger, 1991, An Aboriginal Ceramic Sequence for Maine and the Maritime Provinces, in: *Prehistoric Archaeology in the Maritimes: Past and Present Research* (Michael Deal, ed.), The Council of Maritime Premiers, Reports in Archeology No. 8, pp. 121–178.

Pfeiffer, John, 1980, The Griffin Site: A Susquehanna Cremation Burial in Southern Connecticut, *Man in the Northeast* 19:129–133.

Pfeiffer, John, 1990, The Late and Terminal Archaic Periods of Connecticut Prehistory: A Model of Continuity, in: *Experiments and Observations on the Terminal Archaic of the Middle Atlantic Region* (Roger W. Moeller, ed.), Archaeological Services, Bethlehem, Connecticut, pp. 85–104.

Pfeiffer, John, 1992, *Late and Terminal Archaic Cultural Adaptations of the Lowest Connecticut Valley*, Ph.D. thesis, Department of Anthropology, State University of New York at Albany.

Phenice, T. W., 1969, A Newly Developed Visual Method of Sexing the Os Pubis, *American Journal of Physical Anthropology* 30:297–310.

Piers, Harry, 1889, Aboriginal Remains of Nova Scotia—Illustrated by the Provincial Museum Collection, *Nova Scotia Institute of Science, Proceedings* 7:276–290.

Piers, Harry, 1896, *Relics of the Stone Age in Nova Scotia*, Transactions of the Nova Scotian Institute of Science 9(session 1894–95):27–58.

Piers, Harry, 1912, A Brief Account of the Micmac Indians of Nova Scotia and Their Remains, *Transactions of the Nova Scotia Institute of Science* 132:99–125.

Pollock, Steven G., 1986, Chert Formation in an Ordoviciain Volcanic Arc, *Journal of Sedimentary Petrology* 57(1):75–87.

Powers, Marjorie W., Frank L. Cowan, and James B. Petersen, 1980, Artifact Variability in the Multi-Component Winooski Site, *Man in the Northeast* no. 19:43–55.

Quinn, David B., and Alison M. Quinn, 1983, *The English New England Voyages, 1602–1608*, The Hakluyt Society, London.

Rankin, Douglas W., 1968, Volcanism Related to Tectonism in the Piscatiquis Volcanic Belt, An Island Arc of Early Devonian Age in North-Central Maine, in: *Studies of Appalachian Geology: Northern and Maritime* (E-an Zen et al., eds.), Wiley-Interscience, New York, pp. 355–370.

Redfield, Alden, 1970, A New Aid to Aging Immature Skeletons: Development of the Occipital Bone, *American Journal of Physical Anthropology* 33:207–220.

Regensberg, R. A., 1971, The Savich Farm Site: A Preliminary Report, *Bulletin of the Massachusetts Archaeological Society* 32(1 and 2):20–23.

Reid, Kenneth C., 1984, Nebo Hill and Late Archaic Prehistory on the Southern Prairie Peninsula, Publications in Anthropology No. 15, University of Kansas, Lawrence.

Reynolds, E. L., 1945, The Bony Pelvic Girdle in Early Infancy, *American Journal of Physical Anthropology* 3: 321–354.

Ritchie, William A., 1938, A Perspective on Northeastern Archaeology, *American Antiquity* 4(2):94–112.

Ritchie, William A., 1945, An Early Site in Cayuga County, New York, *Research Records of the Rochester Museum of Arts and Sciences* No. 7, Rochester, New York.

Ritchie, William A., 1946, A Stratified Prehistoric Site at Brewerton, New York, *Research Records of the Rochester Museum of Arts and Sciences* No. 8, Rochester, New York.

Ritchie, William A., 1955, The Northeastern Archaic—A Review, Manuscript on file, New York State Museum, Albany, New York.

Ritchie, William A., 1958, An Introduction to Hudson Valley Prehistory, *New York State Museum and Science Service Bulletin No. 358*, Albany, New York.

Ritchie, William A., 1959, The Stony Brook Site and Its Relation to Archaic and Transitional Cultures on Long Island, *New York State Museum and Science Service Bulletin No. 372*, Albany, New York.

Ritchie, William A., 1961, *A Typology and Nomenclature for New York Projectile Points*, New York State Museum and Science Service Bulletin No. 384, Albany, New York.

Ritchie, William A., 1962, Northeastern Crossties with the Arctic, in: *Prehistoric Cultural Relations between the Arctic and Temperate Zones of North America* (John M. Campbell, ed.), Arctic Institute of North America Technical Paper No. 11, Montreal, pp. 96–99.

Ritchie, William A., 1965, The "Small Stemmed Point" in New England, *Pennsylvania Archaeologist* 35(3–4): 134–138.

Ritchie, William A., 1969a, *The Archaeology of Martha's Vineyard*, The Natural History Press, Garden City, New York.

Ritchie, William A., 1969b, Ground Slates: East and West, *American Antiquity* 34(4):385–391.

Ritchie, William A., 1971a, The Archaic in New York, *New York State Archaeological Association Bulletin 52(July)*: 2–12, Rochester.

Ritchie, William A., 1971b, *A Typology and Nomenclature for New York Projectile Points*, New York State Museum and Science Service Bulletin 384.

Ritchie, William A., 1980, *The Archaeology of New York State*, Harbor Hill Books, Harrison, New York.

Ritchie, William A., and Robert E. Funk, 1973, *Aboriginal Settlement Patterns in the Northeast*, New York State Museum and Science Service Memoir 20, Albany.

Ritchie, William A., and Richard S. MacNeish, 1949, The Pre-Iroquoian Pottery of New York State, *American Antiquity* 15(2):97–124.

Robbins, Maurice, 1959, *Wapanucket #6. An Archaic Village in Middleboro, Massachusetts*, Massachusetts Archaeological Society, Attleboro.

Robins, Kevin, and David W. Black, 1988, Organic Artifacts from the Bliss Islands, in: *Bliss Revisited: Preliminary Accounts of the Bliss Islands Archaeology Project Phase II* (David W. Black, ed.), Tourism, Recreation and Heritage New Brunswick Manuscript in Archaeology 24E, Frederickton, pp. 137–162.

Robinson, Brian S., 1985, The Nelson Island and Seabrook Marsh Site: Late Archaic, Marine Oriented People on the Central New England Coast, *Occasional Publications in Northeastern Anthropology no. 9(part 1)*:1–107. Franklin Pierce College, Rindge, New Hampshire.

Robinson, Brian S., 1992, Early and Middle Archaic Period Occupation in the Gulf of Maine Region: Mortuary and Technological Patterning, in: *Early Holocene Occupation in Northern New England* (Brian S. Robinson, James B. Petersen, and Ann K. Robinson, eds.), Occasional Papers in Maine Archaeology No. 9, Augusta, pp. 63–116.

Robinson, Brian S., and Charles S. Bolian, 1987, A Preliminary Report on the Rocks Road Site (Seabrook Station): Late Archaic to Contact Period Occupation in Seabrook, New Hampshire, *The New Hampshire Archaeologist* 28(1):19–51.

Rouse, Irving, 1958, The Inference of Migrations from Anthropological Evidence, in *Migration in New World Culture History* (Raymond H. Thompson, ed.), *University of Arizona Social Science Bulletin* 27:63–68.

Rowe, John H., 1940, *Excavations in the Waterside Shell Heap, Frenchman's Bay, Maine*. Excavators Club Papers 1(3), Harvard University, Cambridge, Massachusetts.

Sanger, David, 1971a, Passamaquoddy Bay Prehistory: A Summary, *Bulletin of the Maine Archaeological Society* 11(2):14–19.

Sanger, David, 1971b, Deadman's Pool—A Tobique Complex Site in Northern New Brunswick, *Man in the Northeast* 2:5–22.

Sanger, David, 1973, *Cow Point: An Archaic Cemetery in New Brunswick*, National Museums of Canada Mercury Series Paper No. 12, Ottawa.

Sanger, David, 1975, Culture Change as an Adaptive Process in the Maine–Maritimes Region. *Arctic Anthropology* 12(2):60–75.

Sanger, David, 1981, Unscrambling Messages in the Midden, *Archaeology of Eastern North America* 9:37–42.

Sanger, David, 1987, *The Carson Site and the Late Ceramic Period in Passamaquoddy Bay, New Brunswick,* Canadian Museum of Civilization, Mercury Series Paper No. 135.

Sanger, David, 1988a, Maritime Adaptations in the Gulf of Maine, *Archaeology of Eastern North America* 16:81–99.

Sanger, David, 1988b, The Original Native Mainers, *Habitat: Journal of the Maine Audubon Society*, January, pp. 37–41.

Sanger, David, 1991, Five Thousand Years of Contact Between Maine and Nova Scotia, *Bulletin of the Maine Archaeological Society* 32(2):55–61.

Sanger, David, William R. Belcher, and Douglas C. Kellogg, 1992, Early Holocene Occupation at the Blackman Stream Site, in: *Early Holocene Occupation in Northern New England* (Brian S. Robinson, James B. Petersen and Ann K. Robinson, eds.), Maine Historic Preservation Occasional Publications in Maine Archaeology No. 9, Augusta, pp. 149–161.

Sanger, David, and Daniel F. Belknap, 1987, Human Responses to Changing Marine Environments in the Gulf of Maine, in: *Man and the Mid-Holocene Climatic Optimum* (Neal A. McCinnon and Glenn S. L. Stewart, eds.), Proceedings of the 17th Annual Chacmool Conference, Calgary, Department of Archaeology, University of Calgary, pp. 245–261.

Sanger, David, and Daniel F. Belknap, 1991, Archaeological Site Location and Preservation on the Coast of Maine, *Geological Society of America Abstracts with Programs* 23:A199.

Sanger, David, and Bruce J. Bourque, 1986, *The Rise and Fall of the Susquehanna Tradition in Maine and the Maritime Provinces,* Paper presented at the 53rd annual meeting of the Eastern States Archaeological Federation, Dover, Delaware.

Sanger, David, Ronald B. Davis, Robert G. MacKay, and Harold W. Borns, 1977, The Hirundo Archaeological Project—An Interdisciplinary Approach to Central Maine Prehistory, in: *Amerinds and their Paleoenvironments in Northeastern North America* (Walter S. Newman and Bert Salwen, eds.), Annals of the New York Academy of Sciences, vol. 288, New York, pp. 457–471.

Sanger, David, and Douglas E. Kellogg, 1983, Preliminary Report on Sea-Level Rise in the Damariscotta Estuary, Central Maine Coast, in: *New England Seismotectonic Study Activities in Maine during Fiscal Year 1982* (Woodrow S. Thompson and Joseph T. Kelley, eds.), Maine Geological Survey, Augusta, pp. 137–145.

Sanger, David, and Robert G. MacKey, 1973, The Hirundo Archaeological Project—Preliminary Report, *Man in the Northeast no.* 6:21–29.

Sanger, David, and Mary Jo Sanger, 1986, Boom and Bust on the River: The Story of the Damariscotta Oyster Shell Heaps, *Archaeology of Eastern North America* 14:65–78.

Sassaman, Kenneth E., and George S. Lewis, 1990, The Heard Robertson Collection, *South Carolina Antiquities* 22(1&2):49–62.

Schemnitz, Sanford, 1975, Maine Island–Mainland Movements of White-tailed Deer, *Journal of Mammalogy* 56:535–537.

Schindler, Deborah L., George J. Armelagos, and M. Pamela Bumsted, 1981, Biocultural Adaptation: New Directions in Northeastern Anthropology, in: *Foundations of Northeast Archaeology* (D. R. Snow, ed.), Academic Press, New York, pp. 229–259.

Schnitker, Detmar, 1974, Postglacial Emergence of the Gulf of Maine, *Geological Society of America Bulletin* 85: 491–494.

Schnitker, Detmar, 1975, Late Glacial to Recent Paleoceanography of the Gulf of Maine, *Maritime Sediments, Special Publication*, no. 1, pp. 385–392, 1st International Symposium on Continental Margin Benthonic Foraminifera, Part B, Paleoecology and Biostratigraphy.

Schnitker, Detmar, 1986, Ocean Basin with a Past, *Exploration: A Journal of Research at the University of Maine* 3(1):29–37.

Schnitker, Detmar, and Julie B. Jorgensen, 1990, Late Glacial and Holocene Diatom Successions in the Gulf of Maine: Response to Climatologic and Oceanographic Change, in: *Evolutionary Biogeography of the Marine Algae of the North Atlantic* (D. J. Garbary and G. R. South, eds.), NATO ASI Series, vol. G 22, Springer-Verlag, Berlin, pp. 35–53.

Schour, I., and M. Massler, 1941, The Development of the Human Dentition, *Journal of the American Dental Association* 28:1153–1160.

Schweingruber, Fritz H., 1978, *Microscopic Wood Anatomy*, Swiss Federal Institute of Forestry Research CH-8903 Birmensdorf.

Scott, David B., and David A. Greenberg, 1983, Relative Sea-Level Rise and Tidal Development in the Fundy Tidal System, *Canadian Journal of Earth Science* 20:1554–1564.

Sears, William H., 1948, "What is the Archaic?" *American Antiquity* 14(2):122–124.

Shaw, Leslie C., 1988, A Biocultural Evaluation of the Skeletal Population from the Nevin Site, Blue Hill, Maine, *Archaeology of Eastern North America* 16:55–77.

Shipman, Patricia, G. Foster, and Margaret Schoeninger, 1984, Burnt Bones and Teeth: An Experimental Study of Color, Morphology, Crystal Structure and Shrinkage, *Journal of Archaeological Science* 11:301–325.

Shipp, R. Craig, 1989, *Late Quaternary Sea-Level Fluctuations and Geologic Evolution of Four Embayments and Adjacent Inner Shelf along the Northwestern Gulf of Maine*, Ph.D. dissertation, Oceanography Program, University of Maine, Orono.

Shipp, R. Craig, Daniel F. Belknap, and Joseph T. Kelley, 1989, A Submerged Shoreline on the Inner Shelf of the Gulf of Maine, in: *Studies in Maine Geology*, vol. 5 (Robert D. Tucker and Robert G. Marvenney, eds.), Maine Geological Survey, Augusta, pp. 341–364.

Shipp, R. Craig, Daniel F. Belknap, and Joseph T. Kelley, 1991, Seismic-Stratigraphic and Geomorphic Evidence for a Post-Glacial Sea-Level Lowstand in the Northern Gulf of Maine, *Journal of Coastal Research* 7:341–364.

Shipp, R. Craig, Stephanie A. Staples, and Walter H. Adey, 1985, Geomorphic Trends in a Glaciated Coastal Bay: A Model for the Maine Coast, *Smithsonian Contributions to the Marine Sciences* no. 25, Smithsonian Institution Press, Washington, D.C.

Shipp, R. Craig, Stephanie A. Staples, and Larry G. Ward, 1987, Controls and Zonation of Geomorphology along a Glaciated Coast, Gouldsboro Bay, Maine: Glaciated Coasts, in: *Sea-Level Fluctuation and Coastal Evolution* (David M. Fitzgerald and Peter S. Rosen, eds.), Academic Press, San Diego, pp. 209–231.

Skinas, David C., 1987, *The Todd Site: A Case Study of Shell Midden Formation*, Masters thesis, Institute for Quaternary Studies, University of Maine, Orono.

Smart, T. L., and E. S. Hoffman, 1988, Environmental Interpretation of Archaeological Charcoal, in: *Current Paleoethnobotany* (Christine A. Hastorf and Virginia S. Popper, eds.), University of Chicago Press, pp. 167–206.

Smith, Benjamin L., 1948, An Analysis of the Maine Cemetery Complex, *Massachusetts Archaeological Society Bulletin* 9:17–71.

Smith, Bruce D., 1986, The Archaeology of the Southeastern United States: From Dalton to de Soto, 10,500–500 B.P., *Advances in World Archaeology* 5:1–92.

Smith, Harlan I., and William J. Wintemberg, 1929, *Some Shell Heaps in Nova Scotia*, National Museum of Canada Bulletin No. 47.

Smith, Rebecca V., 1990, *Geomorphic Trends and Shoreline Dynamics in Three Maine Embayments*, Masters thesis, Department of Geological Sciences, University of Maine, Orono.

Smith, Walter B., 1926, *Indian Remains of the Penobscot Valley and Their Significance*, University of Maine Studies, Second Series, Number 7, University Press, Orono, Maine.

Snow, Charles E., 1948, *Indian Knoll Skeletons of the Site Oh2, Ohio County, Kentucky*, The University of Kentucky Reports in Anthropology, Vol. 9, No. 3, Pt. 2, Lexington.

Snow, Dean R., 1969, *A Summary of Excavations at the Hathaway Site in Passadumkeag, Maine, 1912, 1947, and 1968*, University of Maine, Orono.

Snow, Dean R., 1972, Rising Sea Level and Prehistoric Cultural Ecology in Northern New England, *American Antiquity* 37(2):211–221.

Snow, Dean R., 1975, The Passadumkeag Sequence, *Arctic Anthropology* 12(2):46–59.

Snow, Dean R., 1976, The Archaeological Implications of the Proto-Algonquian Urheimat, in: *Papers of the Seventh Algonquian Conference* (William Cowan, ed.), Carleton University, Ottawa, pp. 339–346.

Snow, Dean R., 1978, Eastern Abenaki, in: *Northeast* (Bruce G. Trigger, ed.), Handbook of North American Indians, vol. 15, pp. 137–147.

Snow, Dean R., 1980, *The Archaeology of New England*, Academic Press, New York.

Snow, Dean R., 1992, L'Augmentation de la Population Chez les Groupes Iroquoiens, et ses Conséquences sur L'Etude de Leurs Origines, *Recherches Amérindiennes au Québec* 22(4):5–36.

Spaulding, Albert C., 1946, Northeastern Archaeology and General Trends in the Northern Forest Zone, in: *Man in Northeastern North America* (Frederick Johnson, ed.), Papers of the Robert S. Peabody Foundation for Archaeology, Vol. 3, Andover, Massachusetts, pp. 143–167.

Speck, Frank G., 1940, *Penobscot Man*, University of Pennsylvania Press, Philadelphia.

Speck, Frank G., 1977, *Naskapi: The Savage Hunters of the Labrador Peninsula*, University of Oklahoma Press. (Originally published 1935, University of Pennsylvania Press, Philadelphia.)

Spence, Michael W., and William A. Fox, 1986, The Early Woodland Occupations of Southern Ontario, in: *Early Woodland Archaeology* (Kenneth B. Farnsworth and Thomas E. Emerson, eds.), Center for American Archaeology Kampsville Seminars in Archaeology, vol. 2, pp. 4–46.

Spence, Michael W., Robert H. Pihl, and Carl Murphy, 1990, Cultural Complexes of the Early and Middle Woodland Periods, in: *The Archaeology of Southern Ontario to A.D. 1650* (Christopher J. Ellis and Neal Ferris, eds.), Occasional Publications of the London Chapter, Ontario Archaeological Society Inc., No. 5, pp. 125–169.

Spiess, Arthur E., 1985, Wild Maine and the Rusticating Scientist: A History of Anthropological Archaeology in Maine, *Man in the Northeast* 30:101–129.

Spiess, Arthur E., 1990, Deer Tooth Sectioning, Eruption, and Seasonality of Deer Hunting in Prehistoric Maine, *Man in the Northeast* 39:29–44.

Spiess, Arthur E., 1992, Archaic Period Subsistence in New England and the Maritime Provinces, in: *Early Holocene Occupation in Northern New England* (Brian S. Robinson, James B. Petersen, and Ann K. Robinson, eds.), Occasional Papers in Maine Archaeology Number 9, Maine Historic Preservation Commission, Augusta.

Spiess, Arthur E., Bruce J. Bourque, and Steven L. Cox, 1983, Cultural Complexity in Maritime Cultures: Evidence from Penobscot Bay, Maine, in: *Evolution of Maritime Cultures on the Northeast and Northwest Coasts of America* (Ronald J. Nash, ed.), Simon Fraser University Department of Archaeology Publication No. 11, Burnaby, B.C., pp. 91–108.

Spiess, Arthur E., and Mark H. Hedden, 1983, *Kidder Point and Sears Island in Prehistory*, Occasional Publications in Maine Archaeology Number 3, Maine Historic Preservation Commission, Augusta.

Spiess, Arthur E., and Robert A. Lewis, 1993, *The Turner Farm Fauna: Five Thousand Years of Hunting and Fishing in Penobscot Bay, Maine*, Manuscript on file at the Maine State Museum.

Staples, Arthur C., and Roy C. Athearn, 1969, The Bear Swamp Site: A Preliminary Report, *Bulletin of the Massachusetts Archaeological Society* 30(3&4):1–9.

Stewart, David B., and David R. Wones, 1974, Bedrock Geology of the Northern Penobscot Bay Area, in: *Guidebook for Field Trips in East-Central and North-Central Maine* (Philip H. Osberg, ed.), New England Intercollegiate Field Conference Guide Book. University of Maine, Orono. pp. 223–239.

Stewart, Frances L., 1986, *Faunal Remains from the Delorey Island Site (BjCj-9) of Nova Scotia*, Curatorial Report 57, The Nova Scotia Museum, Halifax.

Stoltman, James B., 1974, The Late Archaic in the Savannah River Region, *Florida Anthropologist* 25(2):37–62.

Thomas, Ronald A., 1974, Webb Phase Mortuary Customs at the Island Field Site, *Transactions of the Delaware Academy of Science* 5:119–140.

Thompson, John P., 1974, Stratigraphy and Geochemistry of the Scot's Bay Formation, King's County, Nova Scotia, Unpublished thesis, Acadia University, Wolfville, Nova Scotia.

Thurman, M. D., and L. James Willmore, 1980, A Replicative Cremation Experiment, *North American Archaeologist* 2:275–283.

Thwaites, Reuben G. (editor), 1896–1901), *The Jesuit Relations and Allied Documents*, 73 vols., The Burroughs Brothers, Cleveland.

Todd, T. Wingate, 1920, Age Changes in the Pubic Bone, Part I, *American Journal of Physical Anthropology* 3: 285–334.

Todd, T. Wingate, 1921, Age Changes in the Pubic Bone, Parts II–IV, *American Journal of Physical Anthropology* 4: 1–70.

Trigger, Bruce G. (editor), 1978, *Northeast*, Handbook of the North American Indians, vol. 15, Smithsonian Institution, Washington, D.C.

Truncer, James J., 1990, Perkiomen Points: A Study of Variability, in: *Experiments and Observations on the Terminal Archaic of the Middle Atlantic Region* (Roger W. Moeller, ed.), Archaeological Services, Bethlehem, Connecticut, pp. 1–62.

Tuck, James A., 1970, Port au Choix, *Scientific American* 223(1):112–114.

Tuck, James A., 1971, An Archaic Cemetery at Port au Choix, Newfoundland, *American Antiquity* 36(3):343–358.

Tuck, James A., 1975, The Northeast Maritime Continuum: 8000 Years of Cultural Development in the Far Northeast, *Arctic Anthropology* 12(2):139–147.

Tuck, James A., 1976, *Ancient People of Port au Choix: The Excavation of an Archaic Indian Cemetery in Newfoundland*, Newfoundland Social and Economic Studies, no. 17, Memorial University, St. Johns.

Tuck, James A., 1978a, Regional Cultural Development, 3000 to 300 B.C., in: *Northeast* (Bruce G. Trigger, ed.), Handbook of the North American Indians, vol. 15, Smithsonian Institution, Washington, D.C., pp. 28–43.

Tuck, James A., 1978b, Archaic Burial Ceremonialism in the "Far Northeast," in: *Essays in Northeastern Anthropology in Memory of Marian E. White* (William E. Anglebrecht and Donald K. Grayson, eds.), Occasional Publications in Northeastern Anthropology, No. 5, Franklin Pierce College, Rindge, New Hampshire, pp. 67–77.

Tuck, James A., 1982, Prehistoric Archaeology in Atlantic Canada Since 1975, *Canadian Journal of Archaeology* 6:201–218.

Tuck, James A., 1984, *Maritime Province Prehistory*, Archaeological Survey of Canada, National Museum of Man, National Museums of Canada, Ottawa.

Tuck, James A., 1985, A Summary of Maritime Archaeological Research Conducted at Red Bay, Labrador: The 1984 Season, in: *Archaeology in Newfoundland and Labrador 1984* (Jane S. Thompson and Callum Thompson, eds.), Historic Resources Division, Department of Culture, Recreation and Youth, Government of Newfoundland and Labrador, pp. 246–247.

Turnbaugh, William A., 1975, Toward an Explanation of the Broadpoint Dispersal in Eastern North American Prehistory, *Journal of Anthropological Research* 31(1):51–68.

Turnbaugh, William A., 1977, *Man, Land and Time: The Cultural Prehistory and Demographic Patterns of North-Central Pennsylvania*, Unigraphic, Inc., Evansville, Indiana.

Turnbull, Christopher J., 1983, *A Recent Look at the Mason Cemetery, Maine*, Manuscript on file at the Maine State Museum.

Turnbull, Christopher J., 1985, Reflections on a Ground Slate Bayonet Fragment from the Tantramar Marsh, Upper Bay of Fundy, Manuscript on file, Archaeological Branch, Department of Tourism, Recreation and Heritage, Fredericton, New Brunswick.

Tyzzer, Ernest E., 1936, The Simple Bone Point of the Shell-Heaps of the Northeastern Algonkian Area and Its Probable Significance, *American Antiquity* 1:261–279.

Tyzzer, Ernest E., 1943, Animal Tooth Implements from Shell Heaps of Maine, *American Antiquity* 8:354–362.

Ubelaker, Douglas H., 1974, *Reconstruction of Demographic Profiles from Ossuary Skeletal Samples: A Case Study from the Tidewater Potomac*, Smithsonian Contributions to Anthropology 18, Washington, D.C.

Ubelaker, Douglas H., 1978, *Human Skeletal Remains: Excavation, Analysis Interpretation*, Aldine, Chicago.

van Nostrand, F. C., and A. B. Stephansen, 1964, Age Determination for Beavers by Tooth Development, *Journal of Wildlife Management* 23:430–434.

Ventur, Pierre, 1980, A Comparative Perspective on Native American Mortuary Games of the Eastern Woodlands, *Man in the Northeast no. 20*:77–100.

Verme, Louis J., and Duane E. Ullreg, 1984, Physiology and Nutrition, in: *White-Tailed Deer: Ecology and Management* (Lowell K. Halls, ed.), Wildlife Management Institute, Washington, D.C., pp. 91–118.

Walsh, Joseph A., 1988, *Sedimentology and Late Holocene Evolution of the Lubec Embayment*, Master's thesis, Department of Geological Sciences, University of Maine, Orono.

Waring, Antonio J., Jr., 1977, The Bilbo Site—Chatham County, Georgia, in: *The Waring Papers: The Collected Works of Antonio J. Waring, Jr.* (Stephen Williams, ed.), Papers of the Peabody Museum of Archaeology and Ethnography Volume 58, Harvard University, Cambridge, Massachusetts, pp. 152–197.

Webb, Thompson III, Patrick J. Bartlein, Sandy P. Harrison, and Katherine H. Anderson, 1993, Vegetation, Lake Levels, and Climate in Eastern North America for the Past 18,000 Years, in: *Global Climate Since the Last Ice Glacial Maximum* (Herbert E. Wright, Jr., John E. Kutzbach, Thompson Webb, III, William F. Ruddiman, F. Alayne Street Perrott and Patrick J. Bartlein, eds.), Minneapolis, University of Minnesota Press, pp. 514–535.

Webb, William S., 1974, *Indian Knoll, Site Oh 2, Ohio County, Kentucky*, The University of Tennessee Press, Knoxville,

Whalen, Maureen S., 1989, *Late Quaternary Paleogeographic Reconstruction of the Roque Island Area, Maine*, Master's thesis, Institute of Quaternary Studies, University of Maine, Orono.

Whallon, Robert, Jr., 1973, Spatial Analysis of Occupation Floors, I: Application of Dimensional Analysis of Variance, *American Antiquity* 38:266–278.

Whallon, Robert, Jr., 1974, Spatial Analyses of Occupation Floors, II: Application of Nearest Neighbor Analysis, *American Antiquity* 39:16–34.

Whittall, James, II, 1982, *Work Report: Radiocarbon Dates, Burial Mound, Morrill's Point*, Salisbury, Massachusetts, Manuscript on file, Maine State Museum, Augusta.

Will, Richard T., 1981, *A Study of Prehistoric Bone Tools from the Turner Farm Site, North Haven, Maine*, Master's thesis, Department of Anthropology, University of Maine, Orono.

Willey, Gordon, R., 1966, *An Introduction to American Archaeology, Vol. 1, North and Middle America*, Prentice-Hall, Englewood, New Jersey.

Willey, Gordon R., and Philip Phillips, 1958, *Method and Theory in American Archaeology*, University of Chicago Press.

Willey, Gordon R., and Jeremy A. Sabloff, 1980, *A History of American Archaeology*, W. H. Freeman, San Francisco.

Willoughby, Charles C., 1898, Prehistoric Burial Places in Maine, *Archaeological Papers of the Peabody Museum* 1(6), Harvard University, Cambridge, Massachusetts.

Willoughby, Charles C., 1973, *Antiquities of the New England Indians*, AMS Press, New York. (Original work published 1935.)

Willoughby, Charles C., 1978, *Indian Burial Place at Winthrop, Massachusetts*, Krauss Reprint Co., Millwood, New York. (Original work published 1924.)

Winters, Howard D., 1974, Introduction to the New Edition, in: *Indian Knoll*, by William S. Webb, The University of Tennessee Press, Knoxville.

Witthoft, John, 1949, An Outline of Pennsylvania Indian History, *Pennsylvania History* 16(3):3–15.

Witthoft, John, 1953, Broad Spearpoints and the Transitional Period Cultures, *Pennsylvania Archaeologist* 23(1): 4–31.

Wood, Mark E., 1991, *Maine Salt Marshes and Sediment Accumulation*, Master's thesis, Department of Geological Sciences, University of Maine, Orono.

Wood, Mark E., Joseph T. Kelley, and Daniel F. Belknap, 1989, Pattern of Sediment Accumulation in the Tidal Marshes of Maine, *Estuaries* 12:237–246.

Workman, William B., 1980, Continuity and Change in the Prehistoric Record from Southern Alaska, in: *Alaska Native Culture and History* (Yoshinoba Kotani and William B. Workman, eds.), Senri Ethnological Series No. 4, National Museum of Ethnology, Osaka, Japan, pp. 49–101.

Workshop of European Anthropologists, 1980, Recommendations for Age and Sex Diagnosis of Skeletons, *Journal of Human Evolution* 9:517–549.

Wright, Herbert E., Jr., 1971, Late Quaternary Vegetational History of North America, in: *The Late Cenozoic Glacial Cycles* (Karl K. Turekian, ed.), Yale University Press, New Haven, Connecticut, pp. 425–464.

Wright, James V., 1972a, *The Shield Archaic*, National Museums of Canada Publications in Archaeology, No. 3, Ottawa.

Wright, James V., 1972b, *Ontario Prehistory*, National Museum of Man, Ottawa.

Wright, James V., 1994, The Prehistoric Transportation of Goods in the St. Lawrence River Basin, in: *Prehistoric Exchange Systems in North America*, (John E. Ericson and Timothy Baugh, eds.), Plenum, New York, pp. 47–71.

Yesner, David, 1980, Archaeology of Casco Bay: A Preliminary Report, *Maine Archaeological Society Bulletin* 20: 60–74.

Young, Robert S., 1990, *Geoarchaeology of Johns Bay and Pemaquid Beach, Maine*, Master's thesis, Institute for Quaternary Studies, University of Maine, Orono.

Young, Robert S., Daniel F. Belknap, and David Sanger, 1992, Geoarchaeology of Johns Bay, Maine, *Geoarchaeology* 7:209–249.

Zielinski, G. A., P. A. Mayewski, L. D. Meeker, S. Whitlow, M. S. Twickler, M. Morrisson, D. A. Meese, A. J. Gow, and R. B. Alley, 1994, Record of Volcanism Since 7000 B.C. from the DISP2 Greenland Ice Core and Implications for the Volcano-Climate System, *Science* 264:948–952.

Index

393

THE ARCHAEOLOGY OF GENDER
Separating the Spheres in Urban America
Diana diZerega Wall

ORIGINS OF ANATOMICALLY MODERN HUMANS
Edited by Matthew H. Nitecki and Doris V. Nitecki

PREHISTORIC EXCHANGE SYSTEMS IN NORTH AMERICA
Edited by Timothy G. Baugh and Jonathon E. Ericson

STYLE, SOCIETY, AND PERSON
Archaeological and Ethnological Perspectives
Edited by Christopher Carr and Jill E. Neitzel

REGIONAL APPROACHES TO MORTUARY ANALYSIS
Edited by Lane Anderson Beck

DIVERSITY AND COMPLEXITY IN PREHISTORIC MARITIME SOCIETIES
A Gulf of Maine Perspective
Bruce J. Bourque

CHESAPEAKE PREHISTORY
Old Traditions, New Directions
Richard J. Dent, Jr.

.